PHILOSOPHY
OF EDUCATION

PHILOSOPHY OF EDUCATION

Studies in Philosophies, Schooling, and Educational Policies

EDWARD J. POWER
Boston College

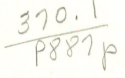

Prentice-Hall, Inc., Englewood Cliffs, New Jersey 07632

Library of Congress Cataloging in Publication Data

POWER, EDWARD J.
   Philosophy of education.

   Bibliography: p.
   Includes index.
   1. Education—Philosophy. I. Title.
LB1025.2.P653   370'.1   81-4312
ISBN 0-13-663252-1   AACR2

Editorial/production supervision by
  Cyrus Veeser and Chrys Chrzanowski
Cover design by Zimmerman/Foyster Design
Manufacturing buyer: Edmund W. Leone

Printed in the United States of America

10 9 8 7 6 5 4 3 2 1

PRENTICE-HALL INTERNATIONAL, INC., *London*
PRENTICE-HALL OF AUSTRALIA PTY. LIMITED, *Sydney*
PRENTICE-HALL OF CANADA, LTD., *Toronto*
PRENTICE-HALL OF INDIA PRIVATE LIMITED, *New Delhi*
PRENTICE-HALL OF JAPAN, INC., *Tokyo*
PRENTICE-HALL OF SOUTHEAST ASIA PTE. LTD., *Singapore*
WHITEHALL BOOKS LIMITED, WELLINGTON, *New Zealand*

CONTENTS

FIGURES

PREFACE

Almost from the time men and women began to occupy this planet, historians tell us, they paid heed to the education of their children. They expected it, among other things, to prepare for life and sometimes to improve the conditions and quality of life in society. As men and women evolved in history and as their social order became increasingly complex, they gave greater attention to the education of succeeding generations. As education matured in a maturing social order, the people generally expected it to be more effective personally and socially. It is an easy exercise to demonstrate how the entire educational process has been improved in succeeding historical periods and it is possible to make a confident assertion that the means for education have never been superior to what they are today.

Yet elements of uncertainty and discord remain to plague us. Despite high expectations for education, on one hand, and with a science of education that has never been more perceptive, productive, and dependable, on the other, the schools are frequently the center of controversy. Agreement with respect to education's scope, to what it should accomplish, and to how it should deploy its resources and techniques is by no means easy to obtain. Along these lines, it seems clear, the science of education—for all its evident accomplishments—cannot be of much help. The science of education is inevitably descriptive and theoretical. It is never normative. It cannot tell us what to do in education. We must look elsewhere for guidance.

When we do, we come to the most ancient of educational disciplines: educational philosophy. It is the business of educational philosophy to probe the fundamental issues of education and to supply some direction with respect to what ought to be done in order to achieve and maintain educational decency.

This book is intended as a beginning, but only a beginning, to the serious matter of establishing educational priorities both with respect to educational objectives and educational means. It could bear the title *An Introduction to the Philosophy of Education.*

As an introduction to educational philosophy, the book is divided into four parts. Part I introduces readers to the study of educational philosophy, illustrates its varying purposes as these purposes are disclosed in different philosophies of education, and considers the status of educational philosophy as an academic discipline. Since educational philosophy has a long and rich historical record, one of the objectives of Part I is to provide the reader with an historical perspective in connection with this ancient educational discipline.

Part II continues the introduction. The reader is given basic information about principal systematic educational philosophies. Sometimes, on certain points, these philosophies conflict; sometimes they agree. In paying attention to systematic philosophies of education, a sensitivity to a contemporary drift away from the systems' approach and to the assumption that educational philosophy has an intrinsic relationship to general philosophy is developed. In any case, the reason for dealing with these philosophies is to ensure a respectable level of philosophical literacy. Part II, in addition, shows how educational philosophy's place may be taken by a theory of schooling, so the contemporary theories of schooling have also been introduced.

Part III, recognizing the relationship in educational philosophy between principle, policy, and practice, centers attention on educational policies that arise from philosophical and practical considerations relative to human nature, to educational purpose, to the content of the curriculum, and to methods and techniques for conducting the educational enterprise.

Were contemporary society immune to educational controversy and conflict over the fundamentals of educational policy, Part IV would be unnecessary. Such, however, is not the case, so Part IV takes a balanced, prudent, and philosophical view of the most frequently disputed issues in contemporary educational policy.

Few books on educational philosophy, and certainly not this one, could be written without help from others. For the most part this help came from both recent and remote literature. Educational philosophy is not a field of inquiry characterized by intellectual fluidity, so one should be neither surprised nor disappointed to find that some of the references—especially those pertaining to philosophical systems—are old. Although they may be old, ideas of consequence in educational philosophy are never out-of-date. I have done my best to indicate these sources of indebtedness. At the same time, in the readings following each chapter, and in the general bibliography, I have included titles to tempt readers and students who, after being introduced to the philosophy of education, have not yet satisfied their intellectual appetites for probing important, frequently imperative, and sometimes universal educational issues.

Edward J. Power

I

EDUCATIONAL PHILOSOPHY'S PURPOSE AND PERSPECTIVE

I

WHAT IS EDUCATIONAL PHILOSOPHY?

In the course of Western civilization men and women debated the things that mattered most to them. They argued, for example, about politics, war, and economics with varying degrees of insight, zeal, and sophistication. In debating what to do about them they always argued from a platform of conviction. What was the source of this conviction? Sometimes, scholars tell us, it was lodged in myth, sometimes in tradition, sometimes in religious faith, and sometimes in reason. Almost nothing in the unfolding of human history occurred as sheer accident. Even when the course of events proved their exponents wrong, action taken along any one of these lines was always supported by what appeared to be good and convincing justification.

Politics and economics, historians tell us, were controlled by persons of social position and authority, for these subjects, even in their infancy, were wrapped in subtleties and obscurities too complicated for the ken of common men. Military strategy and tactics were soon upgraded to become the business of experts, religion the reservation of theologians, tradition a preserve for scholars, and law, while it might exist in heaven, belonged on earth in the hands of the strong.

Yet, outside the narrow circle where courage and cunning counted so much were the so-called ordinary people. They went about their daily chores with what sometimes amounted to a deadening routine, but as they bowed to the demands of necessity they also paid constant heed to the care and upbringing of their children.

We know enough about the lives of our ancestors to know how seldom their hope for their children was inflated, but they were nevertheless solicitous about their training and education. As often as not this tutelage of children in the bosom of the family never counted for much on a scale of authentic educational decency, but the simplicity and rusticity of its character is only one side of a long chronicle.

The other side, the one catching and holding our attention, is the interest persons in every society invested in the care and training of those who would become the next generation of adults. Neither position of authority nor, for that matter, trained intelligence was needed to recognize that whatever society's arrangement of its priorities, the care and training of children headed the list.

Often inarticulate and seldom profound, sometimes with but frequently without design, generation after generation of our forefathers pondered the issue of how to prepare children for their places in society. Even when they were not fully aware of what they were doing, they were planning for education and, in a sense, constructing a philosophy for it.

In the last analysis, whatever form it may take, and however abstruse or sophisticated it may become, and wherever it is found in contemporary society, educational philosophy is a plan for allowing each succeeding generation to fulfill itself and take its place in an increasingly complex and often confusing world. Such a quick and simple definition of educational philosophy, while accurate enough, nevertheless conceals almost as much as it reveals about the many sides of the educational enterprise.

It is necessary to pause from time to time to get our bearings and to examine in some detail varieties of such plans and the fundamental propositions or convictions on which they are based. A place to begin is with the various purposes either assumed by or assigned to educational philosophy.

PURPOSE OF EDUCATIONAL PHILOSOPHY

One has a right to ask any academic discipline to explain itself and to tell persons about to embark on its study what may be expected from such an expenditure of time and talent. Over the years wise men and some not so wise have asked philosophy to justify its existence; in poring over an abundance of educational literature we find that the same inquiry is commonly directed at educational philosophy.

Is philosophy, regardless of the human endeavor with which it essays to deal, simply an academic exercise that, while tempting in intricacy and generous in conundrum, adds up to nothing? Can it be that the time and effort spent by educators, philosophers, and educational philosophers inquiring into almost every side of formal and informal education, of training, and of character building are wasted, and that, in the final analysis, nothing convincing or illuminating can be said about the whole matter of preparing future generations to take their places in society?

Undertaking to persuade persons of its reasonable and responsible purpose, educational philosophy, along with its more ancient forebear, philosophy, has marked out certain routes that it is capable of taking. We should be clear about these routes, for there are many, and not every educator or educational philosopher is ready to count all of them legitimate. So we find the purpose of educational philosophy being characterized as *inspirational, analytical, prescriptive,* and *investigative.* It is worth our while to spend some time examining the meaning and implications of these characterizations. And this may be done best, we think, by using the writings of educational philosophers to illustrate the various purposes at work.

Educational Philosophy's Inspirational Purpose

As an inspirational enterprise educational philosophy means to put on exhibit as a model some organization of teaching and learning that is judged ideal. As we look for illustrations of educational philosophy expressed in utopian language, we are naturally enough attracted to educational philosophy's two classical and universally recognized utopias: Plato's (427?–347 B.C.) *Republic*[1] and Rousseau's (1712–1778) *Émile.*[2] Both *The Republic* and *Émile* have stood the critical test of classical stature—time—and both can be said to belong on a list of great books no educated person leaves unread, but for illustrating the inspirational function of educational philosophy, they are not equally satisfactory.

Plato's Republic   Writing *The Republic,* Plato meant to describe an educational plan that would always be superior for preparing versatile and responsible citizens, but he did not stop with description.[3] He went on to justify the ideal credentials of his plan and came close to requiring its acceptance by any state wanting to enjoy success in the ancient world.

He took the trouble, moreover, to review and criticize the educational plans of the states with which he was familiar. His extensive travel familiarized him with many, and he ended up with the chilly proviso that any state failing to follow the regimen outlined would not only suffer civic decline but would also strip from its citizens any chance to realize their native talent. Description abounds in Plato's bold work, but direction is abundant as well. To find an illustration of philosophy's inspirational purpose we shall have to leave Plato and turn to Rousseau.

Rousseau's Émile.   Jean Jacques Rousseau generously praised Plato's *Republic* as "the finest treatise on education ever written." Along with Plato he acknowledged that, left uneducated, men are "the most savage of earthly creatures."[4] But he began his educational novel, for a novel is what *Émile* is, with the intention of giving his readers a picture of an ideal education, one designed for the boy Emile, and he never abandoned his original intention.

When we read *Émile* we find an educational plan full of novelty and innovation. We find, moreover, that as Emile lives in a country retreat he learns what nature wants to teach him on one hand and what his own nature says is good and useful on the other. Almost certainly Rousseau means to attract our attention and elicit our approval, but he never sets before his readers any unalterable course or direction for education to follow. He merely describes what he considers to be the ideal and is willing to leave to us the choice of adopting or rejecting it as our own plan.

Most scholars who have studied Rousseau's *Émile* agree that his utopian plan was either hard or impossible to imitate except by people of high social rank able to afford tutors for their children.[5] The most astute of Rousseau's disciples always knew that his educational story was meant only for illustration and that before any of the principles buried away in it could be followed, they would have to work out methods suitable to their own condition. To come to this conclusion they had only to read the preface to *Émile:* "The greater or less ease of execution depends on a thousand circumstances which it is impossible to define except in a particular application of the method to this country or that, to this condition or that; and those particular applications are no part of my plan."[6]

Bacon's New Atlantis. To some extent Francis Bacon's (1561–1626) *New Atlantis*[7] also belongs to this category of an inspirational philosophy, a utopian plan for the education of men and women. But Bacon too often ranges beyond educational to scientific and sociological questions, so it is hard to maintain with any assurance that the *New Atlantis* has any, or many, of the credentials of an educational philosophy.

In any case, scholars allege, Bacon was engaged in demonstrating the worth of induction as a way of accumulating dependable knowledge more than in trying to design a place for or a way of disseminating it. According to Bacon, discovery, reached through inductive rather than deductive methods, was to be a huge cooperative social effort; and he was supremely confident that knowledge was more dependably supported by starting with particular cases in experience and drawing general conclusions from them than by beginning with general propositions, first principles, or syllogistic conclusions and then applying them to the particulars of human experience.[8]

Summerhill. Coming closer to contemporary times, the book by A. S. Neill (1883–1973), *Summerhill: A Radical Approach to Child Rearing,*[9] appears to fulfill the specifications of an inspirational plan, although it has marked deficiencies as an educational philosophy: It stops short of any commitment to instruction and is careless about considerations of considerable import—such as the nature of the person and the nature of knowledge—which are essential to an authentic educational philosophy. Neill, moreover, dismissed methods of teaching "because we do not consider that teaching itself matters very much."[10]

Philosophy's Inspirational Purpose Today. Although educational philosophy has adopted, and sometimes promotes, an inspirational purpose, there is little point in dwelling on this purpose for it is neither popular nor preferred among educational philosphers today. In the long run, too little is to be gained by simply setting forth an ideal, or what is assumed to be an ideal, and then leaving the matter of its being adopted either to good will of persons or to chance in events.

Few educational philosophers are content merely to state their case and put trust in its inner logic and natural appeal for adoption. As a class, educational philosophers want to be influential and to have their plans paid heed, so they refuse to engage in what is only an antiseptic exercise. More exactly, they see, probably more clearly than their utopian predecessors, the relationship between theory and practice, between the ideal and the actual. They refuse to allow themselves to be simply interesting, exciting, and, perhaps, innovative in pronouncement but inconsequential in practice.

To stay too long with or to develop too much affection for philosophy as an inspirational enterprise would give additional ammunition to critics who dispense with all philosophy as only an exercise in toying with language, which in the end neither wants nor is able to affect the course of real life.

Educational Philosophy's Analytical Purpose

Every educational philosopher, regardless of allegiance to one or another philosophy, is prepared to be critical and analytical in separating principle and policy into their component parts and holding them up for scrutiny of their meaning, their validity, and their efficacy. Every systematic educational philosophy also takes pardonable pride in its penetrating analysis of the constituents of educational philosophy before melding them into a comprehensive code relative to educational ends and means.

We need read only samples from Plato's dialogues,[11] for example, to hear Socrates ask question after question of famous Sophists, never to be entirely satisfied with their answers. He always wanted more. He wanted definitions of justice, truth, temperance, and prudence rendered precisely. He wanted thickets of linguistic confusion cleared away and complex ideas clarified so meaning could shine through. Socrates' detractors charged him with quibbles over words, and they said he wasted time chasing the elusive "god of certitude" when he should have been helping them find solutions to the practical problems of life in the town of Athens.

They missed Socrates' point: He was as eager as they to attend to everyday affairs, but he wanted to stand on a dependable ground of truth before turning his hand to action. Plato's work may stand as the finest example of analysis in philosophical discourse. But every book ever written on educational philosophy, from the best to the worst, has employed analysis as a method of sorting out the good from the bad, the dependable from the undependable, the true from the false, and the prudent from the imprudent. Some philosophers have shown more talent than others in exercising critical judgment and using methods of analysis, but none has ever abandoned either in drawing on the data of human experience to find signs pointing in the direction education should take.

Linguistic Analysis and Logical Empiricism.   Yet, paying attention to analytic technique as the common currency of philosophic exchange will not lead us to a clear understanding of what is currently called educational philosophy's analytic purpose. It is better to depend on the assertions of exponents of the analytic school (either linguistic analysts or logical empiricists) of educational philosophy: Analysis, they say with almost one voice, is educational philosophy's sole purpose.

As a method, analysis is a way of looking at educational issues and nothing more. It entertains neither pretensions about establishing goals for education, about saying what should be taught and how, nor enthusiasm for telling educational institutions how to meet critical social issues face to face. After stating disclaimers as precisely as possible, analysts go on to embrace one principal commission: to clarify the language used to express thought in order to be as accurate as possible about the meaning (or its lack) in connection with anything said about education. Although it is probably unfair to charge analysts with indifference to thought (say, the content of educational philosophy), the burden of their study clearly rests on the use of language as a medium of expression.

Moreover, when analysts start with the assumption that most educational propositions are either propaganda, or at least unscientific assertions, they are confident that linguistic analysis will reveal their weakness. When they allege that most statements about educational ends and means are clumsy and inexact, both in form and formulation, they feel that analytic technique can help supply definition and precision. When the complexities of the educational process conceal the distinction between, for example, cognitive achievement and the formation of sound ethical character, they point to analysis as the technique for disclosing the distinction.

Skillful analysts can be called on to testify against vacuous theories and hypotheses which, it is said, abound in educational discussion and discourse. Used adroitly, analysis can illustrate the difference between dependable knowledge and whim, exhortation, or mere guess, which it is alleged all too often pass under the guise of truth. In the end, by concentrating on analysis of language and meaning, the enterprise of educational philosophy can become a scientifically enlightened human undertaking with wishful and unscientific thinking pared away.

Justifiers of educational philosophy's analytic purpose are diffident in their promise for it. They tell us how much logic and grammar can contribute to clarity of educational purpose, how a systematic deployment of the arts of mind and expression can illustrate meaning or indict propositions without meaning, but they never define educational purpose. They never set forth those principles on which curricula can stand, or recommend methods of teaching for schools and classrooms. They appear content to leave all this to others. As methodologists, as practicing critics of education, they refuse to proceed beyond an analysis of what has been said about education, and they seem comfortable with their declaration that analysis "has no direct implications for education."[12]

After taking into account the disposition of all educational philosophers to be critical and analytical, and recognizing that this disposition alone does not illustrate philosophy's analytic purpose, we are tempted to close our histories and begin our search for models in education's contemporary literature. If we renewed our review of educational philosophy's history, however, and were careful to interpret what we found, we should very likely conclude that Francis Bacon's

The Advancement of Learning[13]—a book on education frequently consulted whenever our colonial ancestors wanted to find confirmation for their own educational policies, and regularly and lavishly praised by them[14]—was conceived along analytical lines. Bacon's thesis was that most knowledge in man's possession had elements of validity that could be made useful in the practical conduct of affairs if it were purged of those misconceptions that had been grafted to it over the years. Bacon's formula for a kind of cognitive catharsis was inductive logic, and he used induction in *The Advancement of Learning* as a critical, or analytical, technique for discovering dependable educational meaning.

Recent Illustrations of Analytic Philosophy. Still, Bacon's model, so remote from our experience, can have contemporary analogues. And here interest in analytic philosophy is probably more pronounced in Great Britain than in the United States.

Analytic philosophy began with the work of George Edward Moore (1873–1958),[15] Bertrand Russell (1872–1970),[16] and Ludwig Wittgenstein (1889–1951).[17] Alfred Jules Ayer's (b. 1910) *Language, Truth and Logic*[18] and Gilbert Ryle's (1900–1976) *The Concept of Mind*[19] continued and developed this philosophical movement. R. S. Peters (b. 1919), in *Ethics and Education* and *The Philosophy of Education,*[20] made a contemporary British application of analysis to education.

In the United States Israel Scheffler's *The Language of Education*[21] may be taken as representative of philosophy's analytic purpose at work. Scheffler characterizes his book as an essay in educational philosophy; he uses linguistic analysis to clarify ideas in educational literature. His book is an object lesson in the exercise of critical judgment, and he tries to show students of education the methods they should use to draw meaning from an educational literature not yet immune to mental confusion and linguistic obfuscation. As well as any writer in this enigmatic field, Scheffler states his position from a conviction that an analysis of concepts and statements in education constitutes a philosophy of education.

Prescriptive Purpose for Educational Philosophy

Educational philosophers who see prescription as the principal purpose of their discipline begin, in most instances, with the assumption that the universe is characterized by order: All reality, including human beings, fits into a grand cosmic design. Acting intelligently, men and women use their talent to discover the nature of this design and then try to conduct their lives in ways consistent with it. Physical and social reality have differences that cannot be neglected, and these differences account for the rise of discrete sciences and divergent philosophies. In the last analysis, allowing for human freedom to accept or reject what reason prescribes, these differences do not mean that one kind of reality is subject to the law of nature and another is not. The business of philosophy is to interpret all of reality and to bring these interpretations down to the level of daily life.

The role of philosophers, and philosophy, is easy enough to recite, and in this connection the commission for all philosophy, whatever its special branch of inquiry (speculative, normative, or applied)[22] is the same. So, we see, the purpose of educational philosophy in this interpretation is fairly clear and straightforward: to prescribe educational ends and means. What is more difficult, as philosophers of all systems and preferences have learned over the centuries, is to find the fundamentals of cosmic design and then to interpret their meaning in an authentic and persuasive way.

Searching for the fundamentals of cosmic design, some philosophers are led to the conclusion that order is imposed on the universe by a rational being, God, and that in the unfolding of God's plan human beings have duties and obligations that He expects them to fulfill. Other philosophers, while acknowledging order and design in the physical and social worlds, remain unconvinced about divine authorship. With no God to create and manage the world, nature is the source for an unalterable law that does so. In either case, order in the world is confirmed by the data of experience, and it is up to philosophy to relate the evidence of order and design to persons from all walks of life whose destiny it is to find temporal and perhaps eternal satisfaction from their lives.

The role of the general philosopher is broad and comprehensive, taking into account all of reality and all of life; the educational philosopher assumes a somewhat less ambitious charter. His role, when he subscribes to philosophy's prescriptive purpose, is to discover man's nature, capacities, and responsibilities, to find and elaborate dependable intellectual and moral knowledge, to unlock the secrets of the learning process, and, finally, in a comprehensive and prescriptive code, to map out the direction education should take. Such direction is given with accompanying declarations about its worth and authenticity: Grant that the analysis of human nature and the nature of learning is sound and one is rewarded with a logically conceived plan for education that elicits assent and demands adoption.

All this has a harsh sound to contemporary ears unused to hearing so much confidence put in rational processes on one hand and the validity of empirical data to justify these processes on the other. But when one is prepared to acknowledge the dogmatism of truth (a stance these philosophers find comfortable), the credentials of a prescriptive educational philosophy are hard to contradict.

Aristotle, a Pioneer.   Over the centuries educational philosophers have been in the habit of writing directions for education, so illustrations of a prescriptive educational philosophy at work are fairly easy to find. The persuasive deductive logic of Aristotle (384–322 B.C.)[23] started education in this direction. But for some reason unknown to us Aristotle never wrote a philosophy of education exemplifying a prescriptive purpose. He left this commission for others who, over the course of nearly twenty centuries, did their best to carry it out.

Our purpose here, however, would be served better by turning away from ancient models to more modern illustrations, for their currency alone adds a dimension of reality and significance.

Herbart and Nineteenth-Century Educational Philosophy. Reviewing our books on educational history, we meet Johann Herbart (1776–1841),[24] a philosopher, psychologist, and educator remembered most for his pioneering work in educational psychology. But before Herbart turned to psychology he had an established reputation as a philosopher. With a keen philosophical insight for the social and moral dimensions of education, he paid close attention to educational theory. His study of extant educational theory brought him to the abrupt conclusion that, for the most part, theory was deficient. Its principal deficiency, he alleged, lay in the weakness of a foundation constructed on doubtful assumption and misty tradition. This foundation needed prompt reconstruction and reinforcement from science.

The whole structure of educational philosophy could stand confidently on a solid theoretical foundation; and he wanted this structure fully elaborated: He wanted it known and understood. Although Herbart felt uncomfortable as an educational crusader and rejected the role, he wanted educational philosophy to make a difference in the schools. Teachers, he said in his *Science of Education* (an extraordinary title for a book on educational philosophy), should have dependable information about educational goals and processes before entering classrooms. Where were they to get this information?

"The one and the whole work of education may be summed up in the concept —Morality," he wrote, and this concept of morality, he went on to say, is explained and clarified by ethics.[25] So as Herbart pursued his goal of laying down an authoritative standard for education, and to keep a constant check on the validity of the standard, he appealed to moral philosophy and always drew the bulk of his educational wisdom from its huge reservoir. Recognizing, moreover, that education must begin with knowledge of persons—what they are and what they are capable of becoming—ethics (moral philosophy), he maintained, needed help from psychology.

A competent knowledge of ethics would enable educational philosophers to establish proper goals, but such knowledge could do little to show teachers how to construct courses of instruction and develop the appropriate teaching techniques to train the intelligence most effectively. A trained intelligence, it was asserted, is the only adequate and secure safeguard to morality, for the will is a blind faculty able only to choose from among those alternatives the intellect presents. Sound and effective instruction must have guidance from psychology, because the science of psychology possesses those principles on which learning and pedagogic method are based.

Adopting the disinterested stance of a scholar, Herbart spent his several years as a German university professor building what he expected would be a complete and comprehensive theory of education. In effect, he told his students—many of them inquisitive Americans taking their doctorates in German universities—and readers what ought to be done, but perhaps with misplaced confidence in the power of logic to persuade, he neglected to solicit support for a vast array of educational conclusions and allowed them to stand on their own merit.[26]

In some cases merit was good enough to keep his ideas alive among his most zealous disciples,[27] but for the most part, without an enthusiastic and persuasive justification from their author, these conclusions withered from lack of cultivation and promotion and eventually died. Herbart, we believe, was eager to set an educational standard. His hope that this standard would make a difference in schools the world over was almost certainly genuine, but he refused, for whatever reason, to embellish his product with a kind of artistry that gives permanent appeal to an educational rank and file.

In company with Herbart, other educational philosophers sticking close to an orthodox code of scholarly objectivity and pronouncing their educational dicta in clear but unemotional language have suffered a similar fate. They learned too late, if they learned at all, that educational philosophy must campaign for devoted adherents, and that in its campaign, appeals to reason must be supported and sometimes be superseded by appeals to economic interest, social respectability, political expediency, religious orthodoxy, and emotional disposition.

Mortimer Adler and Robert M. Hutchins in the United States. Mortimer Adler, (b. 1902) meticulously distinguishing philosophical knowledge from faith and opinion, certified the credentials of a prescriptive philosophy of education in an essay on educational philosophy in a yearbook of the National Society for the Study of Education: "There cannot be many equally true, though opposed, philosophies of education. With respect to education, as with respect to every other matter the philosopher considers, there can be only one set of true principles and conclusions."[28]

Convinced of the possibility of only one true philosophy, only one capable of guiding education down the long road to the proper and excellent formation of human beings, Adler, alert to the vagaries of human reason, nevertheless conceded that his philosophical conclusions were susceptible of error, although he was prompt to add that he would not be advancing them were he not convinced of their truth.

But the point is larger than this, and it bears on almost every prescriptively conceived educational philosophy: Truth in philosophy is as possible as in any other field of knowledge. Once truth about education is discovered, all have a heavy obligation to adhere to it assiduously.

Adler elaborates what we recognize as a philosophy of education with a prescriptive purpose. We see, moreover, the supreme confidence he exhibits in the power of the human mind to arrive at philosophical truth, affirmed to be natural knowledge without any dependence whatever on faith. And if natural knowledge can be independent of faith, it is also and always superior to opinion.

In company with Adler, Robert M. Hutchins (1899–1977), in almost all his books on education but principally in *The Higher Learning in America,*[29] demonstrated the approach of a prescriptive philosophy of education in connection with what schools teach and what students should be expected to learn.

Regularly deploring the decline of American education into a cult of vocationalism and professionalism, Hutchins employed his educational philosophy to confirm the distinctive human abilities of thought and expression and then to describe the kind of educational program most likely to develop them. When Hutchins wrote about the liberal education of human beings, he refused to restrict it to an elite aristocracy, one without much need to plunge into the practical affairs of life. Rather, he saw it for all citizens who every day are charged with not only making a living but with making decisions affecting their society.

Critics of Hutchins' educational philosophy have been disposed to call a curriculum filled with the world's finest literature and one aimed at the development of thought and expression an exercise in academic irrelevance, but Hutchins argued that any educational program aimed at producing men and women capable of profound and clear thought and precise and persuasive expression was a practical education without peer. Throughout a long and ornamental educational career, Hutchins demonstrated time and again that he meant his brand of educational philosophy to give positive direction to the educational process.

Maritain's Basic Liberal Education. It is often asserted, probably correctly, that both Adler and Hutchins centered their prescriptive educational doctrine on liberal learning, which they defined as being primarily literary in scope and purpose.

Another philosopher who shared most of Adler's and Hutchins' misgivings about modern education, Jacques Maritain (1882–1973), undertook to broaden the meaning of liberal education. In his *The Education of Man* and *Education at the Crossroads,* [30] Maritain scrupulously acknowledged the prescriptive purpose of educational philosophy and introduced the phrase "basic liberal education." This, he declared, is a kind of education essential for everyone. To it he assigned the role of cultivating natural intelligence by beginning with reading, writing, and speaking and then moving forward to prepare persons for those situations they are likely to meet in contemporary society. He rejected the notion that liberal education appeals only to future gentlemen or to a privileged social class, and that it should concentrate almost exclusively on language and literature. Rather, he argued, it should be universal in scope and pay solicitous attention to all future citizens, to free persons who cannot help but make independent judgments in an evolving society and in their personal lives. In effect, Maritain said, the needs of society were changing, and the curriculum of the schools—and the meaning of liberal education, too—were compelled to keep pace with change.

Maritain's liberal education, a policy implicit in his prescriptive educational philosophy, abandoned a traditional liaison with literature and language to embrace any kind of knowledge people needed to lead full, responsible, and satisfying lives. A prescriptive philosophy, however, was commissioned to define the meaning of a full, responsible, and satisfying life.

When prescriptive educational philosophy tells us the meaning of education, it also tells us what schools and colleges should do if they are to keep faith with the commission society has given them to educate children and young people. Educational philosophy is in the vanguard of all those educational subjects concerned with the formation of human beings.

Educational Philosophy's Purpose of
Investigation and Inquiry

An educational philosophy whose purpose is investigation and inquiry refuses to accept or practice leadership. It finds its proper role, instead, in a prudent exercise of the art of delay: It tells educators to organize various kinds of educational experience of their own choosing and to devise pedagogical techniques for introducing students to them. After this has been done, educational philosophy can be called on for evaluations, for justifications, and for commentaries on practice. Educators expecting more than this from educational philosophy will surely be disappointed, because an inquiring educational philosophy is committed to being a moderator of educational and scholastic experience rather than a judge of what is right or wrong in educational goals and practices.

Educational philosophers convinced that their proper role is ratified in cultivating the credentials of an inquiring discipline arrive at this conclusion from an appraisal of the world's reality: To them this appraisal, instead of convincing them that reality proceeds according to an unalterable plan on a fixed course, or that the universe has the kind of structure their prescriptively oriented colleagues like to talk about, presents a picture of a world in the process of evolution: All reality is in a constant state of flux. Even if they wanted to, these philosophers would be unsure of what could be said about knowledge, about how society is held together, what human nature is, or what the end of education should be. As a consequence, practitioners of philosophy as an inquiring discipline choose to help teachers and students meet various challenges in the educational enterprise. They encourage teachers to be experimental and flexible in their approach to learning, and they solicit attention to the interests and needs of students.

Examples of prescriptive educational philosophy are easily found in education's long history, but any quest into the distant past for examples of educational philosophy as a discipline of inquiry and investigation is bound to be disappointing. Most philosophers belonging to this camp joined it by following in the footsteps of its charter member: John Dewey (1859–1952).

John Dewey and Philosophy's New Charter.   John Dewey began a long and illustrious association with pragmatism, a philosophy of education steadfastly committed to inquiry, doubting that any general theory of reality is possible or necessary as a foundation for philosophical inquiry. From this position of doubt, only a short step brought him to an equally skeptical view of the status of knowledge: Truth eludes the grasp of human beings.

With equivocal attitudes about reality and with similar reservations about the possibility of arriving at dependable knowledge, Dewey wrote the twentieth century's most famous book on educational philosophy, *Democracy and Education.* [31] In it he gave educational philosophy's inquiring purpose its first real lease on life.

The broad thesis of Dewey's great book is not easily summarized, but in it he clearly undertakes to authenticate the principle that experience is the ultimate test of all things.[32] Experience, then, may be taken as the banner under which all inquiry-committed educational philosophy marches, and the philosopher's function is to sort out varieties of experience, trying to find those conspiring to promote social efficiency. The point is, and Dewey was always eager to make it, no one could know prior to wading in the pool of life experience how education should try to promote social efficiency. Trial alone might not be a valid test, but in the last analysis it is the only test possible.

In this conception of purpose, educational philosophy's role is to assess trials of teaching and learning, and to assess them according to scientific testing procedures, and then make some comment about their worth. Even these comments, however, should not be taken as authoritative or prescriptive. It is not educational philosophy's business to tell educators what should or should not be done, or what should or should not be taught. Educational philosophy should instead inquire into the consequences of teaching and learning and thus be in a position to give us some insight into what has been done, what the shortcomings are, and how we may do better when we try again to recruit education to the cause of social efficiency.

A Summary of Educational Philosophy's Purposes

Each philosophy of education, we have seen, defines its purpose in a different way, and the definition put forth makes a difference in the way each philosophy approaches fundamental educational issues. What purposes do educational philosophies acknowledge? The question can be answered this way:

1. Educational philosophy is committed to laying down a plan for what is considered to be the best education absolutely.

FIGURE 1.1
Purposes for Educational Philosophy

CHARACTER-IZATION	SUMMARY	PHILOSOPHER AND EXAMPLE
Inspirational	To express utopian ideals for the formal and informal education of human beings	Plato's *Republic*; Rousseau's *Émile*; Bacon's *New Atlantis*; Neill's *Summerhill*
Analytical	To discover and interpret meaning in educational discourse and practice	Peters' *Ethics in Education*; Scheffler's *The Language of Education*
Prescriptive	To give clear and precise directions for educational practice with a commitment to their implementation	Herbart's *The Science of Education*; Hutchins' *The Higher Learning in America*; Maritain's *Education at the Crossroads*
Investigation and Inquiry	To inquire into policies and practices adopted in education with a view to either justification or reconstruction	Dewey's *Democracy and Education*; Kilpatrick's *The Foundation of Method*

2. Educational philosophy undertakes to give directions with respect to the kind of education that is best in a certain political, social, and economic context.

3. Educational philosophy is preoccupied with correcting violations of educational principle and policy.

4. Educational philosophy centers attention on those issues in educational policy and practice that require resolution either by empirical research or rational reexamination.

5. Educational philosophy conducts an inquiry into the whole of the educational enterprise with a view toward assessing, justifying, and reforming the body of experience essential to superior learning.

Dimensions of Educational Philosophy

Having briefly examined the various purposes of educational philosophy, and recognizing from the outset that two—prescription and inquiry—attract the most attention from educational philosophers today, we should go on to inquire into the academic character of educational philosophy.

It is common enough, even in colleges and universities where it is cultivated intensively, to refer to educational philosophy as a theoretical study with little if any practical application to teaching and learning. Philosophizing about education may be fun; it may even test the intellectual mettle of students. But if the essential issues in teaching and learning are to be faced and mastered, an appeal, we are told, must be made directly to educational science.

Philosophy, its most eloquent critics assume, supplies no skill, and teachers need skill. Science, these same critics too quickly conclude, enlightens us about what we should do in connection with all sides of education, and it can tell us a good deal about how we should do it. Philosophy, so they say, belongs to another level of learning. Despite its ornamental and ancient credentials, philosophy can say almost nothing about the problems that every day face classroom teachers, school administrators, boards of education, and all others who have some responsibility for the education of children. Educational philosophy has been caricatured so often, even by persons from whom better might be expected, that its image of impracticality and its assignation with pure theory is almost impossible to erase.

When these dimensions to the study of educational philosophy are put in perspective, we should want to know why there are several philosophies of education. Although only three or four prominent contemporary philosophies of education catch and hold our attention, a complete recitation of the current philosophies would make a long list. It is only natural to be curious about why there are so many.

Nature of the Study

Students, we said earlier, have a right to know what to expect from subjects studied. The point reminds us of an enthusiastic and excited Hippocrates who raced to Socrates' house early one morning to tell Socrates of the arrival in town of the great Sophist, Protagoras (481–411 B.C.). Hippocrates announced his intention of taking a course from him.[33]

Socrates asked young Hippocrates what Protagoras taught, what his special branch of knowledge was, and what Hippocrates expected to know when he finished his study. Unprepared for the question, Hippocrates confessed ignorance about Protagoras' scholarship. Safe to say, we should not want to be forced to admit to a similar ignorance of a subject we are about to tackle. Let us begin by asking whether the philosophy of education is a theoretical (a speculative) or a practical subject.

Our task would be considerably simpler if all educational philosophy stood on common ground and if educational philosophers spoke with one voice on this matter of theoretical vis-à-vis practical knowledge. In fact, though, there are two ideological camps. The first enlists proponents of the view that any distinction between theoretical and practical knowledge and, therefore, any distinction between knowing and doing is either purely fictional or logically artificial. They assert the validity of a kind of knowledge capable of helping us make decisions. Inquiry-oriented philosophers flock to this camp and, in general, find an intellectual climate suitable to their philosophical temperaments. The second, with one foot in the camp of practical knowledge, keeps up philosophical appearances by putting the other in a camp where theory is given solicitous attention: both theory and practice are accredited.

Educational Philosophy as a Practical Study. By erasing any possible distinction between theory and practice, this contingent of educational philosophers leaves itself with the burden of deciding whether the discipline under cultivation is theoretical or practical, whether its academic duty is to tell us only what is or only what we ought to do.

They make this choice eagerly and quickly. Every claim they make for educational philosophy stands on the solid conviction that they are engaged in an eminently practical undertaking, one that gives an abundance of guidance to the problems facing contemporary educators.

John Dewey, for example, spoke with the credentials of an authority when he rejected the dualism of knowing and doing—of theory and practice—as being nothing more than an intellectual remnant from discredited philosophical systems.[34] The crucible of experience, he averred, demonstrates how artificial such a distinction is, and educators who followed Dewey's well-blazed philosophical trail have been disposed to adopt his thesis.

Were we to take our cue from an educational philosophy captivated by a purpose of inquiry, debate on the matter would cease here, and students would be left to ponder the practical dimensions of educational philosophy because there are no others. Yet hastily leaping on this bandwagon of practical knowledge could leave us in the position of experimenting with a variety of current educational techniques or of wrestling with critical social issues facing education without any substantial criteria for assessing their worth.[35] We would have foreclosed our chances to cross the threshold of authentic educational philosophy.

Still, such an outcome would only be the most likely one. The possibility exists, as many prominent educational philosophers have illustrated, of building a philosophy of education on a fundamental premise asserting the pragmatic character of knowledge. To allege educational philosophy's practical mission is one thing, and we should want to subscribe to such an allegation, but to arrive at this definition of mission by dismissing the distinction between different orders of knowledge is another, and on this latter point we want to demur.

Educational Philosophy as a Theoretical and Practical Study. A long and respectable philosophical tradition recognizes the existence of a valid and essential distinction between theory and practice. Prescriptive philosophies of education belong to this camp. According to traditional philosophical convention, theoretical (or speculative) knowledge is capable of informing us, for example, about the nature of reality. Its concern is with what is or was. Metaphysics, as a branch of philosophy, contains theoretical knowledge about ultimate reality. The history of education, a common subject in a professional course of study, parades before us the schools, the teachers, the curricula, the institutions, and the theories that filled out the picture of past education.

Neither metaphysics nor history contains the kind of knowledge that tells us either what should be done or how to do it in situations that may arise in life.[36] Metaphysics may supply data with respect to what *is,* and history may faithfully record what *was,* but no one who recognizes the nature of these disciplines and the kind of knowledge they husband expects them to lay down guidelines for action. The fact, however, that neither metaphysics nor history is practical should hardly tempt us to dismiss both as studies unworthy of our time and attention.

Practical knowledge, in whatever discipline it is found, is ready to tell us what we ought to do and how we ought to do it. There are, however, different levels of practical knowledge: An architect may know how to build a house heated by solar energy, although he might lack the special skill of a clever carpenter.

This leads us to say that although there is theoretical knowledge about education (for example, the history of education—a record of past educational events —and the psychology of learning—a scientific explanation of how learning occurs), the philosophy of education is not a part of its corpus. Educational philosophy is not theoretical or speculative in its purview. Rather, if its purpose is prescriptive, it essays to construct a broad design to give direction to educational practice. Its purpose is to tell educators, students, parents—in fact, everyone interested in education—what ought to be done. The educational philosopher is similar to the architect: He may know a great deal about the design, the purpose, and the policies of education without being a clever or an accomplished pedagogic technician.

The practical knowledge in the discipline of educational philosophy is remote rather than immediate, for it deals with educational action in general: It is essentially practical because it is always concerned with action. Immediately practical knowledge—what is to be done in a given instance—is a kind of knowledge which, while depending on the remotely practical knowledge of educational philosophy, must call upon prudence for help. Where prudence is concerned—knowing what is to be done here and now—experience has no substitute.

If, coming this far, we are persuaded of educational philosophy's practical nature with a principal function to formulate plans for governing the educational process, we should go on to identify the various steps essential to a translation of philosophical knowledge about education to a level where such knowledge can make a difference in schools, where formal education is concerned, and in society generally, when informal education is being considered. Although the bulk of philosophy's attention is normally paid to schools, the belief is common, and undoubtedly correct, that an entirely adequate philosophy's scope must extend to out-of-school education as well.

Limits to the Competence of Educational Philosophy. Before we go much further we must be clear about the limits of philosophy's competence: What can and cannot be expected from it? Educational philosophy is a practical discipline with its eye firmly fixed on giving remote and proximate guidance to the educational enterprise. But this does not mean that every problem in education is philosophical or that every question to be asked about the operation of schools, about the care and custody of learning, can be answered by educational philosophy.

The point should be elaborated: Education is filled with questions whose answers come, if they come at all, from the science of education. When one asks, for example, about techniques most suitable for teaching a reading lesson to a class of students whose disposition toward learning is slight or whose talent for mastering the skill of reading is somehow impaired, the answer should be sought not from the educational philosopher but from the reading specialist—a person conversant with this branch of the science of education.

A professor of educational measurement, of child psychology, or of school administration is attentive to special aspects of the science of education, and knows better than to pretend a philosophical character for his study. And the philosopher, unless he also possesses such scientific knowledge about education, should abstain from making positive assertions about the content of these specialties.

Yet even these limits, sensible as they appear to be, leave ample room for philosophy. Philosophy's commission is to deal with those educational questions whose resolution depends on philosophical knowledge—who is being educated (the nature of persons), what the ends or purposes of education are, and what general means (curricular and methodological) should be used to achieve the goals set.

Translation from Principle to Policy to Practice. Philosophical knowledge has its initial formulation, its first elaboration, in general principles. What can the philosopher say about educational ends and means that has universal application? These declarations with universality—ones that apply to all manner of classes of persons regardless of their locale in geography or history—have the status of principle. Yet, if philosophy always stayed on the level of principle, it could be accused, and probably convicted, of having not practical but only theoretical knowledge about the education of human beings. There would be no way to enlist its knowledge for action. So another step toward action must be made, and when it is made educational philosophy begins to operate on the level of policy.

The translation of philosophical principle to policy is an application of universal knowledge about education to general classes of persons who live in certain places, under certain conditions, at certain times in history. Educational policy plays its part when it tells educators how to organize and operate the multiple sides of a broadly conceived educational plan.

After principle is used to construct policy, and policy makes principle speak directly and immediately to time, place, and person, the next step is to apply policy to the operations of teaching and learning, to bring it down to a point where it directly affects educational practice. The question is: What is to be done in this particular case? Any fully developed philosophy of education should be capable of moving, although not always effortlessly, from principle to policy to practice, and when it does it is worth an educator's time to pause long enough to hear what it has to say.

Where policy and practice meet, however, is where differences between philosophical knowledge and scientific knowledge about education must be recognized and respected. There is the possibility, however, that scientifically based technique will violate the nature or the dignity of the person or tread roughshod over dependable knowledge. Should this occur, it becomes the obligation of educational philosophy to call attention to the deficiencies in educational science and to do its best to redress them. This may be done, we think, without educational philosophy adopting the pretense that its proper boundaries extend far enough to include educational science.

Of the three steps in philosophy's compact with education, the one most difficult to negotiate, the one where most hazards appear because most social issues are complex, is policy. The difficulty is not so much with acknowledging the validity of one or another principle as being socially and politically operable, but rather with adapting universal declarations about education to particular social circumstances.

So as educational philosophers work at their desks or in their classrooms, they inevitably appeal to experience to teach them how to promote prudent educational policies in their own land and time. The message of experience varies in its impression on different persons, even those with the solidest philosophical temperament, and the rendering of prudent judgments about so varied an activity as education is almost bound to have different and sometimes discordant sounds. Even with the firmest principles to guide it, philosophy is seldom spared from incisive and urgent disagreement.

Yet to dwell on or magnify the possibility of philosophical disagreement is also to cloud the issue of philosophy's true dimensions. Playing down discord and looking at philosophy as we have, we can see how its universal elements can stay fresh and effective: Philosophical principle knows neither the limiting influence of place nor the obliterating force of time, but in its translation and application to various historical periods in distinct social and political settings, it can come alive as an influential and effective force in a great social undertaking. Its policies can take on different hues as they are shaped and reshaped from country to country or for different areas within a country, but the universality of its basic principles can carry all the way to the classroom.

Now, if Socrates were asking us what we expected to do when we finished our study, we should be ready with an answer.

Philosophical Variety

If educational philosophy contains genuine, valid knowledge about educational purpose and process, and if such knowledge can be authenticated logically or empirically, it is obviously different from opinion about education. Why, we must ask, does educational truth find so many diverse philosophical outlets and have such a variety of outspoken, zealous adherents? Why are there so many philosophies of education?

If the content of educational philosophy were opinion, right opinion, to use a Platonic expression, rather than vulgar opinion, it would be easy for us to see why one philosopher's opinions about education could differ substantially from those of others. But if the content of the discipline is knowledge about education —as almost all educational philosophers eagerly allege—then our quandary becomes all the greater, for genuine knowledge, we should think, would not reveal one story today and another tomorrow or, moreover, alter the thrust of its meaning to suit the fancy and temperament of a particular audience.

The Nature of the Person. When Jacques Maritain established the nature of man as the unavoidable preamble to any and all philosophies of education, he supplied us at the same time with the answer to our question about philosophical variety.[37] There are different philosophies of education, some of which shall be met and studied in subsequent chapters, precisely because different interpreta-

FIGURE 1.2
Theoretical and Practical Knowledge in Educational Philosophy

KIND OF KNOWLEDGE	APPLICATION TO EDUCATION
Immediately Practical	To guide educational practice in the classroom and laboratory
Theoretical	To express educational principle or, as in the history of education, to record past educational event and practice
Combination of Theoretical and Practical	*Principle:* To make universal declarations about the education of men and women
	Policy: To translate educational principle for application to contemporary social and educational conditions
	Practice: To implement principle and policy on the level of teaching and learning

tions are made—all with the assumed status of dependable knowledge—about the fundamental capacities of human nature.

When naturalistic philosophers probe the nature and capacity of human beings, they find persons who have ascended step by evolutionary step from lower forms of life. Here are biological organisms composed of matter and nothing more, although as a consequence of biological evolution they have reached a highly refined and complex stage of development. Considering capacity, they find the answer in what human beings are capable of doing. Hidden spiritual potentialities are absent and the mystery of human nature waiting for discovery by reason and experience is the vain hope of philosophical absurdity. Human nature is an open book written in language anyone is able to read.

This interpretation of human nature, which the naturalistic philosophers assert is as capable of verification as any other, is where their educational philosophy begins. Step by step thereafter, although taking into account the possibility of shifting in one or another direction depending on philosophies of reality and knowledge encountered, this starting point affects every educational judgment that can be made on the level of objectives and practices. It influences every proposition that can be advanced about social education and its consequences, and it infuses those immensely complex matters of character education with a pragmatic or an experimental system of ethics. It tells us, for example, that ethical decisions must be resolved in familiar, personal contexts, and it leaves us in a world where truth is described as relative.

When humanist philosophers open the book of human nature they read of capacities missed by naturalists. Human beings, they find, are more than highly developed biological organisms produced by an evolutionary process. Their minds and wills stand ready to be perfected by the good offices of a decent education.

It is the business of educational philosophy, humanists maintain, to set fundamentally human standards for education, standards worthy of human nature, and to develop an educational process confirmed by the stability of dependable knowledge about a real material and spiritual world wherein these standards can be realized. Human life, different and more precious than any other kind of life, makes its own natural and logical demands on education. Every educational judgment humanists make is infused with and dominated by this interpretation of human nature.

These naturalistic and humanistic conceptions of human nature are only preliminary general illustrations of why educational philosophy takes different directions when it begins to deal with educational ends and means. The general positions illustrated here as naturalism and humanism are subject to still further subdivision and analysis. Such subdivision multiplies educational philosophies and makes the intelligent outsider, without any philosophical axe to grind, wonder how educational truth can serve so many masters.

NOTES

1. PLATO, *The Republic* (Cambridge, Mass.: Harvard University Press, Loeb Classical Library, 1930–1935).
2. JEAN JACQUES ROUSSEAU, *Émile* (London: J. M. Dent and Sons, Ltd., 1943).
3. Scholarly studies of Plato's educational thought are abundant. Good examples are: John E. Adamson, *The Theory of Education in Plato's "Republic"* (New York: Macmillan, Inc., 1903); R. C. Lodge, *Plato's Theory of Education* (London: Routledge & Kegan Paul, Ltd., 1947); and Walter Moberly, *Plato's Conception of Education and Its Meaning Today* (New York: Oxford University Press, 1944).
4. WILLIAM BOYD, *The Émile of Jean Jacques Rousseau*, trans. and ed. William Boyd (New York: Teachers College Press, 1962), pp. 11, 13.
5. ROUSSEAU, *Émile*, p. 17.
6. *Ibid.*, p. 3.
7. FRANCIS BACON, *The Works of Francis Bacon* (Boston: Brown and Taggard, 1860–1871).
8. The syllogism is a method of deductive reasoning. It consists of a major and a minor premise and a conclusion. The conclusion necessarily follows from the premises, so if the premises are true, the conclusion must be true.
9. A. S. Neill, *Summerhill: A Radical Approach to Child Rearing* (New York: Hart Publishing Company, 1960).
10. Ibid., p. 24.
11. PLATO, *The Dialogues*, trans. B. Jowett (New York: Charles Scribner's Sons, 1872).
12. HERBERT FEIGL, "Aims of Education for Our Age of Science: Reflections of a Logical Empiricist," in the Fifty-fourth Yearbook of the National Society for the Study of Education, *Modern Philosophies and Education,* (Chicago: University of Chicago Press, 1955), p. 304.
13. FRANCIS BACON, *The Advancement of Learning,* ed. Joseph Devey (New York: American Home Library Company, 1902).
14. EDWARD J. POWER, *The Transit of Learning* (Sherman Oaks, Calif.: Alfred Publishing Company, 1979), pp. 79–88.
15. GEORGE EDWARD MOORE, *Principia Ethica* (Cambridge: University Press, 1903); *Ethics* (New York: Henry Holt, 1912), *Philosophical Studies* (London: Routledge & Kegan Paul, Ltd., 1922); *Some Main Problems in Philosophy* (New York: Macmillan, Inc., 1953).
16. BERTRAND RUSSELL, *The Basic Writings of Bertrand Russell,* ed. R. E. Egner and L. E. Denonn (London: George Allen & Unwin, 1961).
17. LUDWIG WITTGENSTEIN, *Tractatus Logico-Philosophicus,* trans. by D. F. Pears and B. F. McGuinness (New York: Humanities Press, Inc., 1961).
18. ALFRED JULES AYER, *Language, Truth and Logic* (London: Victor Gollancz, 1946).
19. GILBERT RYLE, *The Concept of Mind* (New York: Barnes & Noble Books, 1949).
20. RICHARD S. PETERS, *Ethics and Education* (Glenview, Ill.: Scott, Foresman & Company, 1967); and *The Philosophy of Education* (London: Oxford University Press, 1973).

21. ISRAEL SCHEFFLER, *The Language of Education* (Springfield, Ill.: Charles C. Thomas, Publisher, 1960).
22. Speculative philosophy considers the nature of reality and the possibility of our having knowledge of reality. It is descriptive. Normative philosophy, concerned with the true, the good, and the beautiful, formulates principles in connection with them. Applied philosophy seeks to deal with conduct in the various fields of human life.
23. ARISTOTLE, "Posterior Analytics," in *The Works of Aristotle,* trans. under the editorship of W. D. Ross (Oxford: Clarendon Press, 1910–1930), vol. I.
24. J. F. HERBART, *The Science of Education,* trans. H. M. and E. Felkin (Boston: D. C. Heath and Company, 1893).
25. Ibid., p. 57.
26. HAROLD B. DUNKEL, *Herbart and Herbartianism: An Educational Ghost Story* (Chicago: University of Chicago Press, 1970), p. 28.
27. Ibid., p. 80.
28. MORTIMER ADLER, "In Defense of the Philosophy of Education," in the Forty-first Yearbook of the National Society for the Study of Education, *Philosophies of Education* (Chicago: University of Chicago Press, 1942), p. 199.
29. ROBERT M. HUTCHINS, *The Higher Learning in America* (New Haven: Yale University Press, 1936).
30. JACQUES MARITAIN, *The Education of Man: The Educational Philosophy of Jacques Maritain,* ed. Donald and Idella Gallagher (Garden City, N.Y.: Doubleday & Co., 1962); and *Education at the Crossroads* (New Haven: Yale University Press, 1943).
31. JOHN DEWEY, *Democracy and Education* (New York: Macmillan, Inc., 1916).
32. Ibid., p. 92.
33. PLATO, *Protagoras,* 310 af. Trans. B. Jowett in *The Dialogues of Plato,* 3d ed. (London: Oxford University Press, 1892).
34. DEWEY, *Democracy and Education,* pp. 378–379.
35. BOYD H. BODE, *Fundamentals of Education* (New York: Macmillan, Inc., 1921), pp. 241–242.
36. ADLER, "In Defense of the Philosophy of Education," pp. 206–209.
37. JACQUES MARITAIN, "Thomist Views on Education," in the Fifty-fourth Yearbook of the National Society for the Study of Education, *Modern Philosophies and Education* (Chicago: University of Chicago Press, 1955), p. 63.

READINGS

ADLER, MORTIMER J., "In Defense of the Philosophy of Education," in the Forty-first Yearbook of the National Society for the Study of Education, Part I, *Philosophies of Education.* Chicago: University of Chicago Press, 1942. This essay develops the idea that a philosophy of education, if properly constituted, contains dependable knowledge about educational ends and means.
"The Aim and Content of Philosophy of Education," *Harvard Educational Review,* XXVI, No. 2 (Spring, 1956). The entire issue is a report of a symposium on the nature

"The Aim and Content of Philosophy of Education," *Harvard Educational Review,* XXVI, No. 2 (Spring, 1956). The entire issue is a report of a symposium on the nature and purpose of educational philosophy. As one might expect, a variety in view and analysis is represented.

BROUDY, HARRY S., *Building a Philosophy of Education.* Englewood Cliffs, N.J.: Prentice-Hall, Inc., 1961. In Chapter 1 the author explores the ways one should go about constructing a philosophy of education.

ELVIN, LIONEL, *The Place of Commonsense in Educational Thought.* London: George Allen & Unwin, 1977. Chapter 1 is a bold effort to restore common sense to educational discourse.

FISHER, ROBERT T., *Classical Utopian Theories of Education.* New Haven: College and University Press, 1964. Choice here should be made on the basis of the reader's interest.

LUCAS, CHRISTOPHER J., ed., *What is Philosophy of Education?* New York: Macmillan, Inc., 1969. For a challenge to philosophy's and educational philosophy's credentials, read Lewis Fuer's chapter, "American Philosophy Is Dead."

MARLER, CHARLES D., *Philosophy and Schooling.* Boston: Allyn & Bacon, Inc., 1975. In Chapter 1 the author deals with the nature of education, the nature of philosophy, and the nature of educational philosophy.

PETERS, RICHARD S., *Education and the Education of Teachers.* London: Routlege & Kegan Paul, Ltd., 1977. The role of philosophy in teacher education is considered in Chapter 7.

PHENIX, PHILIP H., *Philosophy of Education.* New York: Holt, Rinehart & Winston, 1958. In Chapter 1 the nature of philosophy, the meaning of education, and the value of educational philosophy are discussed from a philosophical point of view.

SCHEFFLER, ISRAEL, *Reason and Teaching.* London: Routledge & Kegan Paul, Ltd., 1973. In Chapters 1 and 2 analytical philosophy and the relationship between philosophy and education are discussed.

2

EDUCATIONAL
PHILOSOPHY
IN HISTORICAL
PERSPECTIVE

E very early society, even the most primi-
tive, historians tell us, paid some heed to the proper training and instruction of
youth. But the record, despite the obliterating forces of time, is fairly clear: This
heed was never cultivated to the point where it could mature into a body of
knowledge about what education and training should do or how it should proceed. Our ancient ancestors were satisfied with broad opinions—some of them
lodged in myth—about education, and they give evidence of having been guided
by them, but they never codified these opinions into special categories of thought.
It was enough for these views about what instruction was needed for oncoming
generations to be grafted to and remain alive in a general social tradition.

The march of time, however, made these pleasant educational informalities
obsolete. When the clock of social evolution reached the Greek Classical Age
(450–350 B.C.), competing loyalties and conflicting social forces issued a vigorous
challenge to old-fashioned educational habits: Should persons be tutored to serve
the state's interests first and in any time left over tend to their own? Or should
the private, personal motives of citizens have priority and in their realization the
legitimate interests of the state, of the body politic, could take care of themselves?
Other alternatives may occur to us now, but in ancient days these were the ones
whose resolution was considered imperative. By adopting the thesis that men and
women have a primary obligation to serve the state, schools and other social
agencies with educational functions were commissioned to superintend civic
training. And for civic training or citizenship the best and most dependable

guidelines were certain to be found in political theory. When personal formation was accorded pride of place, however, lurking in the background was the premonition of individual appetite becoming so ravenous that civic and social virtue would be put in jeopardy. The cultivation of personal talent could be justified, but character needed a safeguard that, it was stipulated, moral philosophy (ethics) would have to supply.

With civic and personal objectives competing for education's attention, moral and political philosophers took their first hesitant steps toward educational theory and, as we have said before, their scholarly incentive in making educational policy complement either politics or ethics carried all the way to the invention of an infant, immature, and dependent philosophy of education.

THE BEGINNINGS OF EDUCATIONAL PHILOSOPHY

The first foundations of educational philosophy were crafted by hundreds, perhaps thousands, of scholars whose perception of education's significance both to persons and societies was clear enough to take them over those inevitable hurdles of convention on one hand and unavoidable human inertia on the other. Among these legions of philosophical pioneers, a few were always in the vanguard, and the trail they marked turned out to be an indelible one for their successors to follow. Since our interest here is intensive rather than comprehensive, this chapter will call for testimony only those witnesses whose record of accomplishment leaps to our attention, so we recognize them at once as the best and most articulate spokesmen for an educational philosophy slowly coming of age.

Relativistic Humanism

The need for the steady hand of theory might have been less urgent had politics and war not intruded on an otherwise serene Athenian society at about the middle of the fifth century B.C. For hundreds of years the ancient tradition prohibiting anyone other than a fully pedigreed citizen from bearing arms in the state's defense had been followed to the letter, but now the Persian army was infiltrating Athens by land, and her men-of-war were sailing down the Greek coast to blockade the port of Athens. The soldiers of Athens were courageous and intrepid campaigners who could be counted on by land, but Athens lacked a naval fleet, and one was desperately needed to save the city from a Persian siege. Necessity, we have often heard, is the mother of invention, and the Athenians were inventive enough to induct their merchant mariners—none of them citizens—into a naval force that succeeded in turning back the Persian threat.

With the conclusion of hostilities Athens went through a period of political and social unrest, so common as an aftermath to war, and during this period the men who had been conscripted to the navy declared their conviction that Athens owed them a debt that could be repaid only by the grant of full citizenship. Nothing like this had ever been heard of before, so without the stability of precedent to guide them in their hour of political need, the citizens of Athens awarded the franchise of citizenship to the men of the navy. All this was well and good, and we are tempted to praise the liberalism of Athens in cutting through the red tape of convention to create a new class of citizens. But Athens was a small city-state governed directly by a few thousand citizens, and every citizen was expected to carry his own social, cultural, and political weight. This weight was too great for the new citizens whose whole lives had been spent outside the circle of a society that took considerable pride in preparing its youth, although usually informally, to handle the responsibilities of citizenship.

The Appearance of the Sophists.   At this point, history introduces us to the Sophists. Hearing what was going on in Athens and knowing that the conventional educational system of the city-state had no place for these new citizens, the Sophists—a cadre of intelligent, clever men—came to Athens to educate them for citizenship, to prepare them fully and quickly to take their places in the ranks of the governors of Athens. While Athenians by the hundreds applauded the Sophists for their ingenuity in devising an abbreviated educational program for men already mature, too old to sit at the feet of schoolmasters, other hundreds were quick to condemn them for their intellectual arrogance and educational presumption. They charged the Sophists with moral nihilism and intellectual relativism, and to a great extent, they were right, for the Sophists refused to acknowledge that morality was anything more than what most people thought was right or that truth had any credentials better than those found in the art of persuasion. If the meaning of virtue was a mystery, then "might makes right" became, in their view, the ultimate operable moral principle; if truth was buried too deeply ever to be discovered by men, then the banner of skepticism had to be carried by the force of the better argument. Sophists were shrewd enough to realize how often the appearance of truth served citizens just as well, and sometimes better, than truth itself. In an opportunistic creed of nihilism and skepticism the Sophists earned and deserved their characterization as relativistic humanists.

The moral and intellectual relativism that we meet today in educational philosophy had its origin at least as early as the Sophists, but this is not the central point we want to make in connection with their work in forging the discipline of educational philosophy. Their positive contributions to the subject must of course be acknowledged, because they belong to the clear record of history, and we shall get to them, but by appearing to be educationally shallow and philosophically naive, the Sophists stimulated others—for example, Plato, Isocrates (436–338 B.C.), and Aristotle—to greater activity in speculating about educational ends and means and thus both promoted the fortunes and speeded the development of educational philosophy. Had Plato and Isocrates been in full agreement with sophistic school practice, the likelihood is that they would have found other urgent matters on which to exercise their almost boundless intelligence and wisdom. As it was, they thought the Sophists were on the wrong educational track, and they would have to do their best, by elaborating an educational philosophy of their own—even by opening schools of their own—to destroy sophistic influence.[1]

Were we to adopt Plato's indictment of sophistry as dangerous and irresponsible, we would still have the obligation to commend Sophists for their humanistic motives. They saw an entire class of mature citizens who by reason of social accident was being put at political and cultural disadvantage. They did their best, as many Athenians would gladly testify, to redress the shortcomings of an educational system that lacked room for anyone unable to meet the qualification of full Athenian ancestry. In addition, they made instruction quick and direct and practical. Refusing to waste time on the frills of tradition and the hoary tales of myth, the Sophists taught their students what they needed most: the art of speaking well. Inventive, innovative, and ingenious in their approach to pedagogy, they conducted their classes by encouraging their students toward literary accomplishment, and despite all we have heard about the excellence of classical education, up to this time literary accomplishment had been paid scant heed.

Primed by enthusiasm and intoxicated by success, the Sophists sometimes went too far, and when they did their more conservative colleagues were ready to lash them with invective. How did they go too far? Although dozens of Sophists flocked to Athens to peddle their scholastic wares, those who made the deepest impression on the history of educational philosophy were Protagoras from Abdera, Gorgias (circa 483 B.C.) from Sicily, Hippias (circa 473 B.C.) from Elis, Prodicus (circa 473 B.C.) from Ceos, and Antiphon (circa 440 B.C.) who, rare for Sophists, was a native Athenian.[2]

Taking their philosophical and ethical cues from their leaders who, from all appearances, were Protagoras and Gorgias, the Sophists adopted theses enabling them to teach anything to anyone—anyone, that is, who could afford to pay their fees. Protagoras intoned the doctrine that "man is the measure of all things," a doctrine so obviously skeptical that it enabled sophistic schoolmasters to advance their own opinions as substitutes for knowledge. This attitude naturally enough offended men like Plato, who had dedicated their scholastic lives to a quest for certitude. Worse yet, Gorgias proclaimed that "Nothing exists beyond the senses; if anything existed beyond the senses it would be unknowable, for all knowledge comes from the senses; if anything suprasensual were knowable, it would be uncommunicable, . . ."[3]

So far Protagoras and Gorgias sound alike, for neither is prepared to invest knowledge with certitude, but where Protagoras would delegate each person to take for himself the measure of experience, Gorgias follows his dangerous doctrine to its ultimate end: Distilling meaning from experience and using it as a guide to action is the proper role for the eloquent or the mighty. Citizens of Athens, if Gorgias had his way, would become the abject followers, first, of orators persuasive enough to convince them to follow a certain course of action, and if oratory failed, force would replace it: In the last analysis, the course of right action belonged to the most powerful. Recognizing the subversion of reason by might in this insidious doctrine, Socrates and his disciples had every right to be horrified.[4]

Scholastic Innovations of the Sophists.   The connection between sophistic school practice and policy and basic principles of knowledge and morality must not be dismissed as being inconsequential, nor should the Sophists be indicted for ignorance of where their skepticism and nihilism would lead, but the Sophists chose to regard themselves as teachers rather than thinkers and showed little or no disposition to convert their students to their philosophical thought. Their aim, they said, was to teach social and political success; so, giving them the benefit of every historical doubt, we should assess the extent of their accomplishments on the level of educational policy, where they were progressive, and on the level of pedagogic practice, where they were innovative. On both levels they made lasting contributions to educational philosophy.

As professional teachers expecting to make a living from their work, the Sophists set their fees according to what scholastic traffic would bear: When competition for students was keen, fees were lowered to attract students; when students were plentiful, fees were high enough to make them prosperous. Protagoras, for example, whose reputation for excellence may have allowed him to do so, charged as much as ten thousand drachmas for a course in civics, and at that time a drachma was the daily wage of a worker in Athens.[5]

But while this side of sophistry is interesting, other sides have more claim to our attention. Assuming that knowledge (or what passed for knowledge) could improve character, the Sophists discarded the aristocratic notion that virtue is a natural endowment. They adopted the policy of investing instruction with the responsibility of forming effective and successful citizens and, moreover, introduced a liberal influence to educational theory by giving nurture precedence over nature. Knowledge, they declared, is virtue, so if citizens or anyone else knows what ought to be done, they will do it.

After placing this burden on instruction, a burden almost too heavy to bear, they proceeded to reform the entire structure of classical education by giving it literary and intellectual objectives. Sport was evicted from the old gymnasiums and, eventually, as sophistic teaching was more widely heralded, schoolboys began to abandon the conventional playgrounds to take their places in classrooms. In the wake of sport's decline, the Sophists, by the end of the fifth century B.C., had founded what we recognize now as a literary secondary education.

Generalizations about sophistic teaching can be hazardous; the Sophists, who were never a closely organized body of teachers, may not have followed a common teaching plan, and with the exception of a few historical fragments, we have little firsthand knowledge about them. However, a few points can be made with confidence. Even their enemies, who tell us most about the Sophists, give us a glimpse of their merit. Beginning with the admission that the Sophists failed to develop a philosophy of education, they nevertheless hastened the day when educational philosophy was able to assert its independence. And in this connection they were responsible for a new type of higher education—literary secondary education—the most advanced instruction in fifth-century Athens.

They sponsored, moreover, new curricula and new fields of knowledge: Language and logic were upgraded in their custody, and studies in grammar and literature were promoted as essential prerequisites to the art and science of rhetoric. Literature and mathematics were commissioned to serve two masters: knowledge and discipline. So the Sophists began by promoting the disciplinary value of education, and their influence was strong enough to keep this value alive to affect the work of their successors. All their pedagogic innovations were riveted on practical results, and here the Sophists' reputation for effective teaching appears to have a perennial dimension. Their theory, although largely anticipatory and severely fragmented, was forced to compete in following centuries with the scientific humanism of Plato and his disciples on one hand and the literary humanism of Isocrates and his successors on the other.

Scientific Humanism

Condemned to moral doubt and intellectual uncertainty by the Sophists, the first foundations of educational philosophy were rescued from the slough of relativism by Plato and were invigorated and rehabilitated in the temperate climate of scientific humanism. Where relativism left everything in doubt and allowed education to take what at any time appeared to be the most expeditious course, scientific humanism followed an azimuth whose critical points were truth and virtue, and neither truth nor virtue was held hostage by the accident of time or place. Both stood on the solid bedrock of science and philosophy.

Citizens must act; neither Plato nor anyone else doubted that. But action always needed an indispensable and incorruptible antecedent: authentic knowledge about what ought to be done. Under this circumstance, the educational program Plato was ready to recommend and the philosophy of education he wanted to promulgate had almost nothing in common with the Sophists' preoccupation with the art of speaking well. The place for all education to begin, Plato declared, is with the most talented youth. Once they have been selected, their good minds must have a common intellectual meeting place to ensure the full and complete cultivation of their capacities. The common scholastic meeting place is dominated by science and mathematics. Or, put differently, the core curriculum of the school, those subjects to which all others must pay deference, should be constructed from the fundamental elements of ancient science: arithmetic, music, geometry, and astronomy.

Plato's Attention to Education.   We first meet Plato, a young Athenian aristocrat, in the company of Socrates, and when we do we are almost certain of his determination to follow a career of practical politics. Wanting to be a political leader, Plato had studied in Athens' best schools and, moreover, had taken every opportunity his enviable social position afforded to reap those educational rewards offered in the cultural capital of the ancient world. He also had Socrates, sometimes credited as the world's wisest man, to tutor him. Yet, neither fine schools nor good teachers, not even one of Socrates' caliber, should be praised for Plato's undoubted genius; it was a personal, private gift.

Even the motives of genius can be altered by the hand of fate, and this is exactly what happened to Plato. When he had reached the age—about twenty-eight—for his political ambition to mature, his close friend and almost constant companion, Socrates, was indicted for what amounted to treason, was convicted in a famous trial, and was sentenced to death. Plato's chance to pursue a political career was canceled because his close association with Socrates made him suspect too. Moreover, he would have jeopardized his own personal security if he had remained in Athens. Filled with grief over the loss of a friend and burdened by anxiety about his own safety, Plato left Athens for about a dozen years.

While Plato was away from Athens the Sophists were busy poisoning the well of educational wisdom, so upon his return, he opened his famous Academy to compete with the Sophists on their own level, and he wrote *The Republic,* a book on political philosophy filled with educational theory, and the early dialogues, among them *Protagoras,* Plato's first direct contribution to educational philosophy.

Recognizing from the outset the obvious impossibility of reviewing every Platonic discourse on education to find the essential elements of his scientific humanism, we shall concentrate our attention on the *Protagoras,* for in it Plato comes to grips with the problem of education and in it, too, he isolates the one central question that started educational philosophy on the way to disciplinary independence. Ever sensitive to dramatic impact, Plato has Socrates ask the question this way: "Can human ingenuity make men good?" He is taking aim at the sophistic assertion that "knowledge is virtue" and he wants Protagoras, the most illustrious of the Sophists, to explain and defend it.

The Dialogue Protagoras.   Readers familiar with the dialogue will remember how it begins and how Plato sets the stage for this famous confrontation between Socrates and Protagoras. The excited Hippocrates, after announcing to Socrates Protagoras' arrival in Athens, ushers Socrates to Callias' house where Protagoras is to be a guest. On the way Socrates tries again to discover what Protagoras' special branch of knowledge is and what young Hippocrates will know if he pursues a course of study with him.

Hippocrates, Socrates ventures to say, should seek out a physician to whom he might become an apprentice if he wants to be a doctor, or he should study under the tutorship of a sculptor if he wants to be an artist. Protagoras might be the right teacher for a young man who aspires to being a Sophist.[6] Although this sounds like good advice to us, Hippocrates remains unconvinced: He doubts that the sophistry of Protagoras represents a narrow technical specialty. Everything he has heard about Protagoras' teaching leads him to believe that it is aimed at preparing public men; his students, Hippocrates believes, should be able to take responsible positions in public life after their course of study is finished, but in addition to this, their broad cultural grasp will enable them to function effectively on an entirely private level as well. This is a large order, and Socrates knows it, but if what Hippocrates expects can be realized in a sophistic school, Socrates wants to know more about it. We can almost sense Socrates' eager optimism as he hurries along to meet Protagoras and learn directly from him this pedagogical formula for revealing the secret of genuine and effective civic education.

Protagoras is obviously a man of ability, and his reputation as an innovative and excellent professor has preceded him; a chorus of admirers has gathered just to be near him to soak up any drops of wisdom he might let fall from his lips. But his brilliance is coupled with a certain shrewdness, and Plato does not want us to miss this: Whatever the substance of Protagoras' educational theory, Protagoras appears to be more a publicist for a point of view from which he can harvest notoriety and financial reward than a careful, dedicated teacher whose only motive is the advancement of knowledge and its dissemination. Plato may be hastily sketching the portrait of a talented professor who has sold his academic soul to the "devil's workshop of opportunism," one indifferent to the welfare of his students but always ready to look out for his own. If this is so, it is also so that Protagoras is a man worthy of Socrates' dialectical steel, for Plato would never have allowed Socrates to spend so much time debating a person of little consequence or one whose influence in educational circles was insignificant.

At first Socrates appears to be a bit uncertain about how to elicit from Protagoras what he really wants to know: If Hippocrates takes Protagoras' course, what will he learn? Put another way, what does Protagoras profess to teach? Either because such a direct inquiry lacks dramatic appeal, or perhaps because Plato wants to show how the civility of cultured persons operates, he has Socrates ask Protagoras to explain his educational theory and practice. This is just the opening Protagoras wants, because he is noted for his eloquence and obviously believes that a long and ponderous speech is the best way to answer Socrates' question.

The speech, though, is disappointing: Protagoras is long-winded and, although he is a master of language, about all he tells his audience is that education is important, that everyone should be concered with it, and that what he has to teach is not so much different from what most teachers were doing. It is important, he goes on, to preserve the best from the past, to learn what we can from the ancient poets, but as we work with an educational program that is old-fashioned in its fundamentals, we must always try to be more effective than our pedagogical predecessors. When all this has been done, Protagoras declares, his students ought to be able to deliver a speech whose principal thrust is to convince an audience that what the speaker has said is sound.

All this is familiar to Socrates, for the Sophists had been saying the same thing for a generation, and it obviously lacked the substance from which educational innovation springs. So Socrates tries again, and this time he is more direct: "I will begin again at the same point, Protagoras, and tell you once more the purport of my visit: this is my friend Hippocrates, who is desirous of making your acquaintance; he wants to know what will happen if he associates with you. That is all I have to say."[7] Although Protagoras is sure he was clear before and is unable to see where Socrates is about to lead him, he answers quickly, perhaps too quickly: "Young man, if you associate with me, on the very first day you will return home a better man than when you came, and better on the second day than on the first, and better every day than you were the day before."[8] Now sophistic arrogance, for this is what Plato called it, is out in the open. By saying that his teaching could make Hippocrates better, Protagoras was affirming the possibility of teaching virtue. And here was a problem even the best of the Sophists had yet to master: Before they could teach virtue, they would have to know its meaning.

Socrates moves in for the dialectical kill: What special virtue does Protagoras teach, and what is its nature? Unprepared for so intense an interrogation and beginning to suspect that he has overmatched himself, Protagoras hedges by saying he would not presume to speak for all Sophists. But Socrates refuses to let him off the hook with so shallow a response. Indifferent to what all Sophists believe, Socrates wants to know what Protagoras believes. Which virtues are his specialty, what is their nature, and how is he able to teach them to the students he recruits?

The Teaching of Virtue. Socrates concedes how the popular education of the Sophists could raise people above their old stations in life by giving them a certain skill with words, by embellishing them with various appurtenances of culture, and by communicating to them the various crafts of politics, but he refuses to concede limitless bounds to educational achievement. By promising to teach virtue, the Sophists were invading the field of moral education and appeared to be ignorant of the distinction between knowing what ought to be done and doing it. Their boundless optimism about what education could do seduced them to adopt the theory wherein the virtues of the soul could be communicated as effortlessly as the arts of mind. They went around claiming, as Protagoras was doing, that they were in possession of the secret for teaching political virtue, for teaching persons how to be good citizens. Socrates wants to be sure to steer the debate in the right direction. His dispute with Protagoras is not over pedagogic technique, for it was entirely possible to praise the Sophists for technical cleverness, but with the fundamental meaning of virtue. The puzzle he wants Protagoras to unravel is how, without any reference whatever to technique, teachers who profess skepticism—who refuse to trust in truth—can certify the validity of the virtues they teach? Protagoras promised to make Hippocrates better day after day. Who, Socrates wants to know, is to define the meaning of better?

Up to this point Protagoras has exuded confidence; he was the authority on such matters, and he had not expected his authority to be challenged in this way. Socrates, he knew, could be a troublesome debater, but he had not expected to have to defend his educational position, only to explain it. Still, he must try. With respect to knowledge of virtue—what some philosophers, he says, call the science of good and evil—there is only the guidance of social science. A social scientist, Protagoras declares, is what he is. And it is the business of the social scientist to find out by regular correspondence with citizens what is considered to be best, what, in the last analysis, is the meaning of political virtue. The ultimate test of what is right or wrong in the political arena is what most people think is right or wrong, for with respect to virtue there is no truth, but only opinion. What most citizens think ought to be done is right, and what most citizens declare to be wrong is wrong. The teacher, in Protagoras's theory, does not have to know anything about virtue's nature, assuming it has one, for he is responsible not for truth but for what the majority of citizens think is truth.

Socrates knew, as do we, how hard it would have been to plumb the various angles of public opinion in ancient days. Neither the Sophists nor anyone else could have been confident of apprehending a majority judgment. Yet this was only a minor defect in Protagoras' argument: The larger—in fact, the fundamental—defect was the dethronement of human reason's ability to grasp truth at all. This defect was the one Plato most wanted to attack.

After some prodding from Socrates, Protagoras grants that reason is man's highest power and that by using it properly the course of right action can be defined. Granting this, though, the great Sophist has contradicted his earlier embrace of skepticism. So Socrates pushes on: He maintains, at least as a working hypothesis, that no one errs knowingly; faced with a choice between two alternatives, a person will always select the one he believes to be right. If Socrates' hypothesis is correct and knowledge of what ought to be done can be mastered, proper instruction can indeed insulate men from evil by motivating them always to do what is right.[9]

Unless we are badly mistaken, this was the substance of Protagoras' earlier confidence in his ability to teach Hippocrates to be better day by day. Now, however, and partly because Socrates is following Plato's doctrine with respect to an aristocracy of ability where truth can become the proud possession of, or is in fact reserved for, persons of the highest intelligence and education, Protagoras demurs. Although the Sophists were far from being true democrats, they resented the superiority of the Athenian aristocracy, and Protagoras shares this resentment. He refuses to concede that success and virtue belong only to the most worthy, so again he recants. The kind of knowledge Socrates is extolling is reaped from long, disciplined years of scientific and philosophical study by persons gifted by nature with superior minds, and this was not the kind of knowledge Protagoras meant when he claimed to be able to teach virtue. Nothing is left for him to do but to admit that he had spoken too quickly earlier: He had, he said, meant to say that Hippocrates would learn to be more effective by studying with him.

Now we begin to see sophistry confusing morality with effectiveness and, moreover, confirming its basic alliance with relativism. At the same time, Plato has demonstrated with surprising skill the shifting ground of sophistic teaching. If Protagoras, the best of the Sophists, was unsure of the purpose of his teaching, could the people of Athens trust the formation of their children to him?

When the debate is over and the book of this dialogue is closed, we know where Plato and scientific humanism stand. Knowledge is indeed the basis for action, and knowledge, moreover, may dispose us to choose the better course, but knowledge is purchased at the high price of effort and ability. It comes to only a few good minds. These good minds are capable of lifting society above the level of right opinion, the best most people can ever achieve, and directing it on a course of action fortified by the solid canons of truth.

Plato's scientific humanism was adopted in its fundamentals by his most famous pupil, Aristotle. In the Lyceum, Aristotle's great school,[10] and in his careful deductive philosophy, Aristotle departed from the philosophical idealism of Plato and found truth, on which action could be based, as the result of intellectual accomplishment rather than as a cultivation of intuition. Plato's truth was spiritual and rational; Aristotle's was material and experimental. In both, however, scientific humanism was sustained as the only sound basis for the education of human beings. From its origin in Athens scientific humanism made its way into the Hellenistic world to compete, although not always on even terms, with the literary humanism of Isocrates.

Literary Humanism

Committed to the equality of opinion—any one is as good as any other—the Sophists bet their educational reputations on the force of the "better argument." Social and political life should be shaped by persons able to use words persuasively. Little wonder then, when all was said and done, that the Sophists spent their time teaching their students how to speak convincingly and debate successfully. At the other end of the educational spectrum, Plato and his scientifically humanistic disciples downgraded the arts of persuasion without destroying them by elevating dependable knowledge, either right opinion or truth, to the pinnacle of human accomplishment. Before persons act, they must understand the nature and consequence of their action, and this is impossible unless they have been properly educated. A proper education, always taking a long time in Plato's view, would concentrate on the development of reason, the human ability of thought, and for this rational development the fields of science and philosophy were most rewarding.

To steer a safe course between these two conflicting educational shoals, and to end up at a port of scholastic call where knowledge and virtue on one hand could be respected and where full participation in social and political life on the other would be open to everyone, was the commission Isocrates assigned to the educational theory we characterize as literary humanism.

Isocrates' Preoccupation with Language. As a contemporary of Plato, Isocrates was profoundly interested in the political life of Athens, so from early youth, with all the resources a wealthy family could muster, he attended the best schools, studied with the best teachers—many of them Sophists—had an intimate association with Socrates, and took full advantage of the cultural opportunities Athens had to offer. When the time came for him to enter the arena of politics, however, he discovered his personality was unsuited to the give and take of public life. His voice was weak, his manner unprepossessing and, worst of all, when he rose to speak he was overcome by nervousness and stage fright. With such personal shortcomings, Isocrates recognized the futility of pursuing an active political career, so he decided to use his talent another way. He began to write political speeches—what today we would call journalistic commentaries—for private reading rather than public delivery, and he began to write for hire speeches to be delivered by others. Sometimes these speeches were intended for the Athenian assembly, the place where public policy was made, but more often they were written for citizens engaged in lawsuits. Over a period of about twenty years Isocrates made a good living and honed his oratorical skill by following a professional writing career.

Writing for others could be profitable and satisfying, but it limited the range of Isocrates' influence, and he wanted to be influential. Therefore, he opened a school outside Athens—his biographers say in Chios—to test, and perhaps improve, his skill as a teacher before establishing himself as a schoolmaster in his home town. Opening a school in Athens in 392 B.C., when he was forty-four years old, Isocrates was faced at once with strong competition from the Sophists, who had been around for a long time, and Plato, whose views on education were known in Athens, although his famous Academy had yet to be founded. Taking a leaf from the Sophists' manual on public relations, Isocrates promoted the fortunes of his school by circulating a prospectus to explain the nature of its educational program and his own theory of education. *Against the Sophists* was this book's title.

Isocrates rejected sophistry because it was irresponsible: Political success and oratorical skill were too precarious a foundation to support the political life of any society. Neither skepticism nor nihilism was countenanced when Isocrates abandoned what he called vulgar sophistry. But another kind of sophistry, which he said was paraded in the educational theory of Plato, was no more promising: Students were encouraged to spend the greater part of their lives seeking after truth, yet their search was unrewarding for the most part; they were left to make their decisions on the basis of common sense. In the long run, Isocrates inquired, do philosophers who pretend to wisdom have any better advice to give about what should be done than persons who day by day follow a practical political career? Time wasted by studying on into old age trying to find a bedrock of truth would be better spent, Isocrates declared, by immersing students in the world of affairs at an early age and letting experience teach them prudence.[11]

Plato's educational program, one designed for political leaders, was so long that few persons lived long enough to finish it; the Sophists invented an abbreviated scholastic program of about one year, but Isocrates settled for a school course of three or four years, one reminding us of a contemporary high school. What should be taught during these years?

Isocrates began by indicting the Sophists and the other teachers of political discourse (he must have meant Plato and his followers) for fraud: The former professed to teach clever oratory while admitting to their total indifference to truth; the latter pretended to search for truth but, for some reason or other, it escaped them, and they were left to conduct their students on a long, fruitless, and unending journey. His school, Isocrates maintained, would redress the short-comings of his competitors. So without describing the techniques involved in teaching it, he gave information first place in the curriculum. And without wasting time trying to defend the validity of the information communicated in the school course—he supposed ultimate truth impossible—he set the goal of preparing students capable of holding their own in political dispute and debate and, at the same time, dedicating them to the proposition that political life should be dominated by a preconception of what was best for Athens. He commissioned a broad curriculum of at least a dozen subjects that would teach students what they needed to know, and these subjects were filled with a knowledge that had passed the rigid test of life experience. In addition to being well informed, Iso-crates' students were to have their ingenuity and imagination whetted by paying close attention to the literature of the great Greek poets, starting, of course, with Homer. Both information and imitative skill, however, were means to an end, and the end was an ability to use written and oral language effectively.

Had Isocrates stopped here his critics could have charged him with dressing up the educational practices of sophistry and trying to peddle them as something new and different, for the Sophists never made any secret about their assignation with oratory. But Isocrates went on. Oratory needed more than effectiveness, more than always winning debates; it needed responsibility, and this brought Isocrates face to face with the issue that Plato had wrestled with in *Protagoras:* Could teaching produce virtuous (responsible) persons?

For the first time Isocrates assumes an uncharacteristically bold stance to reject once and for all the propositions so far advanced on the subject of virtue by Plato and the Sophists. We recall their positions and need not repeat them. Yet it is hard to see what position Isocrates could carve out for himself without undermining any chance he had for making his brand of oratory responsible. Orators, public men and private persons alike, all should try their best to do what is right. How would they know? Knowledge of virtue, Isocrates declared with supreme confidence, is innate; it is nature's bequest to a person. Not everyone is endowed with a natural knowledge of right and wrong, but some are, and they are the ones to be educated. They alone are qualified to lead a state by imposing their judgment on public policy. The extent of their success at public and private leadership, however, would depend on how highly their powers of expression were developed. The purpose of Isocrates' school was to select students whose moral character was sound and educate them in oratory. The more persuasive they were in public and private, the better, and we would never have to worry about their virtue if we were careful at the outset to educate in oratory only those persons whose moral stature was above reproach. In adopting this theory with respect to virtue, Isocrates put a heavy burden on schoolmasters to select their students carefully and to exclude from their classrooms any who showed signs of moral deficiency. Naturally good persons can become effective as a result of a superior education, but naturally evil persons, who would be innocuous if left uneducated, could, with a decent education, spread their immorality and con-taminate a whole society.

With this issue settled to his satisfaction, Isocrates went on to promote a development of the arts of expression. Intelligent, naturally virtuous students, he said, sounding something like Plato, should have a common scholastic meeting place, and this meeting place, the core to literary humanism's curriculum, was always language and literature. These studies above all others educated students in the use of words.[12]

Education in Oratory.   From this start in the ancient world, literary humanism swept into Hellenistic civilization—that long historical interlude between the end of the Greek Classical Age (300 B.C.) and the Fall of Rome (A.D. 500)—where it dominated all educational practice. The schools of this long, complicated period were delegated to perpetuate classical literary culture and for this a concentration on language and literature was judged imperative. If education were unable to make persons morally good, it could, at least, make them eloquent.

And now, with society changing almost too fast for education to keep pace, we meet the champion of eloquence, the great Roman schoolmaster, Quintilian (A.D. 35–97), who concentrated solely on the education of a public man in an unforgettable book, *The Education of an Orator.* Reading through Quintilian's book, we are certain, first, of his indebtedness to Isocrates' literary humanism and, second, of his conviction that more than anything else educational decency rests squarely on a perfection of the human ability of expression.

Following in the footsteps of Cicero (106–43 B.C.), whose earlier commentaries on education made a partial translation of the principles of literary humanism to Roman educational practice,[13] Quintilian set out to describe an educational program, beginning at birth and going on through the highest training in rhetoric, that would guarantee an abundance of public men for Roman society. These orators, these "good men skilled in speaking," were the superior products of an educational program whose supreme objective was eloquence. Naturally enough, the curriculum was filled with subjects whose relationship to language, literature, grammar, and rhetoric was clear. These orators should also be good men— Quintilian is sure of this—but we are always left in doubt about the source and

FIGURE 2.1
The Advent of Educational Philosophy

THEORY	PRINCIPAL EXPONENTS	DEFINITION OF EDUCATIONAL PURPOSE
Relativistic Humanism	Protagoras (481–411 B.C.) The Sophists	Truth is unattainable, so the appearance of truth may serve as well as truth itself. Opinion must be supported by the better argument.
Scientific Humanism	Socrates (469–399 B.C.) Plato (427?–347 B.C.) Aristotle (384–322 B.C.)	Knowledge may not be virtue, but knowledge is an essential foundation to ethical conduct.
Literary Humanism	Isocrates (436–338 B.C.) Cicero (106–43 B.C.) Quintilian (A.D. 35–97)	Virtue is a natural endowment that can be improved with cultivation. Education in the use of words can make naturally virtuous persons more effective and produce the perfect orator: "A good man skilled in speaking."

cultivation of their moral goodness. No time is spent searching for an elusive moral truth, for Quintilian lacks confidence in the worth of philosophy, and whenever philosophy is discredited moral certitude is victimized. From the outset, sounding more like a Sophist than like Isocrates, he excludes ethics from the curriculum. He does so not because orators should be indifferent to morality but because Quintilian is certain philosophical knowledge is incapable of cultivating character.[14]

We have no way of knowing, then, how moral responsibility is to be cultivated, if it is to be cultivated at all, unless, to follow Isocrates' line of thought, it is innate. Yet Quintilian scrupulously avoids such an admission. Perhaps the high ideals expressed in so much of classical literature were infectious enough to shape character as they were expected to shape the arts of oratory. In any case, the old debate over character formation is pretty much forgotten in the maze of advice Quintilian gives on the development of literary and oratorical accomplishments. And in the last analysis, these accomplishments mattered most, for by the time we have come to the end of the ancient genre, educational theory and practice had hoisted the flag of literary humanism over the schoolhouse where, even into the twentieth century, it continued to fly.

NEW PROBLEMS FOR EDUCATIONAL PHILOSOPHY

During the first centuries of the Christian era, Christians were distracted by other pressing issues from pondering questions of educational philosophy. Believing, as a majority did that Judgment Day was close at hand, they spent their time looking out for the condition of their souls and neglected almost everything not directly connected with religion and eternal salvation. If this fatalistic attitude was less prevalent among Eastern Christians than among those who lived in and around Rome, it was because cultural roots were sunk deeper in the East, and Eastern Christians had fewer reasons to fear an educational legacy whose apparently dangerous philosophical presuppositions were entirely familiar to them. Still, paganism was a problem no Christian could ignore, so when the time came for Christianity to shed its introvertive character and become a religious crusade, and when Christians abandoned their enclaves, where in earlier days they had fled to safety, to participate on equal terms with other citizens in social and political life, then and only then were they motivated to consider heretofore neglected educational issues.

The Purpose of Christian Education

We know of the investment earlier educational philosophers made in trying to unravel the secrets of virtue's nature, but from the outset Christian educators were absolved from grappling with so vexing a question. A revealed deposit of faith told them simply and directly everything they needed to know about virtue; moreover, it raised their sights from temporal and civic goals, which had preoccupied such men as Plato and Isocrates, to the edifying objective of eternal salvation. No longer were they content to think only about the formation of citizens; they were obliged now to superintend the education of saints.

This heavy obligation had to be taken seriously by every parent and, for that matter, by every teacher whose Christian commitment was clear, but until Constantine (288?–337) legalized Christianity in the year 313 Christians were discouraged from sending their children to Roman schools. Whenever they spoke of Christian education they meant moral and religious formation, and for a long time they harbored legitimate doubt about the schools' ability to help them. Without trying here to review all the problems Christians had with classical education as it was practiced in Rome and her environs, the doctrine of literary humanism, we know, was in vogue and the schools were filled with a literature whose purview, if not actually anti-Christian, was, at least, un-Christian. The exciting, lurid tales of gods and godesses competing with one another for material rewards and pleasures were bound to present a most repellent face. The pretensions of philosophy, moreover, inflated reason to a point where Christian faith became only a fiction for ignorant, unschooled, and prosaic minds. Besides, no pagan classic contained a single word about heaven; everything belonged in a totally temporal context, and this attitude was held in abhorrence by all Christians. Little wonder then, as often as not they refused to send their children to the regular Roman schools; if they did, special care was taken to immunize them from the contagion certain to be found there.

The Transit of Religious Humanism

While Christianity was in its infancy and Christians neither numerous nor influential, they could find good excuses for boycotting the schools and spending all their educational energy instructing their children, usually in the home, in the ways of faith. But Christianity was destined to grow up, and the time came when Christians wanted to make their way in the world with secular educational credentials while practicing their faith and thus ensuring their place for eternity. Put quickly, Christians outgrew their taste for cultural rusticity: Wanting to be persons of God, they wanted also to reap temporal success by competing on even terms with their pagan counterparts for the material rewards of life. For this a good education was indispensable, and for a long time the only kind of education available was husbanded by the schools of Rome.

To compete favorably in Roman society Christians needed all those appurtenances to literary culture that, for centuries, had been the favorite themes in discourses on educational philosophy. Grammar, logic, and rhetoric were the basics of a decent education, and now Christians were determined to have them. But could they obtain the usual literary education, one immersing them in classical literature, without at the same time being infected by paganism? Christian educators, confident of man's nature and certain of education's ultimate purpose, turned to the difficult question of what to teach in order to give their students an equal chance for temporal success.

Although a few Christian leaders refused to support any concession allowing Christian students to study the classics, maintaining it better for them to lose their chance for success in secular society than to lose their souls, the weight of Christian opinion shifted to the side of some literary education. Christianity began to make a steady exodus from Rome and in doing so, it became more and more a religion of the book; all the help a literary education could supply stood as an essential condition to its missionary zeal. Christians themselves wanted to fathom the fundamentals of their faith; Christian missionaries were dedicated to converting their unregenerate brethren; Christian pastors needed a literary training to perform the liturgy and to preach the gospel to the faithful. No longer could Christians afford to follow intemperate counselors warning them of the snares and delusions in literary learning. And now, for the first time, we meet prominent Christian educational spokesmen who, while never thinking of themselves as educational philosophers, were nevertheless tackling authentic philosophical issues. What they had to contend with was not what to teach, for there was only one choice: the classics. Their problem was more complicated: How could the classics be taught without at the same time doing injury to faith?

Forging a Curricular Compromise.   In the East, most likely in Alexandria, Clement (150?–220?) took the side of the classics. Taught properly, he said, a curriculum filled with classical literature could contribute to tolerance and, moreover, its ideals were compatible with Christian faith. Rather than being an impediment to moral and religious virtue, classical learning, Clement averred, could make a positive contribution to Christian character.[15] Yet this opinion, although it was adopted centuries later, was too progressive for conventional Christians: Surrender to classical learning was rejected in favor of a compromise.

St. Jerome (340?–420) may have been the first Western Christian to offer a compromise solution to what the schools should teach. A man of many parts, Jerome was at once a great scholar and a person so dedicated to faith that his example of asceticism portrayed an ideal Christian life. He could pronounce at one time the worth of literary education and at another time raise doubt about the injury classical study might do to faith. He could read his books and prosecute a vigorous personal scholarship at one time and then abruptly throw away his books and manuscripts and flee to the desert to live in caves. In more temperate moments, however, he advised Christians to go to school and exploit the literary material found there, paying attention only to elements of style—such as illustrations of grammar and rhetoric—and ignoring the content—the stories—classical authors told.[16] Jerome's formula, one allowing Christian students to use the classics, was designated from the beginning as "formal study" and, despite its obvious deficiencies, formal study was practiced in some Christian schools whenever the classics were studied for the next thousand years.

Jerome's educational advice, however, was vulnerable, as any schoolboy could see, for it was impossible for students barely able to read to separate illustrations of style from the story a classic contained. Contamination might be avoided, but its likelihood was too apparent to ignore. Noticing the difficulties in formal study, St. Augustine (354–430), whose educational inconsistency sometimes matched Jerome's, advanced a more realistic and manageable formula for compromise.

Thoroughly schooled in the classics before he converted to Christianity and entirely familiar with literary humanism as it was practiced in Hellenistic and Roman schools, Augustine's compromise plan was simple enough to follow and comprehensive enough to be effective. Its simplicity, in fact, tended to conceal its worth, and we are surprised that such a practical plan had not been advanced before. He told Christian scholars to go through the pagan classics, those books generally considered to be reservoirs of universal wisdom, and from them winnow out everything conflicting with Christian faith and morals. What was left over from this process of selection, with its tasteless, immoral, and vulgar elements pared away, could be compiled in anthologies readily available to students. With illustrations of good style on display, and with a fund of knowledge in these anthologies, Christian students could master the rules of correct writing and speaking by going to specially prepared grammatical and rhetorical textbooks.[17] In addition to finding a workable solution to the problem of paganism, Augustine's compromise ushered in the pedagogical instruments of anthologies and textbooks.

Although Augustine's formula for handling the most pressing problem facing Christian educators filled a temporary need and succeeded in preserving Christian contacts with classical culture, it continued and, to some extent, increased the separation between Christian thought and genuine classical learning. This may have been exactly what Augustine wanted. In any case, each succeeding generation of Christian students, depending for the subjects they studied on the work of scholars who had gone through the classics picking and choosing uncontaminating parts, moved further and further away from the genuine treasures the classics contained, treasures too rare to be salvaged by techniques of expurgation and excerption.

So Augustine's compromise, despite its general adoption by Christian schoolmasters until about the middle of the twelfth century, had its worth discounted as Christian educational theory matured in a changing world. Looking back, we see how Jerome and Augustine spoke to a Christian society ready to follow any good advice, for their educational problem was in urgent need of solution. After the fifth century, though, their compromise plans tended to lose the luster of relevance. After all, whether they knew it or not, they were following in the footsteps of Quintilian and failed to perceive how educational objectives were drifting away from the public oration toward private accomplishment in a school, a study, a government office, or a church. Ornamental oratory, the kind Quintilian trumpeted in his great book, was out of date, for men no longer conducted affairs in the Forum where platform eloquence counted most; the educational program with current appeal was one capable of preparing persons to serve the church, the state, the marketplace and, most of all, themselves. Work left to be

done in the broad framework of Christian education, although the brave beginning of Jerome and Augustine unquestionably paid dividends, was undertaken by
Cassiodorus (480–575). Orthodox in his commitment to religion and education,
Cassiodorus gave the classics a new perspective, keeping them, of course, but
narrowing their influence to make them directly practical in application.

The Seven Liberal Arts.   Cassiodorus, a complex man with a sound classical
education and extensive experience in public affairs as well as a devout Christian
spirit, sensed the urgency of the Christian educational problem. By now Rome
had fallen and Roman schools had disappeared in the wake of political decline.
The directing and steadying hand of dependable educational theory was needed
more than ever before. Catering to this need, Cassiodorus wrote a famous little
book, *An Introduction to Divine and Human Readings,* wherein he freed the arts
from their long captivity in pagan literature and put them in the mainstream of
Christian educational practice. The arts, he said, were seven in number—grammar, rhetoric, logic, arithmetic, geometry, music, and astronomy—and they were
the foundation to all learning. Christians should use them without developing
affection for them, for they were the gateways through which all secular and
divine learning had to pass. Without embracing the arts, Christian education was
impossible.[18]

Although in Book II of the *Introduction* Cassiodorus argued for secular learning—he meant the liberal arts—and was convinced of their literary worth, he
declared the oratorical tradition of Quintilian out of date and abandoned it. The
arts were to form the curriculum of every Christian school, so much is certain,
but their study was to lead to efficiency in conducting everyday affairs of church
and state and commerce; eloquence was sold at discount. Even without Cassiodorus' important work, Christian education may have drifted away from the
oratorical tradition, for Christian educators had from the first raised questions
about its relevance. Still, Cassiodorus was not merely endorsing what may have
been a trend: He was not content only to describe current educational practice;
he meant to improve it.

This implied, first, that the linguistic disciplines (grammar, rhetoric, and, of
course, the Latin language) should be set within the framework of the time.
Neither Ciceronian Latin nor Quintilian's rules of grammar and rhetoric had
much meaning for the sixth century, so Cassiodorus, never worrying much about
classical purity, recommended a sound literary education with a special concentration on the Latin language. Concentrating on Latin as a living language had
the effect of severing many old literary and linguistic connections with the classics, but at the same time it inflated the importance of schools: If correct Latin
were to be mastered, schools were essential. So, perhaps more clearly than before,
Cassiodorus commissioned schools as principal agents for perpetuating the cultural and literary inheritance, although now the inheritance was Christian rather
than pagan. Remnants from the great literary past were retained in Cassiodorus'
syllabus of the seven arts, but their influence was pretty well restricted to literary
style. After all, what could Christians learn from pagans about man's duty to
God? With this revised commission, one making schools responsible for transmit-

ting a Christian intellectual and literary inheritance, it is easy to see why educational theory and method were the objects of assiduous Christian attention.

The Restoration of Learning.   Shortly after Cassiodorus pronounced an educational theory for Christian use, the effects of the fall of Rome and the disappearance of the Roman educational program began to take their toll. Western civilization was engulfed in a three-century period of scholastic retreat. Scholars lost their way and schools were neglected; the state of learning, except in isolated pockets here and there where a few scholars went about their work as before, was deplorably low. These pockets of scholastic activity, for all their flashes of brilliance, were always insufficient to restore quickly what had taken so long to lose. In time, though, due to the work of intrepid scholars and schoolmasters—Alcuin of York (735–804) is probably the best example[19]—and farsighted monarchs—and here Charlemagne (768–814) stands out impressively[20] —schools were reopened and learning began a long climb back to respectability. By the time we reach the twelfth century most of the loss had been recovered, and the world of learning, scholarship, and education was ready to make another great leap forward. Latin, the only linguistic medium hardy enough for scholastic use (handled then with about the same skill and efficiency as students in American colleges today use English), and the classics, approached now without fear of corruption, were studied and read by serious students aspiring to service in church or state. Schools and universities became commonplace in European towns and cities, and the ignorance and illiteracy that had so long prevailed slowly began to recede.

Throughout these long centuries fundamental Christian temperaments had not changed. Every person's first allegiance was to moral rectitude, and faith was always superior to reason. But reason had a place too: It was man's best ornament with a right to be polished by a good education. And now the calendar of educational preference turns back to ancient days, to days when the classics were given pride of place in the curriculum of every school. The old compromises of Jerome and Augustine were forgotten and the cautious counsel of Cassiodorus was neglected. Reason, man's highest natural gift, should be shaped by the best —and what was better than the classics? From time to time conservative Christian educators opposed this open-armed embrace of the classics and went around denouncing pagan learning, but the weight of opinion was on the other side: All secular knowledge, the theory ran, is in classical literature. How could students spend their time better than by excavating its treasures?

This healthy respect for the excellence of classical learning, however, was not without some danger. Motivated to get the best learning without delay, students began to slight the fundamental skills on which literary learning stands. They leaped over grammar and language to get to ornamental studies, such as philosophy, and are said to have attended university lectures on Plato before they could read and write.

With the prospect for all decent learning being violated again, although now by enthusiasm rather than neglect, the humble auxiliaries of classical study needed another defense: The liberal arts needed restoration to their place of rightful significance as the foundation for education. John of Salisbury (1120–1180) became their champion. Grammar, logic, and rhetoric, he said in the *Metalogicon,* needed attention first. Once they were mastered students could go on to invade the fertile field of classical learning. So, we see, John shared the assumption so often made before and later: The classics contain all knowledge worth having. Taken at face value, this assumption relieved all schoolmasters and all educational theorists, too, from wrestling further with the question of curriculum. But where others, in making this bold assumption about the classics, left too much unsaid about the actual and potential worth of classical literature, John was clear.

Scholars should not stop with the words of the ancient authors; they should begin with words and from them make interpretations of their meaning and thus "be lifted up and borne aloft by their gigantic stature."[21] This was no doctrine for a reactionary educational philosopher, but it guaranteed a healthy respect for traditional classical learning. Yet John's theory, while it restored the classics to their earlier eminence, limited the purview of educational practice to reading, for if everything was in the books waiting to be known, reading was bound to be the superior means for obtaining this knowledge. John, in the *Metalogicon,* confirmed this position. Students should read both the classics and interpretations of them, for this was the only sure road to education: "Let him [the student] go on [to read], as authors mutually explain one another, and all things in turn help to explain other things. For which reason there is little or nothing that lies concealed from one who is well read."[22]

Christian educational theory had moved a long way from its early doubts about the worth of the classics, and John is a good witness, but it is not yet ready to stop. Medieval educational theory made the classics welcome, but always restricted their worth to levels of secular learning where the intellect was to be formed. No one thought that books could take the place of the church and the home in building moral and religious character. So when medieval students read their books, they did so with the intention of filling out their perceptions of a world God had made; the books they read did not teach them these perceptions.

Religion's Adoption of Humanism.   Almost ready to step over the theshold to the modern world, we meet a band of educational theorists led by Erasmus (1469–1536) and Philip Melanchthon (1497–1560), whom we shall call religious humanists. Taking for granted almost everything their forebears had said about the classics being deposits of secular wisdom, they went on to endow the classics with an ability to form character as well. Erasmus, although not the first to promote this bold theory, was its most eloquent advocate. The classics, he said, if read properly and understood fully, contain ideals similar to those elaborated in Christian faith. And if this alone were not convincing, as it may not have been to some of Erasmus' Christian confreres, he went on to declare that the hard work involved in studying and mastering the classics fortified a student with a discipline that, in the last analysis, was complementary to moral character.[23]

Erasmus's command of the classics was too good, however, for him to forget those lurid and lascivious tales, those immoral occurrences, and those violent intrusions on decency made by so many classical heroes. Students could hardly be fed a steady diet of indecency and immorality without having their characters affected, so he directed Christian schoolmasters to be selective and prudent in their assignments of classical reading. Nothing was to be left out of course, for Erasmus rejected expurgation and censorship, but classical reading assignments should be made with one eye on the intellectual and moral maturity of the students. Timing was the key: All the classics should be read, but only when students were ready for them.

Timing might immunize students from moral contagion, but it was helpless to ensure denominational allegiance, at least so it seemed to a cadre of religious humanists led by Philip Melanchthon. A great rupture, in 1517, had split the Christian community into hostile factions of Protestants and Catholics, and now education was called upon to sustain general religious orthodoxy and something else: denominational allegiance. As an educational adviser to Martin Luther (1483–1546), Melanchthon recommended that the curriculum of the schools—especially of the secondary schools now becoming more popular—preserve the classics, for on the level of theory he took the position that an abundance of knowledge is the best guarantee against misinterpretation. Students who knew the classics thoroughly could not be misled by them. On the level of practice, however, Melanchthon's progressive theory was reduced to a policy of timid caution: The school's syllabus should pare away any book or part thereof whose interpretation did not explicitly confirm denominational belief.[24]

At the beginning of this long and often disorganized period in the history of educational philosophy, we saw how Christians were ready to jettison the classics and put all their confidence in a pristine faith. True, Christian educational theory eventually found a place for classical learning—some contemporaries said too large a place—but they meant to keep secular knowledge subservient to Christian

FIGURE 2.2
Educational Philosophy in Christian Hands

CURRICULAR EMPHASIS	PRINCIPAL EXPONENTS	EDUCATIONAL POLICY
Christian Education	Christian leaders	To prepare Christians for eternal life and avoid contamination from paganism.
Religious Humanism	Clement of Alexandria (150?–220?) St. Jerome (340?–420) St. Augustine (354–430) Cassiodorus (480–575) Alcuin (735–804)	To use the classical inheritance in the schools' curriculum, but to surround it with proper safeguards.
Classical Humanism	Erasmus (1469–1536) Melanchthon (1497–1560)	To use the classics to educate good citizens and faithful Christians. Education for character is stressed.

wisdom and seldom took seriously any recommendation wherein character or faith was made to profit from classical study. At the end of the period, though, religious humanism made classical scholarship a central plank in educational policy and was prepared to keep it intact so long as a positive contribution could be made to denominational religion. Paganism lost some of its ugly sound and dangerous ring, but education lost something too: Now it heeled to Protestant and Catholic sectarianism. If nothing else is learned from this part of educational philosophy's history, this lesson, at least, is clear: The hard knocks of life and the shifting currents of society conspire to make educational thinkers clever, resourceful, and sometimes so flexible as to put them precariously close to the sharp thorns in the thicket of contradiction.

EDUCATIONAL PHILOSOPHY IN THE MODERN WORLD

Religious discord, an old assumption runs, altered the face of Europe by dislodging past loyalties, and so, burning their bridges behind them, our ancestors struck out in a new direction to blaze a novel social and political trail. No doubt religious revolt and attempted reform had a part to play in the social and political changes sweeping over European horizons, but it would be hard to believe that the breezes fanning the flames of religious conflict were strong or steady enough to generate the power to rebuild society. That European society had its eyes opened in the sixteenth century and began to follow a new course appears certain, but we would be closer to the truth in crediting this new beginning more to geography than to religion. Had the religious humanists had their way they would have persisted in the belief that the future is shaped by the past and that the precious elements of the past, those most in need of perpetuation, are locked securely in the books. They were, for the most part, prepared to acknowledge the veracity of the dogmatic assumption that knowledge is buried in literature, but even more valuable than knowledge for shaping the direction of society is a simple faith found in the precepts of religious orthodoxy.

Geographic novelty—the discovery of the New World—opened the gateway to change. So long as most people thought the physical world was accounted for in the astronomy and geography they had grown up with, they were content to leave things alone and live their lives as before. But suddenly and unexpectedly the world was enlarged almost beyond the range of human imagination, and with this enlargement much that had passed for dependable knowledge was called into doubt. Indictments of ignorance and indifference flew hither and yon, and the educational systems that had been most responsible for keeping traditional assumptions alive and intact were everywhere vulnerable.

Slowly at first and then gaining momentum as time went on, a new theory of knowledge began to captivate the educated elements in European society. Rather than confirming the old doctrine about knowledge being buried away in literature, where with a decent literary education it could be mined, this new theory argued for a kind of knowledge that is found in the physical world. People make their way in the world, a corollary to this argument went, not by searching out a past wisdom but in finding from their own experience, in the real world around them, knowledge enabling them to live more profitable and satisfying lives. At the outset, of course, this new epistemology, for this is what it was, had little or no effect on the common people; yet, it influenced the thinkers and philosophers and, in time, altered the direction of educational philosophy and practice.

The first signs we have of a change coming over education were in the constant complaints being made about the schools. Critics wondered, for example, and we too must share their wonder, why the whole of education should be secreted in a language other than a vernacular. Schools had been in the habit of teaching Latin as the language of scholarship and, although in most countries common people achieved some small level of literacy in their native tongue, no one could go very far up the ladder of scholarship, to the secondary schools and the universities, without a mastery of Latin. This hold Latin had on scholarship was not without some good justification, as we know, but with or without justification, the stark fact remained that worthwhile knowledge was being kept from the very people who needed it most. Language was not alone at fault, as the more perceptive critics were quick to realize: A curriculum totally dependent on ancient literature, they charged, was bound to be deficient.

So as discontent with education raged and as new theories circulated about what knowledge was of most worth, the educational philosophers began again to ply their intellectual trade.

Religious Realism

God created men, gave them the gift of faith, and endowed them with reason, but He also created a physical world and left it to human beings to fulfill their duty to Him by living and working in the physical world. Could they afford to be indifferent to it? This, in a nutshell, was the fundamental world view of John Amos Comenius (1592–1670), a religious minister of a small Protestant sect, a schoolmaster of extraordinary sensitivity and pedagogical skill, a political nomad wandering from one to another European country, and an educational thinker responsible for setting in place the first stanchions of educational realism.

Comenius wrote dozens of books, from schoolbooks intended for mothers teaching their children at home to wise treatises on educational philosophy, and in all of them he preached a novel, optimistic doctrine: Learning begins with those experiences that make an impression on the senses. The first sensory impressions come from a child's physical environment. The child's first textbook, then, is the world around him, and from this book of experience he begins to learn.

The bulk of Comenius' educational thought can be found in *The Great Didactic*, and it must be counted as a book belonging to the first order of importance in educational philosophy. However, we should be careful to admit that for all Comenius' pioneering zeal, *The Great Didactic* was composed in an eclectic spirit enabling its author to draw on the work of earlier philosophers and educators who had reassessed the credentials of knowledge. Translated to schools, this new theory of knowledge encouraged students to know and understand the world in which they lived and not just the world known and interpreted for them by classical authors. Adopting this thesis did not lead Comenius to an outright rejection of classical humanism; it served, however, to broaden the curriculum of the schools and eventually reshaped school learning from bookish classicism to realistic naturalism.

Educational predecessors who inspired and guided Comenius in making a translation of educational purpose to realistic naturalism, and to whom he was careful to give credit, were Juan Luis Vives (1492–1540), Francis Bacon, Wolfgang Ratke (1571–1635), William Bath (1564–1614), and Thomas Campanella (1568–1639). By opening the doors of learning to the physical world and its contemporary issues and by recognizing the infant but energetic physical sciences, Comenius embraced a philosophy of realism and, in turn, was instrumental in forging a realistic philosophy of education. Yet, the realistic naturalism of which we speak and with which Comenius can be credited concentrated on the learning process itself and did not limit the source of knowledge to a natural, physical world. Learning, he said, was natural, and once its natural processes were known, the methods of teaching could be accommodated to it. This accommodation, however, was not meant to exclude from the school's syllabus either traditional culture or orthodox religion. Both, from Comenius' point of view, had a claim on men's allegiance, but so did the physical world. So whether we consider Comenius as a theorist or as a reforming schoolmaster, he must be given a place in the vanguard of the realistic movement in education and thus be recognized as a person of considerable significance in the history of educational philosophy.

In its progress through the modern world, realism often kept company with scientific naturalism, and for the past hundred years or so it has embraced positivism; that is, only knowledge supported by the weight of experimental evidence is acknowledged as valid. Whether or not this association of realism and positivism is inevitable in contemporary realism is a point worthy of later consideration, but for now we should absolve Comenius' educational doctrine from positivism. His starting point was neither naturalistic nor scientific: Man is a child of God and must be educated to serve Him in this and the next world. So Comenius rejected the intellectualism of medieval and classical humanists and replaced it with piety. Yet, astute enough to know that piety is not generated in a vacuum, he adopted the thesis that its principal promoter is dependable knowledge. In endorsing knowledge he subordinated it to virtue (piety) and endowed it with instrumental character. He steadfastly refused, moreover, to countenance knowledge for its own sake—what today is called liberal learning—or for independent application—what might be called practical or professional learning. The virtue that Comenius' philosophy of education aimed for was supernatural rather than natural. It is impossible, therefore, to take Comenius' realism seriously without adverting to his unalterable commitment to supernatural religion and to his determination to make formal education serve religious objectives. From this point on, though, Comenius sounds more like an orthodox educational philosopher than a Christian bishop.

Comenius' Plan for Universal Education.   The sound of his educational orthodoxy echoed all the way to contemporary times. In an educational age where such a recommendation was so avant-garde as to ensure its rejection, Comenius spoke of universal opportunity for schooling. Boys and girls, rich and poor alike, were to be given those instructional opportunities suited to their talent. And nothing is said about segregating boys and girls, for coeducation seemed to him to be nothing more than a natural consequence of social convention. When men and women lived together in the same world and were faced with so many of the same problems, what reason could be found for separating them for schooling or, what was worse, completely ignoring the legitimate expectations of women to be educated? In these schools where boys and girls learned together, all instruction was to begin, Comenius insisted, with the vernacular language. The requirements of later scholarship might demand something more, but the elements, the first instruction toward human wisdom, should start with a language whose social affinities were grounded in the students' life experiences.

This plan for universal instructional opportunity, for all its appeal, would be sterile, however, unless a school system was organized. So Comenius called for a system of public schools, beginning with the first instruction children received at their mothers' knees, through village and town elementary schools, to secondary schools in the cities, and then a university for every province. Although we know how far ahead of his time Comenius was—national school systems were still a century or more in the future—such schools could never have been conducted without the help of a new theory of classroom management: Comenius made a bold and resolute plea for class methods of teaching. Up to this time, of course, most instruction in the schools was conducted on an individual or tutorial basis. Teachers dealt with their students one by one. Following Comenius' plan, an entire class of students could be taught at once.

In class teaching, in taking as many as one hundred students and instructing them in the basic elements of knowledge, a method superior to anything so far available had to be found. And at this point, a point where Comenius stops being an educational philosopher and becomes a pedagogic technician, the first awkward steps were taken in the formation of modern educational method. These first steps, awkward though they were, were justified by Comenius' perceptive but unscientific analysis of learning as a natural process.

Whatever Comenius had to say about upgrading educational practice would have been deprived of meaning, however, if students were kept in isolation from reality, so his final recommendation was that schools prune from their courses of study all useless things. Only useful learning had a place in Comenius' school plan, but in settling for useful learning he did not mean to adopt a doctrine of narrow utilitarianism. Instead he admonished: "Nothing should be learned solely for its value at school, but for its use in life. . . . Whatever is taught should be taught as being of practical application in everyday life and of some definite use.''[25] This plea for relevance was probably the most important plank in Comenius' educational philosophy, for the whole of his educational theory was built on returning relevance to school learning.

Educational Empiricism

By alerting teachers and students the world over to the importance of sense training and realistic school instruction, Comenius put succeeding generations in his debt. Yet, for all their historical luster, both his theories and school practices were modest beginnings, and education had a long way to go before its accomplishments could measure up to the longings of the people for a more responsible performance from their schools. It may be overstating the case to argue that everyone suddenly perceived the worth of a school program filled with knowledge having practical and useful credentials, for educational revolutions simmer a long time before they erupt, but it is not wrong to argue that education began to go in this direction. As it did, enthusiastic riders leaped on the bandwagon, and few demonstrated greater enthusiasm for practical learning than John Locke (1632–1704).

Meeting Locke for the first time tempts us to label his educational and philosophical outlook empirical, although his empiricism, qualified by a recognition of the possibility of internal experience, kept him from becoming a narrow sensationalist. The point he stressed, one that his disciples tended to overstress, made sensory experience the single avenue to knowledge of the physical world: All ideas are grounded on what enters our minds through our senses. This doctrine, especially in our more pragmatic age, does not strike us as being particularly hard, although in the seventeenth century, when philosophers still invested confidence in the belief that fundamental ideas are innate, it was subjected to severe criticism.

Before Locke, Comenius stimulated scientific thinking and tried to infect education with naturalism on the level of learning, but Comenius' theories were largely intuitive; being neither an accomplished philosopher nor a skilled psychologist, Comenius never went much beyond analogical reasoning and deductive logic to certify his conclusions. Locke, however, abandoned intution as a means for solving problems and embraced what is now called the Baconian thesis: Dependable knowledge is the outcome of an inductive process.

Despite what might appear to be poor credentials for an educational philosopher, for Locke was never a professional schoolmaster or even in a broader sense an educator, his comprehensive social and political philosophy, along with profound psychological convictions, qualified him to speak with authority on matters of educational theory and practice. And everything he had to say about education was tempered by his fundamental allegiance to the doctrine of utility, a doctrine fully supported, he supposed, by an authentic scientific empiricism. Locke's educational thought is two-dimensional: one dimension, lodged in his psychology, is concerned with the origin of ideas and the stature of knowledge; the other, based on his perceptions of man's social nature, is an expression of his attitude on schooling. The first dimension is elaborated in *An Essay Concerning Human Understanding;* the second, in *Some Thoughts Concerning Education.*

Born into a middle-class British family, Locke's father, a country attorney, managed the education of his children until they were ready for the secondary school. John Locke had his first school experience at fourteen when his father enrolled him in the Westminster School, a famous but old-fashioned humanistic secondary school that prepared its students, supposedly, for life by taking almost every precaution to immunize them from it. Locke must have had this Westminster interlude in mind when he wrote, in *Some Thoughts Concerning Education,* that the time wasted on learning languages could have been better used for teaching students practical subjects. Whatever merit Locke's secondary schooling had—and it must have had some—he is silent about it and is eager to recite the negative effects of schooling. Could Locke have had his way, the education of young men—and he talks only about young men—would have been handled entirely on a tutorial, private basis.

Although Locke's reminiscences disparaged schooling, his education must have been better than he thought or would admit, because he ended up, after having tested diplomacy and medicine, as a professional philosopher. His philosophical study impressed him with the work of Sirs Robert Boyle and Isaac Newton, and from both he borrowed something for his own empiricism. Beginning with an acknowledgement of reason's place in philosophy, he went on to assert an audacious doctrine: All knowledge, all man's beliefs, even those involving revealed religion, must be subject to reason's test. To many, at least to devout Christians, this seemed to be going too far; almost from the beginning of his philosophical career, Locke was declared an enemy of religion. Locke did not want to be religion's enemy, nor was he concerned merely with scuttling awkward superstition; he wanted to submit vital social and political issues to the cold and objective test of reason. Still Locke could not qualify as a conventional rationalist, although he put trust in reason, because he found reason's substance in empirical data and not in self-evident propositions or innate ideas.

Locke clearly limits the origin of ideas to sensory experience, and by ideas he meant the immediate objects of perception and thought. The senses carry sense perceptions to the mind, but how this is done, physically or psychologically, is left for others to determine. As they enter the mind, perceptions are either simple or complex, depending on their objective nature. But the mind is not a mere passive instrument; in a process involving the mystery of internal experience, the mind manipulates experience and in the end makes it something different from what it was as a perception. This may have been a compositional theory of mind, one where the mind composes from raw material to arrive at meaning or to impose meaning on original perceptions. And this leads us to ask: What precisely was the nature of Locke's empiricism?

The Empiricism of John Locke.   It is at least implicit in Locke's famous *tabula rasa* theory: The mind is originally a blank tablet on which nothing is written before the stylus of experience begins to make impressions; yet these impressions, consisting of sensation and reflection, are neither narrow nor limited. Put another way, the mind is capable of great departures from sensory experience, although these departures always stand on the foundation of sensory experience. This, perhaps, is the substance of Locke's empiricism: "All those sublime thoughts which tower above the clouds, and reach as high as heaven itself, take their rise and footing here: in all that great extent wherein the mind wanders in those remote speculations it may seem to be elevated with, it stirs not one jot beyond those ideas which sense or reflection have offered for its contemplation."[26]

Now we should try to see how Locke's rational psychology influenced educational theory. Did his argument against the doctrine of innate ideas alter the course of education? Did this *tabula rasa* theory influence the work of the schools? First by discrediting any claim for innate knowledge and self-evident propositions, Locke put both tradition and authority in jeopardy—or, at the very least, on the defense. Reason replaced both as the instrument for assessing the meaning of all experience. Reason, properly used, could sift truth from error; reason, not authority or tradition, was the ultimate judge of what was true, practical, and useful. When the implications of this assertion were taken seriously, the school's curriculum was stripped of reams of old literature, and the way was open for empirically verified knowledge to gain a foothold.

But if reason were the only guide to truth, it had to be properly formed, and in Locke's commission to education, training or educating reason became the principal duty of schools. Training reason meant a number of things. It meant perfecting understanding; this was done by having an abundance of experiences to form and temper it. It meant immunizing understanding from emotion, for Locke knew that emotion could color experience, distort its meaning, and be an obstacle to the dependable functioning of reason. Information, of course, was grist for reason's mill, for without information it was pointless to talk about training reason. So in this connection Locke stressed the senses as avenues of knowledge from the outside world, but even Locke's cogent argument was unable to generate a curricular revolution. When the classics were studied, as they were in most schools, and when a knowledge of them was counted the equivalent of educational decency, the senses appeared to be employed as much as if students were experimenting in laboratories. So Locke demurred from enjoining reading or condemning all traditional knowledge, yet he campaigned for scholastic innovation. The books used, he said, were out of touch with reality and perpetuated unexamined, irrelevant assumptions. The mind, he asserted, should be informed by fresh, valid knowledge produced by careful study of the physical and social worlds. Despite Locke's prominence as a British philosopher, however, the schools resisted his advice about what knowledge was of most worth. When Locke was listened to, as in time he was, he raised new goals for education, and when they were adopted, empirical rather than rationalistic educational methods began to make headway.

Finally, Locke's theory on innate ideas and its corollary *tabula rasa* introduced the notion of human equality: All persons are created equal with no one having a head start. His theory of human equality, although he may not have intended this outcome, endowed education and training with additional importance: If everyone begins with nothing, nurture must take precedence over nature. Although Locke would not have cherished the distinction, he must be credited with having whetted the appetites of later generations with a supreme confidence in the power of education to improve the condition of human beings.

Romantic Naturalism

Beginning with Comenius' realism in the sixteenth century and continuing through Locke's empiricism in the seventeenth, educational philosophy made slow but steady progress in reforming and expanding the content of schooling. Books containing treasuries of ancient wisdom were still being read, and language, mainly Latin, was studied with unrelenting attention, but the physical world was being recognized too, and students spent more of their time preparing themselves for the practical occupations of life. However much the syllabus of learning might respond to the constant urgings of educational theory, the purpose of education remained intractable: In or out of school, education was meant to prepare persons to find suitable places for themselves in society. In a word, the goal of education was preparation for life.

Had it not been for Jean Jacques Rousseau, educational philosophers might have continued their speculations aimed at refining this general purpose and honed their arguments over the conflicting claims of liberal or useful knowledge for the prominent place in the school's curriculum. But Rousseau appeared on the educational scene with the intention of inciting a scholastic revolution. He began his book *Émile* with a long indictment of the schools, and he held educational philosophy responsible for an educational program indifferent to the natural needs and interests of children. He held up before his readers a picture of schooling wherein students were forced to capitulate to social and educational artificiality. The end of it all, he proclaimed with the intensity of a crusader, was a society filled with misfits, persons unable to recognize and fulfill their responsibilities to themselves and their fellows. All of education—indeed, all of society—was in urgent need of radical reform.

In 1762, the year *Émile* was published, nothing much had been done on a large scale toward educating most of the children of any country. What was evident to Rousseau in France was common the world over. Elementary schools here and there opened their doors, for the most part, to students able to pay for their instruction; secondary and higher education were still special preserves for the wealthy and the aristocratic. Regardless of the stand any educational philosopher might take, even one as outspoken as Rousseau, without some drastic shift in social and political policy toward the education of the people, the reform of education's fundamental structure appeared to be extremely unlikely. Germany, in the vanguard of public schooling, had created a system of schools for the common people with the intention of shaping them as good and cooperative citizens, but those schools where personal talent could be cultivated and where the skills of professional leadership could be developed were outside the boundary of popular aspiration. We see signs in the eighteenth century of educational vitalization, but they are faint and flickering. Public policy had not yet reached that point where it gave the education of the people serious consideration.

In this climate of relaxed indifference, Rousseau's reflections on educational reconstruction sounded harsh and uncompromising. Extensive opportunity for the education of the people was without much prospect; therefore, following a philosophical thesis compatible to him, Rousseau called for an abandonment of schools. Schools and everything taught in them, he declared, were based on the supposition that human beings have a natural disposition toward evil and that the bulk of education's attention must be directed at correcting the deficiencies of nature. Besides, schools operated on the dogmatic assumption that the principal, perhaps the only, purpose of education is to prepare persons for some occupation in adult society. On both counts, Rousseau declared, education was on the wrong track. As they come into the world, in their original natural state, children are naturally good, Rousseau wrote. Evil is a habit learned in society itself, and social institutions, schools chief among them, are most culpable. The end of education, moreover, if we follow Rousseau, is not the formation of a diplomat, a priest, a teacher, or a soldier but a person.

A common enough misconception in connection with Rousseau's theory is that he was an enemy of education. In the first part of *Émile,* where he is most philosophical in tone, Rousseau affirms the necessity of education with a clear and uncompromising statement that without education "things would be worse [for] mankind cannot be made by halves."[27] It would be plainly impossible for any person without education to cope with life in a complex society, so unless persons can escape society they must be educated in a way immunizing them from the contaminating influences of social life. Emile was lucky when his tutor and nurse took him to the country where he could live in rustic simplicity, but everyone, Rousseau knew, could not follow in Emile's footsteps.

Rousseau's Doctrine of Natural Education.   Education, Rousseau said, is three-sided and all sides are essential: It "comes to us from nature, from man, or from things. The inner growth of our organs and faculties is the education of nature, the use we learn to make of this growth is the education of men, what we gain by our experience of our surroundings is the education of things."[28]

So everyone has three teachers—nature, people, and things—who when they work in harmony produce the well-educated person. The trouble is, according to Rousseau, they seldom work in harmony. Two of the teachers have a relative independence from human influence, and they—nature and things—should probably be counted on most. It is education from human teachers that causes the most trouble. Here the educational trick is to keep the education from other people at as low a profile as possible: This is best done by removing the learner to an environment free from human complexities and contradictions—ideally the countryside—and putting him under the care of one teacher.

Lacking the ring of relevance, this part of Rousseau's educational charter was most susceptible to the sniping of critics who characterized the products of such an educational program "noble savages," and they got a good deal of mileage from their caricatures of "back to nature education." If we analyze his plan carefully, we shall see beyond the critics: By eliminating or reducing the effects of the teaching from persons and things, nature's teaching could be more direct and effective. Natural education was meant to be highly personal, of course, so the whole business of preparing persons for places in society is slighted. But Rousseau meant to forfeit social education, and does so without apology. Yet no one is entirely independent and, with or without Rousseau's blessing, everyone must sometime become part of society and live with others. Caught up here in a dilemma of educational purpose—whether individual or social good is to have priority—Rousseau sounds convincing: "Drawn this way by nature and that way by man, compelled to yield to both forces, we make a compromise and reach neither goal."[29] So, instead of trying to resolve this dilemma, a perennial one, he rejects it: He sacrifices public good and invests all his attention in the education of persons as individuals. Declaring manhood the common vocation, Rousseau will aim at nothing less: "Before his parents chose a calling for him nature called him to be a man. Life is the trade I would teach him. When he leaves me, I grant you, he will be neither a magistrate, a soldier, nor a priest; he will be a man."[30]

The trail to natural education is blazed in the five parts to *Émile,* each concerned with a different period of human development. But without looking at those different periods here, we should return to Rousseau's basic philosophical assumption and recognize it as the chief obstacle to the acceptance of, or even a fair hearing for, the educational plan he advanced: "God makes all things good; man meddles with them and they become evil."[31] This bold assertion challenged the doctrine of original sin and laid the foundation for Rousseau's reconstruction of education. Where conventional educational practice followed a theory making teaching responsible for correcting flaws in original nature, Rousseau's audacious doctrine committed teaching to immunizing an originally untarnished human nature from the perversion of social life. Without any human fault needing correction, Rousseau could promote a heretofore unheard-of liberty in education. The eighteenth century, however, was indisposed to countenance educational liberty, so this progressive theory of romantic naturalism was for a long time sentenced to lie fallow.

National Education

Educators, for the most part, turned a deaf ear to naturalism and listened instead to the declarations of religious humanism, but in other fields—in literature and social philosophy, for example—naturalism became an infectious doctrine with an influence too intense to be stifled. Crossing the threshold of the nineteenth century we see prospects for natural education dimmed and Rousseau's theories discarded, but nationalism was fast coming over the political horizon, and in this new political climate where strong loyalties to a national state were cultivated, the educational precepts distilled from religious humanism began to lose appeal. Religious preference, still keenly felt, continued to make some claim on the schools, and sectarianism was sometimes catered to, but education was about to enter a new era, one where it was commissioned to train citizens to serve the principal interests of a national state.

Quickly, perhaps too quickly, France, Germany, Great Britain, and other European states, captivated by the possibility of reaping political reward from a greater distribution of schooling, turned their hands to creating educational systems. Measured by contemporary standards, the outcome of their effort was disappointing, but we know from our educational history how schools were multiplied and how teachers were recruited to conduct them. What is less clear, however, is the driving force behind this new educational philosophy. The generalization about education serving a national purpose is almost certainly correct, yet this reveals only one side of political motive. Was this investment in education, an investment great enough to include large numbers—in some cases a majority —of a nation's children, generated by a determination to preserve the status quo? Was it made because at long last political leaders, becoming sensitive to the people's needs, were captivated by an altruism leading them to provide means wherein personal talent could be realized? Or was it that the great and powerful persons in these countries wanted to exercise control over the people and found in schools and schooling an excellent way to do so?

Without pausing here to test these motives further, we see a kind of public education marching forward to the cadence call of nationalism. Sustained by political zeal or fancy, schools were delegated to prepare citizens to take their proper places in society; after the interests of an exigent national state were satisfied, schools might introduce studies tending toward personal fulfillment. This huge order was premature; schools lacked the ability to meet it. If education were conscripted in a national crusade, it needed clearer and more precise direction from a philosophy based on a solid foundation of ethical and psychological truth and a method capable of ensuring the objectives of citizenship. This, at least, was the thesis advanced by Johann Herbart as he set out to become the architect for German, and eventually for all, national education.

Advent of the Science of Education.   Distressed with talk about naturalistic education, Herbart laid the foundation for a revival of the realism and empiricism of Comenius and Locke. Education's objective, the moral and civic development of persons, was clear enough, and additionally, according to Herbart in his *Science of Education,* it could be demonstrated by the facts of moral philosophy. From this point on, then, Herbart's educational theory centers on the social and political purpose of schooling. In connection with this purpose, the questions of what to teach (curriculum) and how to teach (method) needed considerable help from the expanding resources of science. The boundaries of the curriculum of the schools could be filled with information essential to personal, social, and political morality. At the same time, students would be taught their duties to society and how to comply with them. Instruction (teaching a body of truth people need) was the school's principal commission, and this instruction should be fortified with a pedagogic technique ratified in a sound psychology of learning. All this Herbart proposed in his various books on education, and when his theory of education was followed, spurred on by zealous disciples who sometimes took liberties with it, we come face to face with the teacher-centered school. Authorities in knowledge and experts in method, teachers made all school learning revolve around them; students, unquestionably and unquestioningly, were under their command.

Education was intended to prepare persons for life, for life in a society whose foundations were already set in place, with a body of knowledge fully accredited in an empirical realism. Standing aside, uninvolved in the educational events of that time, and uninhibited by the threat of reprisal from nineteenth-century politics, we see personal interest, motive, and genius sacrificed on the altar of nationalism. And educational philosophy, especially Herbart's, took part in this sacrifice. Yet, one can go too far along this line; one can be swept away by an enthusiasm for personal objectives and forget that teaching for social solidarity, for national interest and patriotism, is a legitimate, perhaps praiseworthy, function of schools maintained and supported by the state. Herbart's educational philosophy endeavored to protect educators from such memory lapses.

EDUCATIONAL PHILOSOPHY IN AMERICA

The remaining chapters of this book will center largely on educational philosophy in America, so our historical perspective here can afford to be brief and general.

FIGURE 2.3
Educational Philosophy in the Modern World

THEORY	PRINCIPAL EXPONENT	EDUCATIONAL POLICY
Religious Realism	John Amos Comenius (1592–1670)	Education for life and for eternity by following principles of natural learning; book learning supplemented by knowledge of the physical world.
Empiricism	John Locke (1632–1704)	Nothing is in the mind that is not first in the senses; the purpose of education is to develop the ability of reason.
Naturalism	Jean-Jacques Rousseau (1712–1778)	The natural goodness of human beings may be preserved and protected by education from nature.
Nationalism	Johann Herbart (1776–1841)	Scientific knowledge about learning and teaching is essential if education is to serve the interests of the national state.

What we want to illustrate is how educational philosophy began by occupying a humble and subordinate role in American colonial education (far more subdued, in fact, than at the same time in Europe) and then matured as the nation matured to translate social and political objectives into educational policy. Never entirely immune to philosophical and cultural influence from Europe, educational philosophy in this good land had the additional obligation of interpreting doctrines of European origin for educational use in this country. In the end, however, about two and one-half centuries later, educational philosophers wrote a distinctively American educational prospectus. We will review some of the principal antecedents to this noteworthy accomplishment.

Colonial Beginnings

In the early years of the seventeenth century Europeans by the hundreds set sail for the New World. Their reasons for leaving the lands of their birth and early nurture were diverse, although a prominent motive, we know, was religious. When they landed on America's shores they tried, with few exceptions, to build a society wherein distinctive religious temperament and belief could be satisfied along with other multiple appurtenances to civilized life. Once they had tended to the most pressing problems of settling in what amounted to a wilderness, they turned their attention to the education of their children. They had a long and rich educational tradition to guide them, one inherited from and tested by their ancestors in Europe. Although practicing educational philosophers among seventeenth-century colonists were rare, the educational theory of religious humanism was compatible to them, and they did their best to promote it.

By this time, of course, amendments had been made to educational philosophy, and some European schoolmasters were in the habit of following the advice of such perceptive educational thinkers as Comenius, Locke, and somewhat later, Rousseau. Realism and naturalism were in the wind, but the wind seldom blew hard enough to carry either across the Atlantic Ocean. For most of the colonial period colonial educators paid allegiance to a code that listed, in order, as educational goals: religious orthodoxy, civility, and practical accomplishment. No child should be allowed to go through life molested by the devil, so parents, preachers, and teachers did their best to see that everyone had his or her faith bolstered by sound instruction in religious duty. But religious duty, to be fully understood and followed, needed some help from those humble cultural auxiliaries inherent in literary learning. This was the principal justification for some colonies enacting laws requiring everyone to be literate and for the founding of schools. Neither religious rectitude nor the first ornaments of culture, however, could be depended on to keep the economy of the colonies alive. Everyone was told to have enough practical skill to pursue a lawful and profitable occupation and make a living. This code may have been too bare to qualify as a philosophy of education, but it turned out to be the preamble to an educational philosophy that in later years gave direction to the schools of America.

Our colonial forefathers were philosophically literate—this is confirmed in their words and deeds—but all the while they held philosophy suspect. It was a product of human reason, and reason's speculations could become enemies to religious faith. From time to time, though, philosophy might be useful if properly curtailed, and this concession to philosophy's useful character recommended some attention to the writings of educational philosophers. The writer most admired, and perhaps must useful in helping them stabilize the direction of colonial education, was Francis Bacon. Whenever colonial teachers or preachers needed assistance from educational philosophy, they opened *The Advancement of Learning*. What they found, while not always confirming religious orthodoxy, nevertheless certified their belief that much of the knowledge inherited from the past was undependable and defective; it had been misused and misinterpreted by a logical method originating with Aristotle. In promoting inductive to replace deductive logic Bacon never meant to go as far as his colonial readers went. He expected induction to lead to discovery of truth. They, however, confident that truth was in their religious legacy, were interested in inductive logic as a means for classifying and organizing it. Besides, Bacon's *Advancement of Learning* idealized the utility of knowledge, and on this point colonial educators found him most convincing. In any case, *The Advancement of Learning* told them they were on the right educational road. Under these circumstances, as a helpmate rather than as a leader, educational philosophy was introduced to the scholastic wilderness of the New World.

Education and the Republic

With their colonial years behind them, Americans in the last years of the eighteenth century began to contemplate their political future. They were about to strike out on a new political experiment and were prepared, although not without some misgivings, to embrace a republican form of government. The Declaration of Independence, in affirming popular sovereignty, invested the people of the country with the responsibility for conducting their own political affairs. Old political philosophies were jettisoned forthwith. Yet if the people themselves were to be their governors, if they had no one other than themselves to depend upon, they would have to be trained for this new and heavy responsibility. Political policy needed the steady hand of knowledge widely distributed among the people to sustain it. At this point we see the first faint sign of a democratic philosophy of education coming over the horizon, and marching in the vanguard of this visionary theory is Thomas Jefferson (1743–1826).

Before Jefferson, Benjamin Franklin (1706–1790) had written about the need for educational reform in the colonies. Franklin worried more about the absence of practical education than about its generous distribution, and he must be credited with promoting a drastic revision in secondary education: the study of the English language itself, on one hand, and the teaching of the classics in English, on the other. So, although Franklin hardly belongs to the same class as Jefferson as an educational philosopher for democracy, he nevertheless made a consequential contribution to education by breaking with the tradition that Latin was the only suitable language for school instruction. In addition Franklin, along with Jefferson, declaimed against religion's grip on education. Both coupled educational progress in early America with a diminution of religion's influence over it.

Minimizing religion in education, though, was only one side of Jefferson's progressive view; another side was far more important. This other side dealt with making schooling available to the people. Jefferson's republican political policy rested squarely on the proposition that universal manhood suffrage demanded universal education, and in 1778 he prepared a bill for the Virginia legislature that, had it been adopted, would have gone far toward realizing universal education on an elementary level. If public policy is to be made by the body politic, the people must be trained to understand the meaning and consequence of policy. Jefferson, therefore, in advancing a political doctrine also advanced an educational policy, one that took most of the nineteenth century to realize, and even then only partially.

The Common School Crusade

Although Jefferson's bold theory of universal education mustered a good deal of popular support, it had to compete with a common educational disposition in the early United States that the schooling of the people is not a public responsibility. This theory borrowed from a vigorous British policy that "each person should be educated according to his means"; the common good, it stated, depends for definition and realization on those classes in society who, by reason of position, education, and natural ability, are fully prepared to hold the reins of leadership. Anyone falling outside this category of privilege was destined to follow policies forged by others. For a long time the competition from this theory of natural aristocracy—one whose American elaboration is credited to Alexander Hamilton (1757–1804)—was strong enough to impede the progress of Jefferson's democratic educational theory. And coupled with it was the solid determination to make education a private rather than a public responsibility. Under these theoretical hardships, American educational policy moved into and proceeded through the first four decades of the nineteenth century.

Thereafter, for reasons still debated by historians, the old doctrine making education a private duty began a slow retreat and the conviction became more common that the purpose of schooling is to train citizens in civic duty rather than to convey them to safe denominational sanctuaries. With civic education uppermost in the minds of the shapers of public policy, the schools were accorded support and subjected to supervision from the state, and following the assumption that the common good is ensured by educational decency—which in this case meant literacy—the common-school movement was born.

Still, surrounded by political activity and educational ferment, it would have been hard to find an explicit and clearly formulated philosophy of education. The roll of the crusaders for popular education can be called—Horace Mann (1796–1859), Henry Barnard (1811–1900), James Carter (1795–1849), and others—without hearing the name of any legitimate educational philosopher. Here were men, hundreds of them, all dedicated to the proposition that education is a public responsibility, with its sights set on citizenship rather than on religion; all were intensely humanitarian in their outlook, too confident that education could improve the condition of mankind and enhance the worth of society, but one looks in vain for what we today would call a comprehensive educational philosophy. With or without expositors, however, an American educational philosophy was being forged. Although we cannot follow its details here, this forging was always accompanied by tempestuous, acrimonious debate.

The altruism of educators and public men, some say, explains the progress American educational policy made from an individual to a collective theory: that is, that citizens have a right to education and may expect society's resources to support them in it. The proclamations relative to the common good have a convincing ring, but they may be off the mark. The need for an orderly society, where the traditional interests of the wealthy, the well-born, and the powerful could be protected and where the status quo could be preserved, may have been a more persuasive motive for the erection of a policy making education available to the people. By the last half of the nineteenth century alterations in American society had become profound. The ranks of the common men had been swelled by hundreds of thousands. Should these rude people become unruly, should they decide to upset the tranquil operations of society, should their ignorance lead them to imprudence, all the benefits that over the years had accrued to the ruling classes and persons of high social position would be put in jeopardy. Under these circumstances—and bred more in a fear of what they had to lose than in any authentic altruism, some argue—the cause of public, common-school education was promoted by an aristocracy of wealth and power with the sole intention of controlling the people, of keeping them on the safe and narrow path to social orthodoxy and civic order.

Whether we shall ever be able to find the definitive answer to the basic motivation behind popular education, an American invention of the nineteenth century, is hard to say. Yet there is evidence that as educational philosophy began to come of age in the United States, it took the side of the social and economic status quo. Making education an instrument for social and economic preservation while teaching citizens their duties appears to have been the thesis of William T. Harris (1835–1909) who, it may be said, was America's first professional educational philosopher. Committed to philosophical idealism, Harris assumed a systematic universe and a comprehensive body of dependable knowledge. With supreme confidence in human intelligence to shape an orderly political and economic society, he set American schools on a course to perpetuate the tested social inheritance of America. In a word, the purpose of education was to prepare persons for life, the social and economic life of the United States at that time.[32] No room was made for social reconstruction. For such a philosophy of education, the educational method attributed to Johann Herbart, along with the teacher-centered school, appeared to be tailor-made.

Progressive Education

Progressivism in American life began with reforms in politics, economics, and society and, though to a lesser extent, with reappraisals of traditional doctrines in religion and philosophy. Eventually it affected education too. The fundamental thesis of progressivism was that all social institutions have a commitment to the improvement of mankind. So whether in politics, where amendments to the Constitution put the choice of public officers, such as United States senators, in the hands of the electorate; in economics, where trusts and railroad monopolies were made to conform to the public interest; in society, where such things as women's suffrage and women's rights were being promoted and where labor unions were beginning to win their long battle for legal recognition; in religion, where traditional and orthodox creeds were being challenged by liberal and evangelical sects or, in some cases, by secularism; or in philosophy, where the apparently subversive theory of evolution, heralded in Charles Darwin's (1809–1882) *The Origin of Species* and *The Descent of Man,* was redrawing traditional designs of man's origin, the progressive creed made steady, if unspectacular, headway.

In the wake of a general progressive spirit influencing American life and institutions, educational progressivism made its first appearance. The leader, or at least the first visible elaborator, of progressive education was Francis W. Parker (1837–1902). Shortly after his appointment as superintendent of the Quincy, Massachusetts, public school system in 1873, Parker set out to correct faults in the schooling there. Children were sent to their books and lessons with the admonition to study hard, for their work in school was a prelude to later success in life. All schooling was set in the context of some benefit to be reaped in the distant future. Nothing concerning the needs of the children as they came to school was adverted to, and no effort was made to capitalize on the motivation intrinsic to their own lives. Parker, by reforming the curriculum and modifying teaching methods, hoped to correct these deficiencies. To some extent, scholars tell us, he did.

After leaving Quincy, where his progressive policies ran into trouble because the public was unready for radical educational change, Parker went to Chicago to begin a long and fruitful association with the Cook County Normal School. This school, engaged in the preparation of teachers, became the oasis from which progressive educational doctrines flowed.

While never explicitly a philosophy of education, progressive education became a crusade for improving the schools along lines sometimes rescued from earlier educational philosophers all the way back to Comenius and Rousseau. But progressive educators wanted and perhaps needed a more contemporary source of philosophical inspiration, so whenever possible they turned to the pragmatic educational philosophy John Dewey was then crafting at the University of Chicago and enlisted its support.

From the advent of progressive education in the late 1900s to the middle of the twentieth century, this educational practice, for this is what progressive education was, was criticized and condemned by educators and educational philosophers who refused—they thought with good reason—to abandon a commitment to an educational purpose paying heed first to preparing students for the lives they must live as adults. There is, they argued, a basic core to common culture, and education's mission is to teach the essentials of this common core. Throughout its history in America, progressive education was indicted for its "soft pedagogy" by advocates of essential education. To some extent, these two conflicting theories of schooling, with their inevitable hostility, are with us still. Yet, being theories of schooling more than philosophies of education, both worked on the outer fringe of educational philosophy. In later chapters we shall see more fully the philosophies to which they appealed for help, and at the same time we shall see how this conflict between progressive and essential education led to a further development of systematic philosophies of American education.

FIGURE 2.4
Educational Philosophy in America

HISTORICAL PERIOD	PRINCIPAL EXPONENTS	DEFINITION OF EDUCATIONAL PURPOSE
Colonial (1635–1775)	Ministers and magistrates whose religious zeal dominated educational practice. Francis Bacon (1561–1626) was consulted.	To educate children in the precepts of true religion and prepare responsible and industrious citizens.
Early National (1775–1820)	Thomas Jefferson (1743–1826)	A republican form of government required literate citizens who were responsible for shaping political policy.
	Benjamin Franklin (1706–1790)	A practical English education capable of fitting persons for the duties of life.
Common School (1820–1870)	Horace Mann (1796–1859) Henry Barnard (1811–1900) James Carter (1795–1849) William T. Harris (1835–1909)	Education is the principal means for the personal, social, and political betterment of society.
Progressive (1890–1940)	Francis W. Parker (1837–1902) John Dewey (1859–1952)	Education for personal and social growth and an endorsement of the child-centered school.

NOTES

1. WERNER JAEGER, *Paideia: The Ideals of Greek Culture,* I (New York: Oxford University Press, 1945), p. 291.
2. H. I. MARROU, *A History of Education in Antiquity* (New York: Sheed and Ward, 1956), p. 48.
3. JAMES L. JARRETT, *The Educational Theories of the Sophists* (New York: Teachers College Press, 1969), p. 68.
4. PLATO, *Gorgias,* trans. B. Jowett in *The Dialogues of Plato,* 3d ed. (London: Oxford University Press, 1892), 471 de.
5. MARROU, *Education in Antiquity,* p. 49.
6. PLATO, *Protagoras,* trans. B. Jowett in *The Dialogues of Plato,* 3d ed. (London: Oxford University Press, 1892), 312 a.
7. Ibid., 318.
8. Ibid., 318 b.
9. Ibid., 358 b d.
10. JOHN PATRICK LYNCH, *Aristotle's School: A Study of a Greek Educational Institution* (Berkeley: University of California Press, 1972).
11. ISOCRATES, *Antidosis* (Cambridge, Mass.: Loeb Classical Library, Harvard University Press, 1927–1929), vol II, pp. 180–181.
12. Ibid., pp. 183–185.
13. CICERO, *De Oratore* (London: G. Bell, 1903).
14. QUINTILIAN, *The Education of an Orator* (Cambridge, Mass.: Loeb Classical Library, Harvard University Press, 1921), Bk. I, chap. i, par. 10.
15. CLEMENT OF ALEXANDRIA, *The Writings of Clement of Alexandria,* in *The Ante-Nicene Christian Library* (Edinburgh: T. & T. Clark, 1870), vol II, p. 100.
16. CASSIODORUS, *An Introduction to Divine and Human Readings,* trans. L. W. Jones (New York: Columbia University Press, 1946), pp. 119–120.
17. ST. AUGUSTINE, *On Christian Doctrine,* in *A Select Library of Nicene and Post-Nicene Fathers of the Christian Church* (New York: The Christian Literature Publishing Company, 1895), 1st series, vol II, p. 554.
18. CASSIODORUS, *Divine and Human Readings* p. 146.
19. ANDREW F. WEST, *Alcuin and the Rise of Christian Schools* (New York: Charles Scribner's Sons, 1892).
20. J. B. MULLINGER, *The Schools of Charles the Great* (New York: G. E. Steckert & Company, 1911).
21. DANIEL B. McGARRY, *The Metalogicon of John of Salisbury* (Berkeley: University of California Press, 1955) Book III, Chapter i, p. 150.
22. Ibid.
23. ERASMUS, *De Ratione Studii,* in W. H. Woodward, *Desideruis Erasmus (New York:* Teachers College Press, 1964), p. 164.
24. PHILIP MELANCHTHON, *Melanchthon on Christian Doctrine,* trans. and ed. C. L. Manschreck (New York: Oxford University Press, 1965), p. 340.
25. M. W. KEATINGE, *The Great Didactic of John Amos Comenius* (London: Adam and Charles Black, 1896), p. 341.
26. JOHN LOCKE, *An Essay Concerning Human Understanding,* 28th ed. (London: T. Tegg and Son, 1838), Book II, Chapter i, p. 24.

27. JEAN JACQUES ROUSSEAU, *Émile,* trans. Barbara Foxley (New York: E. P. Dutton 1938), p. 5.
28. Ibid., p. 6.
29. Ibid., p. 9.
30. Ibid.
31. Ibid., p. 5.
32. WILLIAM T. HARRIS, *Psychologic Foundations of Education* (New York: D. Appleton & Co., 1898), p. 282.

READINGS

These readings are illustrative of the development of educational philosophy as a discipline and of the influence of educational theory on educational practice in different historical periods. Neither chapters nor periods are cited here because selection for further reading is best guided by the particular interest of the reader.

NASH, PAUL, ANDREAS M. KAZAMIAS, and HENRY J. PERKINSON, *The Educated Man: Studies in the History of Educational Thought.* New York: John Wiley and Sons, Inc., 1965.

PERKINSON, HENRY J., *Since Socrates: Studies in the History of Western Educational Thought.* New York: Longman, Inc., 1980.

PERKINSON, HENRY J., *Two Hundred Years of American Educational Thought.* New York: David McKay Company, Inc., 1976.

POWER, EDWARD J., *Evolution of Educational Doctrine: Major Educational Theorists of the Western World.* New York: Prentice-Hall, Inc., 1969.

RUSK, ROBERT R., *Doctrines of the Great Educators.* New York: St. Martin's Press, Inc., 1979.

SMITH, WILSON, ed., *Theories of Education in Early America 1655–1819.* Indianapolis: The Bobbs-Merrill Co., Inc., 1973.

ULICH, ROBERT, *History of Educational Thought.* New York: American Book Company, 1950.

II

SYSTEMATIC PHILOSOPHIES OF EDUCATION AND CONTEMPORARY THEORIES OF SCHOOLING

3

TRADITIONAL
PHILOSOPHIES
OF EDUCATION

Most philosophers are eager to express their confidence in a twenty-five-century experience with philosophy showing that no self-taught person, no mind uninformed about the work of its predecessors, has been able to make any valuable contribution to philosophy. Whatever truth is lodged in this assertion should be extended to educational philosophy as well. In the preceding chapter we undertook to sketch the evolution of educational doctrine to ensure a certain level of historical literacy. Now we can go on to maintain that if our grasp of philosophical issues depends to some extent on a mastery of the accomplishments of the past, it depends no less on a knowledge of various contemporary philosophical points of view. So in connection with broadening our knowledge of philosophy, we should take the time to inquire into the most prominent and influential systematic philosophies of education.

Idealism, realism, religious-rational humanism, pragmatism, existentialism, and analytic philosophy have credentials of currency, influence, and prominence. We should be prepared to study their basic philosophical theses. Yet when we do, for reasons becoming clearer as we go on, we should be careful to notice that idealism and realism are the principal philosophical sources on which all other philosophies of education draw. Idealism and realism are not the only authentic philosophies of education but, in one form or another, all philosophies of education eventually work their way back to propositions or to developments of propositions found in these two most ancient philosophical interpretations of our relationship with the world.

Although the philosophies of education named are easily sorted out and can stand as independent systems of educational thought, some educational philosophers prefer to sever their relationship with systematic educational philosophy. As we survey the contemporary philosophical scene, we should be aware of a current but modest tendency in American educational philosophy to abandon preoccupation with idealism, realism, religious-rational humanism, pragmatism, existentialism, and analytic philosophy and give attention, without reference to any historically defined system, to the problems education faces in the modern world. No one system, the promoters of this trend allege, has the means to provide solutions to these pressing problems; in fact, allegiance to any one may succeed only in obscuring the problems. In any case, the time spent in mastering systems of educational thought, they say, could be better used to tackle the problems of education.[1]

We recognize almost at once the signs inherent in this position, and they are signs warning us that theory, in the last analysis, is probably not worth the effort, because it overburdens the educational process and makes its effective functioning impossible.

Although elements of truth are lodged in the contention that blind allegiance to a philosophical system can lead to an indifference to real, imperative educational problems, it is not easy to see how radical eclecticism can be an effective remedy. We should begin with the admission that although no one philosophical system may possess ultimate educational truth, systematic philosophies of education offer us a comprehensive intellectual structure wherein the human enterprise of education can be contemplated. These philosophies do not always call the tune for education, but they do express musical preferences: They are carefully reasoned proposals about how education should proceed. Knowing them, even without embracing any one philosophy or endorsing the system's approach—and recognizing, too, the shortcomings of philosophical dogmatism—is bound to improve our perspective of inevitable relationships between educational philosophy and a fundamental (philosophical) view of the world in which we live. Adopting the proposition that an abundance of knowledge—in this case about systematic philosophies of education—is the best safeguard against misinterpretation, we proceed to review them and begin our review with idealism.

IDEALISM

Neglecting for now the mysticism and idealism in the Oriental philosophical tradition to search for a starting point in Western philosophical history, we come face to face with the origin of idealism in the philosophical writing of Plato. From this point on, although scholars tend to agree that Plato was not a systematic philosopher in, say, the way Immanuel Kant was, idealism began a long and persistent march through history. Plato laid the foundations for idealism and in large strokes painted a philosophical picture to be retouched and sometimes redrawn by later philosophers, but they exhibited their artistry for the most part within the broad structure of Plato's design. While it may be pure exaggeration to allege that all philosophy since Plato is nothing more than an amendment to some part of his doctrine, the well of Plato's fundamental idealism, it seems safe to say, has never run dry.

Foundations of Idealism

Prompted by his famous mentor, Socrates, Plato began by inquiring into the nature of knowledge (what knowledge is) and the nature of reality (what can be known). In company with all other philosophers of his day, Plato was interested in the relationship between knowledge and the proper conduct of human life, but where other philosophers were satisfied with a practical knowledge—one capable of being translated immediately into action—Plato wanted more. He wanted to understand the theoretical dimensions of knowledge and the nature and meaning of ultimate reality. And this determination to fathom the universal character of knowledge, both the act of knowing and the object of knowledge, later recommended his brand of philosophical idealism to Christian and Jewish theologians and philosophers. So, despite Plato's equivocal stance in connection with God's continuing relationship with men and the immortality of man's unitary soul, points always uppermost in the minds of religious persons, Plato's idealism entered a centuries-long compact with Christianity and the philosophy subserving it. Christian philosophers, understandably enough, searched for philosophical underpinnings to their faith, and they thought, though very likely mistakenly, that Plato supplied them.

After making its way through thickets of theological dispute generated in a cult of neoplatonism, and sometimes coming perilously close to being only a philosophy of religion, idealism entered the modern world and almost at once was reconstructed by René Descartes (1596–1650). Although Descartes' famous *cogito*, "I think, therefore I am," was a first step toward a certitude that Plato himself might have rejected as being unsound and untrustworthy, it was nevertheless generally compatible with Platonic idealism. Cartesian idealism stressed the importance of personal experience, an experience capable of introducing and certifying the idea of a perfect being—God. The purity of Descartes' idealism can be debated, for sometimes his philosophy shows signs of conventional realism, but the main line of his thought was close enough to idealistic theses to make him fit into the idealist tradition.[2]

After Descartes had given idealism its modern dress, Baruch Spinoza (1632–1677), Gottfried Wilhelm von Leibniz (1646–1716), George Berkeley (1685–1753), Immanuel Kant (1724–1804), Georg Wilhelm Friedrich Hegel (1770–1831), and Samuel Taylor Coleridge (1772–1834), while not always going in the same philosophical direction or always subscribing to what appeared to be an orthodox idealism, in quick succession propelled idealism to the pinnacle of philosophic notice. Colleges and universities throughout Europe made room for idealist philosophers on their faculties and, while the doors of academic halls were seldom thrown open to the ordinary person and whatever went on behind them never affected much the measure of his thought, idealistic philosophy began to infect political, economic, social, and educational theory. Doing so, it exerted a profound but indirect influence on the lives of the people.

Idealism in America.   Over the centuries religion and idealism had made common cause, so it is perhaps not surprising that when American colleges began to expand their curricula to make room for philosophy, the brand of philosophy most to their taste was idealism. The transport of idealism from Europe to America was made principally in two ways: First, without having a legitimate university in the United States to attend, promising American students went to Europe for advanced study and while there were exposed to one or another idealistic creed. They brought its principles home with them. In addition, there was the work of Coleridge. Coleridge was best known to Americans—teachers, students, and the general public alike—as a poet, so his poetry introduced his idealism. Yet he was also an accomplished philosopher with a vigorous and enthusiastic idealistic outlook.[3] As much as anyone else, Coleridge represented idealism to the American transcendentalists, Ralph Waldo Emerson (1803–1882) chief among them, and from their solicitous cultivation idealism began to gain a solid foothold in American philosophy.[4]

The fundamental optimism so characteristic of nineteenth-century America appeared to be a perfect match for philosophical idealism. Moreover, the temper of the United States in this period of exuberant expansion was still strongly religious, another recommendation for a philosophy with a character so friendly to orthodox religion. Under these circumstances the spread of idealism was rapid and the flavor of its beliefs contagious. Following in a broad and general idealistic tradition, William T. Harris, an educator and a philosopher, gave idealism an additional boost by founding the *Journal of Speculative Philosophy* (1867–1893), America's first strictly professional philosophical periodical. Harris, because of his deep involvement in education, first as a teacher and then as superintendent of schools in St. Louis and, later, United States Commissioner of Education, was in a position to meld education and philosophy in a way no earlier American educator or philosopher could have managed.

While Harris was translating idealism into the language of education, Josiah Royce (1855–1916) was cultivating its speculative side and in some respects was more responsible than any other philosopher for the resurgence of idealism in the United States in the nineteenth century. Finally, with its American foundations in place, idealism in education, now as a systematic educational philosophy, was promoted by Herman H. Horne (1874–1946).[5] From this point on, idealism must be followed in the work of our contemporaries.

Philosophical Principles of Idealism

Idealism followed several tributaries as it flowed from its Platonic source toward the modern world, so the mainstream, if one existed, would have been extremely difficult to discern. Without taking the time to follow the direction or test the depth of all these tributaries, we can look closely at two that appear to have carried idealism's principal intellectual inheritance. One is absolute idealism; the other is critical idealism.

Whether absolute idealism had its origin with George Berkeley or earlier is a point we do not have to resolve. Berkeley, in any case, was its most eloquent exponent, and Berkeley's idealism is, in fact, most often used to illustrate absolute idealism. Here was a philosophy that began by flying in the face of ordinary experience, for with one verbal barrage it eliminated the whole of the material world. With the world of matter out of the way, only God, finite spirits, and the idea of finite spirits remained.

Absolute Idealism. The motivation for absolute idealists to set the philosophical record straight was grounded in a determination to reduce the influence of materialism, an influence growing by leaps and bounds under the auspices of the empiricism of John Locke and Isaac Newton (1642–1727). The materialist, the idealist complains, assumes the physical world to be an independently existing world and, moreover, that matter is the sole material composing the universe. Absolute idealism, on the other hand, rejects the supremacy of matter and introduces what sometimes appears to be a fantastic proposition: Things, the objects of common experience, cannot exist by themselves, and they do not exist at all unless there is some mind to perceive them. How should one answer the question about whether or not a tree falling in the forest makes a noise if no person is there to hear it? There is no noise, the idealist answers, because existence without perception is impossible. This refutation of mankind's common experience has led to the conclusion that absolute idealism is nothing more than an elaborate philosophical joke, and a bad one at that. No one should deny the obvious, and common sensory experience authenticates the obviousness of the world of physical reality; the material world itself exists. Persons can have knowledge of it and experience with it.

Idealists may not want to be quite so blunt: They may not be ready to deny the material form of things, although they are positive that we cannot know them as things, we cannot know them by coming in contact in particular cases with their physical qualities. The essence of all material things is spiritual, so material things can be reduced to clusters of ideas, but these ideas do not exist in their own right apart from some mind to perceive them. Absolute idealism does not tell us that we create the world out of the juices of our own minds; it does not tell us that if we do not like the kind of world in which we live, we can create another one by using our mental powers. It does tell us, however, that our ideas of material things must be presented to us by a mind or a spirit which is greater than and has an existence independent of us. To most absolute idealists this mind or spirit is God.

The famous Dr. Samuel Johnson (1696–1772) kicked a great stone and doing so declared he had demonstrated the foolishness of absolute idealism. We may be tempted to do the same. But before we stub our toe we should consider another thesis in this branch of idealism, one having to do with the problem of knowledge.

The absolute idealist maintains, as a matter of principle, that the human mind, which is spiritual, cannot have a cognitive relationship with matter. Correspondence, he says, between two such diverse entities as matter and spirit is impossible. If we are to have knowledge at all, it must be knowledge of the spiritual nature of matter. In this correspondence the human mind is not the creator of its perceptions. A spiritual force in the world produces our perceptions of what can be called objective reality. This reliance on spirit, the idealist maintains, does not affect the reality of things; however, all that can be said about physical reality is that it is perceived or is perceivable. Its meaning depends on a relationship between the spiritual quality of the human mind and the spiritual essence of the world.

The fundamental aim of absolute idealism is to show that material reality has no absolute existence independent of mind, and when it succeeds the foundation for materialism and atheism is destroyed. Objects of sensation are ideas. First, they are ideas in finite (human) minds. These ideas are not created by finite minds but are imprinted on or presented to them by a perpetual divine activity. An Absolute Mind always capable of perceiving objective reality makes the existence of objective reality possible even when human minds are absent, but in the code of absolute idealism things are not perceived by God, or the Absolute Mind, because they exist, for this would make their existence independent of all minds. They exist because God perceives them. On a lower level, they exist when human minds perceive them as ideas.

We are entitled to ask absolute idealists what becomes of our common world —the one where we live, with its houses, rivers, mountains, trees, even our bodies —if we follow this philosophy. The answer is, keeping carefully in mind the distinction between physical reality and ideas of it, that nothing in this philosophy disturbs one thing in nature. Whatever we feel, hear, or know remains as secure and as real as ever. This answer sounds both strange and unconvincing. What is meant, though, is that the immediate objects of our senses cannot exist without our minds and, in any case, they are properly called things rather than ideas. To persons immersed in the practical world of reality rather than living in the ivory tower of the philosopher, absolute idealism has a basic repugnance; they may find it difficult to understand, let alone embrace, such a philosophy.

It is probably unnecessary here to dwell further on this brand of idealism, except to say, especially in connection with the philosophical work of George Berkeley, that Berkeley was a philosopher with an extraordinary ability to use the written language well. Besides, he was highly sensitive to, and careful with, the meaning of words. Mainly for this reason, Berkeley's work, quite apart from affiliation with idealism, is of considerable interest to philosophers today who see in his work anticipations of the modern movement of linguistic analysis.[6]

Critical Idealism.   Leaving absolute idealism we turn our attention to critical idealism, and now our best guide is Plato himself. Idealism, of course, has grown and matured over the centuries, and fertile minds have always found it attractive, so we must append a word of caution: No one should pretend that a brief representation of critical idealism is entirely adequate or that it is a strict illustration of the position of any one idealist philosopher. Attending to this we shall exercise care in presenting the main lines of its principal doctrines.

Critical idealism shows no more interest in cultivating friendly relationships with materialism and radical empiricism than absolute idealism, yet it refuses to establish its point of departure in any declaration rejecting the existence of sensible things. The material world is too real to be denied. Knowledge, moreover, must necessarily be knowledge of something, and knowledge may be related to or dependent on some object in physical reality. Critical idealists, acknowledging this much, begin their epistemological speculation with the conviction that knowledge of something is possible. But this is not all: It must be infallible knowledge of what is. Inevitably, then, from the very outset critical idealism is faced with two inseparable issues: One, epistemological (an investigation of the process of knowing), must sort out the respective claims of sense perception, belief or judgment, opinion originating in and fortified by perceptual evidence, and valid knowledge; the other, metaphysical (an inquiry into the nature of reality), must make a determination about what, if anything, exists to be known. It would be pointless to maintain the possibility of knowledge if there is nothing to be known; it would be profitless to argue for a reality capable of being known apart from a process rendering it valid and leading to truth.

Any number of simple exercises involving direct sensory perception can demonstrate conclusively that whatever the outcome of a perceptual encounter, it is neither infallible nor necessarily of what is. To deny the validity of knowledge coming from sense perception is, of course, different from declaring the possibility of valid knowledge, but idealists in this camp never surrender to skepticism, so they go on, not to build castles in the air—as it appears absolute idealists do—but to find solid foundations on which dependable knowledge can stand.

If perception alone were capable of accounting for truth, then truth would appear in many guises. Everyone would be in possession of personal truth, because everyone capable of having sensory perceptions would hold some view of reality. What anyone believed to be true would be true for him. Such a shaky foundation for truth, however, would make the social order rest on what should be called whim—at least, a flagrant subjectivism—and a virulent form of skepticism—the abandonment of the search for truth and despairing of its existence—would be an inevitable result.

Belief and judgment are obvious human psychological realities. Do they qualify as valid knowledge? Clearly, all kinds of social, political, economic, and educational decisions are based on what persons believe to be true, and this belief, this confidence in true judgment, is almost certainly genuine. Yet human experience has time after time demonstrated how persons with genuine belief, with an implicit faith in their truth, have been wrong. Whatever perceptual evidence belief and true judgment may have to support them, in the last analysis acceptance or rejection of belief and true judgment rests on persuasion, on an ability of persons holding certain beliefs to convince others of their truth. Even when belief is fortified by descriptive analysis of what is believed to be true—that is, by appending distinguishing characteristics to belief—it is incapable, so idealists argue, of converting belief and true judgment into dependable and infallible knowledge.

Idealism and the Possibility of Knowledge.   In the ordinary course of life's activities, most persons never possess what critical idealists call knowledge, true knowledge. For the majority of persons vulgar opinion marks the end of their search for truth, but some lucky ones get as far as right opinion. In other words, for most of us and for most of what passes for knowledge, we are depending on the content of perceptions, which is often off the mark, or on perceptions supported by experience and evidence. In neither case is there authentic knowledge, but it is an unfortunate fact of life that genuine knowledge is foreclosed to the generality of mankind. Opinion, sometimes right opinion, however, enables us for the most part to live effectively.

The step above opinion and right opinion is high, and most people lack the intellectual strength to lift themselves up to the height of knowledge. Those who succeed in obtaining genuine knowledge are exceptional persons with an ability to go beyond the vagaries of sensory perception to the spiritual character of the reality to which their senses introduce them. This spiritual character is idea or form, and from the point of view of most critical idealists, idea or form has an existence and an essence apart from and transcendent to material objects in the world. The minds of some persons have a capacity, if they are properly educated, for apprehending this transcendental existence and essence. A proper training of the mind is, of course, indispensable, and this proper training is accomplished not by wrestling first with the transcendental qualities of objective reality, for this would be impossible, but by beginning with the ordinary objects of sensory experience and having the mind elevated and disciplined by dealing with them in a scholarly way. The outcome of such intellectual exercise is a disciplined mind rather than a mind in possession of truth.

Idealism and the Mind.   Once the mind has gone through a long and intensive training period, it may be capable of coming in contact with and distilling meaning from the universal concepts—the objects forming the subject matter of science—that exist in a transcendental world of their own, a world spacially distinguished from the world of things evident to the senses. The objects of sense experience are copies of universal reality, but universal reality exists in a world of its own.

It is not easy to understand how the human mind, unless it too is spiritual and transcendent, can have a kind of relationship with universal reality leading ultimately to a solid bedrock of truth. And for critical idealists this problem is not easily explained. Sometimes, in fact, an explanation is either not forthcoming or is skirted. Yet, among the more conventional members of this school of thought there is a willingness to explain: Man's soul existed prior to its union with the body, and during this period it lived in the transcendental realm where it had a chance to share in the knowledge of fundamental reality, where, from the beginning, it was ordained to grasp truth. The soul's ability to find truth, and a quality endowing the human mind with spiritual character, is never lost, although it may be suppressed or impaired for any number of reasons. When the mind is properly cultivated and is free from suppression and impairment, it can recollect, it can remember, it can bring back to the level of conscious knowledge those essences to universal reality of which it had prior experience and that are now buried away in memory.

Doctrine on the Soul. This lofty interpretation of man's mind and the positive declaration that, in the last analysis, truth is dependent on the ability of a rational soul to remember the knowledge from its earlier state of existence outside the body would seem to suggest an abandonment of dualism, of any substantial relationship between mind and body. Critical idealists, however, are unwilling to go so far. Although they insist on making an essential distinction between mind and body, they do not deny the influence of the body on the mind. Yet the idealist position on the soul, a position seeming at first to Christian philosophers to fill the bill for their faith, provides for a soul with different parts, and only the soul's rational part is immortal. But this doctrine of immortality, since even in idealism it depends on logical proof and inference and, in any case, fragments the soul, can hardly be satisfying to Christian theologians. Although idealism gives an outward appearance of friendship to religion, and Christians, because of their fundamental attitude toward altruism, are called idealists, idealism is not a philosophy fully supportive of religious doctrine.

Idealism and the Good Life. Despite the fact that idealism lacks theoretical affinity with religion, especially with Christianity, idealists are sensitive to human ethics and to a cultivation of the natural virtues. If an idealist were to list those virtues most consistent with leading a good life and if the good life, rather than being relative, refers to an absolute and unchanging moral code, he would name wisdom, courage, temperance, and justice. These virtues would, in turn, be unified and made operable in prudence—a knowledge of the good and the means to attain it. At this point, going all the way back to Plato, idealists engage in an interminable debate over whether or not virtue—they mean prudence—can be taught. Some idealists appear ready to stake their reputation on the proposition that virtue, being knowledge, can be taught; others, while they affirm that virtue is a kind of knowledge, positively reject the possibility of teaching it.[7] In any case, all idealists accept what stands as the "golden rule" and discard a more ancient and retributive maxim: "One should do good to one's friends and evil to one's enemies."

This review of idealism may lead us to believe that by following its precepts we can make our own world out of our subjective impressions, interpretations, and reflections. Idealists, however, do not mean to create a world of reality out of subjective evocations; they want to pass beyond the sensible world to the world of thought and there to have a direct association with a transcendental reality. Then and only then will knowledge of what is be infallible.

Educational Implications

Throughout most of the history of Western education, beginning with ancient Greece, flowing through Europe, and transplanted to America, the philosophical school of thought lurking in the background, and the one most often appealed to by educators, was idealism. This must at first strike us as strange, for it would seem to be almost as easy for idealists to dispense with all formal education as to cultivate it intensively. We have seen how little confidence idealists put in perceptions of empirical reality, and this prompts us to wonder why, if dependable knowledge from our contact with the physical world around us is either impossible or extremely unlikely, we should spend much time and effort trying to accumulate a body of information without genuine substance and validity. The creed of idealism, one could argue, begins by closing the door on education.

Yet, historically, idealists have not despaired of profit from learning, and they have, generally, a solid record of encouraging all manner of political societies to extend opportunity for education. Plato, for example, although he was uncertain of the good to be reaped, spoke of the sensibleness in educating both boys and girls, and he took this stand at a point in history when conventional educational opinion declared that a woman without wit is normal. Depending on their native talent, persons of either sex could go all the way to the top of the intellectual ladder by capitalizing on the chances they had for forming their minds. His perception of the need for education was both broad and generous, although his optimism was curtailed: Most people, he thought, lacked the talent to profit from the advanced educational program he envisioned for the ideal state. Still, Plato worked out an educational plan in *The Republic,* [8] and idealists following in his wake have tried to do the same for their own time. Some critics of idealism, however, hold to the opinion that Plato's idealist successors, whether they belonged to the camp of pure philosophy or to educational philosophy, never succeeded in going much beyond the program for education he laid down.

Yet, either by staying close to Plato or by going to the most contemporary of his idealist followers, and taking into account the inevitable changes introduced by social and educational evolution, idealism does have a philosophy of education, and it seems unimportant to us now to say whether it is Plato's educational philosophy all over again or one produced by later generations of idealists. Ancient, modern, and contemporary idealists found an abundance of common ground on which to build a philosophy of education.

Education's Scope.   Naturally enough, idealists begin, as all educational philosophers must, with the person to be educated. Educational philosophers must have some understanding of human capacity before they can say anything about the purposes of education or the kind of learning most suitable for the formation of human beings. We have seen enough of the basic principles of idealism to recognize the superiority of mind over matter, so it must be a person's mind that education is commissioned to cultivate. And when the idealist speaks of education being a cultivating agent, there is no intention whatever to restrict this cultivating function solely to schools. The whole of society is a teacher, and this social teaching, in the last analysis, may be far superior to any other teaching that persons will ever have. A social inheritance is communicated in attitudes and ideals, in ways of acting, in customs and conventions far too complicated for any school curriculum to handle. And this social inheritance contains a kind of information, a kind of knowledge, superior to all the subjects schools profess to teach. At its best, education is a social enterprise, and its principal purpose is to immerse all persons in society in the mainstream of the cultural and intellectual inheritance. A great deal of the teaching idealists see going on is informal, and no school can ever take its place.[9] Moreover, this cultural and intellectual inheritance is not material but spiritual. It exists, if it exists at all, on a level transcending the ordinary perceptions of everyday life, and it has almost nothing to do with making a living. Much of it is transmitted incidentally, but incidental or not, its significance cannot be gainsaid. But some of this inheritance, those parts too important to be left to chance, must be husbanded carefully and communicated directly by the school.[10]

After paying heed to the social purpose of education, after ensuring that every person has an opportunity to participate in the intellectual legacy of the human race, attention in education must center on the development of personal talent. The purpose here is not fulfilled by aiming at the development of skill, or even of knowledge, but of personality. Every person has distinct capacities, and it is up to education to allow every person enough freedom and opportunity to actualize the uniqueness of self. Nothing in the idealist educational outlook, unless it is full participation in the social order, supersedes the development of self. As persons proceed up the ladder of maturity, they become more and more able to understand both themselves and their world. As they become more and more attuned to the transcendental character of a spiritual world, they more fully recognize their proper social role, and when they do they become good citizens of the human race.

Educational purpose, we see, is not always externalized or pointed toward the attainment of social betterment; it is also internalized, to the good of the person. Because human personality is unique, its uniqueness authorizes a demand for personal intellectual and moral development that cannot be provided in society generally, and now the school comes into the picture.

When the school first appears, its task is humble and straightforward. It is not given the heavy responsibility of shaping minds but starts with the humble auxiliaries of reading, writing, counting, and speaking. It is only through an immersion in the physical, perceptual world, the world of stones and sticks, of persons and things, that the foundation for educational decency can be laid. This foundation is not important in itself, any more than the opinions one may distill from contact with physical reality are important in themselves; it does provide persons with those arts of expression enabling them to communicate and understand and thus to share in the inheritance of the race. In laying this foundation, moreover, the first steps are taken toward disciplining the mind, toward giving it an excellence that, for some persons, may pay huge dividends by making it possible for them to interact directly with the spiritual and universal character of truth. The best education, when it succeeds, carries us beyond the world of physical reality to the world of thought. The world of thought, idealists aver, is where a genuine human life is possible.

It is time for us now to take a closer look at the principal elements in an educational philosophy committing itself to an educational program capable of producing genuinely human life.

The Student.   Idealists begin their analysis of human nature with an unequivocal rejection of naturalism and its pervasive materialism. They refuse to countenance the evolutionary hypothesis describing how human beings evolved from lower forms of life all the way back to the simple cell. While idealism is supremely confident of the possibility of human progress and is enthusiastic about the prospect of human perfection, this philosophic creed jettisons emergent evolution: Matter cannot produce mind so, in the end, the possibility of an evolutionary process—no matter how complicated or how long it takes—producing the spiritual mind at the end of the evolutionary trail, a mind capable of profound thought and lofty ideal, is patently out of the question.[11]

Human beings are endowed with a fundamental conviction of the reality of their personality and the spirituality of their minds. Everything involved in human action, the idealist argues, evidences a distinctive nature for human beings. In addition to an intuition of personality or self, everyone has an internal experience of freedom. Persons know, because time after time internal experience tells them, of their freedom as moral agents to choose from among the multiple and often conflicting alternatives of life. An ethical conscience, an inherent power of human personality and one independent of environmental forces, imposes this conclusion. It may be, as idealists are quick to admit, that this interpretation of human nature cannot be authenticated by any accumulation of empirical data; they know without being told that no amount of experimentation will ever prove or disprove their thesis with respect to the spirituality of self and the power lodged in it.

The person described by idealism, with the power of thought and choice, lives in a world with an explicit moral order. It is, moreover, the nature of persons to do good and avoid evil. Certainly, idealists agree, the moral order is sometimes flouted, much as statutes intended to regulate the social order are frequently ignored. But the moral order, although different from civil and criminal law, imposes itself on persons who refuse to abide by it and, in the end, has its way. The consequence of acting correctly, in following the prescription of a fundamental moral code, is human survival; the consequence of evil action, of abandoning morality in favor of expediency, is self-destruction. But even in the face of evident evil in the world, an evil whose authorship is uncertain, the idealist affirms the ends of justice and is convinced of the permanence and the eventual victory of the moral law, of the final victory of justice over injustice, and of good over evil.

To fulfill the promise of human talent, a talent whose reality can be demonstrated despite its uneven distribution, to ensure the progress of human beings toward self-realization, to consolidate the victories of mind over matter, to succeed in mastering the mysteries of the universe, to guarantee the perpetuation of freedom, to extend the benefits of the good life to everyone, and to attain peace and tranquility for all human societies—this is the comprehensive, difficult, but explicit commission idealists assign to education. Rather than dispensing with formal education, these conditions, all imperative to living a genuinely human life, accentuate the necessity and importance of education.

With motives supplied in an internal perception of self, students come to school, the idealist says, with a determination to learn what can be known and to grow in wisdom. They seek after these goals because to do so is the normal disposition of the human soul. Besides knowledge and wisdom, persons naturally crave enjoyment, aesthetic satisfaction, and the approbation of those with whom they live. With social sensitivity, men and women seek to develop those skills and techniques and to master that knowledge enabling them to contribute to the general good. They strive for this kind of perfection because they must; it is the nature of human nature to do so. Even then imperfection sometimes raises its ugly head. Despite the lofty motives attributed to them or even implanted in them by the law of nature, students can become lazy and inattentive; they can become indifferent to learning and engage in mischief or indulge folly. They may at times misinterpret the meaning of their own ideals and take personally and socially unacceptable or immoral directions. Should this occur, schools should have means at their disposal to quickly and directly enforce a code of correct and responsible behavior.

Idealists cannot guarantee that human beings will always act for their own good or the good of their society, despite an internal motivation to do so, but the idealist philosophy of education provides for corrective measures when students stray away from the path of moral and intellectual decency. One part of education's purpose is to put persons in possession of truth, thus enabling them to live more effectively in the human world; since we know something about the idealist perception of truth, we know that no idealist is ready to discount the difficulty of its attainment. But the other part of education, one never neglected by any idealist, is to lay a foundation for moral and intellectual discipline, a foundation on which genuinely human life must always stand.

The Teacher. Although idealist educational philosophy stresses an internal, almost necessary, drive toward self-realization and human perfection and although some idealists have come close to downgrading the role of teaching because of the spiritual and recollective character of knowledge, the bulk of idealist thought is on the side of effective teaching. The trail of truth and ethical character is too long and obscure to be followed by the solitary student; although unaided discovery may very well be the superior method of learning, it takes too long. Good teachers are therefore essential.

A good teacher must first understand the nature of the student. Unless teachers understand the spiritual nature of mind on one hand and the spiritual essence of knowledge on the other, they will concentrate pedagogic attention on the outcomes of the acts of perception and the skills of learning. They may neglect the idealist conviction that perception and skill are only essential conditions for learning; they mark the beginning, not the end, of learning. Teachers must lead their students toward a fuller understanding of their own capacities, help them see more clearly what they may become as persons, and give them confidence for realizing the visions they have of themselves. So, good teachers are expert in assessing human nature. They realize, moreover, how teaching decreases in importance as students climb the educational ladder. In schooling's first years, idealists maintain, teachers come close to creating an educational environment for their students, but as learning proceeds and as students become better equipped to meet learning on their own terms, teachers should prudently withdraw. They should know when students need them and when they are better left alone. Good teachers know they are practicing an art, one where they, like physicians, are cooperating with human nature in the process of human development.

In addition to a competent understanding of human nature and the nature of learning and teaching, the idealist wants teachers to be broadly educated and morally sensitive. Teachers are models for their students, and students can be expected to learn from the superior example teachers exhibit. Good teachers are tolerant not only of the mistakes their students will inevitably make but of opinions differing from their own. Few idealists would demur from holding up Socrates as the ideal teacher, for Socrates never gave final answers to any question. Rather, he guided and stimulated his students to search for their own solutions to the problems life posed. At the same time, however, good teachers will be alert, as Socrates was, to the requirements of logic and the demands of truth and will never be ready to sell either at discount.

Idealist philosophy, no doubt, has a solid and, in some respects, a praiseworthy conception of the excellent teacher; good teachers must be masters of pedagogic technique, too, for real skill is involved in being a cooperative artist. But on one side of school method, idealism takes a position amounting almost to indifference: Modern school method places a great deal of emphasis on the physiological bases to learning, and in some methodologies all the basic skills of learning begin with these bases. Here idealism, because it does not put much trust in perception and because it is inevitably preoccupied with the ability of the mind to apprehend truth, is ready to downgrade without abandoning entirely the physiological foundations to the learning process. From an idealist point of view a psychology of learning means more than a physiology of learning, but the logic of learning is superior to both.

The Curriculum. Although idealism is prepared to acknowledge the rea
of a physical world, it is a shadowy world with truth usually hidden from human view. Over the centuries good minds capable of transcending the existence of physical things to get at their universal essences have discovered truth,
an eternal truth certified time and again by mental experience. In the ordinary
course of life other good minds have arrived at right opinion or true judgment
about the nature of physical reality as it imposes itself on them. The school's
curriculum should draw on both sources—truth and right opinion—for its
subject matter.

Truth has been codified over centuries of human experience and is preserved
in a literary intellectual inheritance. This inheritance, in addition to being true,
is characterized by permanence and stability. Here is where curricular emphasis
should be placed. Put more directly, the bulk of human wisdom is in the books,
so from books students should try to mine dependable knowledge. Standing on
the shoulders of their gigantic forebears, some good minds from every generation
may succeed in adding important parts to this intellectual legacy, but whether or
not they do, the foundation for educational decency is found stored away in the
accumulated wisdom of mankind.

Idealists realize, however, that not all of life is accounted for in an accumulated wisdom buried away in the books. There are practical considerations that
earlier scholars, living in an entirely different social world, could never have
experienced. In most of the practical affairs of life, idealists say, we must depend
on ourselves to translate the treasures of knowledge from the past to contemporary times. We have no choice but to put into the school's curriculum a kind of
knowledge, qualifying only as right opinion, enabling us to conduct everyday
affairs.

Every human experience however, cannot be included in a school's curriculum. Time is too precious and life too short for so ambitious an undertaking.
This leaves educators to employ a process of selection, and when they are prudent
and judicious the school's curriculum will contain the most rewarding and the
most formative experiences. If everything can neither be taught nor learned, then
good sense dictates that the most important things be given attention in school.
The school's curriculum, more than any other side of formal education, bears the
burden of preparing students for life, of communicating to them those things they
must know if they are to live fully human lives in an often cruel and demanding
world.

Idealists never declare school life to be something less than real; yet, they insist
on school life being a preparation for life in society. And despite all the effort one
may make to shape school life along lines of social realism, there is no way,
idealists argue, to convert schools into copies of social life itself. Schools are places
where children and young people learn. While in school they should prepare
themselves as best they can, depending on their native talent, to take their places
in society. When students leave school they should be cultivated human beings
ready to transcend the realm of nature to engage in the world of thought, ready

to assume their obligations as good citizens, and ready to see the beauty and hold in awe the mysteries of the universe. More than anything else, they will be persons ruled by thought.

The purpose of the curriculum more than its content, we should notice, is a distinguishing feature in an idealist philosophy of education. Should we search for what the idealist wants to abandon in today's curriculum—the sciences, the liberal arts, the fine and the practical arts—our search would be in vain, for all are there and all are praised. The justification for this curricular breadth seems clear: A broadly gauged curriculum reveals the spiritual nature of human beings and the spiritual character of the physical world.

Method.   Modern education, idealists are tempted to say, has overstressed the significance of method. Yet they are neither disposed to discount method nor abandon it to mere whim. The science of education can, they allege, devise appropriate methods for every kind of teaching, and they are unready to eliminate from a teacher's repertoire of pedagogic skill any method capable of producing effective results. They enjoin method, however, to a solicitous respect for the dignity of every student. No one best method, they declare, is suited to all subjects for all times for all educational purposes. From this point on, idealists are willing to give ingenious and skillful teachers the freedom to discover and use those methods most effective in a particular scholastic situation.

Idealism's Contemporary Status

Despite the attention given to idealism here, few of today's educational philosophers answer to the call of authentic idealism. Remnants of idealist educational philosophy remain to influence educational thought and, to some extent, educational practice, but idealism's historic form, although clear enough in histories of educational philosophy, is embraced with less and less frequency. Why, then —and the question is legitimate—should a chapter elaborating systematic philosophies of education pay heed to idealism? First, idealism's historic stature is so great and idealism had such a pervasive impact on all Western education over the centuries that to neglect it would be an unpardonable oversight. Second, although idealism as a strict and authentic code seldom finds its way into educational philosophy's current literature, contemporary idealism, which bears some slight relationship to its earlier counterpart, finds current expression and exerts some influence on education.

Contemporary idealism, with its speculative character pared away, is hard to distinguish on a purely philosophical basis from conventional or common-sense realism. It is comfortable with physical reality and carries on no running battle with materialism and empiricism. It adopts a theory of knowledge in which correspondence (a conformity between the mind and empirical evidence) and coherence (an internal consistency to human judgment) are the principal criteria. It predicts an order and a regularity for objective reality and here, more than elsewhere, pays some allegiance to conventional idealism, because the prediction of order is, idealists admit, an act of faith or an ultimate assumption. Acts of faith and ultimate assumptions are mental or spiritual, and although some verification is possible, absolute verification must always be lacking. Yet, however much contemporary idealism may turn its face to realism, it wants to assert its independence; doing so it reveals a character different from realism. The differences in this character are distilled into the educational perspective of contemporary idealism.

Liberal Idealism.   Present-day idealism flies a flag of personal and social altruism. Its adherents are eager to identify themselves as liberal (although this term has a variety of connotations) on social, economic, political, and educational issues. Their overriding conviction—or sentiment—is lodged in an optimism for universal human happiness, and they encourage all social institutions, schools chief among them, to adopt a liberal stance. And this liberal stance may extend to social reconstruction, a reconstruction engaged in creating conditions enabling all persons to enjoy the finest lives. This commitment to social altruism makes contemporary idealists friendly to socially conscious religions and, unsurprisingly, many contemporary idealists have religious affiliations. Their idealism may, in fact, spring from religious sentiment.

Freedom of Students.   On a few points of educational practice modern-day idealists are precise, and although their educational positions may not fulfill entirely the rubric of genuine philosophy, they are advanced nevertheless as the foundation to educational belief. The person is supreme and, alone, is capable of determining his destiny. High praise and careful attention are given to the development of personality. In the language of education such attention to self and to self-determination authenticates and justifies the freedom of students to manage their own educational affairs. Conventional idealism would, of course, have prescribed a regimen of study for students, one broad enough, so it was thought, to take into account personal need and disposition. But the determination of curricular content was not, in the conventional view, the business of students but the responsibility of those who knew the most about education and, in addition, possessed knowledge. Only persons who were themselves fully educated had the qualifications to make prudential judgments about the experience a curriculum should contain. Contemporary idealists are enthusiastic in their advocacy of the right of students to choose the kind of education they want.

If students are to exercise this right to have the kind of education they want and believe they need, the curriculum of all schools must be broad and comprehensive, for right in the absence of opportunity to exercise it is sterile. Nothing should be left out and, moreover, if some experiences cannot be tamed for school use, then students should be free to leave school to find them.

In addition to a broad curriculum and a liberal policy with respect to choice, which is something far more ambitious than traditional electivism, educational policy must be ready to take sides. It must reject neutrality on controversial social questions. Directing the activity of schools, educational policy must urge them and their teachers to keep before all students the vision of an ideal society and through the instrumentality of sound teaching equip them to promote social progress. Such schools—better, such school communities—should be characterized by liberality and freedom; they should, moreover, call a halt to dogmatic teaching and oppose all forms of dogmatism in society.

Liberal Education. They should, for example, reject the dogmatic assumption, so long part and parcel of conventional idealism, that liberal education, an education capable of liberating persons from ignorance and making them intellectually and morally autonomous, is superior to vocational training. The idealist allegation is incisive: Liberal and practical art are naturally compatible, so educational theory and practice should destroy the traditional conspiracy aimed at engendering hostility between them. Men and women must live in a practical world, a world where everyday intellectual and moral decisions must be made. They need all the help liberal learning can give; but they must also make a living, and to some extent mental and spiritual life is dependent on having the means to live well. In a society where all persons must be able not only to think effectively but also to perform efficiently, practical, vocational, or professional skill is indispensable. No contemporary idealist commentator is prepared to discount the worth of either liberal or vocational education.

Liberal learning vis-à-vis practical training poses a problem for today's education, and so does the apparent hostility between the curriculum and the extracurriculum. The whole of experience is the business of education, contemporary idealists allege, so any hard line of distinction between what goes on in a curriculum and what goes on in extracurricular activities is bound to cripple scholastic experience. Learning is learning, idealists say, and it makes little if any difference what the subject of learning is. In this view of education, the boundary line between the curriculum and the extracurriculum should be removed.

Moral Education. Still, there is more. Contemporary idealists take the position that the content of education—the curriculum—should aim primarily at what can be taught. Skill can be taught, and no idealist discounts its importance to future learning on one hand and to social effectiveness on the other. And knowledge is waiting to be mastered, although this does not sound much like the earlier idealist pronouncements we have heard. So both knowledge and skill are the principal business of the school. But something besides knowledge and skill is essential to a worthy life: ideals, attitudes, and values. Properly embraced, all add up to the good life. What should formal education do about them? While contemporary idealists refuse to dismiss ideals, attitudes, and values from the educational process, for the most part, they doubt the possibility of teaching them by following ordinary scholastic pedagogies. Education along these lines is to come, if it comes at all, from informal, incidental, and general learning. Values are infectious when they come from a society itself infected by high ideals and basic moral values. All of society should do its best to instill these values in youth, but the school should not be delegated as the principal agency to do this important work because, in the final analysis, this is a kind of education incapable of submitting to the usual methods of communicating knowledge.

Contemporary idealists admonish education to be flexible, responsible, and comprehensive. They call attention to the dignity and individuality of persons. Unstintingly they praise and defend free societies, for only in free societies are persons capable of becoming themselves. And, finally, in some cases, they make an appeal to religion for support. They are neither seeking religious conformity nor soliciting converts to one or another creed of denominational orthodoxy when they make this appeal, but they base it on their belief that of all human institutions religion comes closer than any to complementing contemporary idealism's perception of human nature and its prospect, or promise, for perfection.[12]

FIGURE 3.1
Idealism's Philosophical Principles

Nature of the Person	A mind endowed with rational ability; a will capable of making choice.
Nature of Reality	Absolute Idealism: Only spiritual reality exists.
	Critical Idealism: Both physical and spiritual reality exist, but dependable knowledge is possible in connection only with spiritual reality.
Nature of Knowledge	Intuition or recollection; truth is possible for some good minds; most people operate on the level of opinion.
Nature of Value	Human nature is governed by moral imperatives drawn from the absolutes in reality.

FIGURE 3.2
Educational Implications in Idealism

Educational Purpose	Formal and informal education aims first at the formation of character and then toward the development of human talent and the social good.
The Place of Students	Freedom to develop their personalities and their talents.
The Role of Teachers	To cooperate with nature in the process of human development; mainly responsible for creating the educational environment for students.
Curriculum	Liberal education for the development of the rational abilities; practical education for making a living.
Method	A dialectical method is preferred, but any method effective in stimulating learning is acceptable. A tendency to discount physiological bases to learning.

REALISM

The great German poet, Goethe (1749–1832), described idealism as an obelisk descending from heaven and realism as a pyramid rising from earth. If this illustrates a difference in spirit between idealism and realism, it is meant, in addition, to draw attention to the empirical and scientific emphasis in realism and contrast it with the tendency in idealism to regard the objects of physical reality as illusory or to attribute their existence to perceptions of them. From its first codification as a philosophy providing for a dependable knowledge of reality, realism has prospered because it conforms to ways of thinking and acting that most people, on a purely common-sense level, believe to be true. The physical world exists independently of knowledge of it; yet if human beings employ their rational powers properly they may come to possess truth of this independent reality.

Foundations of Realism

Earlier in the chapter we assigned the origin of idealism to Plato and with ample justification, although idealism has departed greatly from Platonic formulations. Following the same line of thought, we can assign the origin of realism to Aristotle. Our histories of philosophy tell us how Aristotle, although exhibiting supreme interest in the character of human thought—in what can be called formal logic—began with the assumption that scientific proof reveals dependable knowledge (truth) of external reality. He may, as some scholars explain, have started his philosophical career as a disciple of idealism and, during a twenty-year interlude in Plato's Academy, probably tried to complete some of Plato's unfinished speculation or, in a manner of speaking, tried to tie up some of idealism's loose ends. But the time came for Aristotle to leave the Academy and strike out on a career of his own. As the master of his own school—the famous Lyceum—his continuing interest in completing unfinished business in idealism led to the development of realism.[13] All branches of traditional and contemporary realism appeal to some of the philosophical principles he laid down.

Aristotle's Realism.   Aristotle's realism, and realism generally, regards the human being as a single substance composed of mind and body. The spiritual and material dualism of idealism is rejected, so no longer is there talk about a soul with an existence prior to and independent of its existence in the body. The soul has the initial distinction of being the principle of life; besides, it is active in two ways: It has the power, or activity, of rational thought, which aims at truth for its own sake; and it has the power, or activity, of deliberative thought, which aims at truth for practical purposes.[14] And this soul, despite its spiritual or immaterial capacity for coming in contact with the external world and having knowledge of it, is no more essential to the nature of the human being than the body. The possibility of independent spiritual activity—that is, of the mind going its own way without the body or, what is more, of having any perception of reality without the sensory equipment provided by the body—is foreclosed.

All persons naturally desire to know.[15] This is a clear and positive realist affirmation. If they proceed scientifically (gathering empirical data) and logically (understanding and organizing these data in a rational way), dependable knowledge of external reality is possible. Never left in the position of creating the world, we come in contact with a world created for us, and from this contact we can come to know it. It is often the case, of course, that human beings fall into error; they may fail to perceive and understand the properties of the universe, and mystery is usually hard to unravel. Realism never ignores the possibility of error passing for truth, but it affirms that as human beings search for an infallible knowledge of what is, they have an ability to root out error and certify truth. The key to success is logic and evidence. Neither can be neglected.

Realism and Christianity. Aristotle's philosophy had the misfortune, at least from the point of view of a Christian world just waking up to the need for a rational foundation to faith, to fall into the hands of Arabian commentators. Working in the long shadow cast by Hellenistic civilization, scholars like Averroes (1126–1198) and, earlier, Avicenna (980–1037) infused Aristotle's realism with their own brand of mysticism and pantheism. If there is any truth to the remark attributed to Avicenna that he read Aristotle's *Metaphysics* forty times without understanding it, we have some clue to the likelihood of distortion creeping into Arabian commentaries and interpretations of Aristotle. What these commentators produced, especially as they handled natural philosophy (what we call the physical sciences today), was totally unacceptable to Christian thinkers.

Besides, as interest in philosophy had mushroomed in the post-Aristotelian period and especially in those special schools devoted entirely to it, the cradle of Western thought was moved from Athens to Greater Greece and there began to nurse such diverse and discordant philosophical themes as were maturing in Epicureanism (feeling is the criterion of conduct), Cynicism (the doctrine that true happiness is found in temperance, justice, and piety), Eclecticism (truth can be found anywhere), and Skepticism (the doctrine that nothing can be rendered certain).

These philosophies, if they deserve so formal a designation, were either too shallow to account for Christian faith or contained elements basically repugnant to Christian belief. So the Christian world was left with Plato or, more exactly, Plotinus (205?–270), and idealism; realism was allowed, for good theological reasons, to lie fallow. Except for his books on logic, Aristotle was largely ignored by Christian European scholars until his philosophy was rescued and restored by St. Thomas Aquinas (1225—1274). St. Thomas, of course, rewrote Aristotle to suit the needs of Christian theology, but even then the fundamental spirit of Aristotle's realism was kept intact.[16]

Attention to the Physical World. For three centuries thereafter philosophers fought battles to establish and sustain one or another form of idealism or realism, but until the sixteenth century dawned neither succeeded in certifying its bid for supremacy. Then, due mainly to geographic novelty—the New World had been discovered—scholars began to take a closer look at the physical world.

They began, slowly at first and then more impetuously, to jettison their old assumptions about physical reality and as they did were more and more impressed by what they learned from its inspection. This renewed concentration of interest in physical reality projected philosophical realism to a new level of significance. So again, we meet the men of genius whose names are common enough in the history of both philosophy and education.

John Amos Comenius expressed his compact with realism in simple, easily understood terms: The mind is a passive faculty that receives knowledge impressed on it by physical reality. René Descartes, whom we have met before on these pages in connection with idealism, established an identity with realism by affirming the independent existence of the physical world. Baruch Spinoza who, although maintaining his affiliation with idealism, showed a realist face in his doctrine that the substance of the universe, always independent of the knowing mind, determines the destiny of all things. While determinism (a doctrine abandoning freedom and choice) has no inevitable relationship with philosophical realism, realism has a side where determinism is countenanced.

John Locke advocated a strict empirical realism by rejecting the doctrine of innate ideas and supporting a theory of *tabula rasa* (the mind is blank before experience makes its mark). Immanuel Kant, a proponent of indirect realism, argued that our minds do not affect the objects of experience, nor are these objects dependent on our minds for their existence. So, it would seem, Kant's reputation in philosophy was maintained by his ability to keep one foot in the camp of idealism and the other in the camp of moderate realism.

Modern Realism.   Despite all this activity among genuine realists and philosophers exhibiting some sympathy for realism, the philosophical tune was being called by idealism, more exactly, by the idealism of Immanuel Kant. Yet idealism had its detractors and particularly in England two great exponents of modern realism rebelled against it: Bertrand Russell and Alfred North Whitehead (1861–1947). Both added elements of logic and mathematics to realism and used the power of their gigantic minds to express realist philosophy in ways certifying its compatibility with modern science.[17]

While Russell and Whitehead were active in Great Britain, and Whitehead later in the United States, American philosophers, having at long last discovered their dissatisfaction with idealism, began to cultivate the realist creed. When they did, they soon ran into disagreement on basic principles. In the early decades of the twentieth century, American Realism split into two camps: One was New Realism; the other was Critical Realism. From this point on, however, realist philosophy should be followed in the work of our contemporaries.

Philosophical Principles of Realism

Historians of philosophy would probably agree that realism had its first intensive cultivation at the hands of Aristotle as a refutation of idealism, so, not surprisingly, all realists, especially those who thrived in the eighteenth century, spent a good deal of time undermining idealist philosophical theses. Realists, for the most part, find idealism puzzling and usually end up declaring it a false philosophy. Making this declaration they are prone to appeal to common sense and to employ ordinary, nontechnical language in registering their disclaimers. Realists charge idealists with depicting the universe in a way entirely different from what it seems to be. If idealists are right in giving the universe a spiritual nature and in endowing it with an intelligence of its own, they have failed to prove the truth of their assertion. The realist rejoinder is that the common-sense judgment of the universe being material may very well be, and likely is, correct.

Realism vis-à-vis Idealism. When idealists argue that thought enters into the nature of all reality, they are swimming against the current of a common experience of mankind that physical reality is not mental in character. Some idealists, as we have seen, distinguish between a sensation or an idea and its object, but then go on to insist on an inseparable linkage between them. And from a logical point of view, realists charge, idealism both affirms and denies that the object of perception and the perception of an object are distinct. The proper interpretation, most realists agree, is to distinguish between a consciousness of the object of sensation and the object of consciousness. We are as aware of the reality of material things and of our own bodies as we are of our sensations; material things as well as our sensations of them are real and have a substantial existence. In this way, realism takes a stand in opposition to idealism, and it does so in the name of what can be called common sense. Any philosophical opinion that is plainly in conflict with common sense must be rejected. So, in the end, the common-sense view of the world can be taken as being absolutely true: Material things really exist in space and time; they existed prior to our knowledge of them, and they will exist after we are gone. Moreover, we are not the only ones who have come to this conclusion; generations preceding our own have believed the same thing and held their belief with confidence. Can all of mankind be wrong?

Realists are willing to confess to a lack of complete understanding of all their fundamental beliefs or assumptions, but they are absolutely certain of them nevertheless. In addition, realists are tempted to complain of philosophers—originally they meant idealists, but they now extend the caveat to other philosophical systems as well—who corrupt language and confound the mind by using technical vocabulary in a way that has no relationship whatever to ordinary meaning.

This is not the full story of refutation, but it is enough to show where realism stands in relation to idealism. Hereafter we shall pay attention to what realists affirm rather than to what they reject.

The Nature of Reality. We spoke earlier of the several tributaries to idealism and tried to follow two. The tributaries in realism are so numerous, and some are so deep while others are so shallow, that it is almost impossible to discover the mainstream where they all join. Of one thing we can be fairly certain. The mainstream to realism cannot be found in a theory of reality; most analysts of realist thought agree that it is found, when found at all, in a theory of knowledge. Were it not for a common current of epistemology, realism might be scattered into dozens of philosophical rivulets, none with enough force or depth to buoy up the weight of philosophical opinion.

We ask realism: What is reality? The answers are both vast and various. Some realists cling to an assumption where only matter is real and on it construct a completely materialistic naturalism. The whole of the physical world, human beings too, springs from a common source in nature. Some matter and some organisms, possibly produced in an evolutionary process, exhibit a complex construction and react to the physical environment in novel and complicated ways. But in the last analysis, the differences among the things of the world, even taking into account evidence of extraordinary versatility among them, are differences of degree, not of kind. They are explained as accidents of nature rather than outcomes of nature's design.[18] Materialistic realism never disputes the existence of physical reality but, as a matter of fact, positively declares the exclusiveness of physical reality.

Materialistic monism's definition, however, holds no monopoly here, for realism can also be either dualistic or pluralistic. Dualistic realists hold what may very well be a conventional human opinion: Reality is accounted for in both matter and spirit. The complexities of human knowledge and rational thought, they say, are close to impossible to explain apart from some spiritual quality to mind. The brain of humans, they acknowledge, is a material substance, the generator of all organic response, but its activity testifies to the existence of qualities not fully accounted for in a strictly materialistic psychology. This dualism can have two sides: Everything may be the result of an evolutionary process, and a spiritual character to the human mind, which some realists want to feature, may be nothing more than a highly refined outcome of it. Yet it is also possible, other realists explain, that the difference between mind and matter is substantial; the qualities of the human spirit could never be produced in the froth and foam of evolutionary development.[19]

What, then, is their origin? Here is an access to realism for Christian philosophers, for it is probably as reasonable to assume that not only the human spirit but all of reality is authored by the hand of a divine being, God, as it is to assume that mere chance, an unexplained whim of nature, produced human beings and their physical environment. But the interpretation of spiritual authorship need not go the full way; it need not confirm either the immortality of the human soul or affirm the existence of a God who, after creating men and women, continues to have a personal relationship with them. In other words, realism can be deistic as well as theistic. It can hold that God created everything as part of a grand cosmic design and then declared a hands-off policy with respect to His creation.

Monism and dualism are two directions realism may take, but there is a third: pluralism. And now we are bound to encounter difficulty, for pluralistic realists, although affirming the existence of a number of entities in reality and attributing various material and spiritual qualities to them, hesitate to describe or enumerate these entities. The law of gravity, electrical or other energy, the mind itself, God, good and evil—all are illustrations of the kind of entities conceivable in pluralism, and although different in substantial nature, all are real.[20]

This multiplicity of substances poses hard problems for realists, and it tempts some realists to abandon their preoccupation with the substance of nature; it tempts them to ignore the old argument over the one and the many and to regard substance as simply a logical construction. The apparent gap between the spiritual and the physical is bridged by adopting a theory where the mind is not reducible to matter (materialism) and where matter is not reducible to mind (idealism), but where there is but one substance accounting for all reality. Depending on context, it is sometimes called spiritual and at other times called material. This realist thesis, although attractive principally to monists, may very well be the intellectual threshold over which linguistic analysis and logical empiricism pass.

Mind. Realists have somewhat less difficulty in defining mind (although even here unanimity is lacking) than they do in wrestling with the nature of reality. Disposed to find the meaning of mind in an empirical investigation of what it is capable of doing, some realists are quick to declare that the mind is capable of spiritual thought, for in no other way, they say, can thought be explained. If the mind is capable of thinking, as all experience testifies, then the mind must be something different from the body in which it resides and of which it is a substantial part. Materialistic realists, however, are confident that the thinking mind can be explained as a highly complicated part of the human organism, so complicated that it can carry out what appear to be spiritual activities. In the end, though, the mind is simply a function of the brain, and the brain is a highly complex machine produced from the riddle of an evolutionary process. So even in defining the nature of mind realism leaves philosophers plenty of room in which to maneuver.

Freedom or Determinism. On the most basic level, the doctrine of freedom gives human beings the power of volition, the power of choice to act or not to act, to do a certain thing or to do something else. Determinism, turning the other way, elaborates a doctrine of cosmic order and spins a web of natural circumstances: The acts of every person are subordinate to this order and their range is limited by nature's inelastic web. The reality of personal activity goes undebated, for experience itself testifies to it, but debate is mounted over the direction and the extent of this activity. If determinism is a fact, all human action is utterly dependent on the hand of fate, and the exercise of free choice is forever foreclosed. Men and women are neither the masters of their fate nor the captains of their soul.

A prosaic interpretation or intuition—which hardly qualifies as philosophy— by persons whose everyday experience disposes them toward realism takes the appearance of freedom seriously. Common experience seems to parade alternative courses of action before them and seems to tell them, moreover, that by the simple exercise of will they can select from among these alternatives. Once choice is made the matter is closed. Freedom is attested by the incontrovertible facts of experience. This kind of naive realism, however, runs into enormous logical difficulties and is withered by the assault of more rationally conceived philosophical expositions.

If persons have the experience of freedom, an experience that may be either internal or external (the feeling of freedom or choice itself), they have also, if their view of reality is comprehensive, experiences of external forces working their influence. The body itself is an external factor in connection with the exercise of choice, and the body is subject to the deterministic force, some realists argue, of physical law. The science of physiology has shown time after time how the body can be reduced to various physical components; experience, too, if its consequences are weighed with some care, demonstrates how this physical composition can have an incisive influence on how people think, feel, and act. If man's physical composition alone were not enough to give naive volitionists pause, the force of society should be convincing. Free human action, or choice, is restrained or suppressed entirely from one side by the body and from another by society itself.

Looking closely at the physical and social environment, and being careful to interpret properly what is seen, some realists are left arguing that every decision of the will—or apparent decision of the will—is programmed in the physical and social environment; in the last analysis, causes, motives, and forces, whose determining power accounts for everything we do, are found in the environment. What passes for deliberation and creates the illusion of freedom is nothing more than the inevitable functioning of the calculus of probability. If we knew enough about these causes, about the force of the total environment upon us, we would know, too, what we would do or what we would choose under any given set of circumstances. But our choice—if we may use the word—is preordained or determined. There is no array of alternatives. What most people like to call freedom of choice or of will is, this cadre of deterministic realists says, nothing more nor less than our ignorance of causes. Science, however, if it continues to work at a ceaseless pace to unravel the secrets of reality will redress our ignorance and at the same time demonstrate to us how senseless the notion of freedom is.

Yet even when realism is deterministic we are not left mired in a swamp of despair and futility; a narrow path leaves us some hope that a dignified human life is still possible. If we employ our human abilities properly and circumspectly we shall very likely come to recognize the inexorable course of nature and nature's laws. We will know how and when these laws affect us. Under these circumstances, although we are powerless to repeal any of nature's laws, we shall know what they are and how to adjust to them. Adjustment to the steady, relentless force of nature, adjustment to the fact of determinism in our lives, not freedom or clinging to some fantastic illusion of freedom, is the key to successful personal and social life.

If human choice is only a miscalculation of the weight of nature's constant pressure upon us, pushing us one or another way, and if this nature is both physical and social, we have a glimpse of the philosophical foundation on which modern behaviorism stands. Realism can be, in fact, a friendly and cordial encampment for behaviorism.

This abject surrender to determinism, so characteristic of one brand of realism, runs into trouble among those realists who take pride in distinguishing between the physiological and psychological dimensions to human nature. They wonder, and their intellectual quest is worth a moment's consideration, how this deterministic relationship can exist between a mind and a body. The laws of physical reality may very well work their will on the body, but can the mind be their captive too? If the theory of determinism is to be convincing, it must bridge the gap between mind and body; the bridge these realists are looking for is found in the novel notion of psychophysiological parallelism. The mind and the body are ordained to go in the same direction, propelled by different sets of causes, and they end up acting in concert. This proposition has the defect of abandoning freedom, but it has the virtue, too, of elevating human life above the level of pure physical determinism.

In contrast to prevailing deterministic opinion imposing itself on realism is the doctrine that indeed both physical and psychological factors are at work shaping the context within which choice may be exercised and creating all the alternatives for it. Within this context and from among these alternatives freedom is a reality. Persons are incapable of shaping or fixing their environment; so much is taken for granted. But once they become part of it, they are free agents. They participate as a conscious cause in all personal action and, under these circumstances, can be said to be making decisions.

Finally, although having much in common with the view of freedom—and the rejection of determinism—that we referred to earlier as naive realism, realism can assume a stance favorable to personalism, a personalism wherein consciousness is a vital factor in determining the course of human conduct. In this theory, one rarely embraced by realists, personal choice becomes a vital causal factor imposing itself on the environment and shaping it toward human ends. Of course, the physical order is immune to human influence, for the mind cannot remake the world, but within nature's broad design, this tributary to realism declares, human choice is always possible.[21]

So, we see, neither on the issue of reality, mind, nor freedom does realism follow a blazed philosophical trail. Various philosophical explanations, interpretations, and propositions (some exceptionally complex) creep in. Yet, as we have said, there is one common thread running through the whole fabric of realism, and this common thread is epistemology. We should look now at the realist theory of knowledge.

The Nature of Knowledge.   Realism's common epistemological thesis is expressed in the proposition of independence. Following it, all shades of realist opinion can escape skepticism, on one side, and idealism, on the other. Stated most simply the proposition of independence means that reality exists by itself, totally free from any dependence on or appeal to perceptions or ideas of it, and that this reality can be known by human minds. By declaring for the substantial and external existence of reality, the argument for idealism is defused; and by authenticating the possibility of having dependable knowledge of reality, skepticism is avoided.

Paying allegiance to the proposition of independence, realism in America began to make headway against the prevailing idealism of the nineteenth century. With the advent of the twentieth century, however, this simple proposition that almost singlehandedly provided a common meeting place for realism was subjected to intense analysis and, in the end, although realists continued to present a common public face, realist epistemology began, in fact, to separate into two contingents. One, as we have said before on these pages, was called the New Realism; the other, which appeared shortly thereafter, was Critical Realism.

We have no urgent need here to go into great detail reciting the divergent assertions of New or Critical Realism.[22] Yet, we should give some exposition of their basic stand. And when we do we unavoidably become enmeshed in modern realism's theory of knowledge.

The New Realism's theory of knowledge begins this way. The world appears to exist independently of our knowledge of it. This view, it is maintained further, is a natural, almost instinctive, belief of all human beings. So if opposing views on the matter surface, the burden of proof rests with them. And, the New Realists say, an appeal to the fact that when objects are perceived consciousness of them is always in evidence is insufficient proof for the idealist's assertion that reality is dependent on our perception of it.

The problem posed here is neither simple nor inconsequential. Its final solution, it could be argued, rests on our ability to observe reality when it is unrelated to consciousness. Then we could conclude whether or not knowledge of things makes any difference to them. But this, realists reply, is an absurdity, for a criterion of the human situation is to be unable to exclude consciousness from any relationship between knowledge itself and the object of knowledge. The ultimate test, realists insist, must be made by following the behavior of objects under observation. And experience attests that the factor of consciousness has no important observable effect on the behavior of anything in reality. No law of physical nature depends for its reality on the possibility of experience or direct experience with it. Yet there is a further problem—the dualism of thought and things—and the New Realists avoid it by maintaining that the difference between thought and things—between mind and body—is a relational or functional difference and not one of substance or nature.[23]

The New Realism, however, does not stop here. It proceeds to acknowledge the reality of universals or essences and to maintain them as being independent of thought. Particular things have an existence independent of consciousness, and in this creed, so does universal reality. But this relationship between the particular thing and its universal character is neither physical nor mental; it is simply a natural relationship. The relationship, moreover, is neutral, but it can take on a physical or a mental hue, or both at the same time, depending on how it becomes part of the organization of bodies or the consciousness of minds.[24]

Finally, New Realism endows perception with the ability to have a direct contact with reality. Our view of reality is not one shaped from copies or images of it.[25] The objects we perceive give every evidence of being external and independent of our thought processes, so the burden of proving otherwise again rests with the opposition. This theory of knowledge advanced as a substantial thesis in the New Realism is called "presentative."

For all its apparent appeal to a common-sense view of the world and to a common-sense view of knowledge, however, the New Realism was subject to amendment. And amendment was recommended by Critical Realists who claimed their philosophical first cousins were caught up in error. The principal error, they said, was to maintain that things existing in the external world are perceived directly. Perceptions of things in the external world differ from one to another person, depending upon the condition of the perceiver; sometimes these perceptions are in basic conflict with the qualities of the things perceived. Presentative realism, though, is logically bound to ascribe these varying and conflicting qualities to the things perceived, and this ends up in absurdity. But there is a way out: We can say that instead of perceiving reality directly we perceive an image that in some ways represents reality. This may allow New Realists to wiggle out from a logical conundrum, but it leads to subjectivism or to idealism and either, Critical Realists assert, is contrary to fact.

The true perception, according to the theory of knowledge advanced by Critical Realism, is of the essence of a physical object. It goes past the accidental qualities or characteristics of particular objects in experience and comes in contact with their essence, and essence accounts for a class of things. In the end, we may be dealing with appearances, but we have the feeling, and all experience seems to authenticate this feeling, that these essences (or appearances belonging to a class) are real objects. What is left out here is proof of the reality of these objects. We instinctively attribute the datum of the true perception to the external world. And this datum—an entity, an essence, or an appearance—stands between the knower and the things known.[26]

When we say we know an object, we assign a certain essence to it—a general picture representing all the objects in the class—and this essence has a reality independent of the process of knowing. Truth or scientific certitude is the identity of this essence with the actual qualities of the reality referred to. Still, our perceptions are at best only partially genuine. What appears to us, what we grasp in our perceptions, is never entirely the whole of what exists. This, though, is the best we can do, and it represents the full extent of human knowledge.

Despite our earlier optimism about finding realism's common meeting place in epistemology, a closer inspection reveals a hospitable meeting place only so long as realists do not press too far for a theory of knowledge. So long as they remain close to a common-sense level and are satisfied in asserting the priority of the proposition of independence, their views are compatible. Straying beyond this initial premise, however, realists soon discover, as do we, that their intellectual exertions produce several similar but discrete theories of knowledge. Realism, it is true, succeeds in escaping idealism and avoiding skepticism, and it gives us some basis for trusting in truth, but it refuses to give a single and conclusive answer to the question: What is knowledge?

Philosophy of Value.   Staying entirely on a philosophical level and ignoring those realist positions arising from theological predisposition, realism is capable of carving out two theories with respect to value. First of all, we should be clear about what is meant by *value.* Value is something with worth, and in an ethical or moral context it implies a sense of oughtness. What, on the most general level, is good? What ought one do to pursue the good and avoid evil? What, in other words, is the standard of conduct for a decent human and social life?

Some realists affirm, without any diffidence whatever, that the natural law that prescribes the design and direction of the physical world also imposes its prescripts on the moral order, on human conduct. The natural law contains a code of natural virtue for men and women to follow, and it is as binding on them as it is when it prescribes order in physical reality. When they violate it they do so at their own risk and must be ready to suffer the natural consequences of their acts. So there are moral imperatives and their source is in the natural law. A moral philosopher's principal obligation is to discover this natural moral order and translate it into language everyone can understand. Once known and understood, this moral law must be honored, for to flout it will bring injury both to persons and to societies. Under these circumstances, to protect the integrity of persons and societies, certain codes of conduct or social law are written, or are distilled in social tradition, and they must be followed if the common good is to be safeguarded.

Such a social code, one with its foundation secure in natural law, expresses the highest of natural virtue, but it can have supplements. Besides moral imperatives governing the conduct of human life, customs and traditions are useful for imposing stability, regularity, and dependability on conduct. Customs and traditions contain values attested in the experience of the race. They have a history because they have worth, and their history deserves reflection and respect. Men and women are in the habit of paying allegiance to truth, to dependable knowledge of their world; they must pay the same allegiance to ideals and values distilled in the course of human history and, in the end, use them as their guides to the good life.

FIGURE 3.3
Realism's Philosophical Principles

Nature of the Person	Human nature is defined according to what persons are capable of doing. The mind is a highly complex organism capable of thought. Either freedom or determinism is possible in realism.
Nature of Reality	Materialism: Physical reality alone exists. Dualism: Both material and immaterial reality exist. Pluralism: A variety of entities make up reality.
Nature of Knowledge	The principle of independence: Knowledge of reality does not alter the substance or essence of what is. Dependable knowledge of reality is possible.
Nature of Value	Principles for governing human conduct are found in natural law and, on a lower level, in tested convention.

Another side to realism's moral theory puts confidence in test and experiment. The natural law may have its way with physical reality but, according to this view, human action is exempt. What ought to be done at any given time or place depends on what can be demonstrated to be useful. Convention is embraced or rejected according to the standard of need and utility; moral values essaying to set a standard for human conduct belong to the class of convention and must be verified in the same way. What we do or refuse to do, what we call good or evil, what we praise or blame, depends entirely on circumstances on one hand and on effective outcome on the other. Moral imperatives are abandoned; their place is taken by a human intelligence that is able to sort out the good from the bad and is able to distinguish what has worth from what has none and, finally, to leave mankind's moral destiny neither in human tradition nor in natural law but in its own hands. And in all theories of realism, save those adopting a relentless determinism, human responsibility is a fact that the social order and all its institutions must acknowledge.

Educational Implications

Considering its philosophical conception of the world, realism's strong commitment to education is unsurprising. Reality exists to be known; human beings are capable of attaining dependable knowledge. Whether all reality heeds the call of nature's irresistible deterministic force or whether freedom of decision and action is authorized for human beings in nature's code, the worth of education—of understanding how nature works and how men and women fit into its program —is undeniable.

As an educational philosophy realism makes no apology for its commitment to education's overarching purpose: preparation for life. In times and places where life is uncomplicated and society is simple, education can be informal; boys and girls can learn from the natural physical and social environment, and their learning may be good enough to prepare them for life. But when societies are mature and complicated and where a division of human labor is everywhere evident, informality fails to pass muster. In such social circumstances schools must be organized, and the educational opportunity they create must assume a huge part of the responsibility for preparing students to adjust to the social and physical world where they are destined to live.

Experience, realist educational philosophers are eager to concede, is unquestionably the gateway to learning. Almost every tributary to their theory of knowledge contains an unequivocal confirmation of this principle of learning and, at the same time, carries persuasive arguments for swamping any theory of learning indifferent to experience's indispensable role. Were human life long enough, the experience of pure, unaided discovery could have their unqualified support. But it is fantastic to suppose that anyone can learn everything essential to the conditions of life in the time allowed for such learning without the direction, help, and teaching of others. So realists confirm this proposition: Experience must be nurtured and discovery must be aided. And when realists justify nurturing experience and aiding discovery, they mean formal education in the school. The legacy of human experience coupled with the apparatus for seeking truth defines the boundaries of the corpus of knowledge and skill essential to leading successful personal and social lives. The school's principal responsibility is to transmit this body of knowledge and skill in an organized, unified, and meaningful way. Of all the obligations a society may assume, nothing, realists declare with absolute conviction, is more important than the proper education of the young.

Students. In common with all other philosophers of education, realists begin with the nature of the person to be educated. In general, they acknowledge that this nature is revealed most accurately and is demonstrated most effectively in what human beings do. Much of the mystery to the human condition evaporates before the careful, scientific observation of human behavior. However much one might like to attribute to human beings some capacity hidden away from observation, if it is not evidenced in what they do, it lacks reality and can be ignored in the educational process.

Although educational realists differ in their interpretations on the source of human ability, on how knowledge is actually grasped, and on the extent of freedom, if any, persons enjoy, in the last analysis they present a common face of agreement on observable behavior. Human beings are capable of thought, and it makes little difference in their educational program whether this ability to think is grounded in the mind's spiritual character or is a product of a highly refined and complex material organism. In either case, we are left with a person capable of thought. Human beings, moreover, are capable of expressing themselves in a variety of ways; in language, in action, and in art, as all experience shows, men and women illustrate their skills of expression. So far as the essentials of their education are concerned, it makes almost no difference whether they express themselves within the limits imposed by a deterministic cosmos, whether they function freely within certain circumscribed limits left open by this otherwise coercive physical and social reality, or whether they are entirely free agents to do as they please. They may or may not be the captains of their fate; in either case a dependable body of knowledge and a vast array of essential skill should be in their custody.

It is important, though, to make this point with some precision: Realists, in rejecting such things as innate ideas, as minds independent of and superior to the material world, and as spiritual reality, are left with only one direction to take. Human beings must be trained and instructed; they must learn to think and they must learn to act. Nothing else is possible or praiseworthy. And their thinking and acting can be subjected to the scrutiny of scientific technique. It is possible, in other words, to assemble a body of dependable knowledge about how minds function and how human beings act in individual and social settings. So without subscribing in every instance to scientific positivism, realists are nevertheless confident that dependable knowledge can be obtained about the nature of people and how they function. With this knowledge at their disposal, they set out to create an educational program worthy of the capacities of human beings and competent to supply human needs for full and satisfying lives.

In all this, of course, the realist is disposed to acknowledge the student as being an active agent in the educational process. The mind is not an object at rest; its nature is to search for meaning and to probe the mysteries of life in this universe. Although realism makes a firm commitment to sound instruction, the person being instructed—the student—is an active and responsible agent at the other side of the teacher's desk.

While realists refuse to consider separating a person's mind from his body, for such a separation would lead to interminable confusion, there is a point when some special attention must be given to a kind of observable behavior that in ordinary language is called mental. Both Bertrand Russell and Alfred North Whitehead, with almost impeccable realist credentials, impress the word *mind* into their vocabulary, but for them the word *mind* is a convenient shorthand for laws governing events in the living brain. These laws are discovered by the science of psychology. In any case, these laws govern what Russell calls a peculiar sort of "knowledge-reactions."[27]

Frederick Breed, using the word *intelligence* in place of *mind,* said it is a name for a particular kind of function or reaction;[28] John Wild declared that man has been endowed "with a complex and delicate faculty of apprehension whose basic aspects are named *sense* and *reason* in our language." Describing what we recognize as a cognitive capacity, he adds: "These facts [that persons have the ability of sense and reason] are evident and unquestioned. They lead to certain great advantages as well as to grave dangers."[29]

Perhaps the most eloquent of contemporary realists, Harry S. Broudy, describes the person without trying to distinguish the character of human nature as mind or matter. He speaks, rather, of four principles that, taken together, account for human personality and illustrate its unique powers: the appetitive principle (physical appetite); the principle of self-determination (instrinsic motivation); the principle of self-realization (personal objectives); and the principle of self-integration (unification of goals).[30] These principles are meant to describe the natural functioning of human beings as they are and as they utilize those abilities —call them human, if you will—that nature has bestowed.

In the end, all realists seem to conclude, we know from observation of human beings what they are capable of doing; and if we are careful in appraising the results of what we observe we will have before us the capacities with which education must deal, for there are no others.

The Teacher and the Curriculum.   From what we have seen of realism so far, we know of its recognition of the work of energetic, intelligent, and sensitive scholars who, over the centuries, have harvested secrets from nature to leave an inheritance of knowledge about which we can be confident. Pushing back knowledge's boundaries is an enterprise we can share, for nature has some secrets left, if we follow a carefully prescribed route marked out by scientific technique. The whole point of education, then, is to master knowledge and to perfect techniques for obtaining more knowledge.

The place to begin is with teachers. Not depending entirely on themselves to design curricula, but being masters of knowledge nevertheless, teachers represent the authority of truth. Obviously, they cannot communicate knowledge they themselves do not possess, so the first responsibility of teachers is to be thoroughly educated. With knowledge secure in their grasp, they are models for inspiring their students toward genuine learning. In addition to being masters of knowledge, teachers must command an arsenal of pedagogic technique for making teaching effective. There is no need for details here, for the general principle is clear: Teaching method must follow step by step the natural course of learning, and to accomplish this a body of scientific knowledge about both the nature of learning and the science of teaching must be assembled. Realists are ready to praise the teacher whose artistry is evident and effective, but a teacher's scientific pedagogic skill for directing learning activities in classrooms and laboratories impresses them more. Sound learning and technical competence are imperative qualifications, although some room is left for scholarly inspiration and example, as well as artistry, in the repertoire of teachers.

In any case, a teacher's principal responsibility is instructional: Students must be taught what they do not know but need to know when they leave school to meet life face to face.

So the vital issue is never whether or not instruction should form the core of the school experience, for this is taken for granted; rather, it is to define the boundaries of essential instruction. Although realist educational philosophers are well equipped to discuss the curriculum under the general headings of liberal and vocational education, they prefer not to do so. Knowledge for successful living has an intrinsic unity that is fragmented by such distinctions: It is better to talk about what personal and social life requires than to be swamped in a theoretical debate over the virtues, the shortcomings, the strengths, and the weaknesses of liberal or practical education. Any kind of learning clearly essential to the needs of life is ratified. And such learning, of course, may include parts of the curriculum traditionally designated as liberal.

Surveying the work of realist philosophers, it is hard to find a more concise and direct statement about the scope of the school's curriculum than John Wild's. Following him, we see, first of all, a curriculum filled with the fundamentals: It contains language—the students' vernacular plus at least one foreign language, and it has what he calls "the essentials of humane logic and elementary mathematics." Building on this solid foundation, all the sciences are introduced and should be mastered to the extent of students' abilities. Then come history and the social sciences. This curriculum, which comes perilously close to making the paper describing it buckle under its weight, is completed by studies in the world's great literature and art and, finally, philosophy. Wild recommends this common, essential core for everyone; only by following such a comprehensive course of studies can students be equipped to meet the real world. For students with exceptional interests and extraordinary talent, special branches of practical, professional, artistic, literary, or scientific knowledge may be grafted to this basic curriculum.[31]

The school, we have said, has the principal responsibility for effective instruction, and all the resources of scientific method should be employed to build a curriculum and to develop educational technique for making instruction effective. When students leave school they should be fortified by a foundation of dependable knowledge, but there is more. In addition to knowledge, which has no substitute, the school must assume responsibility for providing its students with discipline. Old-fashioned educational language, dredged perhaps from nineteenth-century idealism, would praise mental discipline. Realists refuse to be quite so narrow. The whole person should be disciplined. Few realists find a distinct mind and treat it as an independent entity; yet, without hesitation, they are ready to proclaim sound learning, and most certainly excellence, as being impossible of realization in the absence of a high degree of personal discipline. Discipline, of course, is not communicated by instruction. It is, rather, an outcome of the total climate of the school, where learning is taken seriously and where, for this period of student life, education is the most pressing of personal obligations. Students are in the process of preparing themselves for the future in a world containing clues to that future, so they must be motivated to invest all their talent in a great educational undertaking. The reward after all will be theirs.

Realists recognize the significance of motivation in all of life and especially in school learning; moreover, they realize how the rewards of learning tend to be remote. They are confident, nevertheless, that if teachers are good, if the curriculum is decent and exhibits a clear relationship to life's future needs, and if the school's climate is serious, responsible, and creative, intrinsic and extrinsic motivation will supply the drive necessary to scholastic success. Adjusting to the realities of life, realists say, is an incentive no one can ignore if the imperativeness of adjustment is taught clearly and persuasively and with zeal and devotion.

Looking back, we remember how contemporary idealists praised the freedom of students to manage their own educational affairs and how the door to education was thrown open wide enough to make schools almost unnecessary. All this is promptly scorned by realists, for they find it impossible to understand how boys and girls just in the process of learning have the competence to define the dimensions of their own education. Such definition, realists declare with absolute assurance, must be left to persons with scholarly qualifications and experience.

Finally, education must declare its allegiance to good character, for without citizens who recognize their civic and social duty and fulfill it, all of society will inevitably suffer. But contemporary realists are not tempted to begin with prescriptive moral or ethical codes for defining personal and social behavior. The life of the school can, in fact, be a training ground for good citizenship and for the general formation of character. Although this commitment to character is not specifically a matter for the curriculum, there is a cognitive side: If men and women know how to react to and adjust to the world—if, in other words, they know what they ought to do—they will very likely do it. And experience in the school, where they can have guidance from their teachers in respecting authority and the rights of others, is bound to be of immense help. With this in mind, realist educators may from time to time recommend that certain kinds of experiences, most likely those contained in the literary legacy, be proscribed or censored. If experience is our best, perhaps our only, teacher, then realist educational philosophy finds it hard to be totally permissive with respect to the kinds of experiences young people may have. Truth sets its own limits and, in the end, is itself a censor.

The School as a Social Agency. One function of the school, a function no realist would ever consider discounting, is instructional. But schools are social agencies too and must assume some role in shaping the character and the quality of life in the societies they are intended to serve.

Schools, especially those in the United States, are delegated by realist educational philosophers to teach, justify, and defend democracy and the democratic way of life. Within the limits imposed by this broad and praiseworthy commission, schools as social institutions should cultivate keen, valid perceptions of the common good. They should be in the vanguard promoting social change whenever social change aims to produce a better, more equitable society, one committed to fairness and justice for all. Schools, then, may become involved in social reconstruction, and this involvement has realist blessing, but when they are engaged in radical social undertakings they must be guided by the strictest rules of dependable knowledge and must be ever solicitous of the common good. Even the best schools are never immune to misplaced loyalties or to misreading the signs of social reality, so any surge toward social reconstruction must be tempered with responsibility and prudence. All realist schools are eager to fly the flag of the common good, and all realist educational philosophers are ready to march in cadence under its banner.

FIGURE 3.4
Realism's Educational Implications

Educational Purpose	Life adjustment and social responsibility.
The Place of Students	Instruction: Mastery of dependable knowledge. Discipline: Good order is essential to learning, and mental and moral discipline are necessary for any degree of excellence.
The Role of Teachers	Masters of knowledge; skillful in pedagogic technique, with authority to demand achievement.
Curriculum	Comprehensive curriculum containing all useful knowledge. A realist curriculum exhibits elements of both liberal and practical knowledge.
Method	All learning depends upon experience, so both direct and vicarious experiences must be presented to students. The method of presentation would be both logical and psychological. Conditioning as a principal method is adopted by realists who are behaviorists.

NOTES

1. This position is given further elaboration by Harry S. Broudy, "How Philosophical Can Philosophy of Education Be?", *The Journal of Philosophy*, LII, no. 22 (October 27, 1955), 617; and Robert S. Guttchen, "The Quest for Necessity," *Educational Theory*, XVI, no. 2 (April 1966), 128–134.

2. RENÉ DESCARTES, *Discourse on Method*, trans. John Veitch (LaSalle, Ill.: The Open Court Publishing Company, 1945), p. 35.

3. SAMUEL TAYLOR COLERIDGE, *Biographia Literaria*, XII, in *Complete Works*, ed. W. G. T. Shedd (New York: Harper & Row, Publishers, Inc., 1884), vol. V, p. 146.

4. See O. B. FROTHINGHAM, *Transcendentalism in New England* (New York: G. P. Putnam's Sons, 1876).

5. HERMAN H. HORNE, *The Democratic Philosophy of Education* (New York: Macmillan, Inc., 1932).

6. GEORGE BERKELEY, *Philosophical Commentaries*, ed. A. A. Luce (London: Oxford University Press, 1944), vol. I, p. 24.

7. THEODORE M. GREENE, "A Liberal Christian Idealist Philosophy of Education," in the Fifty-fourth Yearbook of the National Society for the Study of Education, *Modern Philosophies and Education* (Chicago: University of Chicago Press, 1955), p. 123.

8. PLATO, *The Republic* (Cambridge, Mass.: Loeb Classical Library, Harvard University Press, 1930-1935), vol. I, Bk. ii, par. 377; vol. II, Bk. vii, pars. 298, 536; Bk. x, par. 595; and *Laws* (Cambridge, Mass.: Loeb Classical Library, Harvard University Press, 1926), vol II, Bk. vii, par. 810.

9. HERMAN H. HORNE, "An Idealist Philosophy of Education," in the Forty-first Yearbook of the National Society for the Study of Education, *Philosophies of Education* (Chicago: University of Chicago Press, 1942), p. 173.

10. Ibid., p. 160.

11. Ibid., p. 144.

12. GREENE, "Liberal Christian Idealist Philosophy," p. 135.

13. WERNER JAEGER, *Aristotle: Fundamentals in the History of His Development*, trans. R. Robinson (London: The Clarendon Press, 1934), p. 34.

14. ARISTOTLE, *De Anima*, in *The Works of Aristotle*, trans. under the editorship of W. D. Ross (London: The Clarendon Press, 1908–1931), vol. I, section A, pars. 402a.

15. ARISTOTLE, *Metaphysics*, in *The Works of Aristotle*, vol. VIII, section A, pars. 980ai.

16. See Frederick Copleston, *A History of Philosophy*, II (Westminster, Md.: The Newman Press, 1965), pp. 423–434.

17. Russell whetted the interest of educational philosophers in *Education and the Good Life* (New York: Boni & Liveright, 1926); and Whitehead in *The Aims of Education* (New York: Macmillan, Inc., 1929).

18. Although Charles Darwin (1809–1882) made no pretension as a philosopher, his theory had implications for realism, and this would appear to be one. See *More Letters of Charles Darwin* I, edited by F. Darwin (New York: Appleton and Company, 1903), p. 194.

19. THOMAS HENRY HUXLEY, "On the Reception of *The Origin of Species*," in *The Life and Letters of Charles Darwin* I, ed. F. Darwin (New York: Appleton and Company, 1898), pp. 554–555.

20. GEORGE SANTAYANA, *Realms of Being* (New York: Charles Scribner's Sons, 1942), p. 44.

21. See J. B. Pratt, *Personal Realism* (New York: Macmillan, Inc., 1937).

22. See Edwin B. Holt et al., *The New Realism* (New York: Macmillan, Inc., 1912); and Durant Drake, ed., *Essays in Critical Realism* (New York: Macmillan, Inc., 1920).

23. R. B. PERRY, *Present Philosophical Tendencies* (New York: Longmans, Green & Company, 1929), p. 310.

24. Ibid.

25. W. P. MONTAGUE, "The Story of American Realism," in *The Ways of Things* (New York: Prentice-Hall, Inc., 1940), pp. 238–240.

26. DRAKE,, *Essays in Critical Realism*, p. 25.

27. BERTRAND RUSSELL, *The Philosophy of Bertrand Russell*, ed. P. A. Schilpp (Evanston, Ill.: Northwestern University Press, 1946), p. 281.

28. FREDERICK S. BREED, "Education and the Realistic Outlook," in the Forty-first Yearbook of the National Society for the Study of Education, *Philosophies of Education* (Chicago: University of Chicago Press, 1942), p. 93.

29. JOHN WILD, "Education and Human Society: A Realistic View," in the Fifty-fourth Yearbook of the National Society for the Study of Education, *Modern Philosophies and Education* (Chicago: University of Chicago Press, 1955), p. 25.

30. HARRY S. BROUDY, *Building a Philosophy of Education* (Englewood Cliffs, N. J.: Prentice-Hall, Inc., 1961), pp. 42–72.

31. WILD, "Education and Human Society," pp. 34–35.

READINGS

BREED, FREDERICK S., *Education and the New Realism*. New York: Macmillan, Inc., 1939. Although this is an old book, it sets the tone for contemporary educational realism.

BREED, FREDERICK S., "Education and the Realistic Outlook," in the Forty-first Yearbook of the National Society for the Study of Education, Part I, *Philosophies of Education*. Chicago: University of Chicago Press, 1942. In Chapter 3 of the yearbook Breed offers the reader a fifty-page elaboration of realism and its educational implications.

BUTLER, J. DONALD, *Four Philosophies: And Their Practice in Education and Religion,* 3d ed. New York: Harper & Row, Publishers, Inc., 1968. Part 3 presents the idealist position in philosophy, religion, and education.

BUTLER, J. DONALD, *Idealism in Education.* New York: Harper & Row, Publishers, Inc., 1966. This short book contains four chapters and treats in turn the history of idealism, idealism as a systematic philosophy, idealism as a philosophy of education, and the strengths and weaknesses of idealism. It has an excellent bibliography as well.

FRANKENA, WILLIAM K., *Three Historical Philosophies of Education: Aristotle, Kant, Dewey.* Glenview, Ill.: Scott, Foresman & Company, 1965. Chapter 2 contains the essentials of Aristotle's educational theory.

GREENE, THEODORE M., "A Liberal Christian Idealist Philosophy of Education," in the Fifty-fourth Yearbook of the National Society for the Study of Education, Part I, *Modern Philosophies and Education.* Chicago: University of Chicago Press, 1955. The authors of this yearbook are academic rather then educational philosophers. Greene's treatment of idealism essays to make idealism both contemporary in outlook and consistent with religion.

HORNE, HERMAN H., "An Idealistic Philosophy of Education," in the Forty-first Yearbook of the National Society for the Study of Education, Part I, *Philosophies of Education.* Chicago: University of Chicago Press, 1942. For a half-century Horne was idealism's most eloquent spokesman. In chapter 4 of the yearbook he gives us a brief but competent exposition of idealism as an educational philosophy.

OZMAN, HOWARD, and SAM CRAVER, *Philosophical Foundations of Education.* Columbus: Charles E. Merrill Publishing Company, 1981. Chapter 1 is a good summary of idealism as a philosophy of education.

WEBER, CHRISTIAN O., *Basic Philosophies of Education.* New York: Holt, Rinehart & Winston, 1960. Chapter 9 deals with idealism as an American educational philosophy, and Chapters 13 and 14 deal with realism as a contemporary philosophy and a modern philosophy of education.

WILD, JOHN, "Education and Human Society: A Realistic View," in the Fifty-fourth Yearbook of the National Society for the Study of Education, Part I, *Modern Philosophies and Education.* Chicago: University of Chicago Press, 1955. Chapter 2 of the yearbook introduces realism as an educational philosophy with an exposition by a leading realist academic philosopher.

WILD, JOHN, *Introduction to Realistic Philosophy.* New York: Harper & Row, Publishers, Inc., 1948. For the reader who is interested in a fuller view of realist philosophy, this fine book should be consulted.

4

MODERN
PHILOSOPHIES
OF EDUCATION

In the preceding chapter we saw the basic issues of philosophy and their attendant role in education through the eyes of idealists and realists. We may in another context legitimately doubt how faithfully either side accounts for the full story of philosophy, but for now, at least, we should acknowledge the extent of indebtedness the speculative enterprise owes to these two philosophies whose roots are so deeply sunk in ancient ground. We have read elaborations ranging from a parade of profound transcendental conviction to a portrayal of transcendentalism as being nothing less than sheer folly. Neither side capitulates, and the balanced views of compromise on such fundamentals as reality and knowledge, if advanced, are heard but are scarcely heeded. The lines of philosophical exclusiveness are tightly drawn.

Neither idealism nor realism, though, while tilling its own field of philosophical culture with the inclination to view with suspicion and play down the usefulness of all others, has run dry in the aridities of philosophical conflict. Both have been virile enough to generate new and somewhat different ideologies, so our view of modern educational philosophy is incomplete and perhaps defective when we forget the philosophical grandchildren of idealism and realism. In this chapter we continue our exploration of educational philosophy as we review, in turn, religious-rational humanism, pragmatism, existentialism, and analytic philosophy.

RELIGIOUS-RATIONAL HUMANISM

To begin, a distinction should be made between the religious and rational prefixes to humanism, for without such a distinction clearly before us it may be difficult to keep their emphases in proper perspective. Although this statement may sound sweeping, religious and rational humanist educational philosophers follow the same avenue of thought so long as both depend entirely on the faculty of human reason. They perceive the same physical reality, believe fully in the existence of the material world, and are confident that human beings, by using the spiritual and rational resources of their minds, are capable of arriving at dependable knowledge. Together they assert the impossibility of genuine human life without trust in truth.

Religious humanism puts trust in reason to grasp truth but, in the end, this philosophy goes beyond reason's resources to search for ultimate truth. When it does, it comes face to face with revelation, and revelation contains God's free gift of knowledge to human beings. While keeping the realms of reason and revelation distinct, religious humanists nevertheless accord full and complete status to both realms. But should conflict arise between reason and revelation, we are always certain of the side religious humanism will take, for the credentials of revelation are bound to be superior to those of reason.

Religious humanism is, moreover, an expression of a religious culture, and religious cultures should be distinguished from their secular, naturalistic, empirical, idealistic, pragmatic, even rational, counterparts by their pursuit of values the secular, naturalistic, or rationalistic mind considers arbitrary. The importance of this distinction is manifest, although, it must be admitted, it is not the only one to be made. The supernaturalism of religious humanism has the additional effect of making the culture it infuses not only arbitrary but also altruistic. It locates its purpose in the sphere of human freedom as opposed to any kind of cultural or physical determinism; it tends to encourage men and women to live for ends outside themselves and, conversely, to discourage the idealization of self. Religious humanism takes a stance different from all other educational philosophies not only in its religious emphases but by virtue of its whole configuration. It is impossible, then, to evaluate or interpret religious humanism as being only a philosophy of education; it is a total view of the world, the God who made it, and the human beings inhabiting it.

Rational humanism is dominated by the rule of reason. Its adherents refuse to adopt the spiritual monism of idealism or the monistic materialism of realism. They reject the deterministic force carried on the winds of fate and argue, instead, for a life where choice is possible within the limits imposed by physical and social reality. These limits are codified in the natural law. And on a foundation of natural law rational humanism certifies its perception of decent human conduct. In addition to the rule of reason, the rule of natural law is a legitimate reality that cannot be discounted with impunity. Yet rational humanism parts company with religious humanism when the rule of faith, or that deposit of revealed knowledge, to which the latter must pay heed, is etched into the philosophical picture.

The Foundations of Religious-Rational Humanism

The foundations to religious humanism cannot be distilled easily apart from the history of Christianity, and they represent a philosophy of life whose roots, buried deeply in Hellenistic civilization, are almost as old as classical philosophy itself and, if one counts the influence of Judaism, even older. Yet we do not claim that in order to obtain a satisfactory view of religious humanism one must turn to an examination of the whole of the religious inheritance or even to the whole of Christianity's relationship with philosophy. We know from a reading of our standard histories of philosophy of this tempestuous relationship and of the many false starts Christian philosophers made over the centuries: how they embraced idealism only, in time, to abandon it; how they endorsed realism only, eventually, to find it wanting; and how, finally, St. Thomas Aquinas reorganized and reinterpreted Aristotle to produce a philosophy entirely consistent and, on all points, compatible with Christian faith.

Even Thomistic philosophy fell upon hard days, and in the hands of its Scholastic expositors eventually suffered from the misplaced enthusiasm of its friends, who, parading an arrogant intellectualism, were unable to answer any question about anything without pretending to answer every question to everything, and the recriminations of its enemies, who, in the post-Scholastic age (1400–1600), turned out to be incipient empiricists and naturalists.

Contemporary Religious Humanism.   We should be on safe ground staying with religious humanism's modern foundations, although we should keep in mind the antecedents to these modern foundations. Religious humanists, who are also called Thomists, Neo-Thomists, Scholastics, and Neo-Scholastics, are represented most effectively and most faithfully by a near-contemporary of this school of philosophical thought, Jacques Maritain. In all of his work he undertook to present a comprehensive intellectual and moral philosophy and, at the same time, kept the fundamentals of Christian faith intact. He used philosophy to interpret the physical world, man's rational nature, and the exercise of human moral conduct while consistently maintaining an intellectual commitment to revealed religion. A fundamental point in Maritain's philosophy expresses a difference in nature between the senses and the intellect: The former depend on material action exercised by bodily organs; the latter, spiritual in essence, "attains, through the universal concepts it brings out from sense experience, the constitutive features of what things are."[1] Religious humanism is distinctively a dualistic philosophy, and the elements constituting this dualism are matter and spirit, mind and body.

So much is clear, and for religious humanists, at least conventional ones, dualism poses no special philosophical problem. Yet when we come to the work of Pierre Teilhard de Chardin (1881–1955), we are inevitably put in a quandary, for the conventional dualism of matter and spirit is not a fundamental plank in

Teilhard's philosophical platform. His *Phenomenon of Man*,[2] published after his death, probably because his religious superiors (he was a Jesuit priest) discouraged him from publishing books on philosophy, dissolves the traditional dualism of spirit and matter and substitutes instead a doctrine of dynamic evolution. Spirit exists, so much is certain, but it emerges from matter, and the dynamism of evolution sets the stage for a world that is constantly developing the spirit further. In this view of things human beings occupy a central place in what appears to be an evolutionary process instituted by God himself.

Teilhard's philosophy did not stop with an opposition between matter and spirit but went on to oppose the separation of reality into natural and supernatural realms, or where the supernatural imposes itself by an act of divine will on the natural. There is but one reality, a reality disclosed in the organic unity of a developing universe. Human nature and knowledge converge as the world's reflection in and through human beings who are part of the totality of reality. His conviction that the material world is a creation evolving toward a goal allowed for the source of the whole cosmic process to be vested in a preexistent and transcendent being. Teilhard's doctrine of evolution, which he hoped would enable scholars to take the vast bodies of modern scientific knowledge seriously, was intended to infuse Christianity with new meaning and purpose: Its ultimate objective is to save evolution and take its place.[3]

This melding of science, philosophy, and religious faith is vulnerable, especially when it depends so much on lyrical language, to criticism from scientists, from philosophers, and from theologians, and it is by no means easy to say how influential Teilhard's optimistic vision of the world and evolution's place in it will be on general philosophical opinion. At the same time, it is enormously difficult to understand the relationship, if any exists, between this doctrine of cosmogenesis and the religious humanism we have been reviewing. If there is a common meeting place—but with dualism stripped away this is unlikely—it must be on the level of reverential feeling toward the material world on one hand and a profound religious faith on the other. Although Teilhard's philosophy contains many novelties, its influence on contemporary religious and philosophical thought and especially on religious humanism is unpredictable.

Rational Humanism. What we have called rational humanism also has foundations in the past, although they are less ancient than religious humanism's. The origin of rational humanism would seem to have been in the age of the Classic Renaissance (1350–1550). There, in an age fundamentally Christian in spirit, so Christian in fact that it was unnecessary to pronounce religious belief, scholars of the type of Petrarch (1304–1374) and Erasmus came to invest the talent of their superior minds in conditions for the good life. Their preoccupation with the good life, since they appeared to take the Christian religion for granted, led them to the classics. They expected to discover and unearth in the classical literature those ideals that could convert men and women to a vision of a superior human life. With an embrace of supremely human rather than eternal or supernatural goals, the word *humanism* had its genesis. Reason and expression were man's most precious gifts: The business of all of life, especially of education, is to cultivate these gifts to the end that the full potential of human nature can be realized. Under these auspices humanism got its start.

Although humanists of all types and descriptions continued to flourish from the end of the great Renaissance to the beginning of the twentieth century, we must make a great leap forward to find those threads of humanism that were subsequently woven into a fabric of belief called rational humanism.

At the outset two branches of humanism could be identified: One, staying close to its ancestral classical home, paid allegiance to language and literature. It was represented in the work, both inside and outside educational circles, by such scholars as Nicholas Murray Butler (1862–1947), Mark Van Doren (1894–1972), Paul Elmer More (1864–1937), Norman Foerster (b. 1887), and Abraham Flexner (1866–1959). The other branch, stressing the rational and intellectual character of human nature, was most popularly and eloquently represented by Robert M. Hutchins and Mortimer Adler. They and their confreres played down the religious, the spiritual, and the supernatural and gave attention to what they chose to call the distinctive human abilities: thought and expression. They reacted unfavorably to the sciences and the social sciences as supreme guides to human life and, while they were not prepared to follow the dictates of revelation, neither were they willing to jettison them entirely. Under the circumstances rational humanists have usually had a cordial and friendly relationship with religious humanism.

Philosophical Principles

Following in St. Thomas Aquinas' large footsteps, philosophers enlisting in his school of thought (sometimes styled Scholasticism), have been busy excavating the treasuries of philosophical knowledge lodged explicitly or implicitly in his books. Since this work has been going on for more than seven hundred years, it would be nothing short of intellectual arrogance to undertake to capsulate the general philosophical principles of Thomism in a few paragraphs. Yet it is also plainly impossible to follow every tributary to Scholasticism or Thomism in a book on educational philosophy, especially in one where what we call religious humanism plays only a part. To escape this apparent dilemma, we shall content ourselves with a summary treatment of the basic philosophical outlook of one philosopher from this school of thought. By happy circumstance his work is at once thoroughly orthodox philosophically and theologically and, besides, illustrates a penetrating and provocative mind equipped to range beyond commentary to engage the substance of philosophical speculation. This philosopher, who for so long influenced modern religious humanism, is Jacques Maritain.

The Philosophy of Maritain.   Maritain's religious humanism begins with a theory of knowledge and a theory of reality, a common enough beginning, but with this difference: Knowledge and reality, while they may be distinguished for analysis, are merged; knowledge and reality are indivisible. The human power of knowledge, or intelligence, has the ability to apprehend reality as it is; a particular object in reality can be known in all its singular detail and, at the same time, the intellect is capable of grasping and understanding its universal characteristics. So the human mind has a power, something no mere brain, regardless of its refinement or complexity, could ever have: It can possess abstract knowledge of reality and, in addition, can go beyond abstraction to intuition. It can have knowledge of reality, which is unattainable by abstraction alone; it can have an intuition of being.[4]

Armed with this definition of the human mind's intellectual capacity, Maritain, in *The Degrees of Knowledge*,[5] distinguishes between the natural and the supernatural, between reason and faith, and between philosophy and theology. The point is to keep nature and reason within their proper limits and to show too how both nature and reason must coordinate their purposes with those of the supernatural order ordained by God. Properly coordinated, the natural and the supernatural orders disclose a continuity of being that leads, in an exact and careful interpretation, to a comprehensive and unified understanding of man's place in the world.

Man's place in the world, taking into account the power of intelligence and God's gifts, such as faith and grace, is described best, according to Maritain, as an integral humanism, wherein human beings, using their natural talent, are called on to seek the perfection of their nature in concert with the grace made accessible to them by God. It is a humanism where human beings, employing their power of freedom, seek the destiny God in His wisdom intends for them. Human beings are created with a kind of intelligence enabling them to discern God's intentions.[6]

So, we may suppose, Maritain's ultimate objective was to direct philosophy, all that speculation connected with relating human beings to the world where they live and giving it sense and meaning, along a pathway where its consistency with religious faith could be illustrated. On this pathway faith and reason should have genuine respect and status, and on it, too, human beings would be indisposed to betray either.

Rational Humanism's Philosophical Standard. The philosophical standard to which rational humanism appeals is the essentially rational character of human beings. In common with other forms of natural life human beings have a physical composition, but—and this is the critical distinction—unlike other forms of natural life they can think, judge, and discriminate. These qualities make human beings unique and, better than anything else, portray their essence.

Equipped with the human faculty of intelligence, the principal business of men and women is to know the world in such a way that human life is possible. Using their intelligence properly, starting sometimes with self-evident propositions or unassailable first principles and using the enormous power of logic to discover and classify, universal and absolute truth is possible. Truth, then, always within the reach of man's mind but never guaranteed, must be the supreme guide to all human conduct, for without it as a safeguard to dependability and decency, men and women will act on whim or impulse, and their lives will be stripped of those ideals capable of contributing directly to personal happiness and social regularity.

Rational humanists generally, and especially those flourishing on the contemporary scene, are educational philosophers more than pure or speculative philosophers, but in their appeal to philosophy, it appears that they try to keep up a cordial working relationship with both realism and religious humanism. When realism, in one or another of its several branches, is able to certify the spiritual character of intelligence, rational humanists find it unnecessary to pay attention to the philosophical foundations in religious humanism; in other words, if they make an appeal for help to the philosophical giants of the past, their appeal is to Aristotle, not to Thomas Aquinas. Yet, in view of their relative lack of attention to the purely speculative themes in philosophy, we should expect to find rational humanism elaborated most fully in its theories on education.

Educational Implications

The cordiality exhibited between rational and religious humanism extends to practical educational considerations. Yet each philosophy of education has a point of view discrete enough to recommend a separate treatment of educational implications.

Religious Humanism.   Religious humanists, despite the caricatures of the kinds of schools they are alleged to recommend and maintain, readily acknowledge the pedagogical significance of a psychology of learning, where principles of natural learning processes are translated to teaching technique, and a physiology of learning, where there is a forthright admission of the indispensable place the senses occupy in channeling the data of experience to the mind. Although motivated to stress a discipline of learning and a regularity of moral habit as important outcomes of a learning process presently perceived as being deficient, religious humanists make no plea for turning back the calendar of advancement in scientific pedagogic technique. In a word, religious humanists like to count themselves among progressive educators, although their progressivism must be interpreted as a willingness to include in the curriculum subjects, and teaching methods associated with them, that are clearly committed to the improvement of the educational process and student accomplishment in the schools. Under these circumstances, it seems relatively unimportant to recite litanies of method either acceptable or unacceptable to religious humanists.

This is not to say that religious humanists are unprepared to assert educational priorities, and when they pay attention to these priorities we see the educational implications of their philosophy and theology of life.

The Student in the Educational Process.   In the first place, and without qualification, religious humanism establishes the student at the center of the educational process. Maritain, for example, says: "The *principal agent* in the educational process is not the teacher, but the student."[7] And the authority he cites to substantiate this declaration is St. Thomas Aquinas. The point has intrinsic clarity. Yet to safeguard against misinterpretation, we should add that this principle should not be construed as authorizing an uninhibited freedom for students to chart their own educational course or to define the content of their studies and the intellectual discipline associated with them along lines of personal interest or uninformed perception of what is best for them. Religious humanists, in other words, are not able to endorse intellectual subjectivism and moral relativism.

Schooling lacks meaning apart from students to be formed and informed. Schools are conducted neither for the convenience of teachers nor the welfare of administrators. The medal must have another side: The purpose of teaching and administration is to create and conduct conditions favorable to learning, and the curriculum is to be formed by selecting from among all those experiences of the human race the ones prudence judges most worthwhile. This is the context, then, where students are defined as the principal agents in the educational process.

Social Education. Religious humanists worry about promoting a society enabling all men and women to fulfill their natural and supernatural destiny. Their attention to education as an important factor in shaping both society and the lives of human beings is urgent. But a society where persons can expect to lead decent human lives does not suddenly or accidentally appear. It must be cultivated.

This work of cultivation must begin by discovering a common foundation of social conviction—those practical principles of social and civic conduct embraced by all—and it must then proceed to keep this common foundation in place as the best, perhaps the only, practical creed on which a democratic society can stand. Under any circumstance, such a bond of social and civic purpose is fragile; in addition, it must be promoted in such a way that allegiance to it is encouraged but not coerced.[8]

Because education is one of the principal means by which societies cultivate social solidarity, the school, in the last analysis, must assume a large share of the responsibility for teaching the democratic charter in such a way as to elicit zeal and devotion to it. Yet, because religious humanists are committed to respecting the rule of mind and conscience, they prescribe the teaching of the democratic charter as a secular and practical rather than as a philosophical and religious creed or faith. If there is dogmatism in teaching the democratic charter, it must have its source in practical social principles of justice and equality and not be coerced by rational philosophy or denominational religion.

In view of the allegiance men and women who live in free societies must pay the democratic charter, and especially when its justification is not made on religious or philosophical grounds (because such grounds are either too diverse or too precarious to obtain common assent), then education is the ultimate solution. And the kind of education to be offered in the context of a free society becomes immensely important. The only educational foundation strong enough to support the democratic charter, because it alone can account fully for natural and supernatural abilities of human beings, is a liberal one.

Liberal Education.   Religious humanists are keenly aware of the heavy burden of past association borne by liberal education. Liberal education was, of course, traditionally reserved for a class in society with an abundance of leisure and the necessary material resources to make the use of this leisure pleasant. Not working for a living, members of a wealthy leisure class could afford the luxury of what was often considered to be merely ornamental learning. Abandoning all liaison with past images of liberal learning, religious humanists describe contemporary liberal education as one with two dimensions: One prepares persons for life; the other, of equal or greater significance, cultivates wisdom by educating human beings to think correctly and to enjoy truth and beauty. This, religious humanists declare, is the proper definition of liberal education, the only education suitable for human freedom.

Although liberal education is essential for everyone, religious humanists are quick to realize that everyone, because of the limitations of talent, time, or interest, cannot share equally in its treasures. Some persons may have to stop before the ideal is reached. But everyone should have an opportunity to pursue a basic liberal education, and a basic liberal education offers at the very least an introduction to a course of studies appropriate to the development of natural intelligence. Such an educational program, it is important to stress, should be an introduction to the human sciences and not a preparation for later vocational or professional study.

Liberal education, although indispensable, is not enough to satisfy the educational appetite of religious humanists. It is, they say, the obligation of all schools to enlighten students on moral matters and to allow (and the word *allow* is important) them to have religious instruction. But moral and religious education, once endorsed, are subject to a variety of interpretations with respect to both pedagogy and content. And on these points, religious humanism strays away from philosophy and comes down to a level of day-to-day experience and the possibilities therein of practical application. Some religious humanists, in consequence of practical considerations, are willing to embrace a moral education ratified by principles of reason; others are convinced that moral education without a religious component to validate it is hardly more than waste. In almost the same way, opinion varies among religious humanists about the place religious instruction should occupy in the schools. Some, as a matter of fact, insist on the right of religiously committed persons to have their children instructed in matters of religious faith by the schools they attend; others assign responsibility for positive religious instruction to the home and the church and thus leave the schools free from those conflicts and tempests of policy that religious instruction in public schools would inevitably introduce.

Rational Humanism.   Convinced of the distinctiveness of thought and expression as human abilities, rational humanists develop a cogent educational argument favoring a program of studies whose clear purpose is to cultivate these abilities. From this point on they are disposed to complain of the direction taken by so much of modern education when it trys to prepare students for the complex activities of industry, commerce, and administration. Taking this educational purpose for granted, modern educators are tempted, rational humanists charge, to place the greatest emphasis on school programs whose theory lays a foundation for professional, scientific, or technical training. The disdain of these educators for subjects whose aim is toward thought and expression—the very subjects prized by rational humanists—may not be total, for they admit that educated persons must have some interests outside their work, but their inclination is to restrict the attention students pay to such subjects.

It may well be, rational humanists declare, that modern educators rank the traditional humanistic subjects as being recreational or ornamental in nature. But no one considers play or ornamentation more important than work, so such subjects are always pushed into the background of scholastic priorities. As far as most educational practice is concerned, rational humanists allege, humanistic disciplines are regarded as requiring an expenditure of time and energy out of all proportion to their cash value. And some educators appear disposed to deny even a minimum of cash value to them.

From a strictly practical standpoint, rational humanists argue, such educational suppositions are anachronistic. They belong to a period in the early industrial revolution when technical training was first introduced and when the kinds of skills essential to promote this revolution formed the training programs for a relatively small minority of future specialists. Although such an educational emphasis may have had ample justification then, it has, rational humanists charge, been kept alive in contemporary educational practice, and such technical and scientific curricula are recommended for a majority of intelligent children. If science and technology are sometimes forgotten, or lost, in the froth and foam of contemporary educational debate, a curriculum aimed at social skill and economic mobility replaces them.

Education for Contemporary Society. Rational humanists maintain that science, technology, and vocational knowledge, which belong together, cannot be the best studies for persons living in contemporary society and, moreover, cannot be justified on practical grounds. They admit, too, that their proponents are not asked to justify them on practical grounds. They are justified, rather, by the values embraced in contemporary society. The nature of daily experience has changed and the inferences we have unconsciously or half-consciously drawn from our present social and economic circumstances are leading us to set aside the once admired possibilities of personal development and individual excellence in a broad array of human issues and to replace them with a deference to massive industrial, economic, and social organizations. Values are distilled in and from our experience, and the experience of persons in contemporary society is seriously eroding such values as social usefulness and self respect.

Society, rational humanists say, always wears a double face: It furnishes certain services to individuals and demands certain services from individuals in return. But the services of modern society furnish men and women with only selected needs, while the services required by society in return involve only a small part of persons' capacities. The importance of some limited skill, some narrow specialty or interest, has been overemphasized at the expense of an inner harmony and the integrating power of the human will.

Taking the characteristics of modern life into account, rational humanists abhor the fragmentation of human thought and conduct. To reverse this trend toward fragmentation, they promote a view of life that respects individual responsibility and the personal integration of human experience. Technology, they say, is ethically blind, and science, which stresses the importance of a disinterested search for valid data, says nothing about the personal needs of its technicians and so remains neutral. This neutrality on the fundamental issues of life in society, rational humanists declare, is something no free society can afford. The whole of their educational theory is aimed at redressing educational practice and priority and to turn them toward those things having intrinsic value on the balance sheet of human life.

They are certain, then, that the human abilities of thought and expression are developed best by giving the curriculum a clear commission to concentrate on the great ideas contained in the intellectual and literary tradition and to cultivate the arts of language toward versatility, precision, and eloquence in communication so meaning can become a common currency of practical life. Humanism, they admit, can be convicted of having a long and respected history; yet it stands in close alliance with the needs and impulses generated in the rage for specific

FIGURE 4.1
Educational Implications in Religious-Rational Humanism

	RELIGIOUS HUMANISM	RATIONAL HUMANISM
Students	Principal agents in the educational process.	Rational beings whose minds need careful cultivation.
Social Education	An orderly, moral society is an essential condition to the fulfillment of human destiny.	Intellectual and moral formation is possible only in a society committed to a rational moral order.
Liberal Education	Basic liberal education (reading, writing, thinking) is necessary to a free society.	Liberal learning almost alone is capable of perfecting the human abilities.
The Role of Teachers	To superintend intellectual development and moral formation.	To teach truth and value by example and instruction.
Method	Experience is the best teacher. Learning begins with the senses.	Preoccupation with literary learning. Concentration on the logical method.
Teaching of Religion	Some religious humanists insist on religious instruction in the school; others assign religious teaching to the home.	Rational humanists recognize religion as a cultural fact but do not advocate sectarian instruction in the schools.

competency and practicality that conspire to destroy it. Rational humanists counsel their confreres, and all others who will listen, to bear in mind the ultimate practicality of developing the human abilities of thought and expression before they despair of the worth of their philosophy of education.

PRAGMATISM

In *Four Philosophies: and Their Practice in Education and Religion,* J. Donald Butler finds antecedents to pragmatism in the poetic dualism of Heraclitus (540?–470? B.C.), in the skepticism and moral relativism of the Sophists, in the inductive method of Francis Bacon, and in the positivism of Auguste Comte (1798–1857).[9] This is a long philosophical trail and its markings are far from distinct, so although Butler may be right as he untangles the web of pragmatism's history, we shall make our beginning with a pragmatism of more recent vintage, when it began to take shape as a systematic philosophy under the solicitous supervision of American architects. It is fair to assume that pragmatism, even in the hands of illustrious American heralds, is a meeting place for many lines of philosophical thought, ranging from empiricism, utilitarianism, and positivism to a kind of idealism where practical reason and action supersede the functioning of the speculative intellect. In the end, however, its principal exponents transformed them all so completely that pragmatism deserves to be called an American philosophical creation.

Pragmatism's Foundations

It is impossible to give a direct account of pragmatism's foundations and philosophical principles, for its nature is neither to prescribe formulas accounting for the whole of experience nor to solicit allegiance from its adherents to various sets of philosophical propositions. Pragmatism is like a great house openly hospitable to all manner of travelers willing to demonstrate their use of philosophy as a practical social instrument. Once admitted, they are free to move without restric-

FIGURE 4.2
American Pragmatism's Foundations

PHILOSOPHER	PRINCIPAL CONTRIBUTION
Charles Sanders Peirce (1839–1914)	Developed the pragmatic criterion: a way not to find truth but to discover meaning.
William James (1842–1910)	Popularized the idea that knowledge based on experience should be useful: *instrumentalism*. His credentials in philosophy and his affinity to common-sense realism helped make pragmatism philosophically respectable.
John Dewey (1859–1952)	Shaped pragmatism as a distinctively American systematic philosophy. According to Dewey, philosophy's mission is critical, constructive, and reconstructive.

tion among its many rooms and to use them as they choose. Eviction for noncon-
formity is hard to imagine when conformity lacks definition. So pragmatism,
much like contemporary existentialism, comes precariously close to defying definition.

It is best, we think, to represent pragmatism in the work of its founders,
who themselves could not always agree on its meaning: Charles Sanders Peirce
(1839–1914), William James (1842–1910), and John Dewey. These philosophers'
contributions to pragmatism as a systematic philosophy varied enormously;
neither their place in the history of American pragmatism nor their speculative acumen in shaping its doctrines implies an equality of stature among them.
Still, each in his own way was important to pragmatism's philosophical edifice,
so if we are to have a satisfactory picture of this edifice and a measure of the
long shadow it cast over twentieth-century philosophy, some time should be
spent with each of them.

Charles Sanders Peirce.   Educated in chemistry at Harvard University and
spending thirty years of his life, from 1861 to 1891, on the staff of the United
States Coast and Geodetic Survey, Peirce's interest in philosophy was the interest
of an intelligent outsider without any special philosophical axe to grind; it was
not the commitment of a professional philosopher with a creed to defend or an
academic chair to ornament. His admirers tell us, of course, of his membership
in the Metaphysical Club—an informal group whose participants included William James, Chauncey Wright, Nicholas St. John Green, Oliver Wendell Holmes,
Jr., and John Fiske—which met for philosophical discussions, at Cambridge,
Massachusetts, in the early 1870s; they tell us, too, of his lectureship in logic at
Harvard University in 1870–1871, and at the Johns Hopkins University from
1879 to 1884. These ephemeral, temporary academic appointments, however,
especially with their restriction to the subject of logic, offered a poor platform
from which to disseminate philosophical doctrines and an even poorer one for
inventing a new philosophy.

Apart from a few articles published in *The Journal of Speculative Philosophy*
in 1868 and his book on *Photometric Researches* (1878)—which had nothing to
do with philosophy—Peirce's lifetime publication did little to certify his reputation as a philosopher. The bulk of his philosophical work was published posthu-
mously in eight volumes under the title *Collected Papers.*[10]

In the past quarter century scholars have been busy studying the *Collected
Papers* and, in consequence, Peirce's reputation as a philosopher has grown by
leaps and bounds. Yet both William James and John Dewey acknowledged their
indebtedness to him and are said to have given him credit for originating the
pragmatic movement in America. The term *pragmatism,* as part of technical
philosophical vocabulary, was almost certainly coined by Peirce.

Recalling the preoccupations of idealists and realists, we saw how they wrestled with the nature of knowledge and reality. They wanted to know if truth about
what is could be attained. Although Peirce was never indifferent to a theory of

knowledge (epistemology) or a theory of reality (metaphysics)—there is ample evidence in his work on both—he was eager to move beyond these highly and almost purely speculative matters. He wanted to deal directly with the meaning of perception. He sought to establish an inseparable connection between rational cognition (knowing) and rational purpose (doing): Meaning, to put it differently, lies exclusively in its conceivable bearing on the conduct of life. In practice, then, pragmatism is a rule or a method for determining meaning.

Pragmatism's Basic Principle.   Peirce himself formulated pragmatism's fundamental principle in different ways. The most revealing rendition, we should think, was as follows: "In order to ascertain the meaning of an intellectual conception one should consider what practical consequences might conceivably result by necessity from the truth of that conception; and the sum of these consequences will constitute the entire meaning of the conception."[11] Meaning, we are entitled to conclude from this, has a clear relationship to conduct. However, it is not at all clear that Peirce intends this principle to require us to do something, to put something into practice, if we are to extract meaning from a conception. Honoring this principle does not require an application of the conditions of practice; it is necessary only for them to be conceivable.

In ordinary language the words *meaning* and *truth* have a common bond, but Peirce did not intend this central principle, sometimes represented as the pragmatic criterion, as a test for truth or even as a way of approaching the reality of being. On the latter, although he was frequently critical of conventional metaphysics and could write, "almost every proposition of ontological metaphysics is either meaningless gibberish—one word being defined by other words, and they by still others, without any real conception ever being reached—or else is downright absurd,"[12] he was ready to praise any metaphysical theory of reality capable of finding and assessing the life and light of the precious essence of things.[13] A theory of reality, he declared, even a bad one, inevitably rests on observations of reality, on perceptions of a physical world with an external existence, and a properly conceived theory of reality (a good one) will result in "the absolute acceptance of logical principles not merely as regulatively valid, but as truths of being."[14] So, it would appear, although Peirce was prepared to take the evolutionary hypothesis seriously, reality has an essential and universal character that can be known at least on the level of theoretical knowledge. What this may mean on the level of practical knowledge is far from clear.

Reality Theory.   In any case, a general pragmatic theory of reality is enormously difficult to formulate with any real conviction, as Peirce himself and, more particularly, later pragmatists, such as Dewey were soon to discover. Peirce, we have said, took evolutionary theory at its word, as later pragmatists were also to do. But rather than embracing complete indeterminism in nature and depending entirely on absolute chance to grant nature's design and order, he was ready to describe evolution as "nothing more nor less than the working out of a definite end."[15] As evolution proceeds at a steady but uncertain pace and reaches a certain level of natural development, Peirce's world becomes one where order and design are evidenced, or better, one where order and design eventually, but necessarily, define the functions of the physical world.

Theory of Truth.   His view of truth is equally complex and following him is a tricky business. After separating truth into different categories—transcendental truth (which belongs to things as things), complex truth (the validity of propositions), and logical truth (the conformity of propositons with reality)—he goes on to acknowledge the possibility of objective truth. The commission of scientific inquiry is to search for objective truth and sometimes, luckily, the commission is fulfilled. This assertion has a positivistic ring, but it may be going too far to commit Peirce to positivism. Objective truth, though, consists in a "conformity of something independent of his [man's] thinking it to be so, or of any man's opinion on that subject."[16] But then Peirce retreats from what may be taken as an optimistic realist view of truth to enter a disclaimer: In the end, it seems, truth must be taken as an ideal. Standing always just out of man's reach, he struggles for it, comes close to it, but never attains it. Following this line of thought, Peirce appears to reject the possibility of absolute truth, so naturally enough, dogmatism in any form, or a pretense that absolute truth is our possession, must inevitably be an ominous obstacle to arriving at dependable meaning about anything.

Ethical Theory.   Peirce's ethics is a normative science with but one central aim: to look forward to conduct or action. In the sense that action and conduct can be analyzed, ethics is a theoretical inquiry. But theory is not where the treasure of ethics lies. It is found, if found at all, in a conception of the good. And the good, according to Peirce, appears to be "What am I to aim at, what am I after?"[17] The fundamental problem of determining the end of ethical conduct, which must be interpreted as deliberate and self-controlled action, should be resolved in the consciousness of communities. We must learn by active experience in making moral decisions to coordinate our goals, our purposes, and our conduct with those of the communities where we live. And when our ethical sense is fully developed the scope of our community will be boundless. We verify our vision of moral decency by experimentation, and repeated verifications add up to a universal agreement about right and wrong. These verifications, however, regardless of their universality—a kind of broad social contract—only approach an ideal limit of certainty, so any moral assertion is only a hypothesis, and its truth or validity can never be guaranteed to any person at any given moment in his life. If knowledge and reality evolve in an evolving universe, so do conceptions of moral decency.

Despite his tremendous, though tardily obtained, stature and reputation as a philosopher's philosopher, Peirce draws a philosophical picture where relativism on ethical issues and ambiguities in theories of knowledge and reality are fairly plain. Commentators and admirers who credit his chief contribution to pragmatism in the principle for making concepts clear, for his careful analysis of meaning, and for his method of refusing to allow words to do the work of ideas may be too generous in their appraisal. At the same time, we should admit, Peirce had a highly speculative mind and he sought for, even when he did not succeed in grasping, a general interpretation of reality. In the last analysis, his place in the history of pragmatism is assured by the fact that he goaded his successors to continue cultivating the hard and sometimes infertile field of pragmatic philosophy.

William James. The temptation is strong—and some scholars have surrendered to it—to dismiss James' contributions to philosophy and to think of him only as a herald of pragmatism: a popularizer whose fluent and versatile pen catapulted this new philosophical creed to the attention of educated Americans and Europeans. Undoubtedly James' quick mind, his ability to cast memorable phrases, and his extensive writing—*The Will to Believe and Other Essays on Popular Philosophy* (1896), *Varieties of Religious Experience* (1902), *Pragmatism* (1907), *A Pluralistic Universe* (1909), and *The Meaning of Truth* (1909)—propelled pragmatism to the forefront of public notice. The question for us, though, is this: Did James play a substantial role in shaping pragmatism as an American philosophical creation?

Born in New York City, William James was a precocious child—he is said to have spoken fluently at age two—with all the cultural, social, and educational advantages of a good, reasonably wealthy home. Growing up in the company of gifted, prominent persons, he traveled extensively throughout Europe and obtained the bulk of his early education in London, Paris, and Germany. For a while he flirted with the notion of being an artist and began studying for such a career, but then abandoned art. Next he turned to medicine and in 1869 earned an M.D. degree from the Harvard Medical School. After a brief, unhappy interlude in private practice James returned to Harvard University as an instructor in physiology and anatomy. The great range of his mind, however, soon whetted an interest in psychology and philosophy. His *Principles of Psychology*, published in 1890, is a monument to his scholarship in psychology. As early as 1879 he was lecturing on philosophy and in 1885 was appointed professor of philosophy at Harvard.

In the 1870s, as we have said, James and others met with Charles Sanders Peirce in the Metaphysical Club, and from these meetings James discovered the kernel of pragmatic thought, a kernel later to germinate and mature in his fertile mind. At the same time he cultivated a profound admiration for Peirce and appears to have embraced Peirce's definition of pragmatism. In any case, our impressions of James' early philosophical work lead us to believe that he found in pragmatism the perfect compromise between the conflicting philosophical canons of rationalism (where ideas alone are real) and empiricism (where only matter has existence). At first, in company with Peirce, he took pragmatism to be a method for clarifying the meaning of concepts. And to this extent, it appears, he was a charter member of Peirce's pragmatic cadre. But not for long.

James' Characterization of Pragmatism. In *Pragmatism* James is forthright in characterizing pragmatism as "a method only."[18] It is a way of examining the practical consequences of theories or ideas and thus a way of indicating the differences between them, if any exist, or of maintaining that their differences are merely apparent and verbal if their consequences are the same. When James came to expressing Peirce's criterion, the principle of pragmatism to which reference has been made, he rewrote it to suit himself. His interpretation of pragmatism differed from Peirce's, and Peirce was quick to notice the difference. According to James,

> To attain perfect clearness in our thoughts of an object, we need only consider what conceivable effects of a practical kind the object may involve—what sensations we are to expect from it, and what reactions we must prepare. Our conception of these effects, whether immediate or remote, is then for us the whole of our conception of the object, so far as that conception has positive significance at all.[19]

Peirce had meant to stress the general way in which ideas and concepts influence conduct, but James' criterion came down to the level of particular sensations and reactions. Peirce, to put it differently, wanted to use the pragmatic principle to discover the relationship between a concept and the consequences of the concept; James, on the other hand, so his critics said, paid attention to the concept and the consequence but forgot about the relationship between them. This led Peirce and, later, John Dewey to allow their philosophical affinity with James to cool.

Both thought James misused the pragmatic criterion, and this disappointed them, but what bothered them more was James' effort to make pragmatism a theory of truth. Neither Peirce nor Dewey wanted anything more from pragmatism than a certification of meaning. Truth was, they thought, too much to expect. Still James marched forward, and when he did we are uncertain that his promotion of pragmatism kept him in the mainstream of its thought. In any case, this, in summary, was his theory of truth.

James' Emphasis on Experience.   James began with the assumption, for this is what it was, that experience alone counts; it is always pointless to talk about or to act on anything falling outside our experience. And the experience he referred to was to make an appeal to the senses, for experience is always of or about something. It is equally pointless to talk about or to act on a reality that can be known only by categories imposed from without. There is a universe to be known, although James appears to have been enough a moderate realist to doubt the possibility of knowing the things of the physical world directly. Reality, he said, is neither true nor false. It is. And truth is a belief about this reality. Truth, then, is a property of belief, not of things.

Along the same line, although at first this comes as a surprise, James is willing to endorse the correspondence theory of truth: A true belief or idea is one agreeing with reality. From this point on, though, James' theory of correspondence becomes highly complex and difficult to follow. Truth is not merely a copy of reality; it is, rather, a relationship between one and another part of experience. There are subjective and objective aspects to experience, and truth is to be found in the relationship between these two aspects. Put another way, the truth of anything is arrived at by a process of validation or verification. If the process of verification results in establishing the validity of an idea or a concept, the process of verification constitutes the truth of the matter. James, we think, elaborated a theory of truth wherein the matter to be tested and affirmed to be true or false was the correspondence itself and not a subjective conclusion or an objective fact.

Although James wants us to remain on the level of direct experience when we try to arrive at truth, in all this he admits to the possibility of truths existing, and forming codes of conduct, that are not yet verified or that, by their nature, are incapable of verification. And it is James's opinion, whether or not we like to face this reality, that such unverified truths "form the overwhelmingly large number of the truths we live by."[20]

Verification and Use.   Verification is one side of James' picture of truth; the other side is usefulness. It must have been this interpretation of truth—one that neither Peirce nor Dewey found satisfying, but one that was nevertheless becoming widespread—that prompted critics to charge pragmatism with preaching a doctrine wherein truth was anything that worked. Although James had no intention whatever of promoting any doctrine of expediency, the popular conception of pragmatism came down to workability as the test for truth: Anything producing desirable or workable consequences is true; conversely, anything failing to work is false.

James no doubt meant to keep usefulness as part of the test for truth and believed profoundly in it, but he meant, too, to employ *use* in a broad sense, in the sense that whatever is useful must fit into the totality of our experience. He put it this way: "Any idea upon which we can ride, so to speak; any idea that will carry us prosperously from any one part of our experience to any other part, linking things satisfactorily, working securely, simplifying, saving labor; is true for just so much, true in so far forth, true *instrumentally.* "[21] Taken literally, such a proposition elaborating the meaning of truth is almost certain to cause trouble, for it seems to allow any person to define the truth to his or her own satisfaction. And trouble for pragmatism arose, for despite all their best efforts pragmatic philosophers have never been entirely successful in stripping from their philosophy the notion that it is preoccupied with testing truth, and that the ultimate test is anything that works at any given moment in time. James, of course, may have been guilty of overpopularizing philosophy and, in consequence, his language lent itself to easy misinterpretation. Yet he never endorsed, and actually disavowed, the proposition ascribing truth to anything found to be satisfactory. Elements of satisfaction from any given case in experience would have to fit the total ambit of experience. If they did not, regardless of the satisfaction given, they could not be called true.

There is a bit more to James' theory of truth, and it does not, we must admit, make it much easier for us to understand or follow him. Reality, he maintained, is independent of our knowledge of it—so he was something of a conventional realist—and it is with this reality that our belief begins. This, however, is about as far as he could go with realism, for, in the last analysis, although we begin with things, we do not stay forever with them. Our ideas of things and the things themselves are interacting parts of our experience: Truth is mingled with reality; our experience changes both the truth of things and the things themselves. The universe we meet in our experience is constantly on the move; we, too, must move to keep pace with it. In any case, and despite his protestations to the contrary, James was making a strong case for relativism; not a flagrant relativism, he would say, for belief must have some basis in reality, but a relativism that takes into account the various satisfactions and needs from one to another person. When all is said and done, James may indeed have slipped into the conclusion that truth is what works.

James' Popularity.   This, however, is not the side to James' philosophical pragmatism that caused him to be regarded as the most respectable of the pragmatists. Peirce was hard to understand and easy to misinterpret; Dewey, later, capitulated to naturalism and was therefore held in disrepute by persons who still preferred to interpret reality as having some spiritual characteristics. James, though, could speak a language of humanism—he refused to concede that human beings were merely highly developed physical organisms—and he could find room for religion in his spacious philosophical beliefs. He rejected determinism and established the principle of free will, at least to his own satisfaction, by affirming human liberty. It was, he declared, quite simple: He had an intuitive urge to believe in his own freedom, and he supposed, should he so choose, he could believe just the opposite.

This freedom of persons to act, to do certain things and to avoid doing others, is basic, James concludes, to any system of moral and ethical order. While he admits to the difficulty, even the impossibility, of arriving at unassailable moral imperatives, there is, nevertheless, a body of belief about moral rectitude to which all men and women must adhere if they are to live fully human lives. These beliefs, call them a moral law if you will, are verified in the social experience of the race. In this process of verification, and in this will to believe, men and women are helped a great deal by revealed religion. James is not a conventional theist, nor could he be called an entirely orthodox Christian, yet he found religion useful even when it was embraced on the basis of insufficient evidence. Religious belief, he declared, is no illusion, although he was quick to admit that the substance of belief might lack any foundation in fact. Refusal to believe is more dangerous than belief to the good of human society, for in the abandonment of belief a vacuum is created, and a moral skepticism rushes to fill it. Moral and religious values, precariously hinged as they must be, are always a better foundation for a good and satisfying life than skepticism. Such beliefs that contribute to these values are certified, James says, by the will and not by the intellect.[22]

In leaving a place in his brand of pragmatism for an independent physical reality, in confirming what amounted to a nearly conventional humanism, and in authorizing the usefulness of religious belief, James made pragmatism palatable to an audience temperamentally opposed to naturalism and empiricism. Besides, although he counted himself among the men of science, he forthrightly confessed science's inability to deal with or to illuminate the fundamental values of life. In a word, by refusing to be an outright experimentalist—although experimentalism certainly figures into his philosophical outlook—he gave pragmatism a chance to thrive as a reasonable alternative to realism and idealism. It may be fair and closer to the truth, therefore, to think of James as a trailblazer for pragmatism rather than a contributor to it as a systematic philosophy. Making it a systematic philosophy was John Dewey's great accomplishment.

John Dewey.   Besides his enormous influence in shaping pragmatism as a systematic philosophy, John Dewey, probably more than any other American thinker, brought philosophy to the attention of educated Americans. When Dewey was a student at the University of Vermont, philosophy was commonly held to be a speculative enterprise. Preoccupied with assessing intellectual problems, philosophy was next to helpless in the hands of men and women faced with everyday issues needing resolution. To some extent this view of philosophy's worth was confirmed by the fact that its cultivation was left almost entirely to clergymen, who seldom imagined philosophy as having anything other than a handmaiden role to religion. And religion, except when finding its way into evangelical tributaries, was wary of immersion in the mainstream of life's practical currents. This may indeed have been a violation of religion's true purpose—it had certainly been given a different emphasis by Puritan clergymen of the colonial era who never skirted public issues at controversy— but it was nevertheless the conventional late nineteenth-century view of religion's proper place.

Dewey's career as America's foremost philosopher has been reported so often and so fully that reciting it again here is hardly necessary. We know, for example, of his introduction to philosophy at the University of Vermont, where his professor seldom strayed very far from the conventional doctrines of common-sense realism. And at this point in Dewey's life no one was bold enough to predict philosophical prominence for him: He disliked philosophy's alliance with religion, and he found it difficult to accept intuition as a source of truth. We know, too, of his attendance at Johns Hopkins University, where he received his Ph.D. degree in 1884. His major professor at Johns Hopkins—for by now Dewey's interest in philosophy had matured—was George Sylvester Morris (1840–1889), and Morris was an idealist. Morris' idealism, though, was broad enough in its outlook to try to meld philosophy and science; it tried, at least, to find a basis for some working relationship—some rapport—between them.

For the most part, Morris was unsuccessful in forging a cordial relationship between philosophy and experimental science, but Dewey very likely never forgot the urge of his mentor to use the experimental method to unravel the connection between human intelligence and the natural energy generating it. In any case, during the first years of Dewey's academic career at the universities of Michigan and Minnesota, he remained intellectually faithful to the idealism to which he had converted at Johns Hopkins.

In 1894 he went to the University of Chicago, and for the first time we have some clear sign that a philosophical pilgrimage is about to begin. Slowly but surely Dewey moved away from idealism and, in consequence, came closer and closer to a philosophical stance that he called empirical naturalism. In 1904 Dewey left Chicago to become professor of philosophy at Columbia University. At Columbia he continued his work toward a reconstruction of philosophy, and from this work we have the product of an extraordinarily perspicacious mind— a systematized pragmatic philosophy.

Dewey was familiar with William James' work on philosophy and is said to have been impressed especially with James' *Principles of Psychology.* The extent of James' influence on him, however, is almost impossible to measure. While Charles Sanders Peirce was a lecturer on logic at Johns Hopkins, Dewey may have come in contact with him, but there is hardly any evidence of direct philosophical influence, although the frequently made claim with respect to Peirce's general philosophical influence on Dewey is probably accurate. Charles Darwin's *The Origin of Species,* however, published in 1859, the year of Dewey's birth, made a permanent impression on him. Although no one ascribes philosophical status to Darwin's great book, it fairly dominated the substance of Dewey's philosophical creed.

Our exposition of pragmatism's philosophical principles will depend mainly on Dewey, so we shall not try to summarize his basic philosophical views now. We shall, instead, undertake to represent his view of philosophy's function.

Dewey's Definition of Philosophy's Function. We have mentioned Dewey's entertainment of reasonable doubt about philosophy's worth so long as it remained on an antiseptic intellectual level and ignored the problems of the real world where men and women live and where they must daily face perplexing situations. Dewey wanted to move philosophy from the library and the college classroom to the factory, the farm, and the home. He called it a practical enterprise. The task of "future philosophy," he wrote, "is to clarify men's ideas as to the social and moral strifes of their own day. Its aim is to become so far as is humanly possible an organ for dealing with these conflicts."[23]

Philosophy, in Dewey's view, should be critical, constructive, and reconstructive. Its function is not to seek out and define absolute truth; it must not begin with rationally conceived first principles. Rather, it must begin with things as they are. At its best, philosophy is a method of inquiry and a means for integrating the knowledge produced in various fields by human endeavor. Its task is not to find the truth of things, for this is the work of science if it can be done at all, but to look for interrelationships among the various sides to human life. It must deal with the most pressing problems of human society, and as Dewey looked around he found the burning issues of the day to be social, moral, and educational.

In company with Peirce, Dewey defines philosophy as a method of inquiry, but where Peirce seemed to be content with finding the meaning of concepts and ideas, Dewey is convinced that philosophy has a proper role only when it concerns itself with the most practical considerations of life in society. The method that seemed to him to be most appropriate if philosophy were to succeed in this monumental undertaking was experimental, so he was ready to make a "transfer of experimental method from the technical field of physical experience to the wider field of human life."[24]

According to Dewey, this is philosophy's function, so now we should try to see the philosophical principles this most authentic brand of pragmatism set down to give force and direction to philosophy's function.

Philosophical Principles

Here we have an obligation to be especially forthright: Dewey's philosophy—and to the extent that it is Dewey's philosophy, pragmatism—is both comprehensive and complex. In addition, to follow both the depth and direction of Dewey's thought takes us to a bibliography almost too long to read and digest. Listing the titles of only some of his books alerts us immediately to the difficulties one meets in summarizing Dewey's philosophical principles. In 1887 Dewey's *Psychology* appeared; then *Outlines of a Critical Theory of Ethics* (1891), *My Pedagogic Creed* (1897), *The School and Society* (1900), *Ethics* (1908), *How We Think* (1910), *Democracy and Education* (1916), *Reconstruction in Philosophy* (1920), *Human Nature and Conduct* (1922), *The Quest for Certainty* (1929), *Experience and Education* (1938), *Theory of Valuation* (1939), and *Knowing and the Known* (1949). In these books, and many others, Dewey elaborated the principles he considered fundamental to pragmatism.

Philosophy in Dewey's custody was destined to operate under a new charter. In *Reconstruction in Philosophy* he reviewed the course of philosophy's history and concluded that throughout long centuries its commitment had been to a confirmation of fancy and fact, custom and convention, habit and belief. Philosophers spent their best intellectual resources to maintain these largely artificial citadels, making distinctions between realms of existence, between knowledge and action and, in the end, boasting of their allegiance to a discipline whose credentials were superior to those of any science. For whatever motives, some good and praiseworthy but others base, philosophy pretended to a kind of wisdom it never possessed and represented itself as the grand arbiter of universal reality, knowledge, and value. Dewey dismissed such philosophy as being arrogant and repudiated any system of philosophy making these ambitious claims. Still, philosophy had a proper role. Dewey said it is "to free men's minds from bias and prejudice and to enlarge their perceptions of the world about them."[25]

Armed with this definition of philosophy, Dewey undertook to review human activities, not in isolation but in the context of a changing world. Our purposes will be satisfied by paying attention to what his brand of pragmatism had to say about the nature of persons, about the essence of reality, about the operational character of knowledge, and about the source and significance of value. Doing this we must be careful not to caricature pragmatism or oversimplify it, but in any case, we must recognize that while it is possible to speak of pragmatism as being a systematic philosophy, it is also a fundamental premise in pragmatism that perceptions are generated in personal experience. So pragmatic principles are frequently stated in a way, even by Dewey himself, that makes variations and nuances of meaning almost inevitable.

Human Nature.   Dewey himself described his philosophy as empirical naturalism. We should begin by seeing what this means so far as the nature of human beings is concerned. Knowing, as we do, how seriously Dewey took evolution, we must admit that human beings are products of the evolutionary process. They are one with nature: more highly developed than other forms of natural reality, it is true, but in no way substantially different from them. In an inexorable evolutionary process men and women have progressed to a point where they have an ability we choose to call thought. We know how other systems of philosophy regard thought and how some give it a spiritual character. This human ability, their advocates argue, could never occur from a grooming of physical matter. Neither Dewey nor pragmatism generally makes any concession to thought, or mind, as having a spiritual essence. Thought, unquestionably a power of a human mind, is nothing more than a highly developed form of an active relationship between a living organism and its environment. It is simply one especially important outcome of an entirely natural process.

With the nature of mind explained, although ignoring for the moment the various and complex activities it is capable of engaging in, we turn to the question of will. Are human beings free to choose? When the accounts of life are balanced, are humans the captains of their fate? To what extent, if any, are they in control of their own destiny?

Some human activity, pragmatists declare, is impulsive—merely the tendency on the part of an organism to act when it has the opportunity. Some is habitual, but habits must originate somewhere. And some—the best—is intelligent activity. But in being intelligent, activity is not the same as an exercise of free will, although elements of freedom are at work in the process.

Faced with a problem situation where something must or must not be done, human beings, if they act intelligently, initiate a process of inquiry. And this process makes them interact with their environment. Interaction proceeds at a steady experimental pace, and as it does, both the person and the environment with which he or she is interacting are transformed or reconstructed. "There is no inquiry," Dewey wrote, "that does not involve the making of *some* change in environing conditions."[26]

Looking at the matter this way, we see how determinism is unacceptable to pragmatism, for a person is not merely a victim of circumstances. A person does not stand abjectly before the material world, allowing it to have its way with him or her. On the other hand, neither is he or she a free agent. Being involved in a problem situation calling for some human response, to do or not to do something, the person—and what can be called personal choice—becomes part of a volitional transaction. The environment makes its demands, so much is certain, but so does the person. What can be called choice is, in the end, a judgment directed at action, although it is not imperative for action to follow. The judgment is a direction for possible action, but it is a judgment for which the person is not wholly responsible. Environmental conditions also have their say, but they cannot be compelling or dominating when a person is acting intelligently.

The question must pop almost immediately to our minds: If this is the sense in which human beings are free, are they responsible for their acts? To put it differently, can they be called to account for what they do? Can they be jailed or otherwise punished for a violation of good order? If determinism's grip on pragmatism were total, the answer would be no. But, as we have seen, the deterministic force of the social and physical environment is only partial. So for the part the person plays in making judgments on which action is based, there is responsibility.

Reality. Neither Dewey nor any other pragmatist is indifferent to the existence of physical reality, but together they demur from speculating about its essence. Of course, the evolutionary process has been working, so we know that reality is purely natural, as distinguished from supernatural, but what we do not know and can probably never know is what any part of reality is unless we have a relationship of some kind with it. Since our relationship with reality can at best be episodic—only a quick glimpse of the total picture, as it were—it is pointless and profitless to talk about what reality in general may be.

This is not to say that Dewey is indifferent to general concepts and general theories, for without them it is hard to believe that anyone could be a philosopher. Under the circumstances, though, to ask what reality in general is must be a meaningless question from the pragmatist's point of view. If, as Dewey wrote, reality is everything that happens, no general theory of reality "is possible or needed."[27] He does rule out, however, the possibility of centering attention on a problem and working toward a solution without the help of general ideas. Despite what Dewey says on the subject of metaphysics, it is hard to take him at his word. He does have a world view, although the content of this view can be composed only of working hypotheses, all of which are constantly subject to amendment.

Finally Dewey acknowledges the existence of the physical world as antecedent to any human experience with it. Even on the basis of experience, or especially on such a limited basis, he refuses to say what reality is in general.

Knowledge. Pragmatism's theory of knowledge, as shaped by Dewey's seminal mind, prefers to keep a safe distance from absolutes. One would appear to be on firm ground alleging for pragmatism a discounting of the possibility of grasping eternal verity. It may be difficult to find a substitute in the English language for the word *truth,* but when pragmatists use the word they mean by it something capable of showing its usefulness in application rather than something with an eternal and changeless character. To put it somewhat differently, the truth of anything is to be found in its function. No truth is absolute, but truth can be said to possess in its application a constant functional value.

Everything we believe to be true—that is, everything we perceive to be functional in a particular situation—has a reversible character. If we adopt Dewey's thesis here, we must be ready to submit all our beliefs and prejudices, however cherished they may be, to a test of verification and surrender any that fail the test of consequence.[28] Dewey was quick to recognize how his theory of knowledge —sometimes referred to as *instrumentalism*—could raise the hackles of his critics in other philosophical camps and breed insecurity in the minds of persons who saw danger in an abandonment of absolute truth. As Dewey looked at the world, he could not see objects whose meaning stood out as an independent datum; he did not see objects about which we could have dependable knowledge in the absence of any direct transaction with them.

What Dewey and his pragmatic followers generally object to is called, some-what derisively, a spectator theory of knowledge. This, of course, is the theory of knowledge embraced by realism, and fundamental to it is the principle of independence. No pragmatist wishes to reject the reality of a world to which our senses introduce us, but what pragmatists do reject is the notion that knowledge is standing apart from us waiting to be known. Knowledge, rather, starts with experience and with experience's leading strings comes back to experience. In-stead of talking about acquiring knowledge or possessing truth, pragmatist theory concentrates on a spirit of inquiry or a process of inquiry where "no division between act and material, subject and object [exists], but contains them both in an unanalyzed totality."[29]

Looking for meaning or significance rather than truth, Dewey, for example, is prepared to talk about a relationship between the knower and the object known only when as a result of reflection the object known comes to have significance or meaning. Knowledge, in the end, is a process, not a commodity to be purchased and stored away, so one could hardly be said to possess knowledge or truth. And somewhat along the same line, Dewey and his pragmatic confreres are prepared to dismiss traditional distinctions between theory and practice, between knowing and doing. Knowledge and, to the extent that knowledge is theoretical, theory are represented as being simply a way of doing, of applying, or of making.

The common characterization for this theory of knowledge, which may be as revealing as any one could think of, is *relativism.* To say that knowledge or truth is relative is to say, of course, that it depends for its authenticity—or in the case of pragmatism, for its functional worth—on time, place, and circumstance. Expe-rience is inevitably episodic; the relationship one person has with any part of reality cannot be precisely the same in all its aspects with that of another person, so the outcome of this transaction, this relationship between the knower and the thing known, is bound to be personal and is bound, also, to shift from one to another person. Despite what appears to be a clear and unmitigated relativism, Dewey nevertheless maintains the objectivity of truth and tries to insulate his theory from making truth cater to personal whim, desire, or emotional need. The point is worth considering. This objectivity must come, if it comes at all, by following Peirce's definition of truth, which Dewey apparently approved: Truth is an opinion that has the support of and is finally accepted by all investigators.

Peirce meant this definition of truth to apply to scientific investigation, but Dewey extended it beyond scientific investigation or, better perhaps, translated the method of science to all human activity and gave it a social dimension. What most persons, based on their experience, find to be workable hypotheses can be taken as truth, although they must be ready to change both their ways of acting and the formulations on which their affirmations are based when the outcomes of the hypotheses themselves change. In the last analysis Dewey's opinion seems to be that the functionally effective hypothesis is true, although there is no intention whatever to impose any permanent quality on this functional truth. This is as good a definition of relativism as any. It would seem to be a definition that pragmatists are destined to live with.

Value. Probably more than any other philosophy pragmatism must pay close attention to a theory of morals. At first blush this statement has a strange, almost hollow, ring. If we look more closely, though, we realize the futility of trying to accommodate any prescriptive moral code to empirical naturalism. In the absence of dependable and permanent ethical norms distilled in natural law, in a clear rejection of absolute values, and in a denial of a supreme and supernatural moral legislator, a vacuum surrounds insight into the worth of human experience, and this vacuum remains forever unless it is filled by acquired dispositions to respond to certain kinds of experience in certain ways.

Conventional interpretations of ethical conduct are based on a standard of virtue, a definition of what is right and wrong. As men and women come to understand what is expected of them, as they come to understand the human moral code, they undertake to translate these principles of virtue from the level of objective knowledge to a subjective level where they affect directly the decisions people make in the practical affairs of life. A moral code, then, is expected to function as a compass to prudence, as a brake on the action of the will, and as a safeguard to human decency. Pragmatism jettisons traditional conceptions of ethics. In any case, its exponents are tempted to declare, traditional moral philosophy puts the cart before the horse.

Dewey's empirical theory of value—that is, of recognizing what on a scale of human action has worth and what has none—makes action precede purpose, and habitual action precedes any human ability to weigh the worth of the standard

FIGURE 4.3
Pragmatism's Philosophical Positions

Nature of the Person	The evolutionary hypothesis is taken seriously. Men and women are the products of biological, psychological, and social evolution.
Nature of Reality	Physical reality alone exists. A theory of reality in general is neither possible nor necessary.
Nature of Knowledge	Knowledge is relative; its meaning is disclosed in its application: instrumentalism.
Nature of Value	Standard of personal and social conduct is determined experimentally in the experiences of life.

contained in the purpose.[30] By engaging in various actions, men and women are thus able to make some judgment about their worth; what has worth remains to become part of custom and social habit, and what lacks worth disappears. Again, as with knowledge, pragmatism faces the criticism that morality becomes an entirely personal and relative matter: What is good for one person can be rejected summarily as bad for another. Dewey especially, but other pragmatists as well, recognize the problem, and they seek to avoid either ethical subjectivism or moral nihilism by taking a firm position with respect to the social nature of morality. The point is not that morality ought to be social; it is social.[31]

In any case, whether morality is given a distinctive social face or is otherwise praised in a system of empirical naturalism, value must be translated as being constituted of custom, of mores and folkways, and of collective habits. When value is subjected to the crucial test of intelligent, reflective action, it may be regarded as an expedient moral standard. The alternative is chaos and social disorder, something no pragmatist cherishes. Custom may not be exactly what we want to embrace as a moral standard, but it is all we have, and it is up to us to find a "breach in the crust of the cake of custom [to release] impulses; but it is the work of intelligence to find the ways of using them."[32]

If human society is to offer genuine possibilities for men and women to seek for and reach happiness, it is compelled by the force of natural circumstance to subject its moral philosophy to the crucible of constant reconstruction.

Educational Implications

No general philosophy speaks more directly to education than pragmatism, and in some respects pragmatism is primarily a philosophy of education or, at least, education is philosophy's best testing ground.[33] The educational implications of pragmatism are easy to illustrate. At the same time, however, personal interaction with the environment as a way of determining conduct is an article of pragmatic faith, so we should not be surprised to find a good deal of variety in the pronouncements of pragmatically disposed educators. And because of the inherent flexibility in pragmatism and its determination to capitalize on individual perceptions of experience, we should not be surprised at the tendency of pragmatism's critics to caricature the content and worth of scholastic programs and to direct verbal barrages at teachers who embrace the pragmatic creed.

Earlier in this century hardly anyone would have challenged the assumption that the surest guide to pragmatic educational philosophy is contained in John Dewey's *Democracy and Education* (1916). Praised as the greatest book on education since Plato's *Republic,* its evaluators, caught up in hyperbole or simply in the spirit of a pragmatic age, sometimes set it a notch or two above *The Republic.* At best such kudos are hardly more than guesses, but they illustrate nevertheless the ubiquity of Dewey's reputation. The medal has another side: While Dewey was praised, he was also blamed. Caustic critics indicted Dewey and his *Democracy and Education* for every false educational step ever taken in any school by any teacher.

Despite their undoubted luster, however, Dewey's reputation on one hand and his philosophical discourses on the other were insufficient to keep educational pragmatism pure or to enlist its devotees in dogmatism. In the upshot, although many schools flew the pragmatic flag from their staffs and paid verbal allegiance to Dewey's general educational theses, pragmatic educators tended to go their separate ways. For the most part, pragmatists, rather than making common cause in a concerted, organized assault on American education, engaged in guerrilla skirmishes. Pragmatism, its philosophical opposition said, was populated by predatory bands roaming through American schools destroying traditional standards associated with educational decency.

But this is not the most important part of the picture, and we should not dwell on it. What is important is this: What meaning does pragmatism have for teaching and learning? Pragmatism we know, either in Dewey's competent hands or in the hands of any of his followers, never restricted the meaning of *education* to what goes on in schools. Yet in the nature of twentieth-century life, it was impossible to refuse to pay regular scholastic tribute to schooling.

When first pronounced, Dewey's views on education and schooling were often judged so avant-garde as to be unworthy of serious attention. But not for long. As time passed, and particularly in the 1950s and 1960s, many of Dewey's sympathetic and apparently dedicated followers began to speak of his unprogressivism. Dewey, they were tempted to say, was a pragmatist, there was no doubt of that, but he was not quite pragmatic enough. What could have precipitated such a charge?

The Student and the Curriculum.   We know, of course, that empirical naturalism, banking on the validity of the evolutionary hypothesis, regarded the person to be educated as being neither more nor less than a biological organism. Yet qualities conspiring to produce human dignity, while lodged in physiology, are cultivated, if they are cultivated at all, in the succeeding processes of psychological and sociological evolution. All this caused no trouble, for on these points Dewey and his successors spoke a common language. In both cases, obviously, the key to psychological and sociological evolution was to be found in how experience was employed to stimulate the pace of evolution and even, perhaps, to nudge it in one or another direction. And on this point of experience, as it turned out, Dewey and many of his followers could not agree. When Dewey talked about experience, he sounded most liberal and progressive, but it is easy to be deceived by sound. He meant that experiences used to shape human nature and character should be subjected to the test of worth. With a keen sense of history, Dewey was aware of experiential variety in mankind's long march through time: One experience could not be recommended as being just as useful, just as formative, as any other. So when he wrote and spoke about a curriculum, he meant to fill it with experiences judged, on the basis of every criterion available to help judgment along, most formative, most developmental, and most liberating.

Dewey knew something his followers were sometimes tempted to forget: Boys and girls must be educated to live in a real world and meet the problems of life inevitably arising in it. It would not do to have just any kind of experience in the school and, although students should be allowed a good deal of latitude to capitalize on their own interests, they could never be given an entirely free hand, for they lacked experience—the developed intelligence, Dewey would have said —to direct the course of their experience. As a result Dewey's curriculum was filled with all kinds of tested experience, and the subjects in it were not so different from those in a conventional, unpragmatic school. The principal difference here, though, and one Dewey himself never forgot to mention, was that these curricular materials were being advanced, studied, and mastered, not as eternal truths, but only as tested hypotheses. The validity of their practical functions gave them a character of a merely equivocal permanence.

Pragmatism's theory of knowledge is critical here. In the last analysis, it must be pointless and futile to talk about the constitution of a curriculum in the absence of a theory of knowledge. And we know enough about Dewey's theory of knowledge to know how he was prepared to jettison two old curricular assumptions. The first: liberal and vocational education are different, and the former is always superior on a scale of educational decency to the latter; the second: theoretical and practical knowledge, if not substantially different, are at least distinct.

Kilpatrick's Interpretation of Pragmatism.   Disenchanted with Dewey's curricular counsel to keep tested experience and many supposedly traditional subjects in the curriculum, his later disciples—or if not his disciples, a new cadre of educational pragmatists—began talking about an emerging curriculum. The herald for an emerging curriculum, one generated in the needs and interests students brought with them to school, was William Heard Kilpatrick (1871–1965). There would be no textbooks, "but instead all sorts of reference books. . . . I would give no marks in either elementary or secondary school, and send no regular report cards, especially of a kind intended to compare one pupil with another. I think all such seriously hinder the kind of living the school exists to foster."[34] Kilpatrick took pragmatic theory of knowledge with the utmost seriousness, and to some extent misinterpreted it by making experience of all kinds and descriptions equivalent. What a person wanted to learn was personally worth learning, and it made no matter what anyone else thought about its worth. What counted, it appears, in Kilpatrick's theory of schooling was the method of inquiry employed, and the best one he could think of, one he promoted with a good deal of success, was the project method.[35]

In general, then, in departing from the more solidly based experiences associated with the act of learning that had been elaborated by Dewey, pragmatists of the past three decades or so have been tempted to subscribe to the theses contained in Kilpatrick's expressions on education. And to this extent they have given their support to a kind of education dominated by student whim, felt need, and emotional disposition. They have praised functional learning but have ignored school practices where decent functional learning could be cultivated.

Dewey proclaimed the significance of method as a way of having experience, but experience, rather than being just anything, should be beneficial. And the question of benefit, although students could play some part in its appraisal, was not solely theirs to answer. The later pragmatists adopted method and sometimes improved it, but following the trail blazed by Kilpatrick they tended to ignore the quality of the experiences to which method was applied.

Education and Experience.   Under any auspices pragmatism speaks a language where the educational chase is prized over the conquest of knowledge, for the chase is itself an experience contributing to nurture, whereas capturing knowledge must in every case be an illusion. "Ends are foreseen consequences which arise in the cause of activity and which are employed to give activity added meaning and to direct its further course."[36] The charter for school programs in pragmatic custody is written along lines of interest, felt need, and self-satisfaction, for these are the scholastic realities capable of spurring and sustaining motivation. Without motivation to learn, students halt; when they do the possibility of what pragmatists see as effective learning—that is, becoming fluent and versatile in method—ceases also. Stepping outside the mainstream of experience, or what is worse, supposing that experience has some terminus, leads inevitably to stagnation, for growth cannot cease. In this context we hear Dewey saying: "The educational process has no end beyond itself; it is its own end."[37]

The point to this is, of course, that what goes on in schools should, from the pragmatist's point of view, be real rather than artificial. The end of it all is to produce persons capable of leading full and satisfying lives, and they can never be expected to get very far in achieving this objective unless the school itself is a place where real living can be practiced.

Without its details before us, we nevertheless have the outline of a pragmatic curriculum in mind. We also know that all of life is educational and all of education is life. If this means anything at all, it must mean that our development of methods for successful living must apply equally to cognitive and moral hypotheses. Schools are places where students should learn to live by living, and

FIGURE 4.4
Educational Implications in Pragmatism

Educational Purpose	To provide experience for meeting the novelties in personal and social life.
The Student	An organism of extraordinary complexity capable of growth.
The Curriculum	Contains tested experience that is subject to change. The interests and needs children bring with them to school form an emerging curriculum.
Liberal Education	Dismisses distinction between liberal and practical, or vocational, education.
Method	Considers the activity method—learning by doing—paramount.
The Role of Teachers	To superintend and guide the learning experience without intruding too heavily on student interest and need.

they are places, moreover, where students will learn what is desirable moral conduct by living morally in their schools.

The Role of the Teacher. So far we have left the teacher out of account. In pragmatic educational theory teachers are destined to play a highly important though untraditional role. They are neither hearers of lessons nor instructors delegated to teach students a body of dependable knowledge. They are guides and supervisors in a broad and open educational process. As such they must, of course, be the beneficiaries of rich experience, and they must be masters of method. Flexible and versatile, they must be ready to answer students' calls for scholastic help, but they must not thrust themselves on their students, interfere with their freedom, or interpose themselves between students and the process of experiencing. They must operate according to the strict principle telling them that direct experience is always better than vicarious experience, so by artful means they should encourage their students to taste life directly and never to be content with the second-hand.

With these convictions about the direction education should take, convictions distilled directly and logically from principles of general philosophy, pragmatism came to have an almost natural attraction for progressive education, a pedagogic and scholastic innovation of the early twentieth century. The affinity maturing between pragmatism and progressive education may have been of considerable help to the latter, but it did little more than succeed in putting the former in a bad light. Pragmatism's similarity to progressive education, especially on some points of school practice, is hard to repudiate, although we shall see that it is not only exaggeration but poor philosophy as well to pretend to an identity between them (see pp. 180–181).

EXISTENTIALISM

Having come this far in our review of modern philosophy and education, we are faced with two inevitable realities: One is space; the other is influence. At this point in our study, about to launch into a discussion of existentialism and then analytic philosophy, space and influence are related. Were our space unlimited, we could spend a good deal of time with both, but since space is limited and both the theoretical and practical influence of existentialism and analytical philosophy in education is somewhat curtailed—although promoted enthusiastically in some circles—we feel justified in giving an abbreviated account of the two philosophies remaining on our list.

Traveling through the thicket of philosophical discourse—being sometimes enlightened and sometimes confused—we have seen signs telling us that a philosophy, a theology, a sociology, or an economics of education is just ahead. Now, as we wade into existentialism, we meet for the first and probably the only time what amounts to a poetry of education. This is not to allege that the poetic, even mystical, quality to existentialism excludes philosophical principles; it is to say that distilling these principles and the educational implications lodged in them, depending as they do on poetic, imprecise, and visionary expression, is a herculean undertaking.

It may be best to begin with a clear conscience, so we should all confess to being embryonic existentialists, for all of us begin with an immediate experience of our existence and, for the most part, this pure form of empiricism is neither fully explained nor understood. Unless we are radical existentialists, we do not remain on this level, nor does existentialism mainly. We go on to search for meaning and purpose by wrestling with the world's realities while the existentialist turns inward and becomes introspective. Life's meaning is hidden somewhere within him and the philosophy he cultivates is introvertive. Other philosophies count on the extrovertive tendencies of their proponents to look at the realities of life around them and to find meaning by engaging in a discursive learning process. To say that we are all riding on an existentialistic bandwagon is neither a novel nor a subversive philosophical point of view, any more than it is subversive to say that sometimes we are all pragmatists, and probably could not live effectively were we to completely and totally reject pragmatic ways of acting. But after saying so much, especially in connection with our native existentialistic dispositions, we should not leap hastily to the conclusion that existentialism is an expression of a common philosophical point of view. It is not. As a philosophy, it is relatively young; as a systematic philosophy it is not only young but probably lacks the intrinsic character to be philosophically coherent. Let us see, if we can, why at the outset anyone would so indict this philosophy.

Existential Philosophical Positions

Any modern philosophy must have some roots in the past, and existentialism is no exception, yet however deep its roots were, either from lack of cultivation or intrinsic vitality they produced no crop to harvest until shortly after World War I (1914–1918). Rumblings of existential thought began to appear then, apparently as independent philosophical movements in Germany and France. When existentialism matured into a philosophy is hard to tell, because its origins are imprecise and its expositors seldom made any principal intellectual investment in philosophy. We know, for example, the names of Søren Kierkegaard (1813–1855), Martin Heidegger (1889–1976), Gabriel Marcel (1889–1973), and Albert Camus (1913–1960), and we know they had some part to play in the unfolding of existential drama. But we know, too, that they were seldom philosophers in the full professional sense and, moreover, sometimes disavowed, as Camus did, being existentialists at all.

Jean-Paul Sartre (1905–1980), however, made existentialism a matter of common knowledge, although not of common understanding. We should probably stay close to him as we look for meaning in this philosophy. Yet we must also understand, despite his passion for philosophical expression, that Sartre was a man of many talents. Had he never written a line of philosophy, he would have been famous for his plays and novels, and had he never written a word of fiction, he would have been famous for his philosophy.

Passion for life strikes us first as the existentialist's motto, but then as we read on we are never sure that we are not being led through a manifesto of despair. Life is full of conflict and contradiction from which no human being, however he or she may try, is ever immune, so, to follow the typical existentialist view, any explanation of life, any philosophizing about it, if it is to be faithful to life itself, must make room for conflict and contradiction. It is not the role of the philosopher to iron them out or to explain them away in order to make life neat, orderly, and livable, for this would be fraudulent; it is the philosopher's role to reveal them as they are with all their brutish force and factuality.

Men are finite, of this existentialists are certain. But existentialists, and Sartre chief among them (he spends fifty pages in *Being and Nothingness* on it), have an almost irresistible urge to plumb the absurd. Their preoccupation with the past is intense, although they readily admit—at least Sartre does—that "It is the future which decides whether the past is living or dead."[38] Man himself is at the summit of reality, but a real world with all the power and substance of a being that simply *is* stands ready to swallow him up. And what does man have to protect himself from the being of a cruel nature? He has intelligence, and existentialists, sounding almost like idealists now, refuse to argue about its source; he also has freedom to guide his own destiny. There is nothing else.

Meeting the physical world for the first time, the person, as existentialists see it, is in great danger of being overwhelmed by the fact of experience itself. Experience is, and it is powerful. But this is all on a nonreflective level. As persons learn, grow, and mature they succeed in becoming reflective in appraising their experience, and the more reflective they are, the better their chance for controlling the exigencies of nature, for putting themselves in a position where they can oppose a dumb threatening universe ready to swallow them up.

Humanity's greatest friend is freedom; its greatest enemy is determinism. But either, in the last analysis, may be a state of mind, so belief in freedom is essential to any kind of decent life, and any embrace of deterministic theses is bound to

---

FIGURE 4.5
General Philosophical Principles in Existentialism

Nature of the Person	Dualism of mind and body, with special emphasis on mind.
Nature of Reality	An independent, physical universe exists, and it may prove threatening to the realization of personal goals. Spiritual reality may or may not exist.
Nature of Knowledge	A tendency toward skepticism, yet a willingness to acknowledge the possibility of achieving truth.
Nature of Value	A variety in moral standard is inevitable. Persons are free to choose their own moral standard, but some moral standard as an anchor to personal life is imperative.

be dehumanizing and dangerous. Still, freedom poses a problem, for only a free person can recognize the existence of other free persons whose freedom—when freedoms conflict—may prove to be troublesome. The only way out of this possible conflict over whose freedom has precedence is through the development of a sense of responsibility. Had Sartre, or other existentialists, succeeded in elaborating a doctrine of freedom and responsibility, we would have a better foundation from which to speculate about existentialism's message to education. In any case, it would appear, the threshold over which any existential philosophy of education must pass is freedom and responsibility, so we shall follow this deep tributary of existential philosophy as far as it goes.

Educational Implications

By taking allegations of human freedom seriously, it seems to follow that whatever persons become, whatever destiny they carve out for themselves, is up to them. They are in a position to choose one thing or something else, but they must choose something; no man or woman is absolved from making something of himself or herself. As persons strive to make something of themselves, help is needed, and it comes from education. Existentialism abandons an unalterable commitment to schooling, for it would seem to be entirely consistent with its thought to take full advantage of the possibilities of self-education (a kind of education considered by some philosophies of education to be either enormously difficult or impossible), yet at some point or other it must meet knowledge—or what for convenience's sake is called knowledge—and when it does the most practical place to wrestle with knowledge is in school.

Fulfillment of Personal Goals. The school is primarily a place for having experience with life, for existentialism, almost as much as pragmatism, rejects the so-called spectator theory of knowledge. So schools should try to immerse their students in life, but when they do they must be cautious, for "The existentialist attitude toward knowledge radically affects the teaching of those subjects which are dependent upon systems of thought or frames of reference: it states that school subjects are only tools for the realization of subjectivity."[39]

One huge part of this realization of subjectivity—another way of saying fulfilling one's personal goals—is to adopt a set of values, a code of conduct, according to which personal life will be lived. Values are not something we are authorized to embrace or reject: They are both inevitable and imperative. Whether there are sets of values, apart from those distilled in purely personal experience, that are lodged in the legacy of the race or whether values come under the jurisdiction of natural or supernatural law really makes no difference. The source of value is inconsequential, for there must be a personal endorsement of some values. Values are translated from the objective to the subjective realm by an act of personal choice that under no circumstance can be avoided. Persons are free to choose their moral code, but by the very nature of their existence, they can never refuse to choose some moral code. This should not be interpreted as determinism, which, in any case, existentialism rejects, but only as the natural functioning of human life. Looking at the matter this way, it makes almost no difference whatever to existentialists whether their adherents are atheists or theists. If divine injunctions exist and are capable of being translated into ethical norms, it is, finally, up to a person to choose them or some others. Life is an entirely personal game, and the rules of the game are made up as one goes along.

Freedom and Responsibility.   The temptation, of course, is to translate all this into a kind of moral anarchy: Everyone is free to go his own way. If this is true, one is bound to wonder how education can be of much help. Yet existentialism is not prepared to endorse moral anarchy or to absolve education from pointing its clientele in the right moral direction. The person who chooses a value is in the moral position of choosing what he perceives to be not only an ideal for himself but for everyone. The best education prepares us to will our own freedom and, at the same time, to will the freedom of all others; when we assert the value of any action, we are, if we have been properly educated, asserting a value with universal appeal. "I am responsible for myself and for all."[40]

All this means, according to a leading existential spokesman, "that existentialism is concerned principally with liberal education, freeing man from his isolation and his anonymity, freeing his mind from the confusions that prevent him from seeing his situation and his powers."[41] So, to follow this line of thought for a moment, the teacher who enlists in the ranks of existential schooling is a missionary for freedom and responsibility more than an instructor in the subjects of the school's curriculum. The point is, of course, to have the curriculum designed in such a way that its outcome is always human freedom and never enslavement. And this is where both existential teachers and philosophers have most work yet to do: to tell us how all this may be done.[42]

Despite an intense devotion to freedom, existentialists declare that freedom has rules. These rules are generated in social experience and are enforced under the arbitrament of logic. The good person, the ideally educated person, is able to see beyond personal interest and goal. He must find ways to meld his declarations of freedom and value with those of others whose freedom he, too, must respect. This calls for some moral conclusions, one would think, and we have no reason to suppose that existentialism holds otherwise. But they do make a strong point about the distillation and ratification of general social and moral codes, and here we mean the process of arriving at moral codes and not their substance: Character education is always something more than merely improving skill in group dynamics. It must be arrived at by more dependable means.

Critics of existentialism who charge it with inflating freedom and discounting responsibility may be wrong, but if they are, existential educational paradigms are largely to blame for misleading them. Interest in responsible moral action is, in the end, something quite different from making educational provision for its development. In any case, we must return again to the issue of freedom, and now it takes a slightly different emphasis from what we have seen so far. No educational point of view stresses academic freedom more than existentialism, but it is academic freedom with a novel twist. It belongs less to the teacher than the

FIGURE 4.6
Educational Implications in Existentialism

The Student	A rational being with freedom of choice and responsibility for what is chosen. A commitment to fulfilling personal goals.
Educational Purpose	To provide an extensive and comprehensive experience with life in all its forms.
The Curriculum	Mainly liberal because liberal learning is most likely to lay a foundation for human freedom.
Social Education	Freedom has rules, so it is the duty of social education to teach respect for the freedom of all. Respect for the freedom of others is essential, for freedoms are almost certain to conflict.
The Role of Teachers	To protect and preserve academic freedom, where teachers today may be students tomorrow.
Method	No preoccupation with method, but whatever method is employed must point to ways to achieve happiness and good character.

student, and less to the student than to the entire educational process. Even then we cannot be entirely sure where it finally comes to rest, for the role of teachers and students is interchangeable. The teacher today may be the student tomorrow, or the teacher for the first part of a lesson may end up learning from those he is commissioned to teach.

One looks hard and long at existentialism and even then is not certain of having seen much to help with the practical enterprise of education. Still, there is an educational voice telling one not to despair: "Education can point to the way or ways to both happiness and good character; it cannot and ought not to prescribe or enforce. Education is the journey, not the end of the journey; the recognition, not the decision to accept the recognition and stay at home."[43] This is almost pure poetry. Whether it is also educational philosophy is something we have yet to decide.

ANALYTIC PHILOSOPHY

Up to this point we have been engaged with philosophies whose principal object is to speculate about reality, knowledge, and virtue. Together they want to distill meaning from a broad range of human experience, and to this end philosophy's traditional preoccupation has been speculation. Now, however, in turning to analysis we meet a philosophy, although some critics call it more a method than a systematic philosophy, ready to jettison speculation in favor of excavating meaning from what has already been said about reality, knowledge, and virtue or, in the case of logical positivism, establishing a theory of meaning based on the proposition that only those statements that can be verified by sense experience have meaning.

Analysis aims at clarifying language and thought rather than at fashioning new propositions about the nature of the world. Language, in the custody of grammar

145

and structural linguistics, and logic are the analysts' principal intellectual tools as they look for meaning either in what has already been speculated about and is now buried away in the archives of philosophical thought or, again, as in logical positivism, in a direct sensory contact with the facts of experience. So, although their approach is somewhat different, both linguistic analysis and logical positivism can be introduced in this section. Both, in the end, although with a different spirit and, their proponents would say, a method different enough to make them distinct philosophies, employ critical linguistic and logical techniques commissioned to grasp for meaning.

Foundations of Analysis

The motherhouse of analytic philosophy was built in Great Britain around the middle of the twentieth century. By now it has daughterhouses the world over and, without becoming what could be called a popular philosophy, its cultivation in the United States has been second only to that in England.

George Edward Moore (1873–1958) was most likely the modern architect for linguistic analysis, although we should be careful, as we have said before, not to attribute to this philosophical position any monopoly over the exercise of critical technique, as philosophers do their best to dredge meaning from the realities of life. Every philosophy, of course, claims a severely critical perspective as it lines up its propositions to expose their meaning. Still, Moore, in *Some Main Problems of Philosophy* (1953) and in articles published in *Mind* and *Philosophical Studies,* illustrated the practice of analysis to twentieth-century philosophers.

Although breaking ground for linguistic analysis, Moore was preceded by Bertrand Russell, described by some commentators as a twentieth-century Voltaire, and by Ludwig Wittgenstein, who with great scholarly intensity and determination tried to make analysis a distinctive philosophy. The kernel of Russell's analytic thought, most scholars agree, is in *Principia Mathematica* (a three-volume work published between the years 1910 and 1913), written in collaboration with Alfred North Whitehead, but, for the most part, it lay dormant until the hard crust of analysis was broken by Moore. Wittgenstein's *Tractatus Logico-*

FIGURE 4.7
Contributors to the Analytic Movement

Bertrand Russell (1872–1970)	Promoted the use of mathematical logic for scientific analysis of meaning.
George Edward Moore (1873–1958)	Illustrated the use of linguistic analysis in disclosing meaning in philoshical discourse.
Ludwig Wittgenstein (1889–1951)	Truth is the business of science. Philosophy's role is to clarify scientific meaning.
Alfred J. Ayer (b. 1910)	To be a philosopher one must first have the credentials of a scientist.
Gilbert Ryle (1900–1976)	With speculative truth in its possession, philosophy must discover truth's logical relationships.

Philosophicus (1921) became, in consequence of Moore's heraldry, the general charter for an analytic approach to philosophy. We notice, of course, how Russell and Wittgenstein anticipated Moore, yet had to wait for Moore's promotion before analysis gained much stature.

Logical positivists and linguistic analysts sail down the same philosophical river, but they steer their own boats. Linguistic analysts count Moore, Russell, and Wittgenstein among their heroes. The captains of logical positivism are Alfred J. Ayer, whose *Language, Truth and Logic* (1936) had the effect of catapulting logical positivism to prominence, and Gilbert Ryle, whose *The Concept of Mind* (1949) added considerable luster to this approach to philosophy.

Philosophical Principles

Moore, Russell, and, to the extent that he belongs in this cadre, Whitehead, promoted a return to realism. So it may not be wrong to allege to them a principal motive of refuting idealism as they set out to make new marks on philosophy's trail. This refutation of idealism took them into linguistic analysis, where they concerned themselves with a clarification of a theory of knowledge for an independent reality. In adopting a stance of indifference to the nature of this reality, their neglect of metaphysics was almost total.

Wittgenstein, however, with no supreme penchant for refuting idealism, articulated what may stand as linguistic analysis' manifesto: "Most of the propositions and questions to be found in philosophical works are not false but nonsensical. Consequently we cannot give any answer to questions of this kind, but can only establish that they are nonsensical. Most of the propositions and questions of philosophers arise from our failure to understand the logic of our language."[44] Wittgenstein withheld from philosophy any commission to certify truth, for this was science's business. He gave it the responsibility to clarify the results of scientific investigation.

Moore, it appears, was unable to endorse the whole of Wittgenstein's thesis, for Moore, while clearly disposed to use philosophy to clarify the meaning of philosophical propositions, was on the side of common-sense realism when it came to having experience with reality. Should common sense and philosophy be at loggerheads, Moore would embrace the former.

Russell, however, found it difficult to adopt the position of either Moore or Wittgenstein. He wanted philosophy to unravel the world's secrets, not to diagram sentences to discover their meaning. In the upshot he disliked, without rejecting, Wittgenstein's linguistic analysis and was also cool to logical positivism. Logical positivism, he declared, divorced the world of language from the world of empirical fact, a weakness it seemed unable to overcome. For Russell, philosophy's proper method is analysis, but for analysis to function, an appeal must be made to something more substantial than common sense and a critical appraisal of ordinary language. Analysis must be scientific and employ a rigorous logical technique; the best place to find technique, Russell thought, was in mathematics.

With this conviction uppermost in his mind, he went on to develop a highly mathematical logic tailored especially for use in philosophy.

Logical positivism, as we have said, is at least linguistic analysis' first cousin. This assertion would seem to have ample support from Ayer's *Language, Truth and Logic.* In this book Ayer writes the preamble for logical positivism, and he puts it this way: The work of science—he means empirical science—of course, is to discover speculative truth; the philosopher is left to analyze the language used to convey this truth. Still the philosopher's role is somewhat adumbrated. He clarifies "the propositions of science by exhibiting their logical relationships, and by defining the symbols which occur in them."[45]

Without the ability to evaluate the conclusions of scientists, philosophers are reduced to the role of important helpers. With their help scientists can integrate their theories into meaningful statements and muster enough self-confidence to steer clear of metaphysical assumptions. Without any respect for metaphysics, Ayer nevertheless wanted to stop short of discounting philosophy's worth, although it would seem to us that he goes further along this line than he thought, by affirming in the end that science and philosophy belong together as a single enterprise. Science's job is speculative; philosophy's role is logical. Yet it is hard to suppress the conclusion, and Ayer does not worry much about it, that to be a philosopher in the full sense, one must first be a scientist.[46]

What has been said, one could argue convincingly, hardly counts as philosophical principle. Yet these are the main lines of linguistic analytic and logical positivistic thought, or what we have called analytic philosophy. Depending on critical analysis of philosophical propositions and on the results of scientific investigation, however, we must always be prepared for a variety of individual interpretations under the auspices of this general philosophical outlook. One can never be sure of having elaborated or even discovered every tributary to analytic philosophy or, what is more, done justice to every philosopher who counts himself a member of this camp.

Educational Implications

We had some difficulty in winnowing from existentialism a coherent educational code, but this exercise may have been child's play compared to what we face now. By its very nature analysis not only allows but encourages diversity in interpretation, for it is only in rubbing ideas and interpretations, in creating a friction of mind on mind, that dependable conclusions can be reached. Under the circumstances an analytic educational dogma would be surprising.

Linguistic Analysis. Still there are some general educational principles that most linguistic analysts salute. The purpose of education, they say with almost one voice, is to equip us technically to conduct a tour of reasoned doubt into the hinterlands of all knowledge and value that are now accepted. The bulk of this technical equipment, which we must have if we are to criticize, analyze, and articulate, is found in studies of language and logic.

Education, Kenneth Burke avers, should prepare us to brood, but it must be brooding accompanied by a sound method, and this brooding should conspire to unscramble the assertions that make up the bulk of our culture and civilization.[47] At its best, education is a human dialogue. Anyone participating in this dialogue must be able to handle the subtleties of language and the elements of logic in such a way as to clarify meaning rather than to confuse it further.

How optimistic linguistic analysts are about the outcome of this kind of education is never easy to say. They know, for example, that it must have a pragmatic side, for whatever our anticipations are in connection with human wisdom, the stark fact remains that we must make a living in a society whose basic economic functions are largely immune to our influence. Yet if this were all that is to be expected from education, it would perhaps be better to make schools into direct training academies or, in the absence of schools, to depend entirely on some kind of modern apprenticeship system. There are other sides to education and they should be paid due heed. The futility of using good method to grope for meaning and understanding if all we want is skill in meeting the exigencies of economic life is obvious. We must look forward to a better world and to a better life, one filled with meaning and good will. So to this end the educational enterprise should admonish its clientele both toward greater human endeavor, for meaning either in philosophical propositions or anything else is not likely to come without determined effort, and toward the good life. The key to convincing us about the vital elements of the good life is to be found, if it is ever found at all, in a healthy, profound appreciation for the genius of human life.

None of these pragmatic, admonitory, and appreciative objectives will come automatically. All must be cultivated. And this is the work of education. Because linguistic analysts regard education as being primarily social, they pay a good deal of attention to education for life in society. Now, almost for the first time, we begin to hear some strange educational sounds.

Both formal and informal education begin with indoctrination. Analysts are as able as anyone to see the fault in indoctrination, but they do not stop to argue the case for or against it, for argument would be pointless. However much it may offend us, indoctrination has no alternatives, for the nature of education on the first and more basic instructional levels does not supply any. If education is off to a bad start, analysts are eager to redress it, but this takes time. The next step is openly partisan. What is taught is taught with zeal and conviction, but this partisanship is liberal: *Truth* is taught but other lesser (and, of course, incorrect) points of view are presented too.

Basic education is husbanded by following the trail of indoctrination (what Theodore Brameld used to call defensible partiality)[48] and is succeeded by a rigorous but ecumenical partisanship. If education stopped here, analysts are quick to admit, it would be defective. If it is genuine, however, it does not stop here. It goes on to introduce a systematic humanitarianism. Now everything is examined according to the canons of truth, logic, and scientific accuracy. Some old values may have to be discarded. The objective of this humanitarianism is the

inculcation of an impartial spirit. And with this impartial spirit, the truly educated person is ready to cross the threshold of genuine dialectic. Now no preferences are guarded; everything is submitted to the arbitrament of analysis, and the
basic rule of this dialectical game is fair play. In any educational situation, Burke
declares confidently, everyone would be "on good terms. They would preferably
be under the sign of good will. And is not education ideally an effort to maintain
such an attitude as thoroughly and extensively as possible without loss of one's
own integrity?"[49]

Logical Positivism.   Logical positivists are in the habit of referring to themselves as scientific humanists. This designation is hard to translate, but it must
mean a rejection of absolute values on one hand and a dependence on the outcome
of experience on the other. Besides, it attributes critical abilities to human beings
and takes the implications of intelligence seriously without at the same time being
bogged down in debate about their origin and nature. If these questions, or others
like them, are fundamental, they are also, logical positivists maintain, outside the
boundary where positive method can be applied. In the absence of positive
method, no dependable knowledge is possible.

Despite an inevitable appeal to discipline and rigor when the meaning of
experience is being assessed—for logical positivists regularly exhibit their grasp
of logic, science, and language—this educational outlook is disposed to praise the
methods of progressive education (see pp. 180–181). When it does, however, it
means to emphasize the side to progressivism where experimental method is given
pride of educational place and to play down a lack of standard and commitment
to the discipline of learning.

Almost no attention, beyond the polite bow to progressive education, is given
to elementary schooling. Beginning with secondary education and moving on
through the college, logical positivism promotes a cultivation of the liberal arts
and sciences. Its only amendment to this broad educational charter is an admonition to the educational fraternity to teach the sciences more liberally and more
effectively. Teaching science, the message reads, is a matter of developing a
scientific outlook, so a leaf should be taken from the humanist's book on
pedagogy. It is unlikely that a genuinely scientific outlook can come from a
preoccupation with a mastery of laboratory or other empirical technique.

If high marks were given for candor and also for philosophical self-effacement,
logical positivism would be first in the class. After spending nearly twenty pages
discoursing on the perceptions of logical positivism, Herbert Feigl asks what it
all means to teaching and learning. He answers his own question: "I am inclined
to say: nothing that reasonable people have not known all along without the
benefit of any systematic philosophy."[50] And reasonable people, he goes on, are
prepared to acknowledge as being decent any educational program recommending as objectives such things as clarity of thought, consistency of logical principle,
reliability and objectivity of knowledge, rationality in behavior, and an adherence
to fundamental principles of morality.

Contemporary Analysis' Thrust. Feigl's disclaimer, according to contemporary analytic philosophers, is too sweeping. Israel Scheffler, for example, although rejecting dogmatism relative to educational purpose, sees clear implications for the twin enterprises of teaching and learning in philosophy's capacity for sorting out priorities. From among a variety of possible purposes, all of which may be legitimate under certain circumstances, skillful analysts can recommend the ones that in a given situation have stood the test of critical inspection and can be endorsed as most desirable.

Analytic philosophers begin by abandoning a prescriptive role for educational philosophy, and on this point agreement is nearly universal, yet the rank and file are disposed to adopt prescriptive methods for conducting their inquiry into education. They may wrestle with the same educational problem only to render different verdicts, but when they do they try to use the same linguistic and logical techniques.[51] These verdicts, more often than not, take on the form of paradigms for concentrating attention on particular educational issues. They are meant to guide our thought about education without dictating it. In any case, critics of analytic philosophy are tempted to say, analysts spend their time looking for educational fault. Finding it, they cling to their original disposition to withhold solutions and wring their hands while lamenting the failure in the educational enterprise. This, critics argue, is an object lesson in philosophy's surrender and a sure way of rendering it impractical.

Here, too, there is another side. Critics may be too harsh. Paul Hirsh, for example, is one of many analysts who see this philosophy's major role being played by employing the most rigorous kind of research—for which analysts are usually well equipped—to probe the effectiveness of various teaching methods. But analysis need not stop with method, nor does it. Recognizing the supreme significance of the curriculum in the educational process, exponents of analysis are dismayed to read curricular theories and plans lacking both meaning and precision. Too much of curricular theory, they aver, is filled with and dominated by tired and time worn slogans whose current meaning (assuming a meaning at one time) is either obfuscated or confused. Perhaps most troubling of all is the evidence of superficiality in all curricular planning, ranging all the way from the first grade to the graduate school. The curriculum, we agree, could turn out to be a fertile field for analytic philosophy to cultivate.

In the end an educational program committed to the foregoing objectives and built around the functions of language and logic and the evidences of science is bound to contribute to a higher stage of human maturity.

Mankind has embarked on the adventure of civilization in which scientific knowledge plays the major guiding role. . . . A sustained educational effort, for many generations to come, is urgently needed in order to adapt humanity to the new ways of thinking necessitated by this age of science. A philosophy which does full justice to the scientific outlook can be a powerful ally in our endeavors toward a more mature and more fully integrated life.[52]

FIGURE 4.8

Educational Implications in Analysis

Indoctrination	It is at this level where all education must begin. We may not like indoctrination but we have no choice.
Partisan teaching	What is held to be true is taught with zeal and devotion, but other "truths" are introduced and are given a fair hearing.
Scientific humanitarianism	Everything in the school's curriculum must be scrutinized and verified according to canons of logic and scientific authenticity.

NOTES

1. JACQUES MARITAIN, "Thomist Views on Education," in the Fifty-fourth Yearbook of the National Society for the Study of Education, *Modern Philosophies and Education* (Chicago: University of Chicago Press, 1955), p. 58.

2. *The Phenomenon of Man*, trans. Bernard Wall (New York: Harper & Row, Publishers, Inc., 1959).

3. Ibid., p. 297.

4. JACQUES MARITAIN, *The Range of Reason* (New York: Charles Scribner's Sons, 1952), p. 70; and *Existence and the Existent* (New York: Pantheon Books, Inc., 1948), p. 37.

5. JACQUES MARITAIN, *The Degrees of Knowledge* (New York: Charles Scribner's Sons, 1938), pp. 210–226.

6. JACQUES MARITAIN, *True Humanism* (New York: Charles Scribner's Sons, 1938), p. 86.

7. JACQUES MARITAIN, "Thomist Views on Education," p. 71.

8. JACQUES MARITAIN, *Man and the State* (Chicago: University of Chicago Press, 1951), pp. 111–112, discusses teaching the democratic charter this way.

9. J. DONALD BUTLER, *Four Philosophies: And Their Practice in Education and Religion* (New York: Harper & Row, Publishers, Inc., 1968), pp. 417–431.

10. *Collected Papers of Charles Sanders Peirce*, ed. C. Hartshorne, P. Weiss, and A. W. Burke (Cambridge, Mass.: Harvard University Press, 1931–1935, 1958). References to *Collected Papers* are to volume and numbered paragraph.

11. Ibid., 5.9.

12. Ibid., 5.423.

13. Ibid.

14. Ibid., 1.487.

15. Ibid., 1.204.

16. Ibid., 5.211.

17. Ibid., 2.198.

18. WILLIAM JAMES, *Pragmatism* (Cambridge, Mass.: Harvard University Press, 1975), p. 51.

19. Ibid., p. 47.

20. Ibid., p. 206.

21. Ibid., p. 58.

22. WILLIAM JAMES, *The Will to Believe and Other Essays on Popular Philosophy* (New York: Longmans, Green and Company, 1896), p. 22.

23. JOHN DEWEY, *Reconstruction in Philosophy* (New York: Holt, Rinehart & Winston, 1920), p. 26.

24. JOHN DEWEY, *The Quest for Certainty* (New York: Minton Balch, 1929; Capricorn Books, 1960), p. 273.

25. JOHN DEWEY, *Reconstruction in Philosophy*, p. 21.

26. JOHN DEWEY, *The Quest for Certainty*, p. 225.

27. JOHN DEWEY, *Creative Intelligence* (New York: Holt, Rinehart & Winston, 1917), p. 55.

28. JOHN DEWEY, *Reconstruction in Philosophy*, p. 160.

29. JOHN DEWEY, *Experience and Nature* (Chicago: The Open Court Publishing Company, 1925), p. 8.

30. JOHN DEWEY, *Human Nature and Conduct* (New York: Holt, Rinehart & Winston, 1922), p. 30.

31. Ibid., p. 319.

32. Ibid., p. 170.

33. JOHN DEWEY, *Democracy and Education,* (New York: Macmillan, 1916), p. 383.

34. WILLIAM HEARD KILPATRICK, "Philosophy of Education from the Experimentalist Outlook," in the Forty-first Yearbook of the National Society for the Study of Education, *Philosophies of Education* (Chicago: University of Chicago Press, 1942), p. 78.

35. WILLIAM HEARD KILPATRICK, *Foundations of Method* (New York: Macmillan, Inc., 1925).

36. JOHN DEWEY, *Democracy and Education*, p. 225.

37. Ibid., p. 59.

38. JEAN-PAUL SARTRE, *L'Etre et le néant: Essai d'ontologie phénoménologique* (Paris: Gallimard, 1943), p. 500. Translated as *Being and Nothingness* by Hazel E. Barnes (New York: Philosophical Library, 1956).

39. GEORGE F. KNELLER, *Existentialism and Education* (New York: Philosophical Library, 1958), p. 63.

40. SARTRE, *Being and Nothingness*, p. 30.

41. RALPH HARPER, "Significance of Existence and Recognition for Education," in the Fifty-fourth Yearbook of the National Society for the Study of Education, *Modern Philosophies and Education* (Chicago: University of Chicago Press, 1955), p. 227.

42. VAN CLEVE MORRIS, *Existentialism in Education: What It Means* (New York: Harper & Row, Publishers, Inc., 1966), pp. 147–150, makes a brave beginning. He holds, although tentatively, that A. S. Neill's Summerhill is a good illustration of existential theory put to work. See A. S. Neill, *Summerhill: A Radical Approach to Child Rearing* (New York: Hart Publishing Company, 1960).

43. HARPER, "Significance of Existence and Recognition," p. 253.

44. LUDWIG WITTGENSTEIN, *Tractatus Logico-Philosophicus,* trans. D. F. Pears and B. F. McGuinness (New York: Humanities Press, Inc., 1961), 4.003.

45. ALFRED J. AYER, *Language, Truth and Logic* (London: Victor Gollancz, 1946), p. 32.

46. Ibid., pp. 152–153.

47. KENNETH BURKE, "Linguistic Approach to Problems of Education," in the Fifty-fourth Yearbook of the National Society for the Study of Education, *Modern Philosophies and Education* (Chicago: University of Chicago Press, 1955), p. 273.

48. THEODORE BRAMELD, *Patterns of Educational Philosophy: A Democratic Interpretation* (Yonkers-on-Hudson, N.Y.: World Book Company, 1950), p. 564.

49. BURKE, "Linguistic Approach to Problems in Education" p. 301.
50. HERBERT FEIGL, "Aims of Education for Our Age of Science: Reflections of a Logical Empiricist," in the Fifty-fourth Yearbook of the National Society for the Study of Education, *Modern Philosophies and Education* (Chicago: University of Chicago Press, 1955), p. 320.
51. JONAS F. SOLTIS, *An Introduction to the Analysis of Educational Concepts* gives good illustrations of these techniques.
52. FEIGL, "Aims of Education" p. 341.

READINGS

ADLER, MORTIMER J., *Reforming Education: The Schooling of the People and Their Education Beyond Schooling.* Boulder, Colorado: Westview Press, 1977. In Chapter 3 Adler maintains that true freedom has been lost as the aim of education and that false liberalism, the worst enemy of freedom, is still destroying liberal education.

DEWEY, JOHN, *Democracy and Education.* New York: Macmillan, Inc., 1916. So much has been written about Dewey's educational philosophy that one is tempted to depend on commentaries. Yet the best authority is always Dewey himself, and the reader could hardly do better than to consult this book, which has become an American educational classic.

GEIGER, GEORGE R., "An Experimentalist Approach to Education," in the Fifty-fourth Yearbook of the National Society for the Study of Education, Part I, *Modern Philosophies and Education.* Chicago: University of Chicago Press, 1955. Experimentalism —what we have called pragmatism—is presented clearly, directly, and with some charm in Chapter 5.

HARPER, RALPH, "Significance of Existence and Recognition for Education," in the Fifty-fourth Yearbook of the National Society for the Study of Education, Part I, *Modern Philosophies and Education.* Chicago: University of Chicago Press, 1955. Chapter 7 of the yearbook, written by a leading existentialist, is filled with inspirational language about education and the good life.

HUTCHINS, ROBERT M., *Great Books: The Foundations of Liberal Education.* New York: Simon & Schuster, 1954. An education through the great books had its most eloquent champion in Robert Hutchins. As an exponent of rational humanism, he promotes that common theme here.

KERR, DONNA H., *Educational Policy: Analysis, Structure, and Justification.* New York: David McKay Company, 1976. This book illustrates connections between analytic philosophy and educational policy.

KILPATRICK, WILLIAM H., "Philosophy of Education from the Experimentalist Outlook," in the Forty-first Yearbook of the National Society for the Study of Education, Part I, *Philosophies of Education.* Chicago: University of Chicago Press, 1942. Kilpatrick wrote extensively on education and educational philosophy. His vision of experimentalism, or pragmatism, is represented briefly but adequately in Chapter 2.

MARITAIN, JACQUES, *Education at the Crossroads.* New Haven: Yale University Press, 1943. Over the past several years religious humanists have been relatively silent, so one looks almost in vain for recent books illustrating this position in educational philosophy. It would be hard to believe that any book, either new or old, could state the position more clearly and cogently than this.

MARITAIN, JACQUES, "Thomist Views on Education," in the Fifty-fourth Yearbook of the National Society for the Study of Education, Part I, *Modern Philosophies and Education.* Chicago: University of Chicago Press, 1955. In a briefer, although no less effective, treatment of the subject, Maritain reaffirms the philosophical position taken in *Education at the Crossroads.*

MORRIS, VAN CLEVE, *Existentialism in Education: What It Means.* New York: Harper & Row, Publishers, Inc., 1966. Existentialism, the author writes, "is a theory of individual meaning. It asks each man to ponder the reason for his existing." Yet, despite this inherent subjectivism, Morris succeeds in giving us a clear view of existential educational philosophy in Chapter 5.

PETERS, RICHARD S., ed., *The Philosophy of Education.* London: Oxford University Press, 1973. The reader should pay close attention to the chapters in this collection that undertake to clarify educational aims. All the chapters are written from the perspective of analytic philosophy.

SCHEFFLER, ISRAEL, *Reason and Teaching.* London: Routledge & Kegan Paul, 1973. Chapter 1 considers the prospects for an analytic philosophy of education.

SOLTIS, JONAS F., *An Introduction to the Analysis of Educational Concepts.* Reading, Mass.: Addison-Wesley Publishing Co., Inc., 1968. A brief introduction to the techniques of analysis and their use.

5

CONTEMPORARY THEORIES OF SCHOOLING

W hen we turn our attention, however briefly, away from educational philosophy to theories of schooling, we are confronted with an approach to education whose value is derived not from its quality but from the circumstances that attend its development. Humanism, behaviorism, essentialism, and neoprogressivism, all current and controversial, frequently usurp philosophy's place in the vanguard of education's purpose and dominate the day-to-day functions of schools. If philosophy's voice is mute and if these theories of schooling build their pedagogical castles unwisely, if they rely too much on the lath and plaster of fancy to fill the gaps between the bricks of fact, strictures will be piled on their heads by their critics. Sometimes such criticism will be undeserved, for these theories are almost certainly promoted by good and decent people, but at other times, we must understand, the sentiment of humanity and the urge for personal decency standing alone unsupported by philosophical foundations may be insufficient to give sinew and direction to an undertaking so vast as the education of the people.

At the outset, then, we should try to test the meaning of a theory of schooling and see how it differs from a philosophy of education.

Theory of Schooling vis-à-vis Educational Philosophy

There is a tendency to believe, and this belief may not be far off the mark, that theories of schooling take possession of educational ground left forfeit by educational philosophy. We have seen time and again how long it takes philosophy to travel the short distance from the library to the classroom, and when pedagogical issues are pressing, teachers may refuse to put up with delay. Besides, as we follow the various avenues of educational philosophy, we have some reason to suppose that they do not always lead directly to the school practices in which teachers and students are engaged. In a word, educational philosophy may be too antiseptic; it may either be unable to or refuse to engage in the rough and tumble of daily life in the classroom. There is, moreover, the temptation for educational philosophy to become esoteric, to stay too long on the level of theory, and sometimes to dwell on theory whose relationship to actual school practice is unclear or remote. Dewey may have been right when he charged philosophy, especially philosophies of education, politics, and economics, with being indifferent to the burning issues of the day.

All this may tell us something about lapses into ineptitude and the intellectual indiscretion of educational philosophy. It does not tell us much, however, about the difference between educational philosophy and theories of schooling.

Educational Philosophy's Investment. We know where educational philosophy makes its investment. We know it concerns itself with the nature of persons to be educated. We know of its determination to speak about the objectives of education and about the means to achieve these objectives. We know, moreover, of its interest in method, of its interest in setting purely pedagogical priorities and accommodating them to scholastic purpose without becoming preoccupied with their formulation.

Where educational philosophy plays down method to inflate the importance of goals and curricula, to deal with questions of why and what to teach, a theory of schooling concentrates its attention on method, on the actual practices of teaching and learning.

No theory of schooling could be totally indifferent to the nature of the person to be educated; nor could it dispense with such issues as educational purpose and the knowledge to be communicated in a curriculum, for with a stance of indifference on these points it could hardly qualify as a theory at all. But short of this, a theory of schooling—whether humanism, behaviorism, essentialism, or neoprogressivism—is prepared to take for granted what in the custody of educational philosophers are fundamental issues. No humanist or behaviorist goes much beyond psychology to authenticate a view of the nature of the person; and no essentialist or neoprogressive argues much about the nature of knowledge or tries to erect an epistemological citadel to be surrounded by a curriculum. And none of the theories of schooling appears disposed to submit its pronouncements on schooling to a severe and searching scrutiny of linguistic analysts or logical empiricists.

Emphasis on Classroom Management. True, all these fundamentals may be buried away somewhere in the archives of theories of schooling, but there is no temptation to take explicit philosophical stands in connection with any of them. Exponents of these theories take schools, teachers, and students as they find them and, with a kind of mysticism about the power of education and force of schooling to achieve an immense amount of good, undertake to impose on the schools new, sometimes radical, methods with respect to their conduct. In the last analysis, we may be talking about classroom management more than anything else when we introduce theory of schooling. Yet it is principally in the classroom where the drama of education is played, so one would be wrong, despite the importance of educational philosophy to a decent program of education, to ignore the consequences of a theory of schooling. And this applies, we should think, even when such theories are called exercises in an elaboration of classroom management.

Put differently, a theory of schooling tells a teacher what should be done in the classroom, but it does not overly concern itself with any of the philosophical issues forming a basis for this advice. Theories of schooling may eventually run dry of inspiration and effectiveness, for some time or other pedagogical practice has to draw sustenance from a systematic view of life and education's place in it. But for the time being, fortified by convictions about what is best for children as they meet their teachers in the nation's schools, more attention is paid to theories of schooling than to philosophies of education. This, as we have suggested, is due in part to the inability of educational philosophy to speak a language of pedagogical application, but it is also due in part to the promotion of various theories of schooling and to the popularization of notions about education that conspire to make them attractive.

Novelty and Innovation.   Finally, because theories of schooling remain largely indifferent to abstract and abstruse philosophical issues, they leave teachers—and in the long run all manner of school personnel—free to exploit novelty and innovation. If this educational age has earned any single characterization, it must be innovation. Change is the watchword of educational adequacy; anyone ignoring change is bound, so the story goes, to be inadequate as an educator. Since it lacks a philosophical platform to which it must pay intellectual allegiance, a theory of schooling is able to exploit the image of being up-to-date or, better, ahead of its time. By wearing a face of currency and novelty, theories of schooling have captured the fancy of the nation's educators and are serious competitors with philosophies of education as they wrestle for the prize of scholastic allegiance.

HUMANISM

The word *humanism* has multiple connotations as it is pressed into service in various contexts, so it is easy to be misled by the pretensions of a vaguely defined humanism and even easier when humanism is not defined at all. We have met humanists before. Plato is called a scientific humanist; Isocrates a literary humanist; there were the great classical humanists—Erasmus, for example—of the fourteenth and fifteenth centuries. All together, although the means devised for doing so were different, they invested their best energy and talent to improve the condition of humanity. They stressed the inestimable worth of the good life and sought educational and other means to ensure its realization.

The religious and rational humanists we have met work along the same lines to achieve the highest level of human and social decency. For religious humanists the formula is often hard to discover, since in their search for the good and happy life they must maintain a delicate balance between temporal and eternal values and, as we have seen, these values appear sometimes to conflict. Rational humanists, we know, are confident of the ability of a trained reason to handle the affairs of life in such ways that human decency will be assured.

The humanism we want to illustrate now has something in common with its earlier forebears: It, too, maintains an unalterable commitment to the good life. But where earlier forms of humanism undertook to find models of human excellence in the scientific, literary, religious, or intellectual tradition and imitate them, what we shall call romantic humanism exudes an abundance of self-sufficiency and self-confidence. Tilting on the verge of arrogance it turns its back on the past, finds nothing of much worth in tradition, and justifies the motives of each person to find his own satisfaction in a face-to-face confrontation with reality. In the last analysis, traditional values are jettisoned; life is a personal adventure, and the best preparation for this adventure is the freedom a person enjoys in his education to actualize those potentialities that are distinctively personal. It is not easy to be clear about romantic humanism, but it should be evident at the outset that there is no dependent relationship between it and any of the other kinds of humanism we are familiar with.

Romantic Humanism's Common Theme

The single tree of educational reform circled by all contemporary humanists of this camp is that today's schools are bad and are in grave danger of becoming worse. So the common theme of romantic humanism is exhibited in a criticism of the schools. One does not have to sample much of the literature of the past decade for evidence along these lines. We could begin with John Holt's *How Children Fail* or *Freedom and Beyond*[1] and continue with such books as William Glasser's *Schools Without Failure,*[2] Jonathan Kozol's *Death at an Early Age,*[3] Charles E. Silberman's *Crisis in the Classroom,*[4] Herbert Kohl's *The Open Classroom,*[5] Neil Postman and Charles Weingartner's *The School Book,*[6] George Leonard's *Education and Ecstacy,*[7] and Carl Rogers' *Freedom to Learn*[8] without losing this critical train of thought.

These and other current promoters of romantic humanism touch what is often a tender nerve among American educators and, while there is an abundance of hyperbole to salt the dish of astringent assertion served up about contemporary schools, there is also just about the right proportion of the condiment of truth to make their argument palatable and persuasive. The common front is illustrated best in the charge that schools neglect scholastic individualization. Anyone who takes the trouble to look into the matter knows how overwhelming the

evidence from educational psychology is on the side of individual human differences. We need not recite a litany of these differences now, nor should we be
captivated by the belief that human individuality is a contemporary invention.
We know about it, of course, but our ancestors knew about it too. The point is,
romantic humanists declare, that with all this knowledge at our disposal the schools act in a manner that seems to ignore the fact of individual differences. Schools, they pronounce with the utmost conviction, are little more than
assembly lines perpetuating a conspiracy against individuality by accepting a
commission to produce a standard product. This neglect of individualization is
dehumanizing and makes it impossible for anyone to set a compass course toward
human decency.

This indifference to personal disposition, to unique talent, and to private
inventiveness, if it were the only complaint against current educational practice,
would be bad enough, but there is more. Most of what is paraded as a sound
education is considered by these humanists to be irrelevant. They know, as do we
—for they are clever, highly literate people—that relevance is hard to certify in
general and impossible to certify in particular cases. What is relevant for you may
be irrelevant for me. If this is the case, as it must often be, why should I be put
in a position to prescribe your educational interests and dispositions or, conversely, why should you be allowed to dictate mine? In the end, and for anyone
who distills the meaning of relevance on a purely personal level, there can be no
general answer unless it is that everyone must render a private verdict on educational relevance. Throwing open the door so wide as to allow every interest of
every student, every personal judgment about what has worth and what has none,
to be satisfied in the school is bound to put an enormous burden on schools. To
accommodate such interests and dispositions the curriculum would have to be
designed with an exceptionally comprehensive character, and even then it might
not contain every experience to satisfy the extensive and various appetites of all
students.

Thought, romantic humanists declare, is the genius of educational aim. But
as they survey the country's schools today, they find this genius of purpose sorely
neglected. The point is more psychological than philosophical: Thought, it is said,
is generated in the froth and foam of personal experience; it is shaped on the
crucible of real, not fictional, problems. We learn to think as we learn to do
anything else, by thinking. And if, in the course of scholastic experience, we never
have any practice in thinking, if we never have any real problems to wrestle on
an intellectual level, we shall always be in a position of being short changed
educationally.

The charges against the schools are drawn in indictments of various kinds, and
all have the appearance of substance and the support of some evidence. Yet, the
most serious indictment of all is that schools as presently constituted are a sheer
waste of time. Some humanists, therefore, carry their recommendation for educational reform to an ultimate, and from their point of view a logical, end: the
abandonment of schools altogether, a deschooling of American society.

Justification for Humanism

Sensing the need for some theoretical foundation upon which to rest their educational propositions, humanists repair to philosophy and psychology, but their association with philosophy is brief and disappointing, with almost the single exception of a sane and balanced view respecting the important distinction between schooling and education.

No one who thinks seriously about education is eager to assert any monopoly for schooling, yet the underground of educational thought in recent decades has clearly and perhaps convincingly promoted schooling to the pinnacle of social endeavor. The disposition to believe that the person who is unschooled must therefore be uneducated and, moreover, that the only decent preparation for life, whether vocational life or life in general, is found in schools is current. Humanists bristle at such talk. For them the schools are important—some humanists concede essential—but they are unable to account for everything. Social interaction is the great educator, humanists declare, so most of our education generally occurs in society. The school, if managed properly, can be of immense help to us as we travel the road to educational decency, but too much of genuine value in learning to live well can never be codified in a school's curriculum. Besides, unless schools are very carefully managed, they may in fact be repressive; rather than contributing to education, schooling may too often be an obstacle to it. Not many humanists go so far as to recommend the abolition of schools, but every humanist is serious in admonishing us to curb their pretensions.

Humanism and Philosophy. Few humanists are eager to shape any systematic philosophy of education, and many of them worry about the stultifying effect such systemization could have on educational aspiration.[9] Yet, when one looks around for philosophies of education to which romantic humanism could pay allegiance there is really only one with the temperament to be appealing. It is existentialism.

Before we go too far along this line, however, and become too enthusiastic about a wedding of existentialism and humanism, we should pause to get our bearings: At best, existentialism's advice to education is vague. After adverting to existentialism's fundamental subjectivism and personalism, not much remains on the level of philosophical principle for application to any theory of schooling. And humanists, for the most part, need no reminder from us on this point, so their relationship to existentialism, rather than being one based on theory, is based instead on a sentiment of humanity. In time humanists may claim existentialism as their philosophical creed, but that time has yet not come.[10]

Humanism and Psychology. The psychological foundations for humanism are somewhat clearer and, to some extent, they arise as a reaction to behaviorism's enthusiasm for interpreting the whole of human activity on a purely mechanical basis. Behaviorists refuse to worry very much about how their psychological theories affect the balance sheet of life, for they reject almost totally anything in the conduct of life—in behavior—that is unamenable to the probing of empirical

161

technique. If humanists are unwilling to put their trust in God's hands, they are also unable to invest confidence in the scientists.[11] Laws of behavior, however informative they may be in general, fail to account for particular responses in a person's life. Where behaviorism is irrepressible in accumulating data on which hypotheses about life and education, about living and learning, can be based, humanism slides off in the direction of private experience. Abraham Maslow and Carl Rogers may be taken as spokesmen for a humanistic psychology that rejects the psychology of science in favor of the psychology of the person.[12]

Science can keep a record of what people do; it can never probe the reasons for their action. And when humanists come to the issue of human motive, they pay close attention to the pronouncements of Jean Piaget on the affective side of life.[13] Turning to the matter of schooling and education, they are ready to assign top priority to affective education. The warp and the woof of personal, individualized education is imbedded in curiosity, discovery, and freedom. These are the sides to human personality that the school must allow full range. The secrets of curiosity are not revealed to the scientific psychologist; the clues promoting discovery are hidden from the behaviorist; and the freedom to shape and advance one's motives can only be curtailed and suffocated by the arrogant claims of philosophers. Personal life is more private than any committed scientist can imagine, so if we want an education for our children enabling them to develop wholesome personalities, we must, in the end, depend upon a psychology of the person rather than a psychology of science.

In any case, humanist learning theory makes capital out of the old doctrine so long associated with progressive education: We learn by living. There are stages in human development, no humanist doubts this, so some safeguards to a person's freedom to map out his educational course must be erected. But at every stage in the learning process the one thing that counts most is social interaction. We learn, if we learn at all, from direct social experience. And to have such experience an essential educational condition is freedom.[14]

Humanism and Educational Purpose

Humanism's educational character is implied in psychological principles drawn mainly from Abraham Maslow, Carl Rogers, Jean Piaget, and Jerome Bruner;[15] it is a good deal more explicit when we get to schooling. At the risk of repetition, we recall the nature of humanism's investment in schooling: Affirming its importance, humanists, nevertheless, argue for a comprehensive approach to education and are disinclined to assign to schools anything more than an instrumental role in the educational process.[16] Yet as instruments, schools must coordinate their activities with those of a broadly conceived educational process. How can schools do this unless their current character is modified? So humanism's principal thrust is to alter the character of schools, and to the extent it succeeds, a new American school comes into our line of vision.

Self-Actualization. Throughout a good part of education's history, schools were in the habit of accepting a commission preparing students for life. Had this assignment been properly understood, humanists maintain, contemporary schools would be spared overhaul, but the assignment unfortunately was misunderstood. Schools took their cues from life in adult society and forgot about the needs of children. The standard of scholastic achievement was stated in language with meaning for mature persons.

Humanists are committed to redressing this archaic approach, so they fly the flag of child-centered schooling. The child's school life is to be shaped and reshaped according to personal motive, interest, and disposition. And this shaping is always something more than a transmission of knowledge and skill whose utilitarian value is authenticated in an adult economic world. It takes into account the physical, emotional, and social formation of human beings as well as their intellectual and moral development. Put differently, humanistically inspired education essays to leave nothing out, although there is no pretension here: Everything cannot be crowded into a school's curriculum. Good education also occurs outside schools.

Persons are unique in their capacities; their urges, drives, and motives are private and, moreover, precious. The kind of education promoted by humanists, a kind where schooling plays some role, begins at the child's level of experience, pays attention to his motives and interests, gives him the opportunity to realize his distinctive abilities, and in the end, prepares him to live an effective life in human society. Realizing their own personal objectives makes students sensitive to the personal objectives of others, and this kind of education sets the stage for an open and humane society, one where social and moral decency are ratified in the experiences of a good life rather than by legal codes and rigid conventions.

Affective Education.   To talk about self-actualization and to ignore foundational knowledge and skill on which it must necessarily rest is to recommend a school program whose reward will be hard to find. Humanistic educators are keenly aware of this, so they are eager to endorse what in old-fashioned schools is called solid learning. When they do, however, they mean to put opportunity for this kind of learning in a new context. Cognitive achievement must arise in a learning process where the problems one will meet in out-of-school life are met by students in school, but always on a level where they have meaning and where students may be expected to develop a general intellectual competence.

Knowledge is important, no humanist denies this, but feeling must be attended to as well. The emotions play an immensely important role in our personal and social lives, and unless we have learned to both exploit the latent energy in and control the direction of our emotions, we shall be poorly educated. The environment of the school must be open, warm, and friendly. The school must be a nice place, a place where children want to be, and a place where they are convinced they can learn something useful. It must, moreover, be a place where they shall have every opportunity to develop their self-image, where they may come to understand themselves and, accomplishing this, to understand others. The school's scholastic arena must be openly liberal, one where personal aspiration can be translated to personal reality. But there is more. Individualism is prized and should be allowed to reap its reward, yet individualism must not be licensed to trample the legitimate objectives of community life.

So as students in schools struggle for the realization of self-image, they are aided and abetted by their out-of-school experience. If this total educational experience is successful, it will have developed in them a capacity for self-criticism, and it will have made them amenable to criticism from their colleagues. An open school, after all, is only a prelude to an open society. In both, human sensitivity is exceptionally important.

Sensitivity training in education had its origin with psychological entrepreneurs of the past decade or so, and from that source it was channeled to humanistic education. Sensitivity training is a means, so many humanists think, of enabling persons to develop a sharper insight into their own personalities and dispositions. We need not go into the particulars of sensitivity training here, but we should add that, while humanists are disposed to exploit its possibilities, they are also alert to its dangers. Sensitivity training in humanistic schools, then, must be managed carefully and supervised closely by teachers aware of its potential for good and the danger, when badly handled, of its doing severe damage to some students.

Freedom. The academic watchword of humanism is freedom for students to make the most of their educational opportunity. If freedom is taken seriously, students will not be hemmed in by archaic school practice, and they will not be enslaved by a school syllabus committed totally to the communication of knowledge. We have seen enough to convince us of the breadth of humanism's educational vision. Yet this vision is bound to be clouded in school programs with petty rules and regulations, with oppressive curtailment of personal development, and with a custodial attitude about students being in school in the first place. Nothing infuriates humanists more than an educational creed putting and keeping students in a school's custody until their age or skill recommends their release to the realities of life.

Moral Formation. Humanism is deeply indebted to the naturalism first promoted by Jean Jacques Rousseau.[17] Human nature was dispensed from any need for repair; it never required the help of learning to distinguish good from evil or the exhortation to embrace the former and shun the latter. The written or unwritten manifesto of humanism pronounces the intrinsic goodness of human nature, a nature susceptible of contamination only from social infection. So the school's role in moral formation is to provide those opportunities enabling girls and boys to have experience in weighing matters of personal value; from this experience they will learn how to make their own decisions as to what has worth and what has none.

The thesis of humanism is one wherein moral disposition is learned through experience, and it rejects theological doctrines ascribing natural moral weakness to human beings. Every means at the school's disposal, as it couples its activities with those of education generally, should be recruited to equip students to shape personal moral codes and to base their judgments on them.

Discovery and Creativity. Children, humanists declare, are naturally curious and eager to learn. There is a good deal of testimony from reputable psychologists, not to mention the common experience of mankind, to support this sensible thesis. Curiosity should be capitalized on in every learning situation. It is the school's obligation to allow it full freedom to range and to refuse to curtail it on the authority of some scholastic rule or regulation or of some *a priori* commitment to mastering bodies of knowledge.

Every person has a measure of distinctive talent. On a universal scale of human creativity the talent of a particular person may not be extraordinary, yet it is a prized personal possession and should be accorded a chance to ripen. This is what is meant when humanists talk about creativity; they are not referring to artistic or scientific invention, nor are they preoccupied with the prospect of cultivating genuine genius.

Mental Health. Not only do conventional school practices interpose themselves between students and decent learning, they also put misplaced emphasis on certain outcomes of learning. Since, it is alleged, these learning outcomes only infrequently have anything to do with what children are curious about and interested in learning, failure is too often an inevitable consequence. In those cases where failure is skirted, fear of failure becomes a substitute for genuine motivation. Experience of failure, which is totally unnecessary, and motivation by fear of failure, humanists allege, is responsible for confusion, irresponsibility, and distortion in youthful personality. Mental health is impaired and too frequently jeopardized by convention in the schools; by following humanistic school practice, it is protected, for humanism refuses to perpetuate a split between personal life and school life. By making the two one, the mental health of persons and, as a bonus, the good of communities are enhanced.

Good Citizenship. Humanists want education to form good persons; the better persons are, the better societies will be. Responsible, alert, sensitive, and thoughtful people will make social and political life decent, and such people can only be developed through the good offices of an educational program following the pedagogic creed of humanism.

The Curriculum of Humanistic Schools

Humanists, unfortunately, are not very specific about the kinds of scholastic experiences capable of ensuring the purposes of education they promote. We have the impression that knowing, feeling, and willing are all-important to them. They are certainly sincere when they advocate an education for the good life; they are surely sensitive to the need for knowledge and skill if the good life is to be achieved. They endorse the broadest possible learning, and we have the impression that nothing of interest to students is left out. The point though, and one worth making, is that curricula in humanist schools are not foreordained. What students study should be available to them in the rich environment of a school having more the appearance of a learning laboratory than a classroom. The old subjects so long associated with the curriculum fade into disuse and disappear.

Illustrations of Humanistic Schools

The classic illustration of a humanistic school is, of course, Summerhill, founded by A. S. Neill in the 1920s. Humanists are usually generous in their praise of Neill's institution, and many of their cues for schooling come from Neill's account of Summerhill. Considering that Neill's book is well known and generally available, we shall not try here to summarize the humanistic education it describes.[18]

In the United States, without any special schools on which to depend, humanistic education has been given its best test in the open classroom. The authentic open classroom, its inventors allege, is one stripped of teachers' authoritarianism and academic dogmatism. Students pursue their own interests in an orderly way and observe academic regulations they themselves devise. The environment for learning is rich, and students, attracted by personal motives, are tempted to make the most of it. Teachers stay in the background as much as possible; in fact, they never intrude upon learning. But they are available as versatile and informed resource persons and are ready, when asked, to give students the kind of instruction they want to satisfy their scholastic appetites.

The possibilities for this kind of free and open education are enormous, especially when highly motivated, superior students are involved, but some critics declare, sometimes derisively, "that the popular advocates of open education are struggling to move from one myth to another . . . and that . . . since the struggle is frequently without awareness, numerous fallacies are committed and more numerous blind spots are evidenced."[19]

Figure 5.1
A Synoptic View of Romantic Humanism

Theme	Contemporary schooling neglects personal motive and individualized teaching. As such, it is largely irrelevant.
Educational Purpose	Capitalizing on freedom to learn, education has the goal of promoting self-actualization, affective development, and moral formation. These goals lay a foundation for an effective human life.
Curriculum	The range of study is potentially extensive and comprehensive, but the curriculum is organized on the basis of student interest rather than prescribed subjects.
Method	Creativity and discovery are promoted in order to exploit the natural curiosity of students. Method must be deployed to whet, and never to repress, curiosity.
The Place of Students	By exercising personal freedom in the school's society and in controlling their own education, students will learn the fundamentals of personal and social responsibility.
The Role of Teachers	Teachers are cooperating agents in schooling who, without genuine educational authority, are commissioned to create learning situations and make them available to students.

BEHAVIORISM

Theories of schooling compete for the allegiance of educators but, we should think, none is more active in soliciting their attention than behaviorism. In an educational age disposed to attach a great deal of significance to science, behaviorism has the apparent advantage of almost impeccable empirical credentials.

Foundations in Theory

In Chapters 3 and 4 we heard philosophers arguing about the nature of reality, and we met metaphysical propositions ranging from the most extreme form of subjective idealism to the most basic kind of common-sense realism. Making an investigation into behaviorism, there is little to keep us long with metaphysics, for behaviorists, without exception, belong to the camp of common-sense realism. A real world exists entirely independent of any relationship persons have with it, and its operations are regulated by certain natural physical laws. By using our senses we can have knowledge of physical reality, but no behaviorist raises serious questions about the nature of the psychological, physiological, and physical relationship between knowers and things known.

This common-sense or naive realism is bound to cause philosophers, especially epistemologists, a good deal of trouble, and it leads to considerable criticism of behaviorism's abandonment of philosophy. But behaviorists are little deterred by criticism from philosophers, for they are indisposed to take philosophy seriously. They are eager, instead, to invest their intellectual confidence in the scientific method.

In addition to a human being's ability to come in contact with reality and to obtain knowledge from this transaction, behaviorists assert the possiblity of attaining knowledge about the design and order in nature imposed by physical law. Here, of course, the most dependable, perhaps the only, means for obtaining such knowledge are found in science.

At the outset, then, we find behaviorism discounting the role any philosophy can play in life and education. Under these circumstances, it would be indeed surprising were behaviorists to accept responsibility for designing and promoting educational philosophy. So when behaviorists refuse the title of educational philosophers, we should be careful about thrusting it on them.

Freedom and Determinism. Yet there is a side to behaviorism, despite the demurrals of its proponents, that cannot be dismissed as being totally unphilosophical. This side is freedom or, put another way, it is the contest between freedom and determinism. Behaviorists are entirely forthright: Free will, despite all the good things philosophers over the ages have claimed for it, is only an illusion. We act as if we are free; and we think along lines endorsing the notion of freedom. But if we knew enough about the causes in the world, about those things making us act as we do, we would know that determinism, not freedom, is the right explanation of human conduct. We are determined to do certain things and not to do others by the physical and social environment. We are what we are and we do what we do, not because of any mysterious power of human volition, but because outside forces over which we lack any semblance of control have us caught in an inflexible web. Whatever else we may be, we are not the captains of our fate or the masters of our soul.

Behaviorism's philosophical foundations are not set very deeply, as we see, but there are psychological foundations that provide substance and support for a theory undertaking to explain how human beings function. One need not stop to excavate behaviorism's origin in the archives of psychology's history, but we can be fairly confident that John B. Watson (1878–1958) was its principal modern elaborator; and Edward L. Thorndike's (1874–1949) connectionism played an important role in promoting a mechanistic and behavioral outlook in psychology. The contemporary exponent of behaviorism and its most eloquent herald is B. F. Skinner (b. 1904).[20]

Behaviorism's Appeal to Science.   Whether one pays attention to Watson or Skinner, the general thesis is the same. Whatever can be known about human beings must come from an observation of behavior, for there is no other source, and this observation of behavior, moreover, must be conducted according to the strict methods of scientific procedure that are used in the physical sciences.

Infected by a scientific spirit, behaviorists of all shades of opinion rally in support of the assertion that the modern world stands as the beneficiary of science and technology, and that in the absence of scientific technique we should all be living in a world where progress halted somewhere in the sixteenth century. Experimental science, they say, has rewarded us amply, and to certify this pronouncement all we need do is look around. If we applied the same scientific techniques to human behavior as we have to physics, biology, chemistry, and engineering, we should be rewarded even more handsomely. Where humanists complain about an overemphasis on scientific technique applied to the human condition, leading, they allege, to a brutalizing of human beings, behaviorists reverse this thrust to assert that science has not been used enough, or has not been used properly, for collecting and testing data belonging to the discipline of psychology.

Behaviorists, then, in essaying to be true to their fundamental thesis, refuse to consider as part of psychology anything not susceptible of examination in the laboratory or of validation according to authentic scientific methods. This means, of course, that introspection, mind, intellect, will, feeling, emotion, motivation, and all such things, so long part of psychology's repertoire, must be excluded from serious consideration by behaviorists. What is left is observable behavior. There is no time for speculation or for philosophizing about the nature of human nature.

All this sounds harsh, and its most obvious implication is that human beings are substantially identical with all other kinds of life. They are more complex, it is true, and as a result of the functioning of evolution, have achieved certain skills not practiced by less sophisticated animals. But, critics of behaviorism say, this still leaves girls and boys, women and men, as part of the brute kingdom.

The behaviorist's rejoinder sticks close to the scientific data in his possession and he refuses to recant: If the evidence makes women and men part of the brute world, how can complaining about this condition alter the facts? Is it not better to recognize ourselves for what we are, study the way we function, analyze our behavior, and in the end be in a better position to live effective lives than to be dominated by supersitition and myth concerning the faculties, the predispositions, and the spiritual character of our nature? In any case, behaviorists maintain, the knowledge about human life available to us by employing the methods of science does not mean that we must adopt a charter for dehumanizing life. On the contrary, when we know why and under what conditions we behave, we shall be better able to introduce a superior character to life than we can by stumbling along after assumptions without any basis in fact. To believe that we are free when we are not, behaviorists assert, is far more dangerous and intimidating to the effectiveness of life in society than to meet and acknowledge the reality of determinism squarely.

Theory of Schooling

Humanists, we remember, are at pains to distinguish between schooling and education. The school is important, few humanists doubt this, although it plays only an instrumental role in the total educational process. Behaviorists, on the other hand, are supremely confident when they talk about schools' educational prospects and are ready to assign major educational responsibility to them. Where humanists see the educational process as a many-sided, sometimes mysterious, and always a highly personal endeavor, behaviorists operate from a solid conviction that environmental forces responsible for making us what we are must be organized with extreme care and be reactivated in the school's curriculum with the same scientific precision engineers employ when they design a complicated machine. Schooling is a matter, behaviorists insist, of behavioral engineering and, as such, it must never be subordinated to personal disposition and social whim to which, they allege, humanists appeal.

Certain scientifically crafted principles are delegated to superintend the work of schools and the learning activities occurring in them, and these principles add up to behaviorism's theory of schooling.

Empiricism. Behaviorists are ready to follow the lead of common-sense realism: They have perceptions of reality. But this embrace of realism leaves them with a huge problem: verification. No amount of inspection of a statement about a thing or belief tells us whether it is true or false. And on this point of verification, behaviorists do not by any means meet on common ground. Together, of course, they are agreed that scientific method must be employed to arrive at knowledge about anything, for in abandoning scientific method the possibility of certitude, or better, meaning, is foreclosed altogether. But once the data of science, especially data in the science of psychology, are collected, what do they mean? What do they tell us about human nature?

Verification by Consequence. One camp of behaviorism, to which both Watson and Skinner belong, maintains the position that scientific inference—that is, distilling meaning from empirical evidence—needs only a pragmatic justification: Does it work or is it successful? Plausibility appears to support this position. Scientists are able to make predictions, and many of these predictions are later proven to be reliable. The common man, the behaviorist, and the philosopher must concede that science works, for no sane person disputes the contribution science has made and is making to increasing human knowledge by leaps and bounds. Yet at this very point the question must be asked: How can scientific inferences be theoretically justified?

The cadre of behaviorists formed by Watson and Skinner reject the terms of the question. Their rejoinder is that justification beyond the possession of empirical fact is impossible and, in any case, unnecessary. One may object that such an attitude halts inquiry at the very beginning; yet, even then, the facts are that science has delivered the goods. This purely empirical position of one contingent of behaviorists leads to the conclusion that the factual standing of scientific inference is a matter of luck. But this is a hard position for anyone to maintain, least of all the scientific psychologist, for he is looking for dependable interpretations of behavior, and from them he expects to establish certain educational imperatives that in the end will produce the kind of people his scientific elaborations say should be produced. Pure empiricism, philosophers assert, is an inadequate substitute for a theory of knowledge, for it prevents us from generalizing from the data we collect and test; moreover, it prevents us from using such generalizations to move on to further hypotheses to guide our collection of additional data about the human condition. It limits us, as it limits Skinner and his band of followers, to those data that are directly observable. They refuse on principle to deal with any others.

Demonstrative Inference.   Yet another view of verification is entertained by empiricists—those, we should think, who find logical positivism credible—although, as we have implied, its current status is depressed. Data incapable of being verified or falsified are meaningless; any two empirical propositions verified by the same occurrences have the same meaning or significance. But this implies that physical objects grasped by the senses and handled scientifically are moved out of a purely empirical context whenever meaning is sought. Demonstrative inference belongs to logic and perhaps to mathematics; it is not a natural possession of empirical science. So when this camp of behaviorism undertakes to distill meaning from scientific data, when it tries to explain the nature of human behavior, it does so in terms that are not strictly empirical. It moves from scientific fact to generalization and, in doing so, practices the art of demonstrative inference. It is practicing an art designed to find meaning in empirical data.

In some way or other, though, these generalizations must be justified. Of course, not all generalizations, regardless of the luster of their empirical precision, can be justified, because the acid test of experience sometimes proves them false. Yet the behavioral psychologist, if he is disposed to give a coherent explanation of human action, if he is tempted to draw on scientific data for generalizations that have a high degree of probability and are conceded to be genuine inferences from scientific facts, must press on. Here, this side of behaviorism advances beyond the particulars of scientific investigation that dominate Skinner's thought and puts confidence in a verification process that takes testimony from competent observers whose prudence, judgment, and scientific credentials make them expert witnesses. A body of common, scientifically based opinion is the best verification we can hope for.

This kind of verification is dismissed by Skinner as mere fiction. The brand of behaviorism he promotes means to deal only with observable, measurable behavior, and the meaning of this behavior must be found in particular responses rather than in generalizations about them.

In any case, empiricism, adopting either route to verification, gives behaviorists their view of the person, and this view of the person, naturally enough, dominates the practices of schooling they promote. Human nature, in the last analysis, must be defined according to what human beings do. Skinner's version of behaviorism tells us that they do whatever they are conditioned to do.

Conditioning. We should begin by resisting any temptation we may have to reject conditioning as an authentic explanation of some aspects of human behavior. Yet to concede that some of our responses are based on conditioning is a long way from admitting that all human learning is illustrated in the empirical details of the conditioned response. This, though—to explain learning as conditioning —is what contemporary behaviorism, as it marches under a banner hoisted by B. F. Skinner, proposes to do. Depending heavily, too heavily we should think, on the law of parsimony, behaviorists seek the simplest explanation for learning —indeed for all human behavior—and, after having demonstrated the efficacy of this explanation with respect to experimentally induced animal response and to some types of human response, embrace it as an explanation for all human learning and behavior.

Such reductionism turns out to be offensive to scores of psychologists and philosophers who have been unable to find convincing evidence in human life verifying any proposition making girls and boys, women and men, the abject victims of stimulus–response behavior. Although humanists and others may be profoundly insulted by this explanation of human life, their reaction, however much it may appeal to us, does not give us much insight into a behavioral analysis of human action wherein conditioning is always given pride of place.

Conditioning is a physiological or psychological process, or a combination of the two, where a particular stimulus, originally incapable of producing a certain response, is matched with a stimulus that in the natural course of events does produce this response. An unconditioned stimulus produces an unconditioned response, but the matched or conditioned stimulus, after repeated pairings with the unconditioned stimulus, produces a conditioned response. The point to notice, of course, is that, in the course of training, a stimulus that originally lacked the force to produce a certain response becomes able to do so. The classic instance of conditioning illustrated by Ivan Pavlov's (1849–1936) experiment is almost too well known to bear repetition, yet its very familiarity makes it especially effective as an example.

Type S Conditioning.   Pavlov noticed that a dog with which he was experimenting would salivate when it saw food about to be given to it. By introducing the sound of a bell at the same time the food was offered and by repeating this pairing of the bell and the food several times, Pavlov discovered that the sound of the bell would make the dog salivate. The bell (a conditioned stimulus), was able to produce salivation (now a conditioned response). Technical language later dubbed this as type S conditioning, and it was this kind of conditioning that John B. Watson adopted to explain the whole of learning. It prompted him, moreover, to boast that if a young child were put in his custody he could condition the child to become anything he wanted to make it. Watson, of course, never tested his boast, so his bold claim lacks the essential support of empirical verification—which all behaviorists should honor—yet he set in motion a corpus of psychological belief that has earned the designation of behavioral engineering.

Contemporary behaviorists, Skinner chief among them, are not able to endorse Watson's confidence in type S conditioning; yet they do concede that in the last analysis we are all the products of environmental conditioning. We may be ignorant of the environmental forces shaping us; we may be totally unaware of their molding influence. Shaping nevertheless occurs. The only problem—it turns out to be a great one—is that in the absence of our recognition of the fact of conditioning, we shall be shaped in a haphazard, purely accidental way. The formula for redressing the danger and intimidation of environmental accident is to plan the environment so that it will contain forces—stimuli—capable of making us good and effective human beings. The principal work of schools, for they are chiefly responsible for education, is to mold environmental forces and not leave the development of human beings to chance. This, Skinner and his behavioral engineering compatriots assert, is only a way of acting intelligently and responsibly.

Type R Conditioning.   Yet at this point of environmental determinism behaviorists find classical or type S conditioning inadequate. A more sophisticated and complicated type R conditioning is introduced and is called operant conditioning. According to Skinner, operant conditioning accounts for most of human behavior. And by operant conditioning, which differs from Watson's classical conditioning, he means that behavior operates on the environment to produce a response, and if the response is rewarding in some way, the process of conditioning is reinforced. In operant, or instrumental, conditioning the response is always the critical factor in reinforcement. But this causes trouble for some behaviorists who try to follow Skinner: He refuses to introduce any evaluation, such as satisfying or annoying, to characterize or to measure the quality of the response. If a response is followed by certain consequences it tends to appear more frequently, and this is about as far as Skinner is willing to go.

Thorndike's Laws of Learning.   Edward L. Thorndike, who preceded Skinner in this enigmatic behavioral field, handled the matter of evaluating the quality of responses somewhat more directly and in a way easier for us to understand. Formulating the law of effect, Thorndike demonstrated that certain responses were more satisfying than others and, as a result, were reinforced. This law of effect may have only certified a common belief that we tend to do those things that give us satisfaction and avoid those things that are displeasing, yet it stood for a long time as a central plank in Thorndike's connectionistic platform. Contemporary behaviorists, however, refuse to use any language not describing an observable response, so according to their lexicon such things as satisfaction and annoyance, in addition to having a nonscientific character, introduce the interesting, but entirely unproductive, phenomenon of speculation. When we begin to ask why a person responds in a certain way, we are speculating about human behavior. But all we are commissioned to do, according to a strict empirical dictum, "is to classify the event as reinforcing to the organism under the existing conditions."[21]

In any case, with or without speculation, reinforcement plays an immensely important role in operant, or instrumental, conditioning, and it is here we should expect to find the principal implications for a theory of schooling.

Reinforcement.   Behaviorism begins from a dogmatic assumption that all behavior is conditioned; how we behave depends on the extent to which our responses are reinforced. And they can be reinforced positively or negatively. Contemporary behaviorists are reluctant to use evaluative words, such as *satisfaction, pleasure, dissatisfaction,* and *annoyance,* to describe why some things are done and why others are shunned, but in the last analysis, short of behavior occurring in a vacuum, it is hard to imagine a person repeating action unless its outcome gives pleasure or, conversely, refusing to act or trying to avoid action unless somehow the anticipated outcome displeases him. This may very well be the case, and most behaviorists are probably amenable to this hypothesis, yet they are not disposed to make any analysis of evocative physical or mental states. When such apparently emotional responses accompany behavior, their genesis is not directly observable. Anything outside the realm of the observable and measurable is, of course, unanalyzable, so any conclusions about it would be unscientific and undependable.

In any case, our responses are reinforced by their consequences, and the reinforcement, again using the language of behaviorism, is either positive or negative. If positive, we tend to repeat the response; if negative, we tend to exclude it from our repertoire of behavior. When behaviorists talk about positive and negative reinforcers, they do so, as we have said, without using such psychological terms as *motivation, drives, emotions,* or *feelings,* for, we understand, to introduce such terms is to allow speculation to intrude into an arena of behavior explained solely by an application of scientific method.

Building on the premise that good, effective, decent people can be produced by a scientific application of reinforcement procedures, behaviorists turn to the school and commission it to reconstruct its educational program along lines consistent with the principles of scientific psychology. This leads them to endorse and promote educational programs paying close attention to the rudiments of operant conditioning, and if operant conditioning is to function, a schedule of reinforcement must become an essential part of the science of teaching.

Behavior Modification.   One of the most popular notions associated with contemporary behaviorism is that behavior is amenable to modification. Unless one stops to ponder the implications of this assertion, it has the luster of invention. Yet when one stops to think about it, the idea is not so novel after all. No one has ever doubted that what we learn carries with it the possibility of influencing us, and that such learning is almost certain to penetrate to the level of action. If scholars, scientists, and teachers have not always believed in learning's capacity for modifying behavior, we shall have to look for some other explanation for the investment our ancestors made in education and schooling and, also, for the investment we make today. Yet accompanying this conventional assumption that gives learning a leading role in structuring behavior is the assumption that personal, volitional elements intrude too and, moreover, are influential enough to redirect the course of behavior. We are mainly our own masters, we can argue, and regardless of the force of environmental circumstance, are capable of abstacting meaning from experience and, in the end, choosing our own way.

Contemporary behavior modification theory, planted as it is in empirical psychology, makes learning not the principal force but the only force in directing action. Whatever we are, apart from physiological reflexes, we are as a result of learned response; everything is acquired. So if everything is learned behavior, if nothing is innate, if nothing is left to the control of our will, if choice is eliminated from a human's repertoire, then all behavior can be either learned or unlearned. Watson's bold boast—to mold a child as he pleased—is revived in contemporary behavior modification theory: Following the dictates of operant conditioning and applying techniques of reinforcement, a saint can be turned into a sinner and a sinner can be converted to a saint.

Instructional Implications

For the most part behaviorist theory of schooling eschews arrogant assertions of novelty. What is recommended for learning and teaching, behaviorists say, is nothing more than what good teachers have been doing all along. In the past, of course, good teachers based sound instructional practice on fortuitous intuition, unaffected by the empirical evidence a scientific psychology is now able to supply. Still, elements of empiricism infected their approach to teaching, for following pedagogical instinct they adopted techniques whose worth was tested in their effectiveness. Now, however, behaviorism has an arsenal of scientific pedagogic technique and makes it available for all teachers to use.

Operant Conditioning and Teaching.   Behaviorism puts teachers at the center of the educational stage. As the drama of learning is played, teachers are not merely members of a supporting cast ready to perform when students prompt them. They are neither therapists nor entertainers, although they have a responsibility for making the learning environment pleasant because pleasant surroundings contribute to greater productivity. They are employed to organize a vast array of educational variables in precise and effective ways and thus assure the most essential and dependable results from schooling. We heard humanists tell us to guard against the intrusion of teachers into the highly personal, often private, domain of learning; now we hear behaviorists saying the opposite. Good teaching, they aver, means more, not less, involvement of teachers in directing the learning process.

The old, tired notion of teaching being an art is abandoned. It is a science, behaviorists say, and as with any science, a technical method is essential to its proper functioning. In their proper and prominent role as instructors, teachers are commissioned to communicate a definite, prescribed body of knowledge. Using the technology at their diposal to create conditions favorable to learning, they jettison forever the assumption that trial and error can be justified as a contributor to sound learning. Everything must be done with precision and, of course, with clear purpose. Teachers must know what responses are to be elicited and must know, in addition, what techniques, what elements of conditioning and reinforcement, must be brought to bear in particular situations to achieve the desired results.

Desired results—what the outcome of learning should be and what decently educated students should know—are not within teachers' province to determine nor are they left for students to decide. The range of experience of both teachers and students is too narrow to allow them to make such important decisions. So, in the last analysis, the goals and the purposes of education are to be determined by persons qualified to make such monumental decisions. Only in this way, by putting confidence in the judgment of persons in possession of scientific knowledge about the requirements for a good and wholesome society, can a respectable and responsible educational process be ensured.

In the custody of teachers committed to behaviorism, schools are learning workshops, and teachers are the managers. Having positive knowledge regarding the results to be achieved, they direct their students, using all their knowledge and skill in connection with the elements of conditioned learning, to achieve them. Teachers represent themselves neither as their students' friends nor companions, and never as their equals, but as persons in charge of the serious business of teaching what needs to be known if students are to grow and develop into mature, responsible, moral, and informed persons. Chance in education is repudiated and design takes its place.

Behavioral Objectives. Any educational program following the recommendations of behaviorism is prepared to scuttle the old notion separating knowledge from action, or knowing from doing. Unless knowledge can be translated into observable behavior, it is an orphan in the curriculum of the behaviorist's school.

When this thesis is honored, the curriculum of the school will be organized around clearly stated learning outcomes. Broad, vague objectives will be replaced by specific statements about what students will be able to do when the curriculum is mastered. And this, behaviorists allege, means that teachers must be a good deal clearer about what they are trying to teach than has conventionally been the case. They must abandon such generalizations as *knowing, appreciating,* and *understanding* as objectives and replace them with detailed prospectuses on a behavioral level. Unless teachers define their objectives with precision, unless they demonstrate how their instruction influences behavior, they will be neglecting their commission to educate their students and, what is more, will not be in a position to determine whether their instruction has been effective.

Should teachers object to this approach—should they, for example, argue that some types of learning are immune to behavioral definition—the rejoinder would almost certainly be that unless curriculum content can be illustrated as having application on the level of behavior, it must forfeit its place in the school. "Whatever exists," in the curriculum or elsewhere, behaviorists allege, borrowing a famous line from Thorndike, "exists in some amount. To measure is simply to know its varying amounts."[22] Anything unsusceptible of such identification and measurement perforce does not exist or, if it does, cannot be precise or dependable enough to occupy a role in the curriculum.

Performance-Based or Competency-Based Curricula. These curricula are cultivated by an application of behavioral objectives to college courses devoted to the preparation of teachers. The justification is, of course, that if students in classrooms are to be exposed to a kind of education where behavior figures uppermost in the scholastic process, then teachers in charge of directing this learning must know exactly what they are doing. Their preparation for their profession must be accomplished with the same precision they are expected to employ when they themselves enter the classroom to superintend the learning activities of others. Under these circumstances everything in the curriculum of teacher education must, behavioral engineers assert, subscribe to the general thesis that teachers will have specific skills in their arsenal of pedagogy to direct learning expertly and scientifically.

The moral and cultural appurtenances to the education of teachers, one is persuaded, are not accounted for in technical skill, so Thomas Green is almost certainly on the right track when he endorses practical instructional skill and then asks for something more: in order to direct "successful instruction . . . a teacher is, among other things . . . the occupant of a social role and the holder of a public office. [Teaching's] competent exercise requires more than competence in instruction."[23]

Programmed Instruction. Programmed instruction makes us think of teaching machines or other such devices enabling students to match their responses with those in computers or programmed textbooks. When this technology is used, it is used on the authority of the hypothesis that reinforcement comes quickly, directly, and flawlessly from such machines or devices. Yet programmed instruction need not be defined so narrowly. It may be, most behaviorists say, nothing more than a scientifically prescribed   method used in connection with instruction. And a scientific method is logical, precise, conscious, and deliberate.

In programmed instruction the material to be taught is organized and presented step by logical step. Ample reinforcement is associated with each step, frequent clues keep students on the correct route to learning, and an abundance of drill fixes what is learned or done correctly in the student's mind. Once the parts to a lesson are mastered, they are organized into a single, meaningful whole. Nothing is left out and nothing is left to chance: This is the basic meaning of programmed instruction and, behaviorists maintain, it is the way all good teachers have always taught anyway. They recommend it now as the right method of instruction for all contemporary teachers.

Accountability. Students are sent to school to learn certain necessary things, and schools are accountable to their students, to parents, and to society in general for the character and quality of their performance. When objectives for learning are vague and general—having almost nothing to do with behavior—assigning responsibility for education's failures or rewarding its successes is a confusing exercise. Yet when the outcomes of learning are stated clearly, and when, in addition, the level of student accomplishment is known before instruction begins, it is possible, advocates of accountability argue, to discover who or what is at fault when goals of achievement are missed and who deserves praise when they are met.

Almost every institution in society is expected to deliver the goods, or to fulfill its explicit social commission. The schools' commission is to instruct youth. Now, behaviorists argue, if we know exactly what to expect from instruction on every grade level, we shall be in a position to hold schools, and teachers in them, responsible for their performance.

Competency Testing. We have all read lurid tales of scholastic failure and, in connection with them, we have listened to indictments of the schools. The argument-is often advanced that hundreds of students graduating from high school lack the accomplishment a high school diploma is meant to represent. So a movement, inspired largely in behaviorism, is being mounted in several states to withhold high school diplomas from students unable to pass end-of-course tests. If students fail to demonstrate prescribed competencies, which, it is alleged, encompass what high school graduates should be able to do, they must either remain in school until they meet the standard for a diploma or leave school without one. Although setting a decent educational standard and respecting it in awarding academic honors, such as high school diplomas, has a great deal of good sense on its side, many educators worry about the nature of the competencies to be tested, about who is to define them, and about arrogant claims frequently made for testing.

Although early measurement technique was crude and underdeveloped—hardly more than vague perceptions about student achievement—we can find the genesis of testing among some of history's great teachers. From Quintilian to the medieval university, testing for the most part was an oral exercise. In the eigh-

teenth century written examinations were invented for the schools. In the nineteenth and twentieth centuries testing attained a better status, although never an
untouchable one. Admitting the difficulty of adopting the principles of measurement that were suitable in physical science, educators nevertheless used them to
guide measurement in education. In doing so they were faced with two dissimilar
reactions: One, frankly hostile, declared measurement in education invalid and
demanded its abandonment; the other, more friendly, neglected appeal to theoretical foundations to find support in a "widespread public trust in examinations as
a justification for the kind of measurement used in education."[24] The adoption
of state-wide competency tests for high school graduation depends, we should
think, on the extent to which such testing can be justified in social philosophy and,
also, to the degree of confidence educators can generate in the tests they design
and administer.

A Summary Assessment of Educational Behaviorism

The principal thesis of behaviorism, as we have indicated, makes desirable human
behavior a product of design, not accident. If we want an orderly, humane society
composed of persons well equipped to fulfill various and essential functions, the
case continues, we must depend upon solidly based scientific techniques capable
of educating girls and boys. At this point we should be prepared to admit that
many pedagogic techniques promoted by behaviorists do work: Behavioral engineering's effectiveness in the classroom is a good deal more than educational
myth. Put to the test, although bold and exaggerated claims are sometimes made
by ardent behaviorists, it has delivered on many of its promises. Girls and boys
subjected to a controlled environment can unquestionably be molded; on a larger
scale history tells of the kinds of societies shaped by exigent social and political
methods. This contention may be right: Had we grown up in the Soviet Union
or in the People's Republic of China, we should all be Communists; if the citizens
of those countries had been nurtured in this good land, they would most likely
be either Republicans or Democrats.

Yet, many social, political, and educational philosophers blanch at the prospect of extensive or complete educational control. If human beings are to be
shaped according to the design of behavioral engineers, who is to endow these
engineers with the wisdom to draw their social and human blueprints along
ethical lines? The ethical issues raised by the apparition of behavioral engineering
in education are monumental. It is hard to believe that their resolution is only
a matter of using empirical technique properly, prudently, and precisely. Put
bluntly, who in such a system of extensive social control—where the work of
schools is bound to play a highly significant role—is to define the nature of the
good society?

We have, of course, a fleeting glimpse of what behavioral engineering can do
when we open books on utopian literature. We recall the society described in

Aldous Huxley's (1894–1963) *Brave New World*[25] and are familiar with B. F. Skinner's more recent version of utopia in *Walden Two.*[26] In both books the dimensions of a desirable social order are put on exhibit and illustrate an exaggerated confidence in the ability of society's managers to decide what is best for everyone. The camouflage is effective but not good enough to conceal the suppression of human freedom.

Behaviorism's rejoinder is that freedom is a myth, despite all protestation otherwise. When all is said and done, we are subject to control by something or someone. Is it not better for such control to be exercised by persons whose altruism is evident and who have, in addition, the expert knowledge to shape our destiny correctly?

Moving from broad social and ethical considerations about the kind of society behaviorism would promote if given full control to the level of learning itself, we must wrestle with these issues. For the most part they are called to our attention by humanists, but they have the sympathetic endorsement of other educators as well. Learning, humanists declare, is more than a simple matter of doing certain tasks, of having certain skills, or of behaving in certain ways. Its dimensions and requirements are broader than the kinds of skills behavioral technique is equipped to teach. It must include an ability to think, and it must embrace the immensely complicated matter of affective learning. Neither the ability to think cogently nor the matter of emotional, moral, and personality development is accounted for by conditioning techniques promoted in behaviorism. Some behavior can unquestionably be modified and shaped by conditioning, but human beings are more than mere machines who can be made to operate on the laws of a stimulus–response psychology to which behaviorism must necessarily appeal. In the end, opponents of behaviorism maintain, human life and learning are too complex and too precious to be left in the custody of behavioral engineers, regardless of their

Figure 5.2
Behaviorism in Education

Theme	Good, efficient persons are produced by carefully and scientifically controlled educational processes.
Educational Purpose	Modification of behavior; to prepare persons, according to their capacities, for the multiple responsibilities of personal and social life.
Curriculum	The content of education should be comprised of dependable knowledge organized always according to behavioral objectives.
Method	All learning is conditioning. Type R conditioning: operant conditioning, reinforcement, programmed instruction, competency.
The Place of Students	Freedom is a myth. Our behavior is determined by forces we may neither recognize nor control. Such being the case, education by design is superior to education by accident. Students are being prepared for life. They should be required to learn.
The Role of Teachers	Teachers have authority to design and control the educational process. They are accountable for the quality and character of student achievement.

scientific aptitude and pedagogical credentials and regardless, too, of the abundance of their good will. The evidence of human freedom to choose, the right of the human will to function uncompromised by conditioning, should not be bargained away on the scientifically precarious and the ethically nihilistic block of behaviorism.

NEOPROGRESSIVISM

Throughout most of the nineteenth century, American education was dominated by a theory of schooling whose fundamental principles were lodged in idealism. When, in the last years of the nineteenth century, a spirit of progress infected American society, it gave rise to a new and, some say, a radical approach to the education of children. Husbanded first by Francis W. Parker, and as the years wore on by thousands of others, progressive education came to have an intimate relationship with American education. Praised by some educators and condemned by others, progressive education continued almost unabated until the advent of World War II. Thereafter, although practiced as a tributary to the mainstream of schooling, the luster of its educational vision began to wear thin; in the end, with competition from humanism, behaviorism, and essentialism, progressive education became increasingly hard to discover in the nation's schools. This was due, we think, not entirely to competition from other theories of schooling, but because the thrust of authentic progressive education was altered. Its influence on American education was measured now not by school method or a curriculum closely resembling social life, but by its persuasiveness in directing schools to commit themselves to a changing American society. Progressive education, to put the matter differently, faded away and reappeared as neoprogressivism.

Progressive Education

One must recognize the enormous difficulty in trying to represent such a broad scholastic movement as progressive education quickly and briefly.[27] It began, we know, with the novel pedagogical ideas Francis W. Parker introduced to the schools of Quincy, Massachusetts, in 1873. From Quincy the kernel of Parker's progressive thought was spread the country over, and before a half century had passed it had blossomed into a potent force in American schools.

With most of its ornamental features stripped away, progressive education tried to do the following things: to make school life more nearly representative of real life; to introduce functional learning into the syllabus of the country's elementary schools; to capitalize on the project as the principal method of learning; and to recognize personal satisfaction from school experience as the ultimate value and standard of the learning process. Progressive education always paid some attention to the relationship between schools and the general society, so in the late years of the movement—in the 1930s—some progressive educators, notably George S. Counts (1889–1975), began to promote schooling and education as a vital force in the work of social reconstruction, for remaking society as a better place where all the country's citizens could be prepared for a full and satisfying life.[28] Although the word panacea was seldom heard, this side to progressive education—the social reconstruction side—was ready to acknowledge education as a social panacea.

The note whereupon authentic progressive education ended, social reconstruction, is where neoprogressivism began. So neoprogressivism focuses on a point given only tardy recognition by its older counterpart and, while playing down the revitalization of pedagogic technique without forgetting it, concentrates on the social mission of schools and on the employment of education as an instrument for social reconstruction.

Neoprogressivism and Schooling

Education's social and cultural roles have been demonstrated so often and so conclusively in our intellectual legacy that to debate them now is pointless. Schooling is unquestionably an important vehicle for cultural transmission. Taking this for granted, and at the same time acknowledging that the school alone is not responsible for all cultural transmission, nevertheless leaves the school with an enormous burden to bear. And it is made heavier by the advocates of a liberal social creed that, when translated to education, is best described as neoprogressivism. This creed is disposed to make these urgent inquiries: What is culture? Who has the duty to define it? Is the culture schools are responsible for transmitting singular or plural? Whose cultural values is the school expected to transmit? Are schools part of a cultural conspiracy? And what commitment must schools make to cultural pluralism? With answers to these and similar questions, we shall have in focus a neoprogressive theory of schooling.

The School as a Cultural Agent.   Education is a collective enterprise used by a society to instruct its youth in the values and accomplishments of the civilization of which it is a part. As such it is a secondary activity, subordinate to the life of the civilization in which it participates, yet normally appearing as its epitome. When handled otherwise, when youth are exposed to an absurd education with no relevance to real life, any genuine instruction in and introduction to society's culture takes place outside the regular channels of schooling. This complicates and confuses both the schools and the society they are intended to serve. Yet even in societies where cultural evolution finds normal scholastic tributaries, a civilization must achieve its authentic form—its collective personality must reach maturity—before it can create the education in which it is reflected. Once civilization matures, however, the inertia so characteristic of all achievements of civilization—particularly in connection with everything having to do with education and schooling—enables it to preserve its structure and method for decades—sometimes for centuries—without any substantial change.

Educational Aims.   The emphasis given to educational aims requires no excuse. Some educational theorists maintain that the personality of teachers counts more than the instruction organized into their syllabi, and there is a good deal of convincing evidence to recommend this point of view. Whatever teachers teach, the depth of the impression left on their students derives from their tastes, attitudes, and outlook, but most of all from the quality of their minds. At the same time, however, as all teachers know so well, they are almost helpless without the cooperation of parents. A child's response to what teachers and schools have to offer is decided by the values communicated to him or her at home. These conclusions have the support of practical experience, and they point to the same basic fact: The educational process is dominated by the psychological and sociological background of those who take part in it. What any school is depends in large part on the disposition of its students toward education.

Public and Private Experience.   To understand the real nature of the schools as cultural agents we shall need to pay attention to the disposition of both teachers and students. This is never an easy matter, and in any case such dispositions can be known only imperfectly. Yet the difficulty is not insurmountable. Dispositions and attitudes have their roots in experience, and in every person's life two sorts of experience can be found: private and public. Private experience is found in the impact of circumstances peculiar to the individual. Public experience, however, belongs not just to the individual but to the social group, and much of the content of public experience is lodged in the cultural tradition. To some degree, it appears, societies have a universal outlook, with all of their members thinking along the same general lines; there is a common theme forming the core of endless private variations.

Both these sides to human experience have their influence on education. But the private world of the teacher has an impact only on his or her students; the private world of the student has only personal significance. The common tradition —the public experience—on the other hand, makes its mark on everyone, and its influence is increased in its multiplication. When we speak of the education for an entire country over a long period of time, the private variations are suppressed and the common element, called the "spirit of the age" by some scholars, remains as a cultural determinant. This cultural determinant becomes a public fact, and it expresses the most fundamental values of a society. These fundamental values become the epitome of a culture, and the educational system of a society undertakes to husband and communicate them. Schools are organized to keep these values alive in the lives of everyone in society.

Cultural Transmission.   If this is an accurate recitation of education's cultural legacy, it is also the chapter in the story of culture that neoprogressive educators are eager to rewrite. And their determination to rewrite the story of cultural transmission is lodged in one of two sources: In the first place, all this cultural development we are heir to, they declare with some sign of hostility, may be nothing more than an accidental collection of diverse and disorganized traditions that can be justified neither socially nor psychologically. To make the point in a different way, we may simply be the victims of cultural drift. If this is the case, we should be especially quick to enlist in the ranks of social reconstruction-ists, for no one should want to preserve intact common cultural themes and values whose sustaining principles are accidents of history.

This interpretation has weaknesses, however, and they undermine its plausibil-ity. The chief weakness is an indifference to intelligence itself. History tells us, if it tells us anything at all, that our ancestors were persons of purpose, firm conviction, and determination. They would not have allowed themselves to be swept along by a wind of social drift. They imposed their will on culture and infected it with values they themselves distilled and endorsed and wanted to embrace. Anyone who studies the history of politics or economics must recognize the definition of cultural value made by succeeding generations of persons who had the political authority and the economic strength to make their sets of values prevail. The point to all this, social reconstructionists declare, is that culture, that common core of social value taught in the schools and given the schools' institu-tional endorsement, is imposed on weak and helpless people by those with social, economic, and political muscle.

Finally, neoprogressives argue, social philosophers are prone to the mistake of teaching that there is but one culture, whereas in reality there are many. Now the debate is brought down to the level of American society and the schools serving it. There is no singular definition of American culture, they allege, except as it is pronounced by those who want to maintain control over the masses of the people and keep them in their place. American cultural dimensions are plural and extensive: In place of one cultural tradition that schools should be commissioned to preserve and communicate, there are many and all have substantial value. The creed of neoprogressivism is built on the doctrine of cultural pluralism, and all those pious pronouncements made about cultural unity, they say, are part of a conspiracy to elevate the selfish interests of the few and banish the legitimate interests of the many. An ideal education is one that makes every provision for cultural pluralism to flourish.

Schools and Cultural Conspiracy. The generous interpretation that American culture evolved by the nineteenth century to a point where its maturity recommended it as basic content for the country's schools, and that from then on it was kept in the curriculum by a natural human resistance to change, or by simple social inertia, is plausible and, some educational theorists say, substan-tially correct. This interpretation, however, is rejected in the liberal doctrine of neoprogressivism. Liberal doctrine speaks of a hidden curriculum, subversive of authentic democracy, with foundations deeply buried in an ideology of economic conservativism[29] and in educational policies aimed at social efficiency.

Conservativism, one may argue, is committed to preserving the best elements in tradition and to keeping them alive in the currency of social life. But social reconstructionists are unconvinced. They charge conservatives with camouflaging their motives in pronouncements about the common good, and instead of perpet-uating genuine democratic, and thus equitable, social goals, of operating on principles of expediency and vested interest. Sorting out cultural traditions— separating general from special interest—is always hard and can as easily be an exercise in self-delusion as one of social altruism. So, in the last analysis, the indictment reads, the schools of America, dominated by a conservative ideology, have sought to protect the interests of industry, capital, and wealth, or, to use the words of Michael Katz, have committed themselves unalterably to the forming of company men.[30] In doing so they have forgotten about the legitimate needs and interests of the masses of mankind. Faced with a choice between education for freedom or suppression, they have chosen the latter.

The history of American schooling, the most outspoken neoprogressive critics aver, is a record illustrated by teachers acting as governing agents for their students and passing on the established skills and values from the past in an orderly, stabilizing fashion. And all Americans—city dwellers, recent immigrants, farmers, factory workers, American Indians, and blacks—were caught up in an inelastic scholastic web. Teachers alone were hardly to blame, for they were merely carrying out the directives of their superiors, the superintendents who managed the schools and defined their objectives.[31] But superintendents, too, had a good excuse. They were following policies ratified by boards of education. And boards of education were dealing a social policy from a deck stacked by the vested interests in the United States. All this, although it may have contributed to a degree of social efficiency and solidarity, ended up by victimizing the students who, in such a system, had no choice but to forfeit their own needs and interests as human beings. At the same time the rich and various cultures represented in the American nation were stamped out by the irresistible force of school policy. American society, its principal architects said, was a melting pot, and with few noticeable exceptions educational policy followed the melting-pot thesis to the letter.

This is a harsh, uncomplimentary appraisal of the educational effort of a century, and one by no means having universal scholarly appeal. Yet there are eloquent neoprogressive voices promoting the proposition that American educational policy has been conspiratorial for a century or more. Silberman calls the schools "mindless" in their quest for conformity and in their suppression of the native curiosity and talent of students.[32] Others are even more severe as they draw up an indictment for conspiracy. When the conspiracy works, the schools become instruments for social control or, as Freire alleges, become institutions for pacifying the masses.[33]

Schooling, Illich argues, going a step beyond the charges of some of his liberal confreres, does nothing more than reinforce the status quo and, as such, is constitutionally incapable of promoting social change. If change is worth promoting, and Illich believes it is, then the formula for obtaining social change must include the abolition of schools.[34] What will replace them as social agencies is not entirely clear. Holt takes a similar stance: "I think that schools and schooling, by their very nature, purposes, structure, and ways of working are, and are meant to be, an obstacle to poor kids, designed and built not to move them up in the world but to keep them at the bottom of it and to make them think it is their own fault."[35] Green puts the whole conspiracy issue succinctly: "It is sometimes argued, for example, that it is the intent of educational policy in contemporary America to lead the 'underclass' or the 'disadvantaged' to be content in their position of 'disadvantaged' ".[36]

Some of the criticisms of America's schools as they are elaborated by these and other spokesmen, Richard Pratte concedes, may be correct. The schools have not been and are not now perfect, and educators may very well have lost their way. Yet it is quite another matter to attribute the imperfections of schools to conspiracy. "It is my conclusion," he says, "that the critic's dismissal of unintended consequences and hidden curricula has arisen out of a rejection of sociological accounts of schooling in favor of causal theory that posits free, deliberate, opportunistic, and secretive human courses of action imputed to bring about 'intended consequences.' Hence, conspiracy theory rests on the belief that there is no such thing as a hidden curriculum or unintended consequences; rather, some group has conspired to bring about the 'so-called' unintended consequences of schooling."[37]

The victims of this conspiracy, if one exists, are the people in American society who, in being educated according to the themes of a common culture, have been effectively separated from their own. They have been schooled not by following the precepts of popular educational sovereignty but by an educational program intended to mold them to a common social purpose. And this kind of schooling, neoprogressives declare, is subversive of any policy affirming equality of educational opportunity. Such opportunity, they go on, is possible only when educational policy subscribes to cultural pluralism.

Schooling and Cultural Pluralism.   A neoprogressive theory of schooling begins by endorsing cultural pluralism as an essential requirement for a genuinely democratic society. If, as the principal spokesmen for this theory of schooling allege, American society is deficient in its commitment to pluralism, then part of the schools' reconstructing activity must be aimed at changing these fundamentally undemocratic sentiments in society. Schools can expect to gain moral sustenance from the societies they serve but, according to this theory, schools have an important obligation to write a social agenda based on the tenets of democratic social theory. In this connection, of course, the ancient debate is revived over the school's legitimate function: Is it to lead society to a better, more humane world, or must it set its azimuth on the values, the customs, the traditions already embraced by society? In either case, we should think, amendment to the script of culture is possible, but when schools are in the vanguard, change is planned and expeditious; with schools in the rearguard, reading the compass instead of setting it, cultural metamorphosis is the result of a slow, halting, and sometimes erratic process of cultural evolution.

When society is genuinely pluralistic, schools can take their culturally activist cues from society itself; when social policy is unamenable to pluralism and undertakes to subvert it, then schools must do their best to lead a crusade toward redressing what neoprogressives call a cultural monolith. From the outset a pluralistic society must, according to liberal social theory, meet the following specifications: With a variety of cultural communities extant, persons in the community must have the right to choose from among them, and obstacles to their exercise of free choice should be eliminated. When these various cultural communities are formed and recognized, and when they are readily accessible, they must respect the freedom for cultural variety in other cultural communities. Put differently, when cultural communities have independence of action, they must be ready to afford this same independence to others. And in the evolution of various cultural communities, the support of the general community, say the majority culture, is a right rather than a privilege: Minorities in a genuine democracy can solicit support for their minority status from the majority. As these cultural communities interact among themselves and with the larger community, they are entitled, liberal apologists say, to a balance of influence in the formulation of broad social and political policy and, in turn, are expected to cooperate with the general community in the advancement of common social goals.[38]

With pluralism established as a social practice, schools enter the picture. Their responsibility is to help justify and shape educational policies friendly to pluralism. Besides friendship, however, schools have the obligation to introduce all students to and instruct them in a diversity of cultural patterns and values. Consistent with this cultural excursion, educational programs should eagerly embrace a commitment to the development of culturally autonomous persons. According to this theory of schooling, culturally autonomous persons are equipped to make choices with respect to the cultural community they will enter or to abstain from joining any. In all this, schools are to adopt a social philosophy praising and promoting the worth of cultural diversity and to play down the virtue of uniformity and conformity. Moving from these fundamental bases in scholastic pluralism, schools should undertake to enlist cooperation from all cultural communities.[39] The best way to obtain such cooperation, on one hand, and to give a practical education in pluralism, on the other, is to make the school's population a model of cultural pluralism. Theories justifying cultural pluralism have their worth and should be elaborated, but their worth is dwarfed before day-to-day experience of living and learning with persons of various cultural backgrounds and dispositions.

Principles of Cultural Pluralism. Principles of authentic pluralism applied to schools carry with them endorsements of easily recognized liberal educational policy, illustrated by, but not limited to, the following: School control would become genuine community control, where voices previously silenced because of their minority status would now have a role in forging policy, in shaping curricula, and in defining the values taught. Minority rights and values would be ensured by adopting appointment procedures that would give preference to certain types of teachers because of their sex, race, or religion. The school's population would represent the racial balance of the community, and the school's curriculum would recognize, respect, and teach the various languages represented in the community. Conventional American English would surrender its place as the official scholastic language and heed would be given to the languages and the ethnic values of the students. Regular courses in the curriculum would be taught, of course, but in the language native to or preferred by the students. In the end, schools would be freed from the domination of English, although English, neo-progressives suppose, would continue to have a place of scholastic importance and would still be the linguistic preference of most students.

The Dilemma of Democratic Education

The proponents of cultural pluralism, for the most part from the ranks of neo-progressivism, are convinced that multicultural schooling is essential in a democratic society. If we concede the point, we are nevertheless left with a dilemma, and this dilemma, by no means new to American life and institutions, is found to exist in the legitimate but competing ambitions of personal development and social solidarity.

How can an educational program that adopts the fundamental premise that the common good is best served by following a creed of common purpose aimed at social unity at the same time recommend a plan for schooling that instructs students to abandon a belief in common sets of social principles aimed at ensuring a dependable social order and, in the end, a better life for everyone? The right of individuals to be themselves, to follow their own dispositions, and to realize their native talents must of course be respected in a genuinely democratic education. But society has rights, too, and in the interest of the common good, educational programs should try their best to weld the people of society to common purpose. It is one thing to entertain the hope of cultural pluralism to bring about changes in the attitudes of American youth toward cultures different from their

Figure 5.3
Neoprogressivism as a Theory of Schooling

Theme	Education is primarily a social enterprise. The school's mission is to promote social reconstruction.
Educational Purpose	Education is responsible for creating an ideal social order. Cultural transmission is essential, and in a pluriform society this trans-mission must recognize the fact of cultural pluralism.
Curriculum	The school's curriculum must not be dominated by either a major-ity or a preferred culture. All cultural appurtenances and values are entitled to a place in the curriculum.
Method	As an educational descendant of progressive education, activity methods are endorsed.
The Place of Students	The cultural values students bring to school have worth. Personal dignity and social responsibility are enhanced when respect is accorded all cultural backgrounds.
The Role of Teachers	Teachers must exhibit genuine respect, in instruction and other-wise, for all cultures. A school's teaching corps should be repre-sentative of the various cultures in the community.

own and to provide a balanced account of the contributions made to American society by diverse cultural communities; it is quite another to instruct the children of the country to reject the notion that they are the beneficiaries of a common culture whose aim is universal enough to offer equality of opportunity to every person in society. Neoprogressivism, as we have seen, follows the doctrine of cultural pluralism to resolve the dilemma of democratic education. Essentialism, as we shall see, has a vastly different educational formula for its resolution.

ESSENTIALISM

The theories of schooling we have studied—humanism, behaviorism, neoprogressivism—form a common educational front in their advocacy for change. A common but incorrect assumption puts essentialism on the side of the status quo with a determination to preserve the schools as they are. True, a strain of fundamental conservativism runs through essentialism, but it nevertheless finds schools and schooling in many ways as deficient as its more liberal and, in some instances, doctrinaire counterparts. Its proposed solutions to repair American education, however, while in many respects worthy of the characterization *radical,* seldom qualify as drastic pedagogical innovations. At the same time, it is clear, essentialistic charges leveled at American schools are likely to be as caustic and critical as those made by exponents of any other theory of schooling.

Foundations of Essentialism

Some scholars are disposed to call essentialism perennialism and, in employing this characterization, mean to associate it with past educational practice, a practice that has been repudiated, they allege, by contemporary psychological and pedagogical developments. They may mean, too, to associate it with religious prescription in education, where schools were subordinated to religious denominations and were thus restrained from teaching anything incompatible with the foundations of sectarian belief. Finally, they may intend to associate it with education's classical tradition, where schools were places for an elite and where the mainstream of life was diverted away from schools in order to give complete attention to an aristocratic culture without distraction from the everyday needs and necessities of life. In concert these criticisms add up to a theory and practice of education that are irrelevant in today's world. Whatever merit essentialism may have had in the past is something for historians to argue about, but it is judged by its detractors as a theory of schooling entirely out-of-step with the urgencies of contemporary life.

While essentialists need not be offended by the perennialist label, the term's current use is pejorative. Yet it is wrong to charge essentialists with turning back the educational calendar, although it would be hard to believe that essentialism could be an authentically conservative educational theory unless it found some elements in past educational practice to be retained intact. So, although essentialism's roots are buried deeply in the traditions of Western education, with signs of modernity hidden, one must assign its origin as an independent theory of schooling to the period in American educational history when progressive education called the tune for American education. Put quickly and directly, essentialism as a theory of schooling became a counterpoise to progressive education. The founder of the Essentialistic Education Society was William C. Bagley (1874–1946), a professor of education at Teachers College, Columbia University. As an organ for disseminating essentialistic educational views and values he founded an educational journal, *School and Society.*

Complaints were lodged in the journal and elsewhere against the vacuity of progressive educational practice, and for a long time Bagley was the principal crusader against progressive education. In *Education and Emergent Man*[40] he indicted it for damage not only to intellectual but to moral standard as well. After World War II, the critics of American education became more numerous and more eloquent. The list of critics is long and their allegations were all aimed toward the same conclusion: Education in the United States had lost its way and was neglecting the one thing that it should have prized most: the transmission of the social and intellectual inheritance.

Common Core to Basic Culture.   The central plank in the platform of essentialism is that there is a common core to basic culture and that the school's obligation is to communicate this core in a decent, responsible way. Making persons conversant with society's heritage and values, essentialists declare, is the most efficacious way to educate them. This theme runs through the following books, all illustrative of an essentialistic theory of schooling, and although these books often border on hyperbole, they offer grounds for thought about the prospects and directions of American education: Bernard I. Bell's *Crisis in Education,* Albert Lynd's *Quackery in the Public Schools,* Arthur E. Bestor's *Educational Wastelands* and *The Restoration of Learning,* Mortimer Smith's *And Madly Teach* and *The Diminished Mind,* James D. Koerner's *The Case for Basic Education,* Robert Hutchins' *The Conflict in Education,* Paul Woodring's *Let's Talk Sense About Our Schools,* and H. G. Rickover's *Education and Freedom.*

Some scholars have adopted the thesis that essentialism is a philosophy of education and have tried to make it synonymous with realism or religious or rational humanism.[41] Although philosophers of education from these camps may be amenable to putting their feet in an essentialistic stream, it would be hard to demonstrate philosophical compatibility between any of them and essentialism. So we are on safer and more certain ground recognizing essentialism as a theory of schooling, without any leading strings to one or another philosophy of education.

Essentialism and Conservative Politics.   There is the temptation, too, to look for intimate associations between essentialism and conservative political theory. Many books on the philosophy of education, when calling the roll of architects of essentialist education, recite the names, among others, of such notorious conservatives as Edmund Burke in England, and Russell Kirk and William F. Buckley in America. One would of course be wrong in maintaining that exponents of conservative thought withhold their conservative predispositions from education, so most of them end up on friendly terms with essentialism, but it would be wrong also to exclude from essentialism anyone who strays from the reservation of conservative social, political, and economic theory. It is by no means extraordinary or illogical for politically and economically liberal persons to enlist in the ranks of essentialistic education; the common theme of essentialism is found in the conviction that basic culture has a common core that is capable of ensuring social equilibrium. The principal function of all schools is to take this cultural core seriously and communicate it with zeal and devotion. Such a proposition, we need hardly add, has credentials capable of making it attractive to socially liberal persons, although, quite clearly, it is basically repugnant to humanists and neoprogressives and, since it lacks the certification of scientific hypotheses, is rejected by behavorists.

Essentialism: Purpose and Practice

Education's purpose, according to essentialist theory, is to prepare people for life. But life is complex and the enormity of life's demands ranges beyond the competence of any school. Yet there is no reason to despair, for the school can make a contribution. Those educational functions falling outside its purview should be assumed by other social agencies. The school's contribution, the confirmed essentialist declares, is riveted on the objective of sound instruction. What is specifically rejected in essentialism is the conviction, especially prominent in neoprogressivism, that the school must be an active agent cultivating social change and, moreover, must assume responsibility for the total education of society's youth.

Acknowledgment of Change.   Change, essentialists agree, is an unalterable fact of social life: No essentialist is blind to man's evolution in history. Change, however, should occur as a result of the constant pressure society itself exerts; it should be generated in a human intelligence ready to recognize a need for amendment to ways of acting and to the organization and functions of social institutions. Schooling, like statutory law, should spring from the legitimate needs of the people and accompany their social dispositions rather than anticipate them. This, of course, is neither to exclude schooling nor education from any role in social and institutional metamorphosis, although essentialism is adamant on this point: Education's modifying and reforming purposes are indirect and personal rather than direct and institutional. Schools must not be delegated to lead social crusades, however worthy such crusades may appear to be. This is something for women and men to do on a personal level. The action they take as social crusaders, even the inspiration to enlist in crusading causes, may well flow from a scholastic source. The school, properly enough the home for ideas and idealism, may motivate students through instruction to concentrate on social reconstruction and reorganization. All this is compatible with essentialism; what is not compatible, however, is a doctrine committing schools to leadership as social crusaders.

Yet whatever direction the beneficiaries of schooling may take—whether they become martyrs to social justice and economic equity or stay always on the side of the status quo—they are entitled to school instruction qualifying them to function effectively in society. Personal welfare and the good of a whole society depend to a great extent on the level of trained intelligence attained by the people. One need not advert to the education of an elite, to a class to be educated, or to the superiority of the few, for essentialism seeks, not ornamentation but a basic and fundamental competence in those skills and that knowledge essential to an effective life in society.

Indoctrination. A common complaint lodged against essentialism is that scholastic programs following its lead end up being parties to a process of indoctrination. As such they immobilize their students—and ultimately society itself—in the customs and traditions of the past. The objection is that such programs are bound to foreclose any chance for change. The essentialist rejoinder, however, has a familiar ring: If humanism, behaviorism, or neoprogressivism have their way, students in the schools will be indoctrinated in all kinds of social and behavioral programs antithetical to the tested standard and the basic order of social institutions. The charge of indoctrination goes back and forth, and the outsider can never be quite sure whether some elements of indoctrination, regardless of the theory of schooling adopted, can ever be eliminated from any educational process.

In any case, essentialists argue, the best way to suppress the deleterious effect of indoctrination when it occurs is to have persons well instructed in the basics of education. With the basics in their possession they will be better able to form sound judgments and thus immunize themselves from the continuing threat of indoctrination. In this respect, as we look for signs of essentialism at work on the contemporary educational scene, the most prominent programs for advancing the theses of essentialism are promoted in the "Back to the Basics" and the "Right to Read" movements.[42]

Basic Education. Despite occasional claims that the skill of reading is unnecessary in a society where so much attention is given to visual and oral communication, essentialistic schooling accords reading first place in the school's syllabus of basic studies. It maintains that without an ability to read with facility and understanding a person in the contemporary world is almost helpless. Yet, research reports that there are hundreds of thousands of functionally illiterate

American adults. Essential education, by putting reading skill at the top of its scholastic list, would redress this. Essentialists also argue for an educational program ready to make an investment in writing, in speaking, and finally, in the development of cogent thought. These are the basics essentialists are convinced schools should husband. Schools should be responsible for giving effective instruction in them to all students and, moreover, students should be required to meet the objectives set out in the school's syllabus. In the last analysis both commendable culture and social efficiency depend on effective communication, and effectively honed skills of communication belong in an essentialistic code of basic education.

Essentialism has no room for soft pedagogy. Schools should cater to instructional programs certified by social need and educational decency. They should be organized into sensible, academically sound curricula, and teachers should be equipped with superior pedagogical skills to ensure effective instruction. The schools, essentialists say with one voice, are places for learning, and it is the business of teachers, using the best methods at their disposal, to offer their students competent instruction.

Essentialism Indicts Contemporary Education

The principal indictment drawn against contemporary education by essentialists is, as we have said, its advocacy for social reconstruction. We know how this theory of schooling would tone down social activism in the schools and return them to what is called a proper instructional function in relation to the basics, the tools of learning. But there are other indictments, too, and although we cannot hope to find and report on all of them here, a few should be given our attention.

Essentialists deplore the lack of standards in America's schools. They point to the recent disclosures illustrated by state-wide competency testing and the results of college board examinations. They call, too, on the testimony of high school and college educators themselves and this testimony convinces them that the conventional accomplishments of schooling are being missed by hundreds of thousands of young people. This lack of accomplishment, they affirm, is not due to any diminution in the intellectual capacity of the nation's youth. It is due, rather, to a lack of serious and responsible academic cultivation. And the great scholastic culprit here is innovation. Captivated by innovation, teachers have been tempted to allow authentic educational standards to deteriorate. And essentialists, who countenance pedagogic change when its value can be certified, wonder out loud why innovation must always be accompanied by an attack on the standard of educational decency.[43]

Besides this penchant for innovation so characteristic of the contemporary educational scene, a current educational doctrine promoted by various educational philosophers defines "equality of educational opportunity" to mean that all students should have the same scholastic diet. This dead level of scholastic uniformity, essentialists charge, has victimized persons of talent, and because they are neglected in the schools, they are reduced to a level of common mediocrity.

An educational philosophy or a theory of schooling that discounts merit and talent, essentialists declare, conspires to undermine the instructional effectiveness of the schools.[44]

Lacking a sense of clear educational purpose, school programs, essentialists maintain, are vulnerable to almost every passing pedagogical frill and fad. As a result schools are filled with curricula whose educational value is hard to find, and rather than preparing students for the serious business of life, the schools either allow or encourage them to waste their time on activities without redeeming educational worth.

Essentialists are prone, too, to take a close look at the education of America's teachers. What they find saddens them. Their complaints add up to an indictment of the professional preparation and education of teachers. This is the burden of the charge: If teachers are poorly and inadequately educated, if they themselves are out of touch with the basics of learning and the fundamentals of culture, can they be expected to communicate these essentials to their students?

Essentialists neither advocate an abandonment of schools nor close their eyes to the inevitability of social change, but they make an eloquent plea for a substantial upgrading of education's standards. They want schools to become agencies for serious instruction—for teaching what can be taught. They want the curriculum to include only those subjects with substantial academic worth, and they want teachers decently educated and pedagogically efficient to direct the learning activities of students.

Nothing, essentialists declare, is more important to a society than the education of the people. But this education must be sound, and to the extent that schools have responsibility for it, they must be houses of intellectual culture. Their responsibility, while always something less than the promotion of scholarship, is, nevertheless, to provide competent instruction to students, to those persons who will be society's next generation of leaders.

Figure 5.4
Essentialistic Education

Theme	Basic culture has a common core.
Educational Purpose	Cultural transmission to ensure social solidarity and the general welfare.
Curriculum	Basic education: reading, writing, counting, and computing. Skill in communication is essential to scholastic achievement and a decent social life. The school's curriculum should contain what can be taught.
Method	Strip method of fads and frills, abandon soft pedagogy, and concentrate on sound, traditional instructional methods.
The Place of Students	Schools have the responsibility for providing sound instruction and the authority to demand achievement. Students go to school to learn, not to manage the course of their education.
The Role of Teachers	Teachers must first of all be liberally educated, morally sound persons. They should, in addition, be technically skillful in directing the learning process.

NOTES

1. JOHN HOLT, *How Children Fail* (New York: New American Library, 1967); and *Freedom and Beyond* (New York: E. P. Dutton, 1972).
2. WILLIAM GLASSER, *Schools Without Failure* (New York: Harper & Row, Publishers, Inc., 1969).
3. JONATHAN KOZOL, *Death at an Early Age* (Boston: Houghton Mifflin Company, 1967).
4. CHARLES E. SILBERMAN, *Crisis in the Classroom* (New York: Random House, Inc., 1970).
5. HERBERT KOHL, *The Open Classroom* (New York: New York Review, 1969).
6. NEIL POSTMAN and CHARLES WEINGARTNER, *The School Book* (New York: Delacorte Press, 1973).
7. GEORGE LEONARD, *Education and Ecstacy* (New York: Delacorte Press, 1968).
8. CARL ROGERS, *Freedom to Learn* (Columbus, Ohio: Charles E. Merrill Publishing Company, 1969).
9. JEROME POPP, "Practice and Malpractice in Philosophy of Education," *Educational Studies,* 9 (Fall 1978), 293.
10. See, for example, VAN CLEVE MORRIS, *Existentialism in Education* (New York: Harper & Row, Publishers, Inc., 1966); and RONALD J. MANHEIMER, *Kierkegaard as Educator* (Berkeley: University of California Press, 1977).
11. RICHARD H. WELLER, ed., *Humanistic Education: Visions and Realities* (Berkeley, Cal.: McCutchan Publishing Corporation, 1977), p. 3.
12. ROGERS, *Freedom to Learn,* p. 269; and ABRAHAM H. MASLOW, *The Psychology of Science* (Chicago: Henry Regnery, 1966), p. 9.
13. JEAN PIAGET, *The Origins of Intelligence in Children,* translated by Margaret Cook (New York: International Universities Press, 1952).
14. RICHARD L. HOPKINS, "Freedom and Education: The Philosophy of Summerhill," *Educational Theory,* 26 (Spring 1976), 188–213.
15. ABRAHAM H. MASLOW, *Toward a Psychology of Being* (Princeton: Van Nostrand, 1968); Carl Rogers, *Freedom to Learn,* p. 153; JEAN PIAGET, *The Origins of Intelligence in Children,* p. 7; and JEROME BRUNER, *On Knowing* (New York: Atheneum, 1967), pp. 87–95.
16. JOHN HOLT, *Freedom and Beyond,* p. 126.
17. JEAN JACQUES ROUSSEAU, *Émile,* translated by Barbara Foxley (New York: E. P. Dutton, 1938).
18. A. S. NEILL, *Summerhill: A Radical Approach to Child Rearing* (New York: Hart Publishing Company, 1960).
19. DAVID E. DENTON, "Open Education: Search for a New Myth," *Educational Theory,* 25 (Fall 1975), 397.
20. Although Skinner has written extensively, the fundamentals of his creed are revealed best in B. F. SKINNER, *Beyond Freedom and Dignity* (New York: Alfred A. Knopf, Inc., 1971).
21. B. F. SKINNER, *Science and Human Behavior* (New York, Macmillan, Inc., 1953), p. 73.

23. THOMAS F. GREEN, "Teachers Competence as Practical Rationality," *Educational Theory*, 26 (Summer, 1976), 249–250.

24. C. D. HARDIE, "Measurement in Education," *Educational Theory*, 28 (Winter 1978), 54.

25. ALDOUS HUXLEY, *Brave New World* (New York: Harper & Row, Publishers, Inc., 1950).

26. B. F. SKINNER, *Walden Two* (New York: Macmillan, Inc., 1962).

27. Although revisionist historians are disposed to dispute some of its interpretations, everyone regards Lawrence A. Cremin's, *The Transformation of the School: Progressivism in American Education* (New York: Alfred A. Knopf, 1961), as the definitive history of progressive education.

28. GEORGE S. COUNTS, *Dare the School Build a New Social Order?* (New York: John Day Company, 1932).

29. STEVEN SELDEN, "Conservative Ideology and Curriculum," *Educational Theory*, 27 (Summer 1977), 222.

30. MICHAEL KATZ, *Class, Bureaucracy, and Schools* (New York: Holt, Rinehart & Winston, 1971), p. 33.

31. RAYMOND E. CALLAHAN, *Education and the Cult of Efficiency: A Study of the Social Forces That Have Shaped the Administration of the Public School* (Chicago: University of Chicago Press, 1962), p. 33.

32. CHARLES E. SILBERMAN, *Crisis in the Classroom: The Remaking of American Education* (New York: Random House, Inc., 1970), p. 11.

33. PAULO FREIRE, "Cultural Action for Freedom," *Harvard Educational Review*, Monograph Series No. 1, Cambridge, Mass., 1970, p. 1.

34. IVAN ILLICH, "The Alternative to Schooling," *Saturday Review* (June 19, 1971), p. 44.

35. JOHN HOLT, *Freedom and Beyond* p. 186.

36. THOMAS F. GREEN, *Educational Policy* (Danville, Ill.: The Interstate Printers & Publishers, Inc., 1975), p. 14.

37. RICHARD PRATTE, "Conspiracy, Schools and Schooling," *Educational Theory*, 27 (Summer 1977), 191.

38. J. THEODORE KLEIN, "A Pluralistic Model for Educational Policy Making," *Educational Theory*, 28 (Spring 1978), 85–86.

39. Ibid.

40. WILLIAM C. BAGLEY, *Education and Emergent Man* (New York: Ronald Press, 1934).

41. See, for example, G. MAX WINGO, *Philosophies of Education: An Introduction* (Lexington, Mass.: D. C. Heath & Co., 1974), pp. 86–135.

42. BEN BRODINSKY, "Back to the Basics: The Movement and Its Meaning," *Phi Delta Kappan*, 58 (March 1977), 522–527.

43. FRED M. HECHINGER, "Where Have All the Innovations Gone?" *Today's Education,* 65 (September/October 1976), 80–83.

44. GENE I. MAEROFF, "The Unfavored Gifted Few," *The New York Times Magazine* (August 21, 1977), pp. 30–32.

READINGS

BECHER, TONY, and STUART MACLURE, eds. *Accountability in Education.* Social Science Research Council. Windsor, England: NFER Publishing Copmany Ltd., 1978. Chapters 6 and 7 consider standards and values of accountability and accountability at the school level. Chapter 8 is an American view of British accountability. The book is written with the British experience in mind, but it contains good general insights.

BERNIER, NORMAND R., and JACK E. WILLIAMS, *Beyond Beliefs: Ideological Foundations of American Education.* Englewood Cliffs, N.J.: Prentice-Hall, Inc., 1973. Although this book ranges beyond the theories of schooling we have examined here, Chapter 5, on nationalism, and Chapter 6, on progressivism, provide a broad interpretation of policies shaping American education.

CARNOY, MARTIN, and HENRY M. LEVIN, eds., *The Limits of Educational Reform.* New York: Longman, Inc., 1976. The hypothesis of neoprogressivism, that education is capable of social reform, appears to be rejected. Instead, schools are regarded as institutions mirroring the values of society.

HOLT, JOHN, *Freedom and Beyond.* New York: E. P. Dutton, 1972. Holt argues, if not for the abandonment of schools, at least for the provision of educational resources for learners instead of for schools.

KOERNER, JAMES D., ed., *The Case for Basic Education.* Boston: Little, Brown & Company, 1959. Although now somewhat old, this book contains justifications for essentialism.

KOLESNIK, WALTER B., *Humanism and/or Behaviorism in Education.* Boston: Allyn & Bacon, Inc., 1975. A recent and highly readable account of humanism and behaviorism as theories of schooling.

LEMBO, JOHN M., ed., *Learning and Teaching in Today's Schools.* Columbus, Ohio: Charles E. Merrill Publishing Company, 1972. A cadre of humanists makes recommendations for the improvement of contemporary schools.

National Society for the Study of Education, *Behavior Modification in Education.* Chicago: University of Chicago Press, 1973. Accountability and competence-based education are considered by different authors.

NEILL, A. S., *Summerhill: A Radical Approach to Child Rearing.* New York: Hart Publishing Company, 1960. This book stands as the basic exposition of humanism as a theory of schooling.

ROGERS, CARL, *Freedom to Learn.* Columbus, Ohio: Charles E. Merrill Publishing Company, 1969. Teachers, the author maintains, should be genuine in their relations with students and should be careful not to intrude or impose themselves on their students. To do so would impede freedom to learn.

SKINNER, B. F., *Beyond Freedom and Dignity.* New York: Alfred A. Knopf, Inc., 1971. The most recent and likely the most carefully and scientifically justified exposition of behaviorism.

TROOST, CORNELIUS, J., ed., *Radical School Reform.* Boston: Little, Brown & Company, 1973. Although reform in education is not opposed, the several authors of this volume are critical of radical reform movements.

WELLER, RICHARD H., ed., *Humanistic Education: Visions and Realities.* Berkeley, Calif: McCutchan Publishing Corporation, 1977. This volume—a symposium—is filled with good chapters on humanistic education. The authors' sympathy with humanism is evident.

III

PROBLEMS OF EDUCATIONAL POLICY AND PRACTICE

6

THE EDUCATION OF HUMAN BEINGS

So far we have concerned ourselves with an exposition of the basic positions in the prominent systematic philosophies of education, and we have examined the educational stance of current theories of schooling. It is time for us to shift our attention to some of the critical issues facing educational philosophers, teachers, parents, and students as they wrestle with questions of education ranging from principle to policy to practice.

Earlier in the book we adverted to the starting point for all educational philosophy. Faced with the existence of several discrete and sometimes conflicting philosophies of education, it was only natural to inquire into the reason for so many. Our answer then and now stays close to what has been called educational philosophy's unavoidable preamble: the nature of the person. We should try to see how different interpretations of human nature affect the principles underlying educational philosophy and how these interpretations influence educational policy and practice.

INTERPRETATIONS OF THE NATURE OF HUMAN NATURE

It would be possible to return to each of the philosophies of education we have studied and go into considerable detail explaining how each views human nature. What has this to do with an educational philosophy? There is hardly any way of avoiding the conclusion that the principal agent in the educational process is the student. In informal education the student is offered a climate or an environment for learning. In formal education instruction is organized for the student, and for the student alone. Schools are built, teachers are appointed, syllabi are developed, and techniques are deployed. We therefore must ask: What is the pupil's nature? What difference can the pupil's nature make to the way schools are organized and teaching is carried on?

Two general positions, or interpretations, may be distilled on the nature of the person; for our purposes they can be called supernatural and natural.

The Human Abilities: Thought and Expression

Paying close heed to the record of human accomplishment over long centuries of cultural history leads us closer to the conclusion that the principal human abilities, those standing distinctively above all others and setting women and men on a special pinnacle of reality, are abilities of thought and expression.

An old definition of the nature of human beings, and one to which many though not all educational philosophers subscribe, is: Man is a rational animal. In common with almost all forms of animal life, human beings operate on a sensory level. Their senses put them in touch with the external world and transmit the data of experience to them. On a purely physical level their feelings are probably similar to the feelings experienced by animals. And they act upon impulse—that is, they react on a purely physical level when given the opportunity to do so. Although the sensory level of experience is seldom of primary interest to an educator, it is clear that most, if not all, learning has its basis in sensory experience. It is the rational level of experience that holds the major part of an educator's interest. On the rational level human beings have cognitive, affective, and conative experience. Put another way, human beings think, experience emotion, and engage in action. They do something because they choose to do so.

The Ability of Thought. All supernaturalist education philosophers acknowledge rationality as the distinctive human characteristic. Rationality sets human beings apart from and above animals, yet rational humanists and idealists

FIGURE 6.1

Fundamental Educational Questions

Who?	Who is to be educated? The nature and capacity of human beings.	Discussed in Chapter 6
Why?	Why should human beings be educated? A determination or definition of educational purpose.	Discussed in Chapter 7
What?	What means should be used to achieve educational purpose? Building or organizing a content—a curriculum—for education.	Discussed in Chapter 8
How?	How should educational means be deployed to obtain superior learning? The problem of method.	Discussed in Chapter 9

as well as many realists also subscribe to the doctrine of rationality. Other philosophies, perhaps best illustrated by pragmatism, are lodged in materialism and captivated by the evolutionary hypothesis regarding the origin of human life; they recognize no difference of substance or essence between human beings and any other form of life. These philosophies acknowledge that human beings have achieved a degree of complexity in their nervous systems not yet attained by other animals. We should not expect educational philosophers of this school to put much confidence in the old definition of human beings as rational animals. They regard persons as complex organisms capable of doing a number of highly compli- cated things. One of these capacities, conventionally called *thought,* is understood by naturalistic philosophers and psychologists to be nothing more than the func- tioning of a highly efficient and extraordinarily sophisticated nervous system. This capacity, moreover, has a progressive character; it developed along with the physical organism over a span of many centuries and was, in consequence, always subject to the force and chance of evolution.[1]

The thesis dominating this view of human ability was expressed in the early work of Edward L. Thorndike and has stood as naturalism's manifesto: "No- where more truly than in his mental capacities is man part of nature. Amongst the minds of animals that of man leads, not as a demigod from another planet, but as a king from the same race."[2] This almost better than any other statement explains the position of naturalism on the mental nature of human beings.

The Ability of Expression. The human ability of thought is complemented by the ability of expression. Over many centuries of educational history, theories have promoted either thought or expression as having a greater claim on the teacher's attention. History tells us how Plato's educational recommendations always put thought first and foremost on the scale of educational imperatives. With this conviction it was logical for Plato, and all who followed in his theoreti- cal footsteps, to emphasize a bedrock of truth as essential to a full development of the power of reason. With knowledge secure in a person's possession, Plato supposed, expression could take care of itself. The other side to the historical coin is represented in the educational theory of the famous schoolmaster, Isocrates. Assuming truth either difficult or impossible to obtain, he placed supreme confi- dence in an education in the use of words. Expression, he alleged, is the superior human ability.

Effective communication leading to understanding is one side, and an impor- tant one, of the human ability of expression. But we should add both affective education (education concerned with emotional development) and character edu- cation (education concerned with what can be called right or ethical action) as elements in the human ability of expression.

Affective Education. Affective education, given an immense amount of attention in contemporary educational literature, has the general support of all philosophies of education. Both assumptions and methods for dealing with the affective aspects of instruction vary considerably from one to another philosophy and from one to another theory of schooling. We saw how much attention humanistic theories of schooling pay to affective education and how critical they are of current educational practice when it slights a cultivation of the emotions. And we saw, too, how behaviorism, without excluding affective teaching from its repertoire, was amenable to some discounting of its worth. Emotional life has many unfathomable sides, and despite all the kind sentiments favoring affective development, it is probably fair to conclude that educational science has yet to produce a fully dependable method for its attainment. Equally significant, we should think, curriculum builders are uncertain about how to proceed when they are commissioned to devise a syllabus for the development of students' emotional lives.

Character Education Education for character has a much longer—and strikingly different—history than affective education. If affective education is relatively new to the educator's creed, character education has been part of the creed almost from the beginning. When one introduces the subject of character formation, unavoidably an emphasis must be given to perceptions about doing what is right and avoiding what is wrong. Yet, in connection with appraisals of the human ability of expression, this raises almost as many questions as it answers. If persons can be taught to do good and avoid evil, however this transition is made from knowing what ought to be done to doing it, we are still left with a more fundamental issue: Are human beings capable of free choice, or are they caught in the forces of their environment? Do they act as free agents, or are they simply carrying out concealed directions programmed for them in their environment?

We have no need here to repeat what has already been said about the fundamental conflict between theories of freedom and determinism. The advocate of human freedom does not go so far as to allege that everything we do is a result of an action, a decision, of our will, or that we are immune to the influence of events, things, and persons around us. Rather, the allegation is that it is possible for human beings to direct the course of their lives and to do so even in the face of huge obstacles trying to push them another way.

The rejoinder now, by an exponent of determinism, is that we are simply living with an illusion of freedom. If we knew more about the forces of nature around us, we would know that we are either their victims or beneficiaries. We are not free agents standing above and apart from events but are part of a stream of events from which there is no escape.

Motive, Habit, and Discipline. Animals acquire habits, as any trainer can attest, and they can be disciplined to behave in certain prescribed ways. There is no doubt whatever that animals are prompted to action, but this prompting is by impulses and instincts. Impulse and instinct are part of the human repertoire, too; we all remember times when we acted impulsively or instinctively. The point, however, is this: While human beings have impulse and instinct in common with animals, they also have motives. Animals give no evidence of having motives.

We are motivated to do what we do, and if we are lucky our motives will be illuminated by knowledge. We will be able to act, and when we do we shall know why we are acting. Motive has multiple sources, ranging from social to economic, political, and psychological bases, and is increasingly the object of educators' interest. But this is more an area of inquiry for the educational psychologist than for the philosopher.

In connection with the formation of character, and thus an element in understanding the human ability of expression, habit must also be considered. If animals can develop or acquire habits, so too can human beings. A habit is a highly automatic pattern of action, and habits would seem to be close to essential to our having an effective life. Think for a moment of what life would be like in the absence of habit. We would be constantly faced with making decisions. Everything would appear novel to us, and most of our waking hours would be spent wrestling with what would otherwise be routine matters. As it is, habit frees us from routine. Besides, it is frequently supposed that if habits are carefully screened as they are acquired, they can be a boon to a good and decent character.[3]

The discipline of a good school, it is said, can materially contribute to the development of worthwhile habits. In any case, discipline stands as a generalized habit, a way of looking at things and a way of meeting the exigencies of experience face to face. Many educators are convinced that discipline is an outcome either of learning itself or of the learning process. Either way, we feel no obligation here to search for the source of discipline, although we may mention a few of the conventional disciplines: precision, tolerance, unification, appreciation, independence, and dependability.

NATURE OR NURTURE

Contemplating the nature of human beings, and quite apart from whether their abilities of reason and expression are due to an internal spiritual quality or to progressive refinements of human life in a long evolutionary process, we are left with an issue whose genesis has roots reaching back to ancient times. Our distant ancestors grappled with the problems inherent in the conflicting claims of heredity and environment or, to use a more up-to-date phrase, nature and nurture. Their question, one we repeat in our own day, is this: Are our personalities, our dispositions, and our intellectual and other capacities prescribed for us from the outset by an unalterable genetic inheritance? Or are we what we are because of the opportunity we have in society to develop capacities natural and common to all human beings?

The controversy between hereditarians and environmentalists proceeds at a steady pace, sometimes in an atmosphere laden with hostility, where tempers become short and rhetoric sharp. In some historical periods the ground for this debate stood fallow or lacked intensive cultivation. The decade of the 1970s, it is safe to say, was not one of those periods, and from what can be seen over the horizon the decade of the 1980s will not be spared conflicting, competing, and sometimes acrimonious claims by proponents of nurture on one hand and nature on the other.

The Record of Nature versus Nurture in
Educational History

Without undertaking to give a complete account of the respective standing of nature and nurture in education's long history, we should nevertheless call the roll of a few educators whose testimony should be worth listening to. It is probably accurate to credit idealism as it was cultivated by the talented Plato as being the original home for the theory that nature, or heredity, accounts for human capacity. The assumption is evident, especially if we interpret Plato's idealism along absolute lines, that not only are capacities inborn but knowledge itself is implanted in the soul. While this view might not declare the learning process redundant, it does strip all discursive features from it.

Jean Jacques Rousseau, history's boldest and most enthusiastic romantic naturalist, invested such confidence in the environment's ability to shape human beings that he saw no limit to the attainment of human perfection. The combination of a wholesome nature and an uncontaminated environment was, he thought, unbeatable. In the end, though, his advice led to personal rusticity and an abandonment of social institutions. Modern societies found it hard to follow his recommendations on the education of children.[4]

The British philosopher John Locke, whose justification of empiricism broke ground for Rousseau without recommending his flagrant naturalism, took a more moderate position than Rousseau was to take, one tending to keep him within the tradition of Quintilian, who asserted that nurture can correct and repair the weaknesses of nature. Yet when Locke refused to countenance a theory that had arisen in the wake of Platonic idealism—a theory presupposing the existence of innate ideas—he stopped short of discounting innate capacities.

During the long years intervening between Locke and the development of the mental measurement movement, the belief was common that the ability of persons has its origin in internal quality, which was genetically determined. It could neither swell nor shrink. Persons with good talent could neglect its cultivation, and this neglect, whether from lack of opportunity or some other cause, would explain low accomplishment or even failure. But the fundamental point, from which hereditarians refused to retreat, was clear: Talent, capacity, and intelligence are gifts from nature and are neither produced nor developed by any interaction with the environment. Poor capacity is permanent; good capacity can be cultivated to high accomplishment. Cultivation is never discounted entirely, yet it is always subordinate to capacity.

In the first years of its development, say from 1900 to 1920, promoters of mental measurement took seriously the doctrine advanced by some psychologists: A person's intelligence (capacity for achievement) is constant; if the psychometric instruments invented for measuring it are valid and reliable, something dependable can be said about the innate capacity of the person. It was unnecessary, as the long record of intelligence testing has demonstrated, for the mental measurement movement to begin with an assumption of an unchanging intelligence, yet a majority of the early advocates of the measurement movement took this stance. In the wake of this assumption the proposition defending the constancy of IQ was popularly held and widely believed.[5]

The Impact of Behaviorism

Although principles of behaviorism were grafted to psychology when psychology separated from philosophy (for psychology had no alternative but to depend on an observation of behavior for its data), it was not until such psychologists as John B. Watson entered the field that behaviorism, and the complementary nurture theory of human development, began to make noticeable headway in psychology, social theory, and education. The full stature of behaviorism, we see, was achieved in the twentieth century. So it may not be wrong to maintain that behaviorism —as it promoted a nurture over nature theory—provided most of the ammunition for contemporary disciples of nurture theory.

Watson took the lead in setting the compass for behaviorism and, while his work was extensive and comprehensive, the following statement contains behaviorism's fundamental doctrine: "Give me a dozen healthy infants, well-formed, and my own specified world to bring them up in and I'll guarantee to take any one at random and train him to become any type specialist I might select—doctor, lawyer, artist, merchant-chief, and yes, even beggar-man and thief, regardless of his talents, penchants, tendencies, abilities, vocations, and race of his ancestors."[6] This was a bold claim indeed, and when he made it Watson admitted to going beyond the evidence in his possession. Yet the audacious assertion was made with confidence. He thought he was in good company, for he called attention to assertions of philosophers and psychologists who preceded him. They, too, he averred, had gone beyond their evidence when they tried to explain the behavior of human beings.

A few decades before Watson became notorious for his behaviorism, Lester Frank Ward (1841–1913) was making statements with a behavioristic ring, although, paying relatively little attention to psychology, he applied his environmental hypothesis to social theory. "Every child," he wrote, "born into the world should be looked upon by society as so much raw material to be manufactured."[7] Recognizing and taking seriously the hypothesis of "average natural equality of all men," it was up to society, using universal education as a principal means, to assure every person an opportunity to realize his or her talent. Nature, Ward opined, cannot be relied on for the development of personal capacity. If nature works at all, its results are erratic at best. The formation of human beings must be planned, and for the most part this plan is to be carried out in a good school.

Ward's contention was prophetic. It is hard to deny him a place in the vanguard of social engineering where, when fully implemented, behaviorism ends.

Yet when we stop to think about Ward's thesis, he was generally in step with Quintilian's famous assertion: Preaching a doctrine of optimism, Quintilian said most boys were quick to reason and eager to learn. Curiosity and willingness to learn, he alleged, are instinctive attributes of youth, and boys always show promise of many accomplishments until faulty pedagogy causes natural talent to atrophy and innate curiosity to disappear.[8] These deplorable demonstrations of wasted youth, he continued, are not dictated by depravity of natural gifts but by a lack of care. And when Quintilian used the word *care,* he meant what we call nurture. Failure is explained by lack of opportunity.

B. F. Skinner and Contemporary Behaviorism. Recognizing from the outset the long tradition surrounding current convictions about the influence of nurture (environment) in shaping the abilities of persons and also understanding the degree to which contemporary theory is indebted to the work of its pioneers, we should mention the urgent declarations of behaviorism's most prominent contemporary spokesman. With behaviorism as our subject, we are in the mainstream of environmentalism, for to one degree or another all behaviorists are environmentalists, and all environmentalists are exponents of the nurture theory. The contemporary leader of behaviorism fairly leaps to our notice: B. F. Skinner. No one has a closer association with behaviorism, and no one is more convinced of the influence of nurture in shaping our personalities and our propensities than this intrepid behavioral scientist.

Skinner himself would resent the label of *philosopher.* He has little or no confidence in so-called philosophical knowledge and refuses to spend time cultivating it. He calls philosophy speculation and accompanies this assertion with the charge that speculation is based on undependable data, myth, tradition, hoary belief, and old wives' tales.[9] Such things are hardly able to advance our knowledge about the nature of human beings or anything else. What counts for Skinner as he enters this enigmatic field is observation of behavior. And observation must never be casual or incidental; it must be carefully managed if it is to be scientific.

In what promises to be his most important and revealing book, *Beyond Freedom and Dignity,* Skinner lays the groundwork for his theory of environmental determinism: Environmental forces make us what we are. Whatever knowledge we possess is due to environmental, behavioral, neurological, and physiological factors. The old assumption that there is some mysterious spiritual cognitive ability in the composition of human beings is discarded. Introspection is jettisoned, too. Self-analysis, according to Skinner, may be possible, but one can never be certain what it adds up to, because it is impossible to sort out and control in any scientific way these data from internal experience.

Skinner intends not to scuttle the concept of human dignity but to enhance it by explaining how it comes to be in the first place.[10] If we know how we are formed and if we understand that our behavior is conditioned, our chances of living a dignified human life are greater than if we wander around in the fog of traditional philosophy and attribute to spiritual and mental nature the responsibility for directing our action and motivating our behavior. If we understand

Skinner correctly, his intention is not to dehumanize men and women or remake them as physiological machines, for human beings are still able to influence, to shape and reshape, their environemnt; rather, his objective is to debunk the notion of human autonomy.

We are controlled by our environment, so much is clear in Skinner, and for the most part the environment makes us what we are. Yet we are always able to influence our environment and to some extent control the conditions affecting us: We are at once controlled and controllers. In the end we are better off, Skinner says, if we understand this and conduct our lives accordingly. In the rejection of Skinner's thesis, should he be right, we are left in the position of having an environment exert control over us while we are neglecting every chance to control the environment. To pretend we are autonomous when we are not is more dangerous to the welfare of human beings and all of society than to deal with reality as it is.

It would be hard to find Skinner denying any limit to human accomplishment, for he is almost certainly sensitive to the physical and psychological composition of human beings. So we look in vain for a rejection of individual differences. Not everyone can take advantage of the environment in the same way, and not everyone has the physical and psychological composition to benefit from nurture in the same way or to the same degree. Yet behaviorism has an optimistic side: Cultural evolution has a huge place in shaping our physical and psychological equipment. Over a long period of time, if the forces of cultural evolution are managed properly and not allowed to operate erratically, they will inevitably promote a high degree of equality among persons.

All this argues for a technology of human behavior. If the audacious theory advanced by Skinner is taken seriously, the application of behavioral engineering principles to education is imperative. It recommends, moreover, that social engineering be introduced on all levels of society. In the end, Skinner's theory assures us, we shall have given up our traditional notion of human freedom and natural capacity, but in doing so we shall have increased our chances for living in a society committed to promoting human dignity and equality. It would be naive to believe that behaviorism's embrace of nurture's precedence over nature, of environment's superiority to heredity, does not have important—some would say dangerous—implications for education.

The Resurgence of Heredity Theory

We have indicated earlier how much confidence traditional educational theory put in the hypothesis that nature is ultimately responsible for defining and prescribing human capacity. In the light of what stood as part of conventional wisdom with leading strings to our classical ancestors, justification for a further recounting of the historical development of heredity theory is lacking. We should, however, pay some attention to the resurgence of heredity theory after several decades of dormancy in psychology and education. Doing so we are introduced to a scholar whose work, in addition to kindling fires of controversy, must be given principal credit or assigned the bulk of blame for the revival of hereditarianism: Arthur Jensen, a professor of educational psychology at the University of California at Berkeley.

In an article in the Winter 1969 issue of the *Harvard Educational Review,* "How Much Can We Boost I.Q. and Scholastic Achievement?", Jensen challenged a fundamental assumption in environmentalism.[11] The rich environment of a good school, he conceded, might have a slight influence on intelligence. His research revealed an average fifteen-point difference between the mental test scores of white and black children. But only three or four points, he asserted, could be attributed to environmental and cultural differences; the rest were accounted for by differences in genetic constitution.

Jensen appeared to conclude, and appearance was hardly deceiving, that black children were natively inferior to white children. This disquieting conclusion, especially in a social climate where equality was idealized and differences in opportunity and merit were paid scant heed, generated controversy, recrimination, and sometimes bewilderment. Jensen was charged with racism and the objectivity of his scholarship was indicted. Influential colleagues mounted a movement to disbar him from the American Association for the Advancement of Science. Jensen's findings touched a tender nerve among scholars convinced that conventional intelligence tests were unfair for all minority children because they were based on a white, middle-class culture; at the same time, his findings fomented doubt about the commonly embraced assumption that nurture is the critical factor in the development of human ability. The mental testing movement began to fall on bad days, and less temperate critics labeled all mental tests instruments of social and cultural oppression. Voices were heard calling for a moratorium on all mental testing of the young.

Somewhat along the same lines, and again raising doubt about the authenticity of nurture theory, Christopher Jencks and his collaborators, in *Inequality: A Reassessment of the Effect of Family and Schooling in America,* argued that the relationship between educational opportunity and success in American society is neither high nor certain.[12] Luck and merit, they said, are more important in determining success than academic opportunity. The implication of this study was clear: Education plays only a marginal role in determining patterns of equality, opportunity, and social mobility in America.

Jensen's article and Jencks' book broke new ground for hereditarians to cultivate. As a result social and educational programs geared to an upgrading of the status of certain persons in society were trimmed or abandoned. A troublesome but fundamental point refused to disappear: Were the conclusions of these studies sound? Was there any chance that the data on which they were based were collected with defective instruments? Critics were quick to charge that mental tests were invalid because they ignored cultural differences, and cultural differences are authored by nurture not by nature.

Stung by the sharp rejoinders from critics who challenged both his scholarly objectivity and the reliability of tests used to measure mental ability, Jensen essayed to defend his research. In *Bias in Mental Testing*,[13] Jensen ignores the large issue of heredity and environment and even plays down the conclusions exhibited in his 1969 article. The theme of this huge volume is expressed in the preface: "My exhaustive review of the empirical research bearing on this issue leads me to the conclusion that the currently most widely used standardized tests of mental ability—IQ, scholastic aptitude, and achievement tests—are, by and large, *not* biased against any of the native-born English-speaking minority groups on which the amount of research evidence is sufficient for an objective determination of bias, if the tests were in fact biased. For most nonverbal standardized tests, this generalization is not limited to English-speaking minorities."[14]

Jensen's principal conclusions are these: Combating the argument that mental tests employ a vocabulary that is unfamiliar to black children because of their cultural background, he found that black children do better on verbal than on nonverbal tests. He also maintains that the indictment of tests for cultural bias cannot be defended. Blacks do better on "culture-loaded" tests than on "culture-fair" tests. And the latter, of course, are carefully constructed to avoid references that are more familiar to middle-class white children than to black children. Moreover, the charge has been made that, because mental tests are designed by white scholars, the tests naturally, although perhaps unintentionally, favor white children. Jensen finds this charge unconvincing. In a Japanese-language version of the Wechsler Intelligence Scale for Children, Jensen says, Japanese children regularly outscored American children by an average of six points.[15] Additionally, he maintains, the mental tests used for predicting success in education, government, and industry are found to be accurate for native-born English-speaking Americans. Finally, when black and white children of equal socioeconomic status are tested, white children score twelve points higher than black children.[16]

Aside from the implications Jensen's conclusions have for the issue of race as it appears and reappears in American society—and they have an ominous sound —they tend to close the gap between heredity and environment and, moreover, go a long way toward repudiating the allegations of behaviorists and environmentalists, who, as we have seen, stand confidently by their doctrine making human nature dependent upon nurture and reject heredity as of no material consequence in assigning capacity to men and women.

Educational Significance

Implications of the nature versus nurture theory for educational policy are fairly evident, and they can be illustrated directly and quickly. Nature theory makes schooling and, in fact, all appurtenances of experience somewhat secondary: The mental and moral stature of persons is due not to experience, although experience may help in the realization of innate capacity, but to natural, inborn talent.

When heredity theory is embraced, the commission of educational policy is to discover persons in society who can profit from instruction and give them the best opportunity a good school can offer for cultivating this talent. For persons with limited ability or a different kind of ability, the educational program should be adjusted accordingly. If, as hereditarians are tempted to allege, the mental tests so far developed are valid, if they in fact measure innate capacity for achievement, they should be employed for sorting persons in society and for selecting students for school attendance. The justification for this policy resides in the theory of conservation of social resources: Every society must make a judgment about the amount of its wealth allocated for education. It should, hereditarians argue, invest its resources in a way that will reap the greatest dividends for society. Gifted students should have first call on society's educational bounty. Although heredity theory may find it possible to justify universal education, this justification would seldom go as far as to endorse the principle of equality of educational opportunity.

Exponents of nurture theory are inevitably enthusiastic about the power of education. Over the decades, especially in the United States, they have demonstrated a boundless faith in education, and their faith finds its genesis in the conviction that boys and girls are creatures of the society wherein they reside. If formation is to be sound, praiseworthy, and rewarding, it is essential that schools be open to all and that experiences in them be rich and varied.

In addition to richness and variety, an educational policy grounded on nurture doctrine promotes universal education as an essential condition. And when schools for all the children of all the people are in place in society, environmentalists will be solicitous about the efficacy of their teaching. From the nurture theory perspective this policy is eminently logical and entirely justified. Instruction is, after all, an important auxiliary in forming human capacity.

A policy supporting universal education is essential in nurture doctrine; so too is equality of educational opportunity. Potential for talent is hidden among the people, and children from all social levels are entitled to an opportunity to shape their characters and fortify their minds. In the final analysis, no point in educational policy stands out more prominently, nor is any more important and consequential, than equality of educational opportunity. Faith in education and equality of opportunity are implicit elements in the educational policy of nurture theorists.

The Balance of Compromise.   Although hereditarians and environmentalists attract the bulk of public notice as they promote their views on the principal factors contributing to the formation of men and women, the majority of educators, especially in American schools, tend to adopt the balanced view of compromise. Indisposed to be mired in one or the other theoretical camp and convinced of the importance of nurture, especially in the years of youth, they do their best to promote educational policies and follow practices that their experience tells them are most worthwhile. At the same time they recognize, because practical experience certifies it, the reality of individual differences.

Most teachers refuse to stop to debate the origin of individual difference. Time after time they meet talented students who are eager to learn; but they also meet students whose motivation is poor and whose capacity for learning appears weak.

Although they may be ready to admit that students with poor motive, from uncultured and economically deprived homes, and with limited capacity for scholastic achievement are not natively inferior to more able students in the same classroom, they also realize the futility of trying to ignore the calendar of culture. They are powerless to redress cultural deficiencies that may have been festering for generations. They cannot supply motive when it is almost totally absent, nor can they instill capacity for learning when it is lacking or limited. They try to do their best; they try to meet educational reality face to face, and this means recognizing the fact of individual difference. They feel no heavy obligation to explain the reason for individual difference.

Neither romantic humanists nor behaviorists endorse what appears to them to be scholastic capitulation. Both are committed to the primacy of nurture. Yet educational policy and practice are unable to afford the luxury of an exclusive embrace of either environmentalism or hereditarianism. In the last analysis, the most practical educational policy is based on a balanced view of compromise between the conflicting theories of heredity and environment.

EDUCATIONAL RIGHT AND EQUALITY OF EDUCATIONAL OPPORTUNITY

Throughout the greater part of Western educational history common opinion made education a privilege rather than a right. Seeking confirmation for this assessment is hardly necessary. For long centuries only those persons lucky enough to enjoy aristocratic status or economic abundance were offered the services of learning, either by private tutors in the home or in special schools reserved almost entirely for an elite.

When the doctrine of natural human right was given wide circulation, largely from the promotion of John Locke,[17] the strength of tradition was still great enough to halt change in the schools. Ingrained social habit that associated education with privilege and position proceeded without abatement. The justification for introducing John Locke here may not at once be evident. Yet when we consider Locke's influence on our ancestors who wrote the Declaration of Independence, we can see how the theory of natural right infected the foundation of American social policy. We should realize, though, that Locke's political interpretation of natural right theory took him in one direction on the matter of education while our political forebears went in another. Locke refused to give even a moment's notice to the education of common men. The elaboration of natural right, as expressed in the language of human equality in the Declaration of Independence, came in time to idealize the education of common men and women. The political giants on whose shoulders we stand wrote: "We hold these truths to be self-evident, that all men are created equal, that they are endowed by their Creator with certain inalienable Rights, that among these are Life, Liberty, and the pursuit of Happiness."

Whenever social policy expresses life, liberty, and the pursuit of happiness as fundamental rights, as has been the case for a long time in American history, their realization assumes as a precondition some degree of human cultivation. This introduces education to the picture where, depending on social and political disposition from age to age and from place to place, it attracts different degrees of allegiance. Self-education, one could argue, is all our forefathers intended when they inscribed these memorable commitments to "Life, Liberty, and the pursuit of Happiness" in the Declaration. Yet, although we believe self-education to be within the realm of possibility, it is always and everywhere exceptionally difficult to manage. Actualizing even part of our personal potential for achievement without aid from others is almost impossible to imagine. So whatever our forefathers may have meant when they forged this basic principle whereupon general American social policy is based, common contemporary opinion holds the attainment of natural right futile unless the principle is husbanded by social policy allowing for its free and ready exercise. Right in the absence of any chance to exercise it must be meaningless.

When the subject of exercising human right (without stopping now to debate the origin of right) is introduced, the issue of opportunity becomes paramount. How is opportunity distributed? Does it depend on luck? Does the hand of fate assume the role of a principal determiner? Is opportunity for the realization of life's good things reserved in some artificial way for the few? Is opportunity dispensed by following a principle of aristocracy of ability? Or is opportunity offered to all members of society on an equal basis? And what is equality? These are questions for educational philosophy to ponder. Still, we should admit, educational philosophy has seldom been able to answer any of them in a way eliciting universal agreement.

EDUCATIONAL RIGHT

Without exception modern educational philosophies are tempted to defend the proposition declaring education a fundamental human right. Yet philosophical opinion drains off into deep or shallow tributaries when asked what kind of education this right authenticates. Is education to be primarily intellectual, moral, social, or vocational? Is it to have a broad syllabus melding all of these? Must it stay close to the school, or should it be deeply immersed in the realities of social life as these realities exhibit themselves on a practical daily basis? If the case is convincingly made that education is a fundamental human right, then an obligation is necessarily imposed on society to provide the opportunity implied by this right. So regardless of philosophical stance, social and political policy in the last analysis may be the principal, and possibly the final, arbiter of educational right and opportunity. The object lesson here is almost too clear to need illustration. We need only look around to see how various political entities make different provision, or none at all, for the education of their citizens. If education is a fundamental human right—as we are disposed to believe—then we must admit how frequently this right is honored in the breach.

Source of Educational Right

There is, moreover, no mainstream of philosophical opinion with respect to the source of educational right. Is it lodged in the nature of human beings, as some philosophies allege? Is it assigned to persons as accredited members of certain societies? Does it stand on conceptions of justice that are distilled in the process of life in society?

The Universal Declaration of Human Rights, issued by the United Nations in 1948,[18] is unquestionably an eloquent assertion defining education as a fundamental human right. But it is a policy statement which, one suspects, can hardly be based on a universally acknowledged philosophical principle. In the absence of such a unifying principle, a policy statement such as this is almost certain to look for its legitimacy in what must be called a social compact. The social compact in this instance is a policy-level agreement declaring the educational right to be in the best interest of the world community.

Expression of policy without the support of underlying principle may be illustrated further by calling attention to the American Declaration of Independence again. The language of the Declaration, undoubtedly carefully chosen by its authors, acknowledges that human beings "are endowed by their Creator with certain inalienable rights." Yet it must be evident that whatever our enthusiasm for the generous sentiments expressed in the Declaration, there is not now—and for a long time has not been—any universal appeal to a divine being as the author of fundamental human right. This language is eagerly embraced by supernaturalists; naturalists think it hardly more than literary hyperbole. In a supernatural interpretation of human nature, human ability is a gift from God. Both individuals and societies are obliged to seek for its development. It would be sacrilegious, theists say, for men and women to ignore their minds, their wills, their social dispositions, and their emotions when these qualities are gifts from their Creator and are expressly intended for cultivation and utilization. So from one perspec-

FIGURE 6.2
Is Education a Right, a Privilege, or a Claim?

	IMPLICATION FOR POLICY
If a Right:	Every person in society is entitled to equality of educational opportunity. If obstacles to opportunity exist, they should be removed.
If a Privilege:	Educational opportunity should be distributed according to ability, need of the person, need of society, or social position.
If a Claim:	Opportunity for education should be allocated according to social, political, economic, or other influence and power.

tive, natural right to education—call it fundamental human right if you will—has a divine origin. And the burden of making the exercise of this right possible is shifted to society.

The record of history, however, somewhat dims the luster of this interpretation and its translation to the level of social policy and educational practice. To say the least, the record is filled with conundrum. Although human dignity and its educational consequences are certainly implicit in religious doctrine, such doctrine has not always been explicated in the religious educational tradition. Policy and practice in religiously dominated societies have often left huge gaps in educational opportunity. For illustration we need only consult the educational record of our colonial ancestors. Contemporary religious thought, however, when translated to what we call religious humanism, is particularly solicitous of educational right. And religious humanism as a philosophy of education enjoins all societies to make the exercise of this right possible.

It is not essential, however, to enlist the support of a divine being to authenticate the doctrine of natural right in education or anything else. By virtue of human composition (and now without reference to its origin or evolution) we are persuaded by the voice of experience that human beings possess qualities whose natural design recommends their development. It is simply in the nature of human beings to function in certain ways. If they are to function effectively, both for their own good and the good of society (and society, too, subscribes to the statutes of natural law), then the development of these qualities becomes both natural and imperative. Education as a principal means for such development automatically leaps to the forefront. The kind of education recommended for persons depends, in the last analysis, on their nature. Since their nature is many-sided and complex, all educational means must take these evidences of diversity into account. The record illustrates that a theory of education based on natural right, as right is distilled from natural law doctrine, gives attention first to the development of rational ability. Yet nothing in such a theory opposes preparation for life in society, which would and should include all kinds of practical education.

Another interpretation of educational right is extant and should be adverted to, because it may currently be the most common interpretation. It is heedless to supernaturalism and displays no keen interest in any natural right doctrine. It flows from a recognition that human beings live in organized societies. They must have some common bond if they are to live effectively and successfully and if moral anarchy is to be suppressed. The common bond—hardly anything more than an agreement to live according to a certain standard—is best secured by education.

We must, this point of view alleges, learn how to live, and we must learn to live together, for nothing is implanted in our nature telling us what is best for us or how we should function either individually or socially. We learn from the experience of living. Nothing else is possible. But chaotic experience lacking unifying themes may be profitless. Unifying themes for life in society—the social compact referred to—have a foundation in the simple, undeniable pragmatism of life itself. In the absence of education we would, to paraphrase Plato and Rousseau, all be savages. The business of education is to humanize us, and our right to education—which can be authenticated by the record of human experience—finds its justification in our needs as social beings.

Dependence of Educational Right

So long as one remains on the level of theory in affirming education as a right, as many scholars have expertly done, the citadel of educational right seems impregnable.[19] It can be defended from all sides. Yet, as we know from the record of human experience, it is impossible to always stand on the high ground of principle and to invest all our attention in theory. A closer inspection of the theory of educational right makes us wonder whether or not it is acknowledged and ratified on the policy level. History is filled with accounts of privilege for certain classes of people, and the legal climate in the United States makes us wonder, too, about the enforcement of a policy counting education to be a natural right.[20]

If education is taken to be a privilege rather than a right, then the state or some other social agency has the authority to define the conditions under which this privilege is awarded. Is the privilege of education to be enjoyed on a broad and liberal basis? Are schools to be open without discrimination to all the children of all the people? Despite the noble sentiments expressed by the founders of the nation in the Declaration of Independence and the Constitution, our national history recounts how many times and in how many places education was handled as a privilege and was made available to the classes while being withheld from the masses.

In such a climate of educational restriction, a long time passed before political policy advanced far enough to endorse free schools. Throughout much of early American history, in fact, education was understood to be a privilege, for this is the only way to interpret the practice that prevailed for generations: Each person was educated according to his own private means. All manner of children for various reasons were without means to obtain an education. With the advent of free schools, these intransigent attitudes were somewhat altered, but nevertheless, it is evident that the conception of education as a privilege continues to have substantial popular support.

Even when the United States educational policy asserted that all citizens should be offered opportunity for some schooling, the underlying justification was an appeal to the common good. And when compulsory attendance legislation was making halting progress from state to state (from enactment in Massachusetts in 1852 to—in the case of the first forty-eight states—Mississippi in 1914), eloquent voices could be heard pronouncing the doctrine that any authentic interpretation of natural right allowed persons to remain ignorant if they chose.

But to return to the doctrine of the common good and the general welfare: It stands as a social rather than a personal doctrine authenticating the extension of educational opportunity. It neglects the nobility of individuality and accentuates the worth of community. It does not say that men and women should be educated because of intrinsic recommendations in their nature; rather, it says that, in the interest of having a common, cohesive society and an effectively functioning political system, a certain level of trained intelligence among citizens is essential. In an upgrading of educational opportunity, justified by the greater political demand placed on citizens, American elementary schools eventually went beyond the provision for mere literacy and turned the early nineteenth-century common school into our conventional eight-year elementary school.

It is also possible, our recent experience tells us, to make the exercise of educational right, if one exists, a contest between competing persons or contingents of persons in society. A claim to education—sometimes to general education and sometimes to vocational or professional education—is asserted and, if the petition is sufficiently persuasive or threatening and, moreover, if its proponents are able to reinforce it with various evidences of political influence, the claim is recognized. In the absence of political influence, the best claim for education may go unnoticed.[21]

In any case, whether a right, a privilege, or a claim, education is acknowledged as an imperative need in modern society. And now the question must be met: How much education does a person have a right to claim and how liberally should the privilege of education be distributed? Does educational right or privilege extend to all persons in society equally? Does it put mentally talented persons in a different category from others? Does everyone have an identical claim on public educational resources? Does educational right extend so far as to require an educational opportunity for physically, emotionally, or mentally handicapped persons that is equal to the opportunity accorded all others?

If education is a fundamental human right, as is frequently alleged, it would be hard to justify any differentiation in educational opportunity. If, however, education is a privilege, then opportunity for it should be extended according to a sound policy taking into account the reward society may expect to reap from those expenditures aimed at cultivating human talent. If education is a claim, then it belongs to the political arena, where principle and policy always play second fiddle to expediency and political muscle.

EQUALITY OF OPPORTUNITY

No educational issue in recent decades has stimulated more controversy than equality of educational opportunity. For a long time, of course, American education followed a principle transplanted from Great Britain: Each person should receive the amount and kind of education his economic and social circumstance recommended. Following this principle almost to the letter, thousands of the country's children were left to fend for themselves. If they were unable to make their own opportunity, their talent went uncultivated. With the passage of time and the whetting of a more tender social conscience, this ancient principle was replaced. Thereafter, social philosophy promoted the novel idea that society has a responsibility to its members, and to itself as well, to enhance the quality of social, economic, and political life. A condition for improving life's quality was a more generous distribution of educational opportunity.

At the outset, then, American education began by endorsing a thesis making education a personal responsibility. Later, with this thesis amended, education was certified as a collective responsibility. The policy of compulsory attendance had its origin in this amendment. As this policy matured and as compulsory attendance legislation spread the country over, persons could look to society for the provision of educational opportunity; moreover, in the interest of the common good, society could require children of certain ages to attend school. We know from our histories how compulsory attendance legislation met with opposition and hostility. Eventually, however, this educational policy based on a theory of collective social benefit prevailed, and American educators were disposed to talk boldly about equality of educational opportunity. They used such language even when evidences of educational inequality were apparent in American society.

A recitation of past or current inequality is not our purpose here, so such considerations, important as they are, need not detain us. Yet we should be aware of the educational impoverishment suffered for decades by American Indians, blacks, Mexican Americans and others, even while the principle of equality of educational opportunity was being idealized. Despite its elevated theoretical status, equality of educational opportunity on the level of practice was often little more than educational fiction.

Theory of Equality

A theory of equality based on an assumption of an aristocracy of ability is almost indigenous to American social thought. This appraisal of equality, with strings leading to the social philosophy of Thomas Jefferson, affirms a distribution of talent throughout the population.[22] It prefers to skip over the question of talent's genesis—whether it comes from nature or nurture—but if pressed for an opinion, its expositors usually take the side of nature. Moreover, the theory maintains that, in the interest of the general welfare, persons with talent should be selected and given an opportunity accommodating their talent. Selection, of course, turned out to be a critical point; debate still rages over the validity of various means employed for selection, despite the refinement of means in more recent years. Yet following Jefferson's aristocracy of ability theory (if, indeed, he was its author), society will be rewarded for its investment in the cultivation of human talent. Ideally, anyone capable of making a contribution to society should never be neglected. But we know from experience how often ideals are missed.

Whether Jefferson's theory as he shaped and applied it to American social philosophy was Aristotelian in origin is hard to say. In any case, it resembles Aristotle's famous thesis on equality, one with strong logic to support it: Equality means a similar treatment of similar persons.[23] On the level of educational opportunity this thesis should be translated to mean that anyone with talent should be given an opportunity to cultivate it, without respect to race, cultural background, social status, or anything else. If personal talent recommends academic opportunity, such opportunity comes close to being a right. Talent along other lines—artistic, vocational, professional—can make a similar claim for cultivation. Adopting this definition of equality permits and justifies wide variations in opportunity, but the point to be stressed is this: Everyone should be offered enough opportunity to realize or actualize personal capacity.

This view of equality, especially when applied to education, is almost certain to discriminate, and discrimination is justified by the conviction that talent is distributed unequally among the people. This defense of discrimination in levels of opportunity as a logical consequence of a principle of equality is almost certain to be offensive to scores of social and educational theorists. Instead of following a doctrine of meritocracy[24]—a doctrine recommending rewarding achievement or evidence of ability to achieve—they turn to one of identical opportunity. No one, this egalitarian theory alleges, should be excluded from anything. A chance is the least a democratic society can be expected to offer its citizens. And chance —in all schools and social institutions—should be afforded without any semblance of discrimination.

The meaning of equality, we see, is subject to various interpretations. It ranges from the opportunity to which every person has a right, based on the amount of individual talent possessed, to a claim everyone may make on any opportunity society affords.

And now, although dwelling on the point is unnecessary, the conception of human ability evidenced in various philosophies of education is bound to have some bearing on interpretations of equality. If, as some philosophies assume, persons are endowed by heredity with a certain level of talent, the obligation of society and its schools is to provide the kind of opportunity such persons need to cultivate their innate talent. Should the nurture theory be preferred, however, the justification for identical opportunity is grounded on the conviction that talent is produced in the richness of experience. So, following this line of thought, opportunity withheld forecloses the possibility of genuine human development.[25]

Inequality's Contemporary Signs

Despite the pronouncements in our nation's early political documents, we know how frequently the principle of equality of opportunity was discounted. The contemporary picture of American education blots out the most flagrant practice of inequality, although inequality in one or another form continues to exist. Surveying the contemporary educational scene, we find that the principal evidences of inequality are related to race, sex, and economic and social status.

Racial Inequality. Justification for equality of educational opportunity with indifference to race is elaborated in an interpretation of human nature maintaining that talent of all kinds and descriptions is distributed to human beings in virtue of their humanity. Accidental features, such as race, are powerless to impair or realign this distribution. Although this view of human nature has good recommendations from both divine and natural law, it fails, nevertheless, to elicit universal assent.

When human beings are characterized as products of an evolutionary process, the proposition gains plausibility that as they evolved from one to another stage some organisms succeeded in obtaining advantages denied by the accidents of evolution to others. Based on this assumption of human origin and development, an argument can be mounted that challenges and seeks to destroy the thesis wherein vast and various potential for human achievement is universal. Following this point of view to its logical conclusion, differences in opportunity are justified and, in consequence, policies recommending equality (if equality means identical opportunity) are grounded on nothing better than misplaced sentiment.

In any case, it is clear, equality of opportunity for certain groups of persons in American society lacks uniformity. One reason for a lack of uniform opportunity is found in racial theory, attitude, or prejudice.[26] Due either to nature or nurture, the argument runs, certain persons in society, or an entire race, are less able than others. This native inferiority automatically disallows any claim such persons may make to educational right (if a right) or privilege (if a privilege). Adherents to this view refuse to indict society or any of its institutions for perpetuating inequality. The victim of inequity, in the final analysis, is the best justification for policies sustaining inequities. He is victimized by lack of talent and, although personally faultless—because nature or nurture is to blame—his opportunity must be limited to his ability to profit from it. With talent lacking, the extension of opportunity is a sheer misuse of society's resources and, in the long run, because social resource for education is limited, will inevitably have the effect of reducing opportunity for those capable of profiting from it.[27]

Additionally, it is argued, opportunity may be withheld because certain classes in society are culturally or socially deprived and, as a result, are unable to profit from equality of opportunity and are unready to meet and deal with social institutions face to face.[28] They are encouraged to catch up. When they do, they can expect to receive equal opportunity. On its face, this social hypothesis has every appearance of discrimination. Look more deeply, its advocates say, and it is not discrimination at all, but only a prudent use of society's resources. Still, it is hard to see how any group in society could manage to catch up without a chance to do so.

Such expressions of social policy, apparently outgrowths of rugged individualism—for so long an American creed—have little support from sound logic. They linger on nevertheless and conspire to impede the development of just policy on equality of opportunity. It would, however, be a mistake to reject all interpretations of equality tending to restrict it as being nothing more than a virulent form of racism. On the one hand, reasonable, responsible social and educational philosophers have made, and continue to make, plausible justification for a policy of social and educational opportunity based on the aristocracy of ability theory.[29]

On the other hand, it is never easy to countenance a policy too often bordering on elitism, where the aristocracy is artificial rather than natural and where insurmountable obstacles stand in the way of a realization of natural talent.

Inequality Based on Sex. Even from a quick reading of educational history we discover how for centuries women were excluded from the schools. And this was done as a matter of policy. Here and there, due to some unusual circumstance, women appeared as intellectual and literary ornaments, but these appearances were so rare as to stand always as the small change of history. The exclusion of women from all manner of educational opportunity was based on dogmatic assumption: Women either lacked talent to profit from schooling—and this attitude had wide currency—or any educational accomplishment women might make would be wasted because social convention refused to open the door of economic opportunity to them.

Social illumination relative to the education of women came in short bursts. Eventually the acknowledgement became fairly general that women should be educated. Some social commentators declared that if only one sex could be educated, it should be women. The rationale for this declaration sounds sensible even to contemporary ears. As wives and mothers women are bound to have a penetrating influence on the temper of the home and ultimately on the tenor of society, so on this basis education could be made an imperative requirement for them.

Still, despite progressive refinements in social and educational conscience, evidences of inequality in education based on sex lingered on.[30] The point is not so much that schools closed their doors to women, but rather that the opportunities for women in society after they had completed their schooling—especially in the traditional professions of law, medicine, and theology—were frequently severely restricted.

With the advent of coeducation in American colleges—an occurrence of the 1830s, although progress was slow and not much accelerated until the twentieth century—theoretical justification for closing the doors of halls of learning to women largely disappeared. Yet, old attitudes die hard. And in the case of the higher education of women, which for the most part meant the forward march of coeducation, the attitudes were remarkably slow to die. Although as yet not entirely free from those of older times, contemporary attitudes based on evidence supporting equality between the sexes go a long way toward justifying educational, social, and occupational equality for women.

In the last two decades of the twentieth century a charge of inequality of educational opportunity for women would be hard to sustain, if equality of opportunity is taken to mean access to the schools. The point is more subtle: Restriction appears in economic and social opportunity and thus conspires to render opportunity in schooling, abundant as it is, a somewhat empty benefit.

Inequality Due to Social and Economic Status. Inequality due to economic factors is almost too clear to require illustration or discussion. For a variety of economic reasons, but due principally to lack of financial resources, certain persons in society are deprived of an opportunity to cultivate their talent. Public schools and universities may be available to them; yet it is easy to demonstrate wide variation in educational opportunity from one public school system to another or from one public university to another.[31] And in connection with this kind of inequality of opportunity, some critics allege, the courts of the United States have not been of much help.[32]

Social inequality is more insidious and, in consequence, more difficult to illustrate with confidence. Persons coming from certain cultural and social backgrounds may find it difficult or impossible to obtain the kind of education appropriate to their talent. Should they be lucky enough to find a proper schooling, their talent may neverthelsss go unnoticed because the doors of opportunity beyond the school are too often securely closed. Motivation to strive for achievement and excellence is almost certain to be curtailed when talent is sentenced to disuse.

Provisions to Redress Inequality

Current practices aimed at providing equality of educational opportunity are, for the most part, based on the social and educational policy expressed in *Brown* v. *Board of Education* (1954).[33] In this United States Supreme Court decision a separation of the races in schools was declared inherently inequitable and therefore unconstitutional. Fundamental to this decision was an educational philosophy making school achievement dependent to a large extent on the social composition of the school. The court, in effect, challenged the notion long countenanced by American schools and educators that, if good schools are provided, it makes no matter whether children attending them are white, black, or a mixture of races. In the absence of racial melding, the court held, schools are incapable of promoting educational equality. The constitution of a school's population contributed, the court said, either to equality or inequality of opportunity for educational decency and adequacy. In its decision the United States Supreme Court enjoined all school systems to proceed toward complete desegregation "with all deliberate speed."

In the wake of the *Brown* decision, and to provide theoretical substantiation for the Civil Rights Act of 1964, the Coleman study was commissioned. Assumptions from which the study proceeded can be challenged, as a number of scholars have done,[34] but challenge aside, the report confirmed the social doctrine wherein equality of educational opportunity was made to depend principally on a melding of all classes and races in the schools of the United States.[35] Arguing that all children benefited from such melding, the report proceeded to explain how children suffering from educational and cultural disadvantage in segregated schools (regardless of the quality of these schools) could benefit solely from their association with white, middle-class children if they were removed forthwith from their segregated educational institutions. This conclusion, so baldly stated, could be regarded as offensive to minorities, for, in effect, they were told that superior achievement was probably beyond their reach unless they were to obtain it in association with white children.

In any case, in tandem, the *Brown* decision and the Coleman Report authenticated the proposition that equality of opportunity rests on an embrace of full and complete integration. This policy, as readers need hardly be told, has over the past decade or so led to all kinds of scholastic disruption in several of the country's great cities when federal courts required a racial mixture in the schools. To achieve racial mixture satisfactory to the court, children were bused within school districts and in some instances district lines were ignored so as to achieve compliance with legal directive.

Compensatory Education. The point to be noticed, some social and educational theorists argue, is not the advantage to be gained from a mixing in public schools of all social and racial classes (and they are tempted to acknowledge the benefit accruing from such mixing to a pluralistic society), but that certain disadvantaged children, even when they are mixed scholastically, are unable to achieve in this new, and sometimes hostile, educational climate. The reason for their inability to achieve in schools with a better social and educational environment has nothing to do, it is said, with scholastic opportunity or social setting. It is, rather, that they lack the basic skill to obtain a decent education. Under these circumstances the remedy is to be found not in a mixing of the races but in laying an educational foundation for decent scholastic achievement. And these basic skills—the conventional tools of learning—can come only as a result of remedial or compensatory instruction in specially designed educational programs.

The outward appearance and the principal objection to compensatory instruction is that it smacks of paternalism. Moreover, and quite naturally, persons dislike having their shortcomings paraded in public view. Even when they are artfully disguised, compensatory educational programs have the effect of putting scholastic failure or deficiency on public display.

Preferential Educational Treatment. Compensatory justice, some theorists assert, recommends or requires that certain disadvantaged persons in American society be given a chance to recover their lost educational ground. This can be done, they say, only if disadvantaged persons are allowed to enter the mainstream of schools and colleges, and especially the mainstream of professional education.[36] Having been held back for so long through no fault of their own, persons of this disadvantaged generation should be afforded special opportunity to recover. This may mean, and in some schools and colleges has meant, special admissions criteria for disadvantaged applicants.

A sense of history's faults and social sentiment give credibility to all kinds of affirmative action programs. Yet social critics are quick to call attention to what is alleged to be a misinterpretation of the principle of equality of opportunity. What is missed, they point out, is this: If equality of opportunity, in education or anything else in society, is a fundamental right (in the case of American society, a right justified by the democratic charter), it means the same thing for all persons and social classes. In this critical rejoinder to appeals for affirmative action, one is asked to consider how equality of opportunity as a social principle can be respected and enforced by depriving one class of persons of opportunity while according special opportunity to others.[37]

NOTES

1. A near contemporary of CHARLES DARWIN, the author of *The Origin of Species* (1859), HERBERT SPENCER (1820–1903), formulated what he called the law of evolution in *A System of Synthetic Philosophy: First Principles* (London: 1862–1893), I, 367, wherein he defined evolution as "an integration of matter and [a] concomitant dissipation of motion."

2. EDWARD L. THORNDIKE, "The Evolution of Human Intellect," *Popular Science Monthly*, LX (November 1901), 65.

3. WILLIAM JAMES, *Principles of Psychology* (New York: Holt, Rinehart & Winston, 1890), I, 127, is at his eloquent best when he writes on habit: "The hell to be endured hereafter, of which theology tells us, is no worse than the hell we make for ourselves in this world by habitually fashioning our characters in the wrong way. Could the young but realize how soon they will become mere *walking bundles of habits*, they would give more heed to their conduct while in the plastic state. We are spinning our own fates, good or evil, and never to be undone."

4. The recommendations are selected in *The Emile of Jean Jacques Rousseau*, translated and edited by William Boyd (New York: Teachers College Press, 1956).

5. For the full story of the evolution of mental tests, see FRANK N. FREEMAN, *Mental Tests: Their History, Principles and Applications*, rev. ed. (Boston: Houghton Mifflin Company, 1939) or FLORENCE L. GOODENOUGH, *Mental Testing: Its History, Principles, and Applications* (New York: Holt, Rinehart & Winston, 1949).

6. JOHN B. WATSON, *Behaviorism* (New York: W. W. Norton & Co., Inc., 1924), p. 82.

7. Quoted in CLARENCE J. KARIER, *Shaping the American Educational State* (New York: The Free Press, 1975), p. 151.

8. QUINTILIAN, *The Education of an Orator*, I, trans. by H. E. Butler (Cambridge, Mass.: Loeb Classical Library, Harvard University Press, 1922), Bk. x, pars. 34–39.

9. B. F. SKINNER, *Science and Human Behavior* (New York: Macmillan, Inc., 1953), p. 449.

10. B. F. SKINNER, *Beyond Freedom and Dignity* (New York: Alfred A. Knopf, Inc., 1971), p. 104.

11. ARTHUR R. JENSEN, "How Much Can We Boost I.Q. and Scholastic Achievement?" *Harvard Educational Review*, XXXIX (Winter 1969), 1–123.

12. CHRISTOPHER JENCKS et al., *Inequality: A Reassessment of the Effect of Family and Schooling in America* (New York: Basic Books, Inc., Publishers, 1972), pp. 14–18.

13. ARTHUR R. JENSEN, *Bias in Mental Testing* (New York: The Free Press, 1980).

14. Ibid., p. ix.

15. Ibid., p. 570.

16. Ibid., p. 680.

17. JOHN DUNN, *The Political Thought of John Locke* (Cambridge: Cambridge University Press, 1969), pp. 43–57.

18. United Nations. *The Universal Declaration of Human Rights*, article 26, 1–2.

19. AMERICO D. LAPATI, "Education: Privilege, Claim, or Right?" *Educational Theory,* 26 (Winter 1976), 19–28.

20. TYLL VAN GEEL, "Does the Constitution Establish a Right to Education?" *School Review,* 82 (1974), 323; and BERTRAM BANDMAN, "Some Legal, Moral and Intellectual Rights of Children," *Educational Theory,* 27 (Summer 1977), 171.

21. This point is stressed by JOEL FEINBERG, *Social Philosophy* (Englewood Cliffs, N. J.: Prentice-Hall, Inc., 1973), p. 24.

22. ROY J. HONEYWELL, *The Educational Work of Thomas Jefferson* (Cambridge, Mass.: Harvard University Press, 1931), pp. 10–12.

23. ARISTOTLE, *Nicomachean Ethics,* 1130b–1131a. *The Works of Aristotle,* trans. into English under the editorship of W. D. Ross (Oxford: Clarendon Press, 1908).

24. CLARENCE J. KARIER, *Shaping the American Educational State* , pp. 138–144, discusses the dream and the reality of the meritocratic state. His analysis is clearly unfriendly to meritocracy.

25. ROBERT H. ENNIS, "Equality of Educational Opportunity," *Educational Theory,* 26 (Winter 1976), 13–14.

26. H. J. EYSENCK, *The I.Q. Argument: Race, Intelligence, and Education* (New York: Library Press, 1971).

27. MICHAEL D. CASSERLY and JOHN R. GARRETT, "Beyond the Victim: New Avenues for Research in Racism and Education," *Educational Theory,* 27 (Summer 1977), 197–198.

28. Ibid., pp. 198–200.

29. THOMAS F. GREEN, "Equal Educational Opportunity: The Durable Injustice" in Robert D. Heslep, ed., *Philosophy of Education* (Edwardsville, Ill.: Studies in Philosophy and Education, 1971), pp. 121–143.

30. LLOYD G. HUMPHREYS, "Race and Sex Differences and Their Implications for Educational and Occupational Equality," *Educational Theory,* 26 (Spring 1976), 140–142.

31. DAVID A. J. RICHARDS, "Equal Opportunity and School Financing: Toward a Moral Theory of Constitutional Adjudication," *The University of Chicago Law Review,* XVI, i, 32–71.

32. BERTRAM BANDMAN, "Some Legal, Moral and Intellectual Rights of Children," *Educational Theory,* 27 Summer 1977, 171.

33. *Brown* v. *Board of Education of Topeka,* 347 U.S. 483.

34. ROBERT H. ENNIS, "Equality of Educational Opportunity," *Educational Theory,* 26 Winter 1976, 16–17.

35. JAMES S. COLEMAN et al., *Equality of Educational Opportunity* (Washington, D.C., Government Printing Office, 1966).

36. A highly publicized case, *Regents of the University of California* v. *Bakke,* 438 U.S. 265, involved admissions criteria for a medical school.

37. ROBERT D. HESLEP, "Preferential Treatment and Compensatory Justice," *Educational Theory,* 26 (Spring 1976), 147–153.

READINGS

BANDMAN, BERTRAM, "Some Legal, Moral and Intellectual Rights of Children," *Educational Theory,* 27 (Summer 1977), 169–178. The author concludes that unless we accord rights to children we abandon them for ourselves.

CARNOY, MARTIN, ed., *Schooling in a Corporate Society.* New York: David McKay Co. Inc., 1972. Chapters 6, 7, and 8 are concerned with the problem of equality of educational opportunity and its resolution.

COLEMAN, JAMES S., and others, *Equality of Educational Opportunity.* Washington, D.C.: Government Printing Office, 1966. A report of an extensive study authorized by Congress to investigate the educational opportunity afforded the nation's children, especially opportunity for minority children.

EYSENCK, H. J., AND LEON KAMIN, *The Intelligence Controversy.* New York: John Wiley and Sons, Inc., 1981. This book takes the form of a debate between Eysenck, who is on the side of hereditarianism, and Kamin, who asserts that culture influences test scores and politics affects psychology.

FLEMING, JOHN E., GERALD R. GILL, and DAVID H. SWINTON, *The Case for Affirmative Action for Blacks in Higher Education.* Washington, D.C.: Howard University Press, 1978. A report on several studies of affirmative action.

HAWKINS, DAVID, *The Informed Vision: Essays on Learning and Human Nature.* New York: Agathon Press, 1974. The final essay, "Human Nature and the Scope of Education," examines various theories of human nature and their consequences for education.

HESLEP, ROBERT D., "Preferential Treatment and Compensatory Justice," *Educational Theory* 26 (Spring 1976), 147–153. The author finds the justifications for compensatory justice flawed and incapable of supporting policies of preferential treatment.

HODGKIN, ROBIN A., *Born Curious: New Perspectives in Educational Theory.* New York: John Wiley & Sons, Inc., 1976. The section on curiosity, a natural endowment, has interesting implications for education.

JENCKS, CHRISTOPHER, and others, *Inequality: Assessment of the Effect of Family and Schooling in America.* New York: Basic Books, Inc., Publishers, 1972. This work tends to call into question the liberal concept that schooling is capable of erasing inequality from American life and institutions. Many factors over which schools have no control whatever explain economic differences and other evidences of success.

JENSEN, ARTHUR R., *Bias in Mental Testing.* New York: The Free Press, 1980. The author of the article, "How Much Can We Boost I.Q. and Scholastic Achievement?" *Harvard Educational Review,* XXXIX (Winter 1969), 1–123, that created a tempest of controversy among psychologists and educators assembles evidence convincing him that tests of mental achievement are not biased.

LAPATI, AMERICO D., "Education: Privilege, Claim, or Right," *Educational Theory,* 26 (Winter 1976), 19–28. The author develops the argument that when education is regarded as a fundamental human right, inequality of opportunity can more easily be eliminated.

NOLL, JAMES W., ed., *Taking Sides: Clashing Views on Controversial Educational Issues.* Guilford, Conn.: The Dushkin Publishing Group, Inc., 1980. In issue 12, a judge and a professor of law answer the question: What rights do students have?

ULICH, ROBERT, *Philosophy of Education.* New York: American Book Company, 1961. Chapter 3, entitled "Whom Do We Educate," takes a philosophical perspective of the nature of persons and is well worth reading.

7

DISTILLING EDUCATIONAL PURPOSE

In any inquiry into educational purpose, it is useful at the outset to make a clear distinction between education and schooling. Once made, the distinction seems obvious and usually goes uncontested, yet its very clarity—one bordering on the self-evident—may contribute to its frequent neglect. The declaration is axiomatic: Education is a lifelong process. We should all probably quickly agree that education begins with birth and continues throughout life. So much of education is informal and incidental. Schooling, however, is direct and limited in ambit. The warning is fair: Schooling's limits are more severe than commonly supposed.

Education has been, and may still be, America's common faith.[1] But this faith, with all its expectations and exaggerations, has suffered from a blurring of the distinction between schooling and education. Faith in education is praiseworthy, so on this point we are uncritical. However, if education is regarded as synonymous with schooling, a common fault replaces a common faith and, in consequence, schools run the risk of being commissioned with responsibilities and obligations too great for their scholastic competence. Most of what we know and are able to do is learned outside the schoolhouse and belongs in the custody of an education conceived on the broadest terms. To recognize the penetrating influence of informal education is not to gainsay the significance of schooling or to downgrade it. It is simply a matter of setting the record straight. Schooling is undoubtedly essential. Complex modern society would be rendered helpless without the contribution good schools can make, but schooling, in the final analysis, accounts for only a small sample of the total educational benefits accruing to human beings. Viewed in this light, the ringing contemporary declarations for deschooling of American society have a hollow, artificial sound.[2]

If all social institutions have some educational function—and experience tells us they do—it is all the more important to have a clear vision of educational purpose. It is entirely warranted to expect an adequate educational philosophy to pay close attention to both formal and informal education. Still, one must realize that the bulk of educational philosophy's time is, and probably should be, spent on formal education. We should listen closely to what educational philosophies have to say about the goals of formal education.

Two Hypotheses: Discipline and Knowledge

Two general hypotheses on educational purpose can be distilled from educational philosophy's long history. They have been remarkably durable. One assigns to formal education the objective of disciplining the mind; the other commissions schools to invest their time and attention in communicating knowledge and skill. A full historical accounting of these two distinct, sometimes hostile, educational cultures is unnecessary for a grasp of their meaning, but it is probably worth a moment of our time to see how they have affected American educational practice. The clearest statement from an American source on education's disciplinary purpose was made in the Report of the Yale Faculty in 1829.[3] According to this famous document, whose advice was considered definitive and directive for decades, the purpose of education is to form the mind and strengthen or discipline it, so when school days are over it will be prepared to resolve any of life's problems. The implication is evident: What is studied is of far less import than how the scholastic process proceeds.

Following its American articulation in the Yale Report, this disciplinary view remained at the forefront of educational policy for another half century; thereafter, it had effective competition from a theory that began by jettisoning all talk about disciplining the mind. Instead, education was delegated to fill the mind with useful information or to equip it with certain skills and thus prepare students for the inevitable and predictable tasks of life in society. This theory that promoted utility and considered the complexities of modern life rendered it pointless to suppose that any one course of study could be sturdy enough to have universal worth.

Life in society is filled with vast and various demands. If persons are to respond effectively to these demands, they must be equipped with knowledge and skill for doing so. Under this theoretical code, wide curricular variety was ushered into the schools. Education adopted the proposition that education must be utilitarian, and followed it to the letter; electivism became the American curricular way of life. In the wake of electivism, and in the wake, too, of experimental psychology, which put no stock at all in faculty psychology, an assertion of education's disciplinary purpose lost credibility. In an abandonment of almost all appeals to discipline, American education suddenly began to wear a new and different face.

The battle for scholastic allegiance was won by utility, yet discipline refused to surrender. So these two views of educational purpose continue to have meaning for us. It is clear, of course, that some educational philosophers prefer to invest their intellectual capital in one or the other theory without at the same time being dogmatic and exclusive. They can recommend either discipline or utility as a principle objective and be serious about their recommendation, but they can express it in language flexible enough to allow for a modest cultivation of the objective assigned a subordinate place.

Neither discipline nor utility, however, exhausts the alternatives associated with affirmations of educational purpose. Taken together they may, in fact, do little more than introduce them. As we move on we are faced with other statements about education's ultimate goal. Our philosophical forebears spoke of education for the good, the true, and the beautiful. Contemporary educational philosophers, while generally unready to employ such traditional language, fix their sights on purposes whose foundations belong in the good, the true, and the beautiful. In contemporary educational philosophy these purposes are translated to read: education for character, education for life, education for growth, education for personal fulfillment, and education for the development and refinement of aesthetic aptitude.

EDUCATION FOR CHARACTER

When educational philosophers introduce the subject of character education, whether they mean only good citizenship or a more broadly gauged sense of personal and social responsibility, they enter the field of ethics or moral philosophy. Turning to moral philosophy they expect to discover dependable philosophical knowledge about worth or value as a guide to or determiner of human conduct. Establishing standards for human conduct is the special function of moral philosophy. Armed with ethical knowledge, educational philosophers can call upon the science of education and their own educational experience to guide them in the assertions they make about the possibility of any program of instruction contributing directly to those practical, daily ethical decisions persons must make as they go through life.

Put more directly, educational philosophy is inevitably committed to paying some attention to this question: Can virtue be taught? If virtue cannot be taught and learned as arithmetic can be taught and learned, it is either a natural endowment or is developed haphazardly in the multitudinous experiences of life itself. Adopting this stance relative to the genesis of virtue, schools could hardly be assigned the objective of education for character. Should we be disposed to take this position, we must also be ready to leave everything in moral formation to the wiles of chance or to the exigencies of experience. This is unavoidable unless we want to endorse the assumption, no longer common but once surprisingly popular, that women and men are born with innate moral dispositions: Their nature disposes them to ethical conduct or condemns them to immorality. Should this be the case, and should these moral dispositions mature with the experience of life, it is pointless to ask schools, teachers, curricula, or any parts of the scholastic enterprise to try to do anything to shape them in one way or another.

The Primacy of Character Education

Capitalizing on our sense of history, we can discern the educational objectives singled out for special attention by generations of educators whose dedication to education was no less than our own. Although a good deal of contemporary literature on character education gives the impression of cultivating a new, unbroken field, we know that throughout education's long history hardly any dissenting voices were heard when the purposes of education were recited to be the preparation of youth to meet the standard of adult life, the development of the whole person, moral formation, and liberal learning. These were complementary rather than competing objectives. Even so, their worth was weighed differently. Among the four stated objectives, moral formation was always accorded pride of place. Its primacy, however, was not meant for schooling alone but for all of education, whether in the home, the church, the marketplace, the playground, or the inchoate but penetrating and sometimes insidious instruction of society generally. Character education or moral formation was neither solely nor explicitly a school responsibility.

An ancient tradition in Western culture tells us that it is better to be good than learned, cultured, or skillful. This tradition had its origin in the ethical culture of classical Greece and was, in turn, authenticated and cultivated by the fundamental altruism of Western religion. Both in classical and religious culture the implication was clear: Some standard must exist for distinguishing between good and evil, between ethical and unethical behavior.

This highly significant moral problem occupies a central place in philosophy and, in consequence, turns out to be persistent in educational philosophy as well. It must be evident that if teachers undertake to instruct their students in virtue, if they try to teach them what ought to be done, some standard must be established for assessing the meaning of virtue. Without a standard they have nothing to teach. The admonition to do good and avoid evil has the ring of soundness, and most of us are ready to follow it to govern our conduct. But before we can do what is good, we must be able to recognize good; if evil is to be avoided, we must be able to recognize evil in all its various forms.

Can Virtue Be Taught?   Before a person can make a commitment to the course of virtue, the meaning of virtue must be known. This point is almost too obvious to express. Yet in the first years of educational philosophy's history, this issue piqued the curiosity of philosophers and educators. These early educators were the Sophists, about whom so many scholastic tales have been told, and the philosophers were Socrates, Plato, Isocrates, and Aristotle.

Knowing and Doing.   This basic problem in ethics, one explored by Plato in *Protagoras* and taken up again in several of his dialogues as well as in *The Republic,* turns out to be permanent. It has two sides. The first side grapples with a definition of virtue. What is the standard to which ethically disposed persons aspire? If there is a standard, what is its source? If there is no standard, then all talk about the cultivation of ethical character is pure waste. The second side, assuming the possibility of determining ethical standard, is preoccupied with a translation of ethical standard to the level of personal conduct. Put another way: knowing what ought to be done is one thing (and no one seriously disputes the possibility of communicating a body of ethical knowledge even in the face of profound differences of opinion about the validity and universality of ethical principle); doing what ought to be done is something else. For centuries the world's finest teachers foundered on the rough edge of this point.

If human beings are ethically determined to act in certain ways because of the knowledge in their possession (and this appeared to be the sophistic assertion), they will do what their knowledge tells them is right. They are helpless to do otherwise. But if knowledge does not have determining force and power, the other problem leaps to the forefront: How can people be taught to do what ought to be done?

Plato's Thesis.   This ethical and pedagogic issue, wrestled with by all educational philosophers beginning with the great Plato, has been resolved in various ways. Plato's thesis, one with the apparent confirmation of centuries of human experience, tells us that while no guarantee can be made about right knowledge leading to right action, the chance of action being good or right is greater if it is grounded on a bedrock of ethical truth than if it is left without support from dependable ethical knowledge. Ignorance is always an enemy of the good; knowledge can sometimes be its friend.

Plato's confidence in the illuminating quality of truth to influence action was contagious, so for centuries moral and educational philosophers made huge instructional investments in ethics and came close to adopting the practical thesis —one they would have rejected on principle—that knowledge is virtue. Direct teaching with respect to virtue became, in consequence, a pedagogical preoccupation. But this preoccupation, when faced subsequently with competition, slipped away from prominence.

Vergerius and the Nobility of Character.   Crossing the threshold of the Classic Renaissance we meet a writer and teacher—it is hard to think of him as an educational philosopher—who had a new prescription for character education. Peter Paul Vergerius (1349–1420) took a stand in his little book, *On Noble Character and Liberal Studies,*[4] that was more explicit than anything so far stated. The principal business of education, he wrote, is the development of character. We know, as Vergerius must have known, that for centuries character development had been part of educational purpose, so he was not saying anything novel. But what he did say was different enough to be noteworthy. Character education was given first place on all lists of educational objectives and, moreover, its realization was made to depend principally on the study of literature. Vergerius' colleagues, steeped in the habit of idealizing the acquisition of knowledge as the supreme educational goal, must have been shocked at his audacity. For a short book he spends a lot of time praising good manners. Then he proceeds to tell his readers how character can be an outcome of teaching.

Literature is important, Vergerius agrees, because it occupies leisure hours; additionally, it teaches the power of expression, which is a practical accomplishment for the world of affairs. Vergerius also called literature a moral guide and, as such, essential, basic instruction for everyone. Here was the formula to an integration of individual and social motives and to the translation of right knowledge to the level of right conduct. Henceforth schools were commissioned to educate their students for character and to employ literary means for doing so. They had Vergerius to thank for this.

But they had little else to thank him for. After setting the compass of schooling on a tangent of character and delegating literature to develop it, he stopped. Nothing in his little book qualifies as pedagogical advice helping literature achieve this elevated moral goal. Nevertheless, and despite what appear to us now as obvious deficiencies in his theory, Vergerius' advice was taken seriously. His successors were left to resolve the pedagogical problem inherent to his proposal. The problem was this: How can literature be a moral teacher?

Erasmus on Character. A century passed before a formula worthy of sound educational practice was invented. Its inventor, Erasmus, began from the assumption that the purpose of education is the formation of character and that literature can be of great help. He went on to recommend dependable educational techniques for using literature as a moral teacher. Taking for granted the noble ideals and the ethical standards buried away in classical literature, his problem was first to excavate them and then convert them to personal possessions of students.

If all ethical knowledge worth having is found in literature, the first step, according to Erasmus, was for students to master literature. To achieve this he organized a curriculum filled with all the Latin and Greek classics. Students in the secondary school, for this is where his literary syllabus was located, were assigned to an assiduous study of the whole of the classical corpus. They should, he said, read every book twice. The first reading was for style; the second for content. When they read for content they were to notice everything and analyze everything the books contained.[5]

No memory was strong enough to retain every novelty in the books, so notebooks were introduced. Under proper headings, Erasmus tells us in *De Copia* ("Illustrations of Ideas and Words"), everything learned should be recorded carefully and accurately in the notebook.[6] Thereafter students should occupy themselves memorizing their notebooks.

The point to all this, including its vigor and rigor, is clear. After years of living with the literature of the classical ethical heritage, students would have a flawless grasp of it. But another, perhaps more important, side was attended to: Intellectual and moral discipline were inevitably cultivated through hard and serious study. According to Erasmus' theory this discipline, always essential to scholastic success, was transferred from school study to life itself. After school days were over, students were morally fortified by their education and training to do what they ought to do. Prudence was their possession. They knew what should be done (the intellectual virtue of prudence); they did what they ought to do (the moral virtue of prudence). This was an outcome of the classical curriculum, whose syllabus never wandered from language and literature.

Throughout this long and intensive literary course, however, one safeguard was observed with extraordinary care: The literature selected for the students' use should be appropriate to their moral maturity and level of learning. And in spite of his confidence in literature as a moral teacher, he knew that the classics were pagan, so he adopted another safeguard. In the end it may have been the most efficacious of all cultivators of character: the early habits of morality impressed on youth by the atmosphere of a good home.

Whether Erasmus had discovered the right formula for character development is a point we are dispensed from deciding. In any case, generations of teachers thought him correct and followed his recommendations almost to the letter. So when we look for the justification of literature in the syllabus of the modern secondary school, we know it was put and kept there for moral reasons.

The time came, however, when literature began to lose curricular prominence, although moral formation, or character education, continued to occupy a central place in educational purpose. Something besides literature needed to be found to promote it. And now we meet another of the great educational theorists whose commitment to character education was unmatched: Johann Herbart. "The one and the whole work of education," he wrote, "may be summed up in the concept —Morality."[7]

Plato, Vergerius, Erasmus, and Herbart, we think, were engaged in telling us something worth hearing about the foundations of education in value, about what, in the end, adds up to education for character.

The Problem of Value

We try to determine the worth of things and actions. In the sphere of ethics we are concerned with determining the worth of action. Why do we choose to do one thing rather than something else? The answer would seem to be simple: because we attach greater worth to one thing than to another. Now the question arises: what is the source of this worth? Do we test what we do and, depending on the consequences of our action, arrive at evaluations of worth? If so, we are acting pragmatically. Do we do what gives us the greater amount of pleasure regardless of the consequences? If so, the principle guiding our conduct is not pragmatic but hedonistic. Are there explications of worth certified for us in the natural law? Is it simply in the nature of things to require a certain course of action of us? Is there a universal moral law that transcends nature and appeals for its authority to a divine lawgiver?

Convictions with respect to worth (morality and character) as they stand today depend heavily on two hostile conceptions of ethics. One is ethical humanism, a doctrine that makes social success or failure the final arbiter of right and wrong. The abandonment of any other standard for appraising action is total. The other is a fundamental religious attitude with respect to the nature of the person and the obligations persons in society have to one another because of their sharing in the fatherhood of God. Hostility here is rooted in the essential discord between the secular and the sacred.

EDUCATIONAL PHILOSOPHY AND CHARACTER EDUCATION

Every philosophy of education is interested in character education, but every philosophy of education, as we shall see, does not give character education top priority on its hierarchy of objectives. It is time now to take a closer look at character's place in systematic philosophies of education, and when we do we must pay attention to the theory of value embraced by each of the philosophies.

Idealism and Character Education

Idealist educational philosophy is clear on two points concerning the nature of value: A dependable standard with respect to what has worth and what has none can be erected, and this standard can be communicated and understood. In the broad sweep of human civilization good minds have distilled moral imperatives and these moral imperatives have been certified, clarified, and confirmed time and again by rational processes. An appeal to reason is final in idealism. In consequence, we are all able to fathom the fundamental meaning of morality. We have dependable knowledge for defining good and decent human character. In the end, we see, idealism strips away the mystery surrounding value.

Idealism however, wants to avoid an indictment for oversimplification, so no idealist alleges that a theory of value is easy to construct or implies that crafting a theory of value is employment for everyone. Rather, it is difficult work, work usually reserved for the most able men and women. Any suggestion that moral standard is produced in the froth and foam of popular will—or that what is moral is what most people believe to be moral—is summarily rejected. A universal moral law is buried away in the nature of reality and in the nature of human beings. The right intellectual tools and rational processes are essential to mining it. Once this rich moral ore is excavated, the moral experience of the human race is able to tell us something about how a sense of its worth can be communicated from one to another generation. The moral tradition, part and parcel of human civilization, is itself an effective teacher of character.

Once we have dependable moral knowledge, once we know what ought to be done, we have an obligation both to ourselves and to society to do it. This is less difficult than it sounds, idealists aver, for an original deposit in human nature motivates rational men and women to do good and avoid evil. Individual differences in the success we have in fulfilling the moral law may surface, but in the end everyone is naturally disposed to its embrace.

Should idealism appeal to religion, as some contemporary idealists are prone to do when they label their idealism as Christian or religious,[8] then any violation of moral imperative raises the possibility of divine retribution. The important point to be fixed, though, in connection with conventional idealism is that no appeal to religion is essential to certify the validity of a universal moral law or the natural disposition of men and women to try their best to adhere to it. If appeal beyond reason itself assumes a level of significance—an intellectual stance that few idealists would find comfortable—an appeal to human experience can certify the pragmatic worth of following the prescripts of the moral code. This certification may take various forms, but traditionally its form is characterized in the language of the golden rule.[9]

With a commitment to the shaping of character, to disposing boys and girls to act habitually in certain ways, educators have sometimes resorted to indoctrination. Calling indoctrination a shortcut to the attainment of desirable character, they justify it further by calling attention to the immense amount of good it can do. Evidences of indoctrination are easy enough to find in education. In fact, indoctrination may be almost indigenous to informal education, where its operations are insidious and easily concealed. But concealment, or a kind of academic subversion, of indoctrination has almost nothing to do with its adoption in formal education, where it can be recognized and, with proper safeguards, avoided. Idealism is ready to take a firm stand on any kind of indoctrination, wherever it is found. Because a positive moral code is grounded in reason and is justified by rational processes, indoctrination is rejected as being incapable of educational decency.

Censorship, though, is a different matter. Censorship can be justified as a way of filtering experience, and this filtering is appropriate for informal as well as for formal education. The objective is to supply us with a kind of right knowledge on which moral judgment can be based. All of us, the idealist is certain, are indebted to experience for the forming of our character. It can therefore be argued that experience must be true and dependable. If experience, especially literary experience, is capable of misleading us, it should be curtailed; if nonliterary experience is likely to betray our moral sensitivity and make difficult or impossible our doing what we ought to do, then that experience must be censored too.

Plato himself gave all succeeding idealists an object lesson in the use of censorship.[10] But when Plato recommended censorship of the literature used by students in the classical music school, he meant to protect from contagion their intellects rather than their wills. The poets, he said, engaged in the repetition of myth, and despite the fact that these myths had a long and honorable standing in Greek tradition, they were fiction. To put it bluntly, which Plato was unafraid to do, myth was lie. Students had a right to be taught truth, so the works of the poets were to be excised, expurgated, or banned altogether. Plato's successors in the field of moral philosophy modified his justification for censorship. When they used censorship in education or sought to justify it, they meant to protect the morals of their students.

Idealism is confident of its ability to certify a dependable moral standard and to communicate it to students by means of effective teaching. Still, the matter of character education is not entirely settled: Having a body of knowledge about what ought to be done is different from following a course of conduct implied by that knowledge. Having an objective moral code is one thing; living according to a set of ideals is another. Now idealists, in company with all other educational philosophers, must decide how knowledge can be translated to virtue. Their answer is the good moral example of society, the unimpeachable character of a good teacher, and the continuity of ethical standard and moral conduct sustained in the good order of society itself.[11] In addition, as a kind of bonus, idealism is serious about Plato's interpretation of discipline and its close relationship to moral formation. When Plato stopped short of acknowledging the Socratic doctrine that knowledge is virtue, he nevertheless admitted that the hard work inevitably associated with serious study develops discipline, and discipline is character's first cousin. So, although knowledge may not be virtue, the conventional idealist interpretation is that in its acquisition certain traits of character that contribute to decent, dependable, and morally efficacious conduct are necessarily developed.

Realism and Character Education

Whether realism adopts character as a primary educational objective is uncertain, for the range of realist thought is extensive, yet no realist would dare neglect character as an educational objective. In any case, wherever character may stand on realism's hierarchy of educational objectives, any proposition with respect to it has a foundation in natural law. In order to act ethically, human beings must first be apprised of the meaning of the various virtues that, when taken together, constitute moral behavior. Knowledge of what constitutes ethical conduct is hard to obtain, so it is probably unreasonable to expect everyone to discover the fundamentals of morality without help. And help always takes the form of instruction. Yet persons endowed with sufficient natural intelligence and equipped with proper scientific technique are able to discover and codify a body of dependable ethical knowledge. After submission to tests of verification and validation, this knowledge must be added to the curriculum of every school where it should be taught with commitment, zeal, and devotion.[12]

Realism is supremely confident of the possibility of human beings attaining dependable knowledge; it refuses to shrink from talk about truth, and this confidence in the power of the human mind extends to conceptions of the good and the beautiful as well. Realists working in the field of character education have a standard to guide them: positive knowledge certified by a positive method. They are absolved from waiting for the consequence of conduct to tell them whether human action is ethical or unethical. The banner of knowledge is raised above the schoolhouse where it can be seen by every teacher engaged in the important work of shaping character. When the work in a course of moral instruction is finished, we will know with a high degree of certainty what ought to be done if we are to fulfill the design of personal nature and, moreover, if we are to act virtuously (ethically) in all our social relations. But this is about as far as knowledge can take us, for realist educational philosophy has no secret formula for converting a knowledge of virtue to virtuous conduct.

At this point, realists declare, the moral environment of a good school can be contagious. In the school's environment, and in the social environment generally, boys and girls will come to adopt those attitudes disposing them to act according to the canons of ethics. Knowledge may not be virtue; yet, for conventional realism it is an indispensable condition, so the final step in the education for character, a translation of knowledge to conduct, is completed in the practice of living ethically.[13]

Realist philosophy discovers the fundamental precepts of morality in natural law. The order of nature carries its own penalties and exacts its own compensation for violations of the natural law. But everything in an ethically sensitive society will contribute to the formation of a human disposition to act in accordance with a positive moral code. Structuring an ethically sensitive school society is the principal responsibility of teachers after their work of providing sound instruction is finished. No philosophy of education exhibits greater confidence in the worth of knowledge to guide us in ethical conduct. Yet, we should add, realism does not interpret all human behavior, even all ethical behavior, in terms of an adherence to the law of nature. Natural law is the place to begin and every realist is serious about it, but in all of social life, experience tells us, convention and fashion appear. They contribute to a more effective and efficient social life. Valuable as they are, however, no realist assigns intrinsic worth or value to convention and fashion. Their place in influencing behavior must be sustained, if at all, by a fundamental pragmatism. Convention and fashion are retained when they work and are discarded when they no longer fulfill personal and social expectation or need.

In summary, realism depends on positive methods for arriving at dependable knowledge concerning worth or value, and this knowledge adds up to a foundation for ethical character. So, we see, a cognitive side to value and character is indispensable. From this point on, after instruction has done its duty, good character must be confirmed and fortified in the practice of life itself. But not all conduct has an imperative quality. Some behavior submits to a pragmatic test, and here we find those conventional values that, while they may be highly prized from age to age, do not qualify as or follow from the law of nature.

Conditioning and Social Engineering.   Behaviorism, we have said before, is generally comfortable with the general philosophical theses of realism. Yet, by no means are all realists behaviorists. Those who are pay less attention to the good offices schools or society may generally employ to dispose girls and boys toward ethical behavior and good character. Behaviorists take no stand in opposition to a climate wherein character may be formed, but to depend entirely on moral climate, they declare, is to leave too much to chance. Good character is an outcome of conditioning; to guarantee it, the environment for learning must be filled with situations where good behavior is rewarded and unethical behavior is censored. In the language of B. F. Skinner, operant conditioning is the best, if not the only, formula for developing character, for making people good, decent, and responsible.[14] And if the promise in behaviorism is realized, not only will boys and girls in school be educated to be ethical persons but all of society will be the beneficiary. The amount of good that can come from moral and social engineering programmed into the educational process is limitless.

According to this behaviorist doctrine, there is no doubt whatever that we are what we are, ethically good or bad, because of the formative experiences of our lives. Behaviorism tells us how to control these experiences. Motive enforcing ethical conduct belongs not to those categories of knowing what is right but, rather, to categories of reward and punishment. We learn to do what brings us satisfaction, and we learn to avoid the painful and disappointing. Properly reinforced, this kind of learning is permanent.

Religious and Rational Humanism and Character Education

Religious Humanism.   Religious humanism, as much and perhaps more than any other philosophy of education, makes character formation the primary purpose of education. But here we should remember the distinction between schooling and education, for according to this philosophy the school may be assigned a subordinate role in connection with character. Its responsibility may center on communicating a body of authentic moral and religious knowledge to students. To adopt Maritain's language here, the function of schools is to teach what can be taught.[15] And Martain gives the impression that character can hardly be expected as an outcome of conventional pedagogy. This, however, is only one side of the educational coin, for other religious humanists find arguments to sustain the proposition that moral knowledge is no different from any other kind of knowledge. Knowledge of any kind, they allege, can be taught.[16]

Skirting this rupture in their ranks, we turn to a point where, generally speaking, a common front is formed. Most religious humanists take seriously the theological doctrine of original sin. This doctrine tells them how human beings begin with a wounded nature and, in consequence, are susceptible to the temptation of evil. It is imperative, then, that in addition to having correct knowledge about the standard of human conduct—and the source of this knowledge is both natural and divine law—persons must be disciplined, habituated, and sometimes coerced to do what ought to be done. Anyone engaging in evil or unethical conduct should be punished. Example is a good moral teacher, so schools following this philosophy of education will exert their best effort to maintain moral environments conducive to the development of character. Admonition to do good and avoid evil will never cease, and the curriculum should be filled with subjects whose ethical dimension is clear and precise. Conventional instruction may not, in the end, be responsible for character formation, but no religious humanist ignores the instrumental contribution ethically responsible instruction can make. For the most part, the religious humanist finds the most dependable of all ethical knowledge in religious doctrine itself. And here, of course, the authority is unimpeachable, for the authority is God himself. The appeal here is final and fundamentally religious, an act of faith. Persons who follow a course of conduct outlined for them by a divine lawgiver are bound to reap their eternal reward.

A good school can be a laboratory for the development of moral virtue, but the school alone, regardless of its quality, is incapable of doing everything needed to assure the formation of sound ethical character. The cultivation of religion in the church and the inculcation of piety in a good religious home are superior to anything the school can do. Knowledge is a safeguard to character, for without knowledge one could hardly be certain of the difference between right and wrong, but it is only a safeguard, for no religious humanist expects knowledge alone to protect anyone from evil. If knowledge is one safeguard, the consequence of conduct is another. Social and legal penalty can serve as important deterrents to unethical behavior, but religious humanism goes a step beyond these penalties and exacts one far more severe: the loss of a person's immortal soul.

Rational Humanism. Rational humanism is friendly to the convictions of religious humanism and is ready to confirm its confidence in the use of reason to sustain conceptions of personal duty and social responsibility. Without confidence in reason, nothing of much worth can ever be said about good character nor could anyone hope to organize any educational program to cultivate it. But rational humanism stops short of adopting any religious perspective in relation to the formation of character.

An ideal education can contribute to the development of a person whose life will be dominated by the rule of reason. And, rational humanists argue, the rule of reason has enough force to extend to the certification of ethical character. Rational behavior carries with it the necessary implication of good character, so rational humanism is ready to depend upon the ability of schools, and education generally, to enforce the rule of reason.

Pragmatism and Character Education

Following the pragmatic doctrine to the letter, character education is unquestionably important because it promotes social efficiency, although to say where it belongs on a hierarchy of educational objectives is mainly guesswork in view of pragmatism's reluctance to organize any such hierarchy. In the abandonment of ethical behavior, where we respect the rights of others and they respect ours, we should be swamped in a slough of moral anarchy. No one could stretch the ethical theory in pragmatism far enough to include either immorality or anarchy. But what is moral?

Once acknowledging the worth of character education, although without an appeal to moral imperatives or divine injunctions assumed by other philosophies, pragmatism makes its realization depend on experience itself. We learn to live well by living well, and we learn to live ethically by living ethically. What is ethical in any final or ultimate sense is impossible to determine. And to revive ancient issues where debate rages over the essential meaning of virtue is largely a waste of time. What, then, is moral behavior and what is ethical character? This, pragmatism responds, is up to the public test. And the most dependable public test is always what works most effectively.

In the absence of any ethical standard—other than socially effective conduct, of course—the definition of character may change from time to time and from place to place. Because conceptions of morality are subject to the forces of social evolution, any statement about value and character illustrating morality must be relative. What must be learned, not only in the custody of a good school but in all of society as well, is that acting ethically is doing what the situation requires. We must, to follow this line of thought, be schooled to appraise the circumstances in which we find ourselves and where action is demanded, and then do what is most satisfactory, or, to put it differently, what works best. The only safeguard to ensure or promote ethical behavior is social approval. So, although pragmatism refuses to admit the existence of a standard for conduct based on a natural law and has no time whatever for religion's role in establishing a moral code, it is nevertheless careful to make social awareness and benefit part of its ethical repertoire. The final certification for good character and the justification for education working toward it on all levels, both formal and informal, is that it pays huge personal and social dividends.

Existentialism and Character Education

Existential moral philosophy makes us responsible for our behavior, so the implication is clear: We must do our best to act ethically. We should never be surprised to hear existentialists praising good character. Yet, apart from developing a sense of freedom and responsibility, and developing it according to personal perspective as we come face to face with a hostile world, little in existentialism exhibits clearly either where character stands on its hierarchy of educational objectives or how best to achieve it. In the language of existentialism we are destined to live in a world too often full of incoherency, confusion, and resistance; learning to live well with so many obstacles to hurdle may, in the final analysis, be the existential definition of good character.

While these generalizations have elements of validity, they do not tell us much about existentialism's commitment to character education. Let us see if we can be more precise. In the first place, we know existentialism starts with a personal awareness of existence. Thereafter in the experience of life we are confronted with the possibility—better, the need—to exercise choice. The standard for moral choice, or those moral convictions with which particular decisions must square, is purely personal. Any moral standard may be adopted, although some standard is imperative.

From this point on existentialism regards the person as being potentially autonomous. In this context autonomy is the personal ability to make decisions and to control one's own destiny. The ultimate determiner of value, the fundamental principle superintending it, is always self-actualization. The existentialist would say: I should do always and consistently what I judge best for the full realization of my personal capacity. To this end, school practice should constantly encourage the exercise of free choice. And this is best done, existentialists think, not by idealizing the worth of free choice in an antiseptic way but by encouraging students in the development of competence in free choice at every turn of the educational road and by urging students to assume the responsibility they have to themselves to make choices.

All this must be done in an atmosphere of freedom, for character education, existentialists declare, is not moral training, conditioning, or making students submit to the discipline of authority. In the practice of choice everyone is required to grapple with an urgent, perennial issue. Existential expectation is that this issue is capable of resolution in personal life. This is the issue: How can self-interest be accommodated to the general welfare?

Part of education's responsibility for character formation is accounted for in instilling discipline, or creating an educational climate where it may be developed, in connection with the exercise of free choice. What is chosen is not at stake here; schools are not delegated to tell students what to choose. The point is, rather, that when faced with the need to make choices, persons will have the courage, the social stamina, and the personal vigor to do so. Seen in this light, the school is a place where ethical method—the way to choose and the habit of choosing—is encouraged and developed, and where ample time is allowed for practice in making choices. This, we think, is how existentialism interprets the role of education in the formation of desirable human character.[17]

Analytic Philosophy and Character Education

Analytic philosophy is unprepared to make any independent assertions relative to the place of character in education or schooling, although it would be hard to believe that this philosophy of education is less interested in ethical behavior and desirable social conduct than any other. Its philosophical purpose, however, is not to formulate propositions with respect to anything in education; rather, it is to examine and analyze extant educational statements and discern their meaning. In this enigmatic field of character education, analytic philosophy, we should think, will have plenty to do.

Illustrative of analytic industry is the work of R. S. Peters, especially as it holds up for criticism Kohlberg's theory of moral development. Peters' criticisms are extensive, but they center on what Peters believes is Kohlberg's failure to take habit fully into account as a basis for consistent moral conduct.[18]

But this is only part of the analyst's task as he confronts the problem in moral education. The other part, as it is elaborated by Peters, probes for Kohlberg's meaning of *habit*. Is the term *habit* used to call attention to personal habits without any examination of how they are formed? Does *habit* mean a routine response to certain situations? Or does *habits* used in this context raise the issue, which would seem to be central to character education, of how the psychological process of habituation proceeds and how it can be managed more effectively? In this instance we have an object lesson in an analytic search for meaning.

EDUCATION FOR LIFE

The purpose of education, it may be said, is to prepare children to live effectively in society when they attain maturity. Such a statement, even when translated for adoption in contemporary society, contains few novelties. The durability of this purpose—education for life—is evident, and the best explanation for durability is that it is pointless to contest the obvious: Children mature into adults and are thereafter faced with countless obligations and duties. Any worthwhile educational program should surely take into account preparation for life in society. We may be ready to admit to different evaluations of worth—to different places on a hierarchy of objectives—for education for life, as many educational philosophers and philosophies concede, but when we do it is almost imperative, considering the nature of human life and the nature of society, to give this objective some place on our list of educational objectives.

A historical note should probably be interjected here, and from it we may be able to see how this broad educational purpose is ratified as a modern school objective. Before our forefathers were ready to organize schools for a majority of children in the nation, a large part of education, whether for life or anything else, was handled either in the home under the direction of parents or in the workshop under the direction of a master. But in the course of social evolution it turned out that neither the home nor the apprenticeship system was equipped to educate and train youth for the growing complexities of life in society. So schools, becoming more common, eagerly embraced the thesis (one referred to earlier in the chapter) that the principal general function of education is to satisfy the requirements of utility. Schools, to put it another way, should commit themselves to teaching useful knowledge. And what could be more useful than preparing persons to live in society?

The educational objective of preparation for life has two sides: One side has to do with the preservation of culture, or with those appurtenances to civility enabling us to live decently as human beings; the other side has to do with practical accomplishment, with those human skills that contribute to comfort, success, and physical well-being.

The Civilizing Purpose of Education

With preparation for life narrowed to the level of a school objective, the civilizing function of education is elaborated in this way: A good deal of life experience, as it transcends the purely practical, puts us in touch with a cultural legacy. And this legacy is filled with traditions that speak to every side of human life. These traditions add coherence to intellectual life and give meaning and purpose to practical life. It is the duty of the school to transmit the intellectual legacy to its students enabling them to achieve a respectable level of literacy in it.

Tradition is one side of the scholastic coin, truth is the other. The school's duty, according to this theory of education for life, is to give students sound instruction. The practical purposes of education will add definition to this instruction. With a grasp of theory and a command of truth, we have in our possession what may be the most practical kind of education, although in our pragmatic age respect for intellectual tradition is played down and, sometimes, vigorously withheld. This education, which we can describe as being at least potentially practical and immensely rewarding theoretically, contains the ideas and the idealism for motivating society toward good and great things. Ideas are the power plant for generating the current for social reconstruction and leadership.

It is possible, as recent educational events illustrate, to commit preparation for life to social activism and to make schools camps which social reformers take up their intrepid marches.[20] But the more conventional interpretation is to make the school the home of ideas, so that persons, using a variety of means, will be able to influence society after their school days are over. In this way, though, the school's social influence is indirect rather than direct. Finally, in consequence of an education in traditional civility, confirmation will be given to the democratic charter, which, in the final analysis and with all its fragility, maintains its authority for prescribing regularity and coherence to the social, political, and legal order in the consent and understanding of the citizens.

The Practical Purpose of Education

Educational philosophers are amenable to defending the civilizing functions of the school and at their eloquent best are persuasive. But now we are faced with a common pragmatic rejoinder: We must make a living. And making a living, along with living well, is becoming, as society becomes more demanding and more complex, a full-time obligation. What practical purposes can be distilled from life itself and used to inform schools with respect to their overriding practical objectives?

Few educators debate the efficacy of these practical and necessary educational purposes. Yet debate centers on where such objectives should be placed on an educational hierarchy. In any case, these are the objectives, and it would seem clear that no contemporary school or educational program could afford to ignore them: vocational and professional skill; knowledge of personal and community health practices and habits; skill to fulfill the responsibilities of citizenship on the local, state, and national levels; emotional stability and intellectual perspective to function as a member of a family; knowledge and skill to make necessary decisions in connection with the consumption of goods and services; a grasp of the methods of science in order to make an intelligent appraisal of the scientific and technological age in which we live; a sensitivity to the good and beautiful things of life and the world, including art, music, and literature; an ability to make profitable and human use of leisure time in an economic society where leisure time is becoming more abundant; the ethical sensitivity to assume personal and social responsibility; and, finally, the development of an ability to think in order to resolve day-to-day problems inevitably confronting us.[20]

Social science, the assumption proceeds, contains the information educators need to construct practical curricula to realize these objectives. So educational philosophers should turn to social science for guidance when they undertake to state practical objectives for the schools.

Education for Life Adjustment.   Whether we as individuals play some role in the development of social organizations or are only interested bystanders (and democratic policy strives to make us participants), we are nevertheless faced with the obligation to conform to social, economic, and political order. The social, physical, economic, and political worlds will only infrequently heed our personal pleas for recognition. To live successfully, we must, life adjustment theory tells us, learn to adjust to the realities of all of life. First, though, we must know what they are. And educational philosophy can tell us how to discover these realities. So, calling upon sociology for help, educators resort to an analysis of the broad, comprehensive job of life. What are its requirements? Once we know the needs of life, they can be put into the school's curriculum and children can be prepared for life by mastering the knowledge and skill essential to meeting these needs.

This, the expositors of life adjustment allege, is far less difficult than it sounds. Despite the complexity of social research, it is nevertheless possible to study and analyze the various sides to society. Once knowledge of what society requires for success is acquired, the necessary educational and personal adjustments can be made.

Education for Cultural Pluralism.   Appraising the contemporary status of society, especially American society, we see it beset with problems of race, integration, sex, social mobility, and poverty. In addition, it is beset with educational problems relating to culture, or to those fundamental ideals exhibited in language, literature, song, and social mores. The point of education for cultural pluralism is to withdraw the school's commission for teaching a majority culture, or for transmitting a social inheritance belonging only to one part of society. This social and educational theory begins with the assumption that all cultures, without regard for social setting, have equal worth. And this admission of equality of worth implies two things: First, minority cultures must have a place in the school. They must be part of a broadly conceived social education, and students whose association with any one of these cultures is native must have a chance to study it in a way authenticating its intrinsic worth. Second, a concerted effort must be made in schools to teach everyone to value and respect cultures other than their own.

EDUCATION FOR GROWTH

Education for growth, a statement of educational purpose most generally consistent with pragmatism, had its most explicit formulation in the philosophical work of John Dewey. After Dewey, educational philosophers by the score adopted growth as a principal educational purpose and undertook to shape school policy in ways that would promote it. One must begin with the realization, though, that when Dewey idealized growth he meant it as an end in itself rather than as a process having an end.[21]

Expositors of education for growth begin with two assumptions: First, children are immature and, because of their native ability to learn, are traveling down the road to maturity. Second, as they travel this long road, one frequently filled with all kinds of obstacles (some predictable and others completely novel), they have the right to expect from the schools a course of instruction providing them with habits for meeting and mastering existing conditions and, moreover, for adjusting their skills and their behavior to novel conditions.

Children in school, or in educational circumstances of any kind, have a capacity for growth, and this growth is best when it enables children to use their capacity in connection with new aims. New aims are distilled from the experience of life itself. Such aims must be neither routine nor the inventions of curriculum builders, educational philosophers, or teachers, for such aims have only one consequence: They arrest growth.

Growth is a natural characteristic of life. Nothing in education endows children with it or withdraws it from them, although faulty educational procedures can arrest or modify it. The point is that education, to adopt the language of John Dewey, is one with growing. It has no end beyond itself.[22]

When educational purpose is defined as growth, and when this definition is taken seriously, it means that schools must kindle in students a desire for growth, and this kindling involves applying the artistry of teaching without at the same time descending into any kind of compulsion or routine training. In addition, it requires that the school provide the means of growth. In all its operations—in the curriculum, in method, in the general environment of the school itself—necessary and appropriate means to ensure personal growth must form the seed and the motive force for decent educational accomplishment.

EDUCATION FOR PERSONAL FULFILLMENT

Every philosophy of education pays some heed to the realization of purely personal goals but, with the exception of existentialism and humanism (a theory of schooling), personal fulfillment is seldom accorded a high place in statements of educational purpose. Reflecting for a moment on analyses of the fundamental motives of life, we find that Aristotle was probably the first to identify happiness as the principal goal of human striving.[23] But Aristotle laid down a number of conditions for the certification of a standard of happiness, and when we read him we are fairly certain that he did not intend standard to have merely a personal justification. Happiness was achieved by meeting the world on its own terms and developing both knowledge and skill to function effectively in it. In the end, happiness was a reward of intellectual virtue. It came from becoming what one, according to the intentions of nature, ought to become.

Contemporary educational humanism, referred to earlier as romantic humanism, has a number of illustrations in school practice, but its most authentic and revealing codification is found in A. S. Neill's *Summerhill.*[24] This statement of educational purpose (if this is what *Summerhill* is) appears to take for granted that happiness is the goal of life, so it gives little attention to translating it to education. It stresses, however, that the definition of happiness and success is both narrow and personal. The world, we are told, although the telling is probably unnecessary, is filled with all kinds of cruelties, with all manner of social and physical obstacles, with evil, avarice, greed, illness, war, and suffering. Amid all these serious and sometimes unavoidable impediments, we must try to find our way to a goal giving us personal satisfaction and happiness.

The schools responsible for educating us can be of considerable help along these lines if they begin by understanding that their principal duty is to adopt a hands-off policy with respect to the assignment of educational purpose in particular cases. Schools, in other words, are not to tell us what will make us happy. They should, however, use all the means at their disposal to educate us in such a way that we are capable of making a judgment for ourselves about what is most worth our attention, of what in the end will make us happy. All this, though, must be done without any element of compulsion, indoctrination, or conditioning. To provide for an education along these lines, schools should have the resources to equip us to make the kind of life journey we want to make. Again, the warning must be heeded by every responsible educator and teacher: The school must not force its teaching on us. It must wait; it must be ready to teach when we want its teaching. Chances are, considering the complexity of life in modern society and the essential skills demanded for success, to say nothing of happiness, that schools will have plenty to do.

When the objective of education is personal fulfillment, schools—indeed, all of education—must be ready to withdraw from any exercise of stating their goals. Such determinations are personal and exceedingly private. Yet the schools should do their best to help us form these objectives for ourselves and, as we have said, have those resources of positive instruction ready and waiting if we decide to use them.

Obviously, such interpretations of educational purpose raise huge questions of policy, to say nothing of causing unease, among persons called upon to support the schools whose purposes they are excluded from superintending.

We need knowledge to give direction to our lives and to enable us to make a living; we need a sense of value, a standard of ethics or morality, to enable us to live decently and responsibly; and we need to be able to recognize and understand the beauty of the world, of life, and of creative art to make life more fully and culturally human. The ancient Greeks were frontiersmen in the quest for beauty, although they were concerned mainly with the beauty and grace of the body and, to some extent, with the beauty of a noble character. The humanists of the Great Renaissance taught unforgettable lessons about the aesthetic appeal of poetry and literature and laid, in addition, a secure foundation for the promotion of fine art. In the development of fine art and music, generation after generation of our ancestors came to prize the beauty of things appealing first to the senses and then to the mind. And now we must inquire: On what basis should we make judgments about beauty, about what is and what ought to be appealing to us?

Interpretation of Aesthetic Standard

Is it enough to say that I like or dislike something? Are evaluations of the worth and appeal of the beauty and artistry of the world merely a matter of personal taste? If some work of art appeals to me and is ignored as meaningless by another person, is it possible to conclude that we are both right in our aesthetic judgment? Are we, in fact, making an aesthetic judgment? Or is our reaction merely a matter of caprice or whim?

By now, we know that philosophies of education have theories of reality, knowledge, and value. They have theories of aesthetics as well. And although it is impossible to delve very deeply into various philosophies or theories of aesthetics, we can nevertheless make a beginning by giving a quick summary of where each stands with respect to standards of beauty.

Idealist philosophers were probably the first to concern themselves with standards for evaluating and appreciating beauty. When they did, following with logical precision the standards already established with respect to the operations of the universe, they found the standard for beauty expressed in the absolute mind, or spirit. What is good and true is expressed therein, so it was entirely consistent to expect to find the ultimate definition of beauty in the same place. Idealists discovered, as we have also, that the absolute mind is seldom transparent; it does not divulge its secrets easily. So again, following the usual rational procedures of idealism, it becomes the responsibility of good minds, properly schooled and trained, to bore into the expressions of the absolute mind and to discover what we ought to like by telling us something about the standards essential to making judgments about beauty.

Realist aesthetic theory begins from a different place. It begins with nature. And nature is dominated by order. Natural operations are expressed in the design of the natural order, and our theory of art and beauty, if it is to give us guidance for making personal judgments, must follow the prescription in the law of nature. What is aesthetically valuable and tasteful is, in the final analysis, that which conforms to the order of nature. Incongruity, incoherence, and disorder violate the order of nature and they violate, too, the symmetry and harmony of all works of art. A naturalist school of artists, whether in fine art, music, or literature, most clearly illustrates the realist theory of aesthetics at work. What is best, what we ought to judge best, conforms to reality. Anything unnatural, whether its appeal is to the mind or to the senses, is bound to be rejected by any realist aesthetic standard.

The aesthetic theory of religious humanism introduces a new side, a side accounted for mainly in the intellect and imagination. What is beautiful, what we ought to like, must first have an intellectual content that is an accurate reflection of human, social, and spiritual life. When the intellectual soundness is certified, if the object of art is both good and true, then the human imagination takes over. Imagination is a spiritual power of the mind and it creates, beginning with what is, what ought to be on the level of beauty. The basis for forming judgment about aesthetic worth rests on an intellectual apprehension of the purpose, the nature, and the scope of any artistic endeavor. With a standard for evaluating beauty in nature, in human activity, even in the soul itself, we are absolved from following the ephemeral guidance of taste.

Pragmatism's approach to standard for aesthetics follows the same course as for knowledge, reality, and value. Beginning with personal likes and dislikes, those things with appeal and those with none, we progress to a point where social evaluations made in connection with works of art are recognized. A social consensus with respect to what is appealing, to what has aesthetic worth, is as far as a pragmatic theory is able to go.

Existentialism is dominated by subjectivism and, some say, aesthetic arrogance: My evaluation of beauty and my inclination to appreciate works of art, literature, or music should be entirely my own. As I develop my standard for judgment, I will less and less be dominated by standards employed, and sometimes imposed, by others.

Teaching Aesthetic Standard

When we take the standards recommended in aesthetic theory and put them to work, we have alternative courses of action. First, and following a generally idealist thesis, we should begin with the world's masterpieces, whether in literature, music, or art. The final judgment as to their excellence, their appeal to what is fundamentally beautiful, is their universality in dealing with perennial human issues. Put differently, great works of art, we can call them classics, deal with human themes in relation to beauty that are totally indifferent to time and place. Great art knows no history and is ignorant of geography and time. Its standard of excellence is taught most effectively by following a pedagogy of imitation.

Realist aesthetic theory has no difficulty whatever in recommending the great masterpieces as models for the development of standard. We are, after all, largely creatures of our experience, and this is important to remember. Yet, it is equally important to remember that standard for judgment comes not from the art so far created, although it may illustrate standard, but from the natural design of what is represented by art. So art may speak to our minds, to our emotions, or to our sense of values, and when it does it must represent the order of nature and accurately reflect things as they are. Art is a way nature has of communicating with us. To be authentic, though, art must be a representation of what is. The handiest illustration here is literature where, if it is not to betray things as they are, art must represent reality, with all its crudity, brutality, and meanness, although it must do so in an artistic way. All of life is not beautiful; some sides are sordid. These sides, too, may be the subject of art, especially of literature and drama, and they are aesthetically sound to the extent their representations of reality are accurate.

Religious and rational humanism have an undiminished respect for the intellect. So by using the great works of art as models and illustrating their intellectual soundness, we are able to teach persons the standard of artistic excellence and beauty. Art may take various forms, and it may depart from purely material norms to appeal to the human spirit. But when it does it must contain meaning, and this meaning must be consistent with fundamental ideals of rationality and, in religious humanism, with revelation. Good art never distrusts, destroys, or caricatures the dignity of man, the essentials of reality, or the dependability of knowledge. Men and women have a right to appreciate the beautiful things of life, of nature, and of a spiritual relationship with their Creator, but the appeal of art to human emotion is made through the intellect.[25]

What is a good book? Why do I praise a movie? Why do I admire the great masterpieces of visual art? And what tells me when music is good, pleasant, and satisfying? So far we have seen some answers to these questions. The answers centered on standards for judging beauty and refinement. With these standards in our possession, we have something to teach oncoming generations about what is worth their praise and what merits their blame. Turning to pragmatism, however, we abandon any notion of permanent standard passed on from one to another generation. Each generation is free to make its own appraisal. In doing so it can be guided by the past, but never directed by it.[26] Put quickly, we come to develop standards for appreciating and creating by having experience with art and artistic production. We learn to recognize beauty in the same way we learn anything else: by having experience with it. And we learn something about artistic harmony and aesthetic satisfaction by practicing our judgment. We learn to create by being creative. As an integral safeguard to this learning, we have all around us the general evaluations of society on what is aesthetically appealing and what is not.

The existentialist would feel that we had forsaken freedom and abandoned personal responsibility if we were to adopt any way for learning aesthetic standard other than by immersing ourselves in the practice of artistry. We learn, or come to recognize, what appeals to us, not by looking or listening, but by going to the studio, the study, or the music hall and engaging directly in the work of artistic creation.

One thing is certain and applies, we think, without respect to any association or affinity we may have to one or another aesthetic theory: The possibility of appreciating art and of developing a sense for beauty is impossible without some experience in fine art, music, and literature. Perhaps our ancestors were wiser than we think when they constructed a curriculum for decent liberal education and called it the curriculum of the seven arts. Although they neglected fine art in this litany of artistic objective, they included music and recognized its appeal to the clearly secular as well as to the spiritual nature of men and women.

Human beings, the authority of the science of reason—philosophy—tells us, are seekers after the true, the good, and the beautiful. There is more to human life and physical nature, we know, than knowing and doing. There is also the appreciation for the fine and appealing things of life whose beauty goes unrepresented, and sometimes unnoticed, except through art. Where education for aesthetic value should rank on a set of educational objectives is a matter for debate. What would appear undebatable, however, is that some education for appreciating the beauty of nature and of life is essential education for everyone.

What is to form the content of instruction in aesthetics? Without intruding too heavily on instructional content but concentrating on purpose, these points would appear to command the attention of educational philosophy: First, schooling generally is not engaged in the education or training of creative artists. We should take for granted that schools should lay a foundation for prospective creative artists, but this foundation is built on general educational decency. Except in special schools, technical instruction in art seldom finds its way to the curriculum. Following this line of thought, schooling's connection with aesthetics should be on the level of consumption. We may not paint portraits or compose operas, yet we should have enough instruction to appreciate them.

So the second point adverts to the setting of standards for appreciation. Here, it would appear, if such instruction is to be effective, we should be taught something of the technical skill essential to artistic execution. This is probably the easiest part to the whole process, for there is a good deal of agreement in painting, music, and architecture, in all the arts, as to what constitutes technical competence.

The next two parts to instruction in art appreciation are harder to teach. How well does an artist employ technical skill and thus fulfill the purpose of his composition? Did the artist succeed? Although some degree of objectivity is possible relative to evaluations of artistic success, art, we know, speaks with many voices. After this, the ultimate artistic dividend is the meaning or significance communicated in any artistic illustration. What does it say about life and reality? And whatever it says, does it say it only to me or to everyone? At this point,

FIGURE 7.1
A Summary of Educational Purposes

Education for Discipline	Education should aim principally at forming and strengthening the mental faculties, thus enabling persons to meet and master the exigencies of life when school days are over.
Education for Knowledge	Education should concern itself mainly with the teaching of useful knowledge and skill, which are essential to life in society.
Education for Character	Using any means at its disposal, including discipline and knowledge, education should seek to form morally responsible and socially sensitive human beings.
Education for Life	Civility and utility are essential conditions for personal and social decency and success. Education should concern itself with the teaching of relevant competencies.
Education for Growth	Education should supply opportunity for personal growth. It should always aspire to cultivating rather than arresting growth.
Education for Personal Fulfillment	Happiness is life's ultimate objective, so education should contain the means to promote personal autonomy, an essential condition to happiness.
Education for Aesthetic Refinement	Education should prepare persons to appreciate beauty in all its various forms and supply standards for making aesthetic judgments.

objectivity is fleeting and teachers teaching for the appreciation of beauty are hardly to be envied.

Finally, we should consider the possibility of art itself being a teacher. The subtlety of art's impact, not only on the intellect but on the emotions as well, through music, literature, poetry, sculpture, painting, and architecture can communicate lessons about human dignity, dependence, integrity, and ingenuity that the more prosaic subjects of the curriculum are almost certain to miss. Yet, if we are ready to acknowledge art as a teacher, we should be all the more eager to embrace those aesthetic standards that, it would appear, are essential conditions for the comprehension of art.[27]

NOTES

1. Faith in education is illustrated well by HENRY J. PERKINSON, *The Imperfect Panacea: American Faith in Education, 1865–1976* (New York: Random House, Inc., 1977) pp. 3–12, 219–221.
2. See PAUL GOODMAN, *Compulsory Mis-education*, pp. 10–24, 31–34.
3. "Original Papers in Relation to a Course of Liberal Education," *The American Journal of Science and Arts,* XV (January 1829), 297–351.

4. Reproduced in W. H. WOODWARD, *Vittorino da Feltre and Other Humanist Educators* (New York: Teachers College Press, 1963), pp. 96–118.

5. ERASMUS, *De Ratione Studii,* in W. H. WOODWARD, *Desiderius Erasmus Concerning the Aim and Method of Education* (New York: Teachers College Press, 1964), p. 164.

6. Ibid. ERASMUS' *De Copia* (see D. B. KING and H. D. RIX, *On Copia of Words and Ideals*) (Milwaukee: Marquette University Press, 1963) became an immensely popular textbook and guide. It appeared in fifty editions before 1555.

7. J. F. HERBART, *On the Aesthetic Revelation of the World as the Chief Work of Education* trans. H. M. and E. FELKIN (London: Swan Sonnenschein & Co., 1892), p. 57.

8. THEODORE M. GREENE, for example, uses the title "A Liberal Christian Idealist Philosophy of Education" for his chapter in *Modern Philosophies and Education,* in the Fifty-fourth Yearbook of the National Society for the Study of Education (Chicago: University of Chicago Press, 1955).

9. HERMAN H. HORNE, "An Idealist Philosophy of Education," in the Forty-first Yearbook of the National Society for the Study of Education, *Philosophies of Education* (Chicago: University of Chicago Press, 1942), p. 193, is clear and precise when he asks: "Does idealism as a philosophy = religion?" He answers "No. Idealism is a certain intellectual account of the world. It provides only one possible basis for religious worship."

10. PLATO, *The Republic* (Cambridge, Mass.: Loeb Classical Library, Harvard University Press, 1930–1935), vol. I, Bk ii, par. 377a; Bk. iii, par, 392b; Bk. x, par, 592a; and *Laws* (Cambridge, Mass.: Loeb Classical Library, Harvard University Press, 1926), vol. II, Bk. viii, pars. 810c–811b.

11. HERMAN H. HORNE, *Philosophy of Education,* rev. ed. (New York: Macmillan, Inc. 1927), pp. 179 and 182; and B. B. BOGOSLOVSKY, *The Ideal School* (New York: Macmillan, Inc., 1936), p. 18.

12. JOHN WILD, "Education and Human Society: A Realisit View," in the Fifty-fourth Yearbook of the National Society for the Study of Education, *Modern Philosophies and Education* (Chicago University of Chicago Press, 1955), p. 18; and HARRY S. BROUDY, *Building a Philosophy of Education* (Englewood Cliffs, N.J.: Prentice-Hall, Inc., 1961), pp. 241–242.

13. The difficulty encountered on the level of action is exhibited by SHERMAN M. STANAGE, "Meaning and Value: Human Action and Matrices of Relevance in Philosophies of Education," *Educational Theory,* 26 (Winter 1976), 53–71.

14. B. F. SKINNER, *Beyond Freedom and Dignity* (New York: Alfred A. Knopf, Inc., 1971), p. 136.

15. JACQUES MARITAIN, "Thomist Views on Education" in the Fifty-fourth Yearbook of the National Society for the Study of Education, *Modern Philosophies and Education* (Chicago: University of Chicago Press, 1955), p. 63.

16. See, for example, WILLIAM MCGUCKEN, "The Philosophy of Catholic Education," in the Forty-first Yearbook of the National Society for the Study of Education, *Philosophies of Education* (Chicago: University of Chicago Press, 1942), p. 266.; WILLIAM F. CUNNINGHAM, *The Pivotal Problems of Education* (New York: Macmillan, Inc., 1940), p. 567, defines Catholic education this way: It is "a process of growth and development whereby the natural man baptized in Christ, *under the guidance of the teaching Church* (a) assimilates a body of knowledge derived from human effort and divine revelation, (2) makes his life ideal the person of Jesus Christ, and (3) develops the ability, with the aid of divine grace, to use that knowledge in pursuit of this ideal."

development whereby the natural man baptized in Christ, *under the guidance of the teaching Church* (a) assimilates a body of knowledge derived from human effort and divine revelation, (2) makes his life ideal the person of Jesus Christ, and (3) develops the ability, with the aid of divine grace, to use that knowledge in pursuit of this ideal."

17. WILLIAM F. O'NEILL, "Existentialism and Education for Moral Choice," *Phi Delta Kappan* XLVI, no. 2 (October 1964), 48–53; and VAN CLEVE MORRIS, *Existentialism in Education: What It Means* (New York: Harper & Row, Publishers, Inc., 1956), p. 38.

18. R. S. PETERS, "Reason and Habit: The Paradox of Moral Education," in *Philosophy and Education*, Israel Scheffler, ed., 2nd edition (Boston: Allyn & Bacon, In., 1966), pp. 245–262. A more general critique may be found in BETTY A. SICKEL, "Can Kohlberg Respond to Critics?" *Educational Theory*, 26 (Fall 1976), 337–347.

19. Social activism in education had what may have been its first theoretical justification in GEORGE S. COUNTS, *Dare the School Build a New Social Order?* (New York: The John Day Company, 1932). For a current evaluation of Counts' work, see WILLIAM E. SHEERIN, "Educational Scholarship and the Legacy of George S. Counts," *Educational Theory*, 26 (Winter 1976), 107–112.

20. Objectives such as these are based on the work of the Educational Policies Commission, *Education for All American Youth* (Washington, D.C.: National Education Association, 1944), p. 216.

21. JOHN DEWEY, *Democracy and Education* (New York: MacMillan, 1916), p. 49.

22. Ibid.

23. ARISTOTLE, *Eudemiam Ethics.* In *The Works of Aristotle*, trans. and ed. by W. D. Ross (Oxford: Clarendon Press, 1908–1931), 1214b 25f. ADINA SCHWARTZ, "Aristotle on Education and Choice," *Educational Theory*, 29 (Spring 1979), 97–107, refers to this point in her comparison of Aristotle and Kant.

24. A. S. NEILL, *Summerhill: A Radical Approach to Child Rearing* (New York: Hart Publishing Company, 1960).

25. JACQUES MARITAIN, *Creative Intuition in Art and Poetry* (New York: Pantheon Books, Inc., 1953), p. 100.

26. JOHN DEWEY, *Art as Experience* (New York: Minton, Balch & Co., 1934), p. 40.

27. The educational possibilities of art are handled in a perceptive article by DONALD ARNSTINE, "Learning, Aesthetics, and Schooling: The Popular Arts as Textbooks on America," *Educational Theory*, 27 (Fall 1977), 261–273.

READINGS

ARNSTINE, DONALD, *Philosophy of Education: Learning and Schooling.* New York: Harper & Row, Publishers, Inc., 1967. The author devotes Chapter 7 to learning and the aesthetic quality in experience.

BUBER, MARTIN, *Between Man and Man.* New York: Macmillan, Inc., 1965. Education worthy of the name, Buber writes, pp. 104–117, is essentially education for character.

DEWEY, JOHN, *Democracy and Education.* New York: Macmillan, Inc., 1916. In his great book, pp. 41–53, Dewey describes education as growth.

GOODMAN, PAUL, *Compulsory Mis-education.* New York: Horizon Press, 1964. The design to contemporary education, Goodman argues, pp. 10–24, 31–34; is out of date. He has suggestions for improving it.

HERSH, RICHARD, DIANA PAOLITTO, and JOSEPH REIMER, *Promoting Moral Growth: From Piaget to Kohlberg.* New York: Longman, Inc., 1979. With an introduction by Kohlberg, the book gives a good synthesis of his theory of moral development.

HORNE, HERMAN H., *Free Will and Human Responsibility.* New York: Macmillan, Inc., 1912. Although old, this book sets the tone for educational purpose in American idealism.

LODGE, RUPERT C., *Plato's Theory of Education.* New York: Harcourt Brace Jovanovich, 1947. Plato, more than any other educational philosopher, paid close attention to the goals of education.

NEILL, A. S., *Summerhill: A Radical Approach to Child Rearing.* New York: Hart Publishing Company, Inc., 1960. The aim of life, Neill says, is happiness. Education should prepare for life. Page 24 reveals the purpose of education at Summerhill, the English school that illustrated Neill's humanism.

NOLL, JAMES W., *Taking Sides: Clashing Views on Controversial Educational Issues.* Guilford, Conn.: The Dushkin Publishing Group, Inc., 1980. Various conceptions of educational purpose are treated as five issues in Part I.

SMITH, PHILIP, G., "Knowledge and Values," *Educational Theory,* 26 (Winter 1976), 29–39. The author returns to the old question and asks it this way: "How does rightness relate to goodness?"

WHITEHEAD, ALFRED NORTH, *The Aims of Education and Other Essays.* New York: Macmillan, Inc., 1929. Whitehead ends Chapter 1 on this note: "The essence of education is that it be religious." The reader is bound to want to know how this conclusion is justified.

WINKLER, FRANZ, *Man: The Bridge Between Two Worlds.* New York: Harper & Row, Publishers, Inc., 1960. On pages 205–215 the author shows the importance of knowledge as an educational objective.

8

DETERMINING
EDUCATIONAL
CONTENT

$\mathbf{D}$ebate surrounding educational purpose is perennial, and we are far from being optimistic about finding a way to terminate it now. Yet, reviewing the history of education, including the history of educational philosophy, we find that neither dispute over human nature nor dispute over educational purpose used all of educational philosophy's rhetorical ammunition. Most of it was discharged in connection with the question: What should be taught?[1] What scholastic means should be employed to achieve the purpose agreed upon? And debate over this question, even within the friendly borders of one or another philosophy of education, is with us still. Controversy surrounding the question of curriculum content shows no sign of subsiding. Safe to say, this issue in educational philosophy will affect the work of teachers in contemporary society more directly than any other we can think of.

CURRICULAR THEORY: GENERAL
CONSIDERATIONS

Some correlative questions pertain to a theory of curriculum, so before we inquire about the curriculum as it is perceived in various philosophies of education, we should briefly examine them.

The Possibility of Teaching

We begin with what at the outset might appear to be an audacious inquiry, or some would say, an inquiry steeped in impertinence or nonsense: Is teaching possible? Although the literature on this point is far from being extensive, it is nevertheless large enough for us to see that this question, although never cultivated intensively by educational philosophers, is consequential. It has almost nothing to do with the existence or the validity of knowledge, so it skirts epistemology to deal directly with the psychology of communication.

In this context the term *communication* includes both information and attitude—anything, in fact, conventionally associated with the art of teaching. It does not center on any supposition involving the possibility of learning, for the assumption is clear enough, even among persons who reject the possibility of teaching, that learning occurs. Its occurrence, however, is a result of pure discovery. The mediating influence of the educator and the artistry of the teacher are lightly esteemed. Neither can have any direct bearing on education.

Still, even to adopt the notion that teaching is impossible does not allow educational philosophy to disregard the content of experience, which, it would seem, would have to be pure and immediate. It does, however, remove from serious philosophical consideration any question relative to formal education and, instead, imposes a heavy burden on society, on the generality of human experience to shape the kind of climate where broad and decent learning is possible. It appears obvious that avant-garde critics of American schooling who conspire to deschool American society have missed a theoretical foundation for their bold thesis. Yet, so far as we know, no advocate for deschooling has taken a philosophical stance denying the possibility of teaching. It is enough to allege, they say, that the teaching going on in the schools does not amount to much.[2]

The rejection of teaching as a human possibility can be made a little clearer. Teaching requires communication; if communication is lacking, teaching is likewise absent. The problem has three sides: What is communicated? What are the essential conditions for communication? Under what circumstances can communication be judged successful?

So far as the first side is concerned, teachers can tell students something, and no one rejects the dictates of common experience to abandon this proposition. Yet, mere telling can be antiseptic, so the point of reference becomes meaning. What teachers tell students arises from and finds its meaning in teachers' paradigms of belief; what students are told filters through their systems of belief. If the students' fundamental beliefs are identical to those embraced by teachers, exponents of this thesis argue, the information communicated is unnecessary, for students already know what teachers are telling them. But if the students' systems of belief are different from the teachers', then teaching is impossible, for communication—transmission of meaning—cannot take place. This is Bernard Davis's conclusion: "If teaching is to be of use in the cases for which it is needed, it must be possible in cases in which the assumption of shared systems of beliefs fails. But

255

is this possible? For something to be taught it must be communicated. For it to be communicated it must be a consequence of the material presented by both the teacher's system of beliefs and the pupil's system of beliefs. Insofar as the pupil's and the teacher's beliefs do not coincide, communication does not take place. But, insofar as the pupil's and the teacher's beliefs do coincide, teaching is unnecessary. So, insofar as teaching can occur it is unnecessary. And, insofar as teaching is necessary, it is impossible."[3]

If teaching is either unnecessary or impossible, good sense would tell us to abandon it, and this appears to be Davis' counsel. In fairness to him, however, we should add that he recognizes ways other than through teaching for human education to occur. He encourages us to submit these alternatives to intensive cultivation.

Should this dilemma be allowed to go unresolved? Must we accept the dogmatic assumption that it is impossible to shape, alter, and broaden a student's system of belief? Rather than jumping precipitously on the bandwagon of untested and untried alternatives to teaching and summarily abandoning teaching (which has been occurring with undoubted success for centuries), should we not attend to a more basic kind of teaching? Should we not concentrate less on the transmission of information—teaching as telling—and instead speak directly to a formation or, if need be, a reconstruction of students' systems of belief? The common currency of educational conviction presupposes a similar foundation from which both students and teachers proceed when instruction begins. The art of teaching will be fraught with deficiency if this sound principle of learning is unrecognized. It is quite another thing to argue that in its essential nature teaching is incapable of effectiveness in shaping systems of belief, in laying a foundation whereupon all competent instruction, both in and out of school, begins. It is too late in the educational game, we can say with some confidence, to dispute the possibility that teaching does occur or to maintain that teaching is restricted solely to the communication of information or skill. Part of a teacher's artistry must be engaged in the communication of meaning and in finding substantial bases whereon meaning can be erected.

If we move beyond Davis' apparently bald conclusion that teaching is impossible—a conclusion not very well supported by evidence—to the position taken by Carl Rogers that teaching is dangerous to the development of the whole person and should therefore be avoided, or to Carl Bereiter's thesis that anything other than skill development undermines personal autonomy and is invidious, we come to firmer philosophical interpretations of the nature of teaching. One may argue, of course, about the possibility of teaching causing learning, and there are advocates for both points of view.[4] In any case, Rogers wants teachers to approach their work as "facilitators"; Bereiter wants them to be "skill-trainers."[5] Both, while they seem to disbelieve the effectiveness or the possibility of teaching, are nevertheless apprehensive about its consequences. These critics and others who appear to share their view are either unmindful of or disregard traditional philosophical analyses of teaching, analyses conveniently reviewed in Israel Scheffler's *Reason and Teaching*.[6]

Three standard interpretations of the nature of teaching are grounded in the writings of John Locke, St. Augustine, and Immanuel Kant. Each has made its mark on educational practice.

Locke's interpretation is consistent with his empiricism. We should not be surprised to find him asserting' with some confidence that our senses convey information about reality to us. Some reality is contained in the experience teachers put before us. But our senses are not merely passive reapers of data, nor are our minds simply reservoirs for holding the data of experience. At this point Locke's empiricism is moderate rather than radical. Our minds take over and, heavily indebted to language, arrange, organize, and classify the data of experience and impose meaning on them.[7] In Locke's interpretation of teaching, it is hardly possible for any student to be an entirely free agent in the learning process; on the other hand, because every student has an active, rational mind capable of independent functioning, it is unlikely that any student will be victimized by his experience, whether it comes directly or through the mediacy of a teacher.

Augustine recognized and stated the paradox rehearsed by Davis and others and, in the end, resolved it by admitting, on one hand, that teaching does not result directly in learning but, on the other, that teaching "prompts" students to experiences they might not have were they left alone. Having these experiences they are able to discover meaning in them by using rational vision, a spiritual power of the human mind.[8] The principal difference between Locke's empirical view and Augustine's visionary one is that mental vision, or insight, is not dependent on the particulars of experience. Locke's experiences, taken one by one, add up to something; Augustine's experiences, absorbed in larger coherent units, allow for the operation of an inner vision to translate them from mere information to knowledge.

Neither Locke's interpretation, which depended on the mind's ability to impose meaning on data, nor Augustine's, which depended on the mind being able to apprehend meaning in reality, was entirely satisfactory to Kant. In his interpretation the rule of reason is the dominating factor that safeguards students from the conspiracy of convention and the despotism of teachers. Kant acknowledges experience, of course, and some kinds of experience may be communicated to students by their teachers. We can imagine Kant concluding that teaching is essential for the advancement of the human race; otherwise, we should make precious little progress. Yet reason has its own rules, and when experience makes its mark on us it is always interpreted, evaluated, and judged by inherent human rational principles. Rational principle, in the end, translates mere information, the raw data of experience, into knowledge.[9]

The Curriculum and the Whole Child

Were educational philosophers indisposed to listen to advice from psychology, they would nevertheless recognize the complex constitution of human nature. With few exceptions they would acknowledge this basic principle: The whole person, not just the mind, the body, the emotions, or the will, is the proper object of education. But they would not stop here. They would go on to affirm this: The whole person may not be the proper object of formal schooling. How much are schools capable of doing? And what kind of knowledge can schools communicate most effectively? How much responsibility for human formation can schools reasonably accept? Or, put another way, how much responsibility for the education of the whole person should schools have thrust upon them?

For example, if we were to make a convincing case for the primacy of character education, as countless educational theorists have done and are doing still, would we then be able to demonstrate that the school is capable of achieving this objective? If we were to conclude that it is, then what experience should be pressed into curricular service for the achievement of this objective? Moreover, is it necessary to think of scholastic content in purely conventional terms? Must there be bodies of knowledge to communicate, or can the content of the curriculum be organized around experience to be learned by directly immersing students in the act of discovery? This, of course, is partly a problem of method or pedagogic technique, but one can scarcely disregard the question's pertinence for the curriculum. We shall see more of this—knowledge vis-à-vis discovery—when we turn to a consideration of educational philosophies and the curriculum later in the chapter.

The Transmission of Culture. When intellectual education is accorded pride of curricular place, as it has been throughout most of education's long history, a good deal of confidence is exhibited in the school's ability to transmit, always staying close to their intellectual content, the knowledge and values judged by society to be most worthwhile. One can take for granted that any society, when it commits its schools to a transmission of the social and intellectual inheritance, will pay allegiance to those things it considers most formative and useful for oncoming generations. The content of the curriculum is bound to reflect the society's basic attitude as to what knowledge is of most worth.

In any society competing loyalties and, sometimes, conflicting values arise; when a school's curriculum is formed, these loyalties and values must be either accommodated, suppressed, or ignored. Whatever formula is adopted for handling them, the school itself is subjected to fluctuating moods and convictions. In consequence, debate rages far and wide over what knowledge is of most worth or, at least, of enough worth to be included in the curriculum. It may be possible to answer this question on the level of principle, as we shall see various philosophies of education doing, but it is quite another matter to answer it on the level of policy and practice; here the principles of educational philosophy are only guides, and practical judgment and experience must be counted on to put curricular policies into practice.

In any case, the basic thesis adopted by curricular theorists when they embrace the principle that the curriculum should transmit culture is this: There is a common core to basic culture. And no mystery surrounds the formation of this common core. Its origin is found in the evolution of human beings in history. Over the ages we have learned—and the lesson has been authenticated in the tests history itself imposes—that certain kinds of knowledge are essential to us if we are to live successfully in society. Additionally, certain human and social values are both universal and essential to a decent life.[10]

Some of these essential values belong to the practical order. They contribute directly or indirectly to preservation. Others are, or are called, ornamental. They contribute qualities of genuineness and humanness to life. Yet, whether we dwell on the practical or the ornamental, everything in the social legacy, everything in the cultural inheritance, obviously cannot be put into the curriculum. Recognizing this and intending this content to be mastered by girls and boys in the schools, we must be selective and include in the curriculum those elements qualifying as being most essential to social and personal decency. Sorting out these elements requires a kind of prudence that, for the most part, must be exercised by men and women who are expert on life and education. They, in the last analysis, should define the breadth and depth of the curriculum and translate for it and for the school's syllabus the essentials of the social inheritance. This is straightforward essentialism (both a theory of curriculum and a theory of schooling), which, although it may not sound easy, may be implemented with expedition in a culturally homogeneous society.

Yet if we shift our thought from the general pattern of culture to its variety of reflected forms, we see men and women evolving in history and living in different parts of the world where various demands are made on them. They develop a special culture that satisfies their social and personal needs. The mainstream of culture as it pertains to human life is clear and deep, but as it runs its social course it drifts away into several tributaries. Some cultural tributaries are shallow and are easily filled or blocked; others are deep and cannot be dammed or diverted.

This is the declaration: Cultural pluralism is a natural consequence of social evolution.[11] Seen in this light, its reality cannot be gainsaid, whatever evaluation may be made of the worth of its various illustrations. But when the schools—in the United States the public schools—are delegated to shape a curriculum to communicate the essentials of the cultural inheritance, decision is imperative. Someone must make cultural choices.[12] Naturally enough, different cultural legacies have intrinsic justification, and the beneficiaries of these cultures have deep and sometimes indelible allegiances to them. How much, if any, of a distinctive cultural legacy can persons be expected to forfeit in the name of social and cultural solidarity? The solution to this complex curricular problem, one magnified by the realities of a pluralistic society, may be found in adopting the sound democratic principle of majority rule with minority right.

On the practical level, however, the application of this principle raises two difficult subordinate problems. If it is desirable for a school's curriculum to transmit the social inheritance in a way that will ensure social solidarity, then it is imperative for the school's curriculum to have a common cultural foundation. How is this common foundation to be formed? Should it be formed from an amalgamation of all cultures represented in society—the melting-pot thesis translated to curriculum[13]—or should it be the majority culture?

In connection with the second problem, a solution has been discovered, at least on the level of theory, and is presently recommended. It allows a place in the school's curriculum for all cultures. In some cases, in some places, this solution might work. Yet, when put to work it threatens to overburden the curriculum; in consequence, the schools do poorly what they could do well with a more restricted commission. With too many cultural legacies to organize into a syllabus and promote equally, scholastic confusion rather than decent learning may be the outcome. The law of diminishing returns sets in quickly and almost certainly takes its toll on scholastic quality.

The danger of scholastic confusion may be illustrated by the contemporary educational embrace of bilingual, or multilingual, instruction. We should begin with this admission: Bilingualism is nothing new in education; additionally, language is a highly effective vehicle for communicating culture. Ancient Rome adopted bilingualism and grafted it to the legacy of classical education. Students in Roman schools studied Greek in order to master Greek culture, which many Romans supposed was superior to their own. But wanting to be true to their own cultural tradition, they studied Latin—their vernacular—as well. They never allowed either Greek language or culture to supersede Latin in the converse of daily life and schooling.

A long historical leap takes us from ancient Rome to twentieth-century America. And here educators are recommending bilingualism—not so much as a way of boring into the essentials of the cultural heritage represented by a language but as an acknowledgement of pluriform culture in American society. Linguistic versatility and variety can be praised and should be supported, but the evidence is almost overwhelming: Neither language (English along with any other) in a bilingual curriculum is mastered with any degree of alacrity.[14] The great enemy to mastery, or even habits of conventional usage, may very well be the failure on the part of educators to establish linguistic priorities, or it may be a determination to do nothing more than pander to public opinion. Talk is cheap, we hear said, but we should be careful about embracing such a superficial view. It is not cheap, for language used with care and precision enables us to learn what we need to know, to share and promote our ideals, and to maintain social standards of reason and decency.[15]

There is, of course, considerable utility in having mastery and fluency in more than one language, and this utility is more and more recognized, especially in the international marketplace. But when justification for a revival of language study in American schools is made on this basis, it is largely indifferent to the social optimism of cultural pluralists.

Another justification for intensive cultivation of language is possible, although there is what amounts to a conspiracy of silence surrounding it. Language is a vehicle for thought. We use symbols—in this case words and sentences—as tools for thought, and without them are close to intellectual helplessness. But this justification, while not rejecting the value of various cultural paradigms, is based on the assumption that linguistic fluency and discipline are outcomes of solid language instruction. With attention riveted on language as a tool for thought, no special notice or praise is given to the advancement of cultural pluralism.

The curricular dilemma introduced by the social fact of cultural pluralism and illustrated further by the contemporary rush to bilingual instruction is by no means amenable to quick and easy resolution.

Intellectual Growth. This approach to the curriculum begins with the assumption that intellectual development—which may be taken as the principal thrust of formal education—is not to aim at the objective of conveying the past to the present. The past may be interesting, and an appreciation for past accomplishment and cultural ways may have some elements of worth, but they are always subordinate to the principal aim of the curriculum. This principal aim is to open the minds of students in such a way that persons are made capable of meeting reality in all its various forms. The school's curriculum should equip students for intellectual growth and maturity.

Viewed in this light, the thorny issue of whose culture is to be embraced by the school's curriculum is bound to be discounted. Intellectual formation, bare

FIGURE 8.1
General Curricular Considerations

The Possiblity of Teaching	(1) Teaching is possible but ineffective. (2) Teaching depends on shared systems of belief; when it is possible, it is also unnecessary. (3) Traditional interpretations of teaching: Augustine, Locke, Kant.
Holistic Education	The education of the whole person is commended to educators, but is the school's curriculum capable of bearing this educational burden?
Physical Education	Physical education has nearly universal support in theory, but in practice lacks intensive cultivation.
Emotional Education	Affective education has contemporary appeal, but educators are uncertain about its curricular status.
Spiritual Education	In a religiously pluralistic society, the place of religion in the curriculum is subject to debate.
Social and Civic Education	How can a curriculum provide for the development of social and civic values and at the same time ensure political and social freedom?
Economic Education	Vocational and consumer education stand as essential elements in preparation for life in contemporary society.
Domestic Education	Preparation for worthy home membership has high priority. How can the curriculum promote it?
Cognitive Formation	If the school's function is primarily intellectual, the curriculum should concentrate on means for intellectual formation. It should contain what can be taught.
Cultural Transmission	The curriculum may be assigned the role of cultural transmission, but in a culturally pluralistic society, whose culture should be taught?
Intellectual Growth	If intellectual growth, rather than acquisition of knowledge, has primacy in the curriculum, should this growth be cultivated by reviewing the accumulated wisdom or by wrestling with the burning issues of the day?

and unencumbered by social values, mores, cultural impediments, or ornaments, is what counts. It should be sought, and with some luck achieved, by giving students curricular experience capable of whetting and sharpening their intellects. They should be taught how to think and act intelligently and thus be ready to meet the authentic realities of life, not with ready-made solutions salvaged from the past but with a trained intelligence. To accomplish this huge educational undertaking a number of skills may be essential, for an ability to think is never developed in a vacuum nor is it cultivated successfully apart from fundamental appurtenances to learning. Yet, following this curricular formula, the curriculum can be rendered culturally free. Stripped of affinity or special allegiance to this or that ethnic group or race, the aim of intellectual accomplishment can be achieved without at the same time involving the school in constant debate over what is essential to culture, and without making any commitment to a common core. Put another way, the common core to educational experience is intellectual skill and acumen, and while neither can be developed without some curricular content, such intellectual accomplishments are culturally antiseptic.

This is not to say, of course, that with this approach to the curriculum society itself will be immunized from the pressing issues of cultural choice or preference. It will, however, remove from the school those constant tensions imposed by cultural pluralism. Following such a line schools will be absolved from making cultural choices.

CURRICULAR ISSUES AT CONFLICT

Without pretending to recite all the conflicting points about the curriculum or promising an exhaustive analysis of them, their status nevertheless should be a matter of record here.

Knowledge for Utility versus
Education for Discipline

Some attention was given to this issue earlier in our discussion of educational purpose, but now we return to it with a focus on curriculum. All of life, we are told, makes various demands for knowledge and skill. Clearly, without some essential knowledge for making a living and for living in society, we should all be extremely disadvantaged. Some of life's demands can be satisfied by what we know, but some require skill to do something—to find employment, earn wages or salaries, and make a living for ourselves and our dependents. Can schools entertain such a broad commission? If they can, how successful have we a right to expect them to be in fulfilling it?

In 1979 the Carnegie Foundation for the Advancement of Teaching, under the auspices of the Carnegie Council on Policy Studies in Higher Education, published a study wherein it promised to speak directly to these issues as they affect

American high schools. The commission's long report eschewed any substantial recommendations for elementary education to concentrate almost solely on secondary and postsecondary education.[16]

Beginning with the ominous pronouncement that 25 percent or more of American secondary school youth are wasting their time, talent, and motivation in the schools as they presently exist, this commission's report called for an overhaul of the high-school curriculum and for substantial changes in postsecondary schooling. Moreover it abandoned, at least by implication, any traditional allegiance to liberal learning for all students and, almost without hesitation, depleted the general curricular significance of knowledge and discipline. Its recommendations, in fact, conspired to give American secondary education a new face.

Instead of following old dicta relative to curricula, where the schools displayed a distinctive scholastic purpose—aiming either at knowledge for use or for discipline—high schools were asked to show a scholastic side only to those students with capacity and interest. But this side would be attractive, the authors of the report supposed, only to a minority in the secondary-school population. The curriculum for the rest—if, indeed, it is right to call it a curriculum—would encompass a variety of experiences and allow students to follow those having the most appeal to them. And a striking departure is made from academic convention: Some secondary-school students would spend the years when otherwise they would have been in school in military service; some would go directly into the economic world, where their education would consist mainly of on-the-job training; others, if so disposed, would engage in various types of social service. They too, for the most part, would be learning by doing.

These recommendations, interestingly enough, are offered in the expectation that, if adopted, they will contribute to the salvation of American secondary education on one hand and to the general benefit of American youth and society on the other.

Such a view of secondary education, with an obvious foundation in a comprehensive theory of life adjustment, is almost certain to be offensive to a minority of secondary-school theorists who continue to put confidence in the disciplinary goals of the high school's curriculum. The high school years, they contend, form an interlude, probably the last one in the lives of most students, permitting them to pursue learning in a disinterested manner. A disinterested pursuit of learning should not be interpreted to mean inconsequential, indifferent, or useless. The worth of such learning is not disclosed in the attainment of skills for sale or knowledge for specific use. The outcome from such curricular exposure to sound and decent learning is an ability to think intelligently and to act prudently.

Secondary-school curricula contain the means to shape intelligence and prudence, although neither the secondary school nor any school can guarantee either in particular cases. If the discipline of cogent thought is insufficient to satisfy critics of contemporary secondary education, there is, finally, cultural appeal. A large-scale abandonment of language and literature, of science and mathematics, of social science, history, and art in secondary-school study will almost certainly render American society a cultural wasteland. Is personal and social aspiration and are cultural values so easily discounted or so unimportant that they can be traded over the academic counter for curricular and scholastic rewards so fragile and ephemeral as vocational skill, military efficiency, and social service?

The Core Curriculum

Justifications for a core curriculum can be made on two levels: principle and policy. Justifying core on the level of principle requires us to reconsider the nature of knowledge. Knowledge, we have been told countless times by epistemologists, has an inherent unity. Knowledge is one, although it may be either recorded or mastered in discrete parts. Perhaps, considering the nature of learning, it can be obtained only by tackling it part by part, by adopting, to employ analogy, Caesar's principle of military strategy—"divide and conquer." If, however, the parts are not organized into a meaningful whole, we shall never have a complete and comprehensive understanding of the world and its reality. We need a backbone, a spine, to which the various parts of knowledge may be associated and around which they may be integrated. Without a core—a common body of knowledge —to which all parts of knowledge may be joined, this theory continues, our grasp of reality is almost certain to be defective.

It is not essential, however, to stay on the level of principle to find justification for core. Educational policy is capable of justifying it too. If societies are to function effectively, it is tempting to believe, they must have some common bond. With a common bond, one formed of value and knowledge and social commitment, it is possible for citizens to communicate their meaning, their aspirations, their hopes and their disappointments. Without a common bond, without a uniform and securely held foundation in knowledge and conviction, society will be fragmented, insecure, and uncertain, and in consequence the general welfare will be difficult or impossible to promote. The spirit of any age will be so fraught with conflict and misunderstanding, due largely to an inability of the members of society to communicate, that social and individual decency will be victimized.

Principle or policy, we say, is capable of justifying a core curriculum. Still, a troublesome problem remains. What is to constitute the core? Should it center on the human ability of thought? Should it concentrate on a development of the arts of expression? Should it be constructed out of the social experience and thus be relative to time and place? Should it be contextual or problematic?

History has taught an unforgettable lesson. If a core curriculum is adopted, the most fundamental instruction, the kind most capable of making communication possible and the kind most likely to weld society to common purpose, is language—the vernacular language. Used with clarity, with precision, and sometimes with persuasion, it holds out the best chance and in the last analysis may be an essential condition for social solidarity and an educational accommodation to the general welfare. Yet enthusiasm for the vernacular, especially when it has the standing of a national language, is in twentieth-century America bound to be on a collision course with a similar enthusiasm for bilingualism.

If we move beyond language to adopt common illustrations from the cultural inheritance, we are almost certain to face objections from advocates of cultural pluralism. Although justifications for a core curriculum may be theoretically plausible and convincing, selecting content for the core and obtaining general assent to it is far from easy.

Electivism

Electivism as a guiding curricular principle begins with a dogmatic assumption: All knowledge is of equal worth. Following this line of thought, logic rejects the erection of any curricular hierarchy. Electivism, we should think, would be extremely difficult to apply at the elementary level. In order to implement electivism at the secondary or postsecondary level, the curriculum would have to be broad and comprehensive. Students could elect any subject, any course of study suitable to them. They would, of course, be expected to study something and would also be admonished to study hard. Commanding their own educational ship they would be readying themselves for life by fulfilling their personal needs and expectations. Who, electivists would ask, is better able to translate need and interest than persons possessing them?

Apart from questions relative to a philosophy of knowledge that begins by discounting degrees of knowledge, a curriculum following the dictates of pure electivism runs the risk of overburdening any high school or college to a point of academic impotence. All curricular alternatives would have to be available. In the practical order, especially in the practical financial order where schools would be obliged to support the teaching of everything, pure electivism is probably impossible. Admitting so much, designers of the curriculum would be in the position of making judgments about what should be included and what should be excluded. In consequence they would have no choice but to violate the basic principle of electivism: all knowledge is of equal worth. And this choice is, in itself, a confession that all knowledge is not of equal worth.

Pure electivism is one thing, and it runs the risk of condemnation by educational philosophers and an alert public opinion; elective possibilities for students, granting them some freedom to pursue the attractions of personal interest by choosing some subjects for study, is quite another. It is, we should think, as unphilosophical to recommend a completely required curriculum that allows neither personal talent nor interest any range as to promote pure electivism.

Relevant Study

The language of contemporary education fairly bristles with talk about relevance.[17] When schools or subjects are castigated, and here no level of learning is absolved, they are accused by their tormentors of being irrelevant. But what is the meaning of *relevance,* and in what ways are schools guilty of irrelevance?

Relevant knowledge, if it means anything at all, means that knowledge has a bearing, a significance, for the case at hand, for something in this instance. If relevance is given a more extensive meaning, it must imply a kind of knowledge capable of having a bearing on, a significance for, life. Yet, it would seem that anyone declaring any kind of knowledge or any subject in the curriculum irrelevant would have to speak with exaggerated confidence or unbridled arrogance to make a judgment about the worth of anything for everyone. What may strike me as being purely ornamental knowledge and having little use could conceivably be eminently useful and practical for another person. Conversely, what appeals to you as being immensely practical and useful for the solution of an immediate problem may have no significance or value whatever for me. If we look at the issue of relevance philosophically, the point is that pronouncements about curricular relevance cannot possibly be based solely on personal judgment. The credentials of any kind of knowledge must be, and we think they are, capable of more substantial verification.

How anything other than error—or, if we may use the phrase, faulty knowledge—can be judged generally irrelevant is beyond the comprehension of the educational philosopher. For certain classes of persons some kinds of knowledge may be more interesting and predictably more useful than other kinds of knowledge. But rendering a personal judgment about the whole curriculum or any subject in it is bound to be dangerous to educational adequacy and decency.

It is possible, for example, for the disciple of disciplinary theory to assert the universal relevance of study: Any kind of study, any subject, to the degree that it contains legitimate knowledge, is capable of influencing the minds of students, of forming them, of shaping them and incubating intellectual vigor.

The study of literally relevant subjects and only relevant subjects puts a severe limit on the possibility of future accomplishment by keeping the horizon of personal aspiration low. What knowledge, what intellectual accomplishment will students need a decade after they leave school? If they are guided only by immediacy in making their curricular choices or, what is worse, if educators responsible for designing curricula make these predictions and put into the curriculum only those studies whose illustrations of relevance seem clear to them, students run the risk of being crippled by the very education intended to raise them to the level of intellectual and moral autonomy.

Curricular Innovation

Progress, we are told, is illustrated by change, but what kind of change is illustrative of progress? No one needs to read very much of contemporary educational literature before being confronted with testimony idealizing the virtue of innovation. And, it would seem, educational leaders seldom have enough confidence in their convictions to resist the temptation to be innovative.

The point seems easy enough to make and justify philosophically: If change results in a more generous or a better distribution of educational opportunity, it can be recommended by its consequences. But if change, or innovation (a better word, we are advised, because, unlike change, it is not neutral but value-laden)[18] neither holds out the likelihood of educational betterment nor promotes educational improvement, it lacks philosophical persuasiveness and educational justification.

Educators, the judicious temperament of philosophy tells us, must be cautious about jumping on the bandwagon of innovation. First, many contemporary innovative practices in education are counterfeit: They are hardly more than old ideas or discarded practices rescued from the scrapheap of history. Second, a prudent evaluation of some proposed innovations would frequently lead to their rejection; they would be revealed as barren of any implicit characteristics contributing to educational improvement. Their best recommendation, not necessarily a good one, may be change for the sake of change.

If educational philosophy recommends caution in adopting the innovative educational plan or practice, it tells us also to be prudent about rejecting novel educational ideas before they have a chance to demonstrate their worth. At this point educators have a good guide available: educational history. We have long since learned how difficult it is to be authentically inventive with respect to educational policy and practice. A careful reading of educational history can provide good guidance about what should be embraced and what should be avoided when change is thrust on us in the name of innovation. No word, not even innovation, contains enough magic to induce us to follow an educational proposal blindly.

Jettisoning innovation before it begins is imprudent, yet there is another side to the coin, a side about which educational philosophy speaks also with the voice of caution. When curricular innovation is tested, students in the schools become the subjects of educational experiment. If innovative practice bears good fruit, their reward is better education; if innovation fails the test of consequence, in some instances students are done what may be irreparable harm. Neither parents nor the public at large look kindly on schools when they undertake to become laboratories experimenting with pedagogic content or technique.

The Curriculum and Social Control

To the extent that education helps form intellects and characters, it makes a positive contribution to social order. But when we shift our focus from moral and intellectual formation to direct social education, we run into some trouble.

Should schooling commit itself to teaching us how to live in political and economic society? Should it undertake to teach the positive worth of, say, the free enterprise system? Should it commit itself to the communication of the virtues of a republican form of government? Should it reflect a constant faith in the democratic charter? When the answer to these questions is affirmative, the schools and their curricula are engaged in teaching for social control. Are they justified in doing so?

Political philosophy has consistently justified the ambition of the state to employ the school as its delegate to teach and ratify the political and economic systems adopted. American schools, on all levels, we should think, promote the worth of the American political system in terms of human justice and decency, not always blind to its faults but pointing with pride to its virtues. Would a school system, controlled by public policy and supported by public money, countenance a curriculum wherein instruction conspired to undermine the democratic charter either directly or subversively? And in this connection, where does legitimate instruction start and stop and where does indoctrination begin and end?[19]

Despite the harsh sound, schools on all levels, and without compromising human freedom, undertake through their instruction and their general climate for learning to promote social control and good political order. The educational philosopher would think it strange if this were otherwise, for no one is on the side of anarchy. Yet, while the general principle may be praiseworthy, its implementation is almost constantly a matter for debate. How much teaching for social control is justifiable? At what point does such teaching become corrosive of freedom? When do the benefits to social tranquility and order atrophy into social paralysis?

The Cocurriculum

Educational philosophers are not of one mind with respect either to the purpose or the maintenance of a cocurriculum. Philosophies of education whose principal focus is on an experience rather than a subject-matter curriculum see little or no reason to make what must be a nominal distinction between the curriculum and the cocurriculum.[20] Should the distinction be made, it turns out to be artificial. Everything is accounted for in experience, so to call one a curricular experience and another a cocurricular experience is pointless.

Shifting from the experiential arena, however, we find educational theorists making and defending a distinction between the curriculum and the cocurriculum. They justify the distinction in one of two ways. The cocurriculum, many critics of American education declare, is a tributary to schooling, one just deep enough to carry the weight of leisure-time activity. In this view, whatever is done in the cocurriculum on any educational level is recreational and, at best, a scholastic diversion. If such diversion can be defended, defense must depend on the need students have for organized recreation in conjunction with the hard and serious work of study. But no distinct benefit to decent learning, they say, is a certified outcome of the cocurriculum.

Another position, however, ratifies the cocurriculum with legitimate educational purpose without discounting the opportunity for recreation and leisure-time employment it contains. We may, it is possible to argue, learn some very important things at our leisure. In this view, the activities of the cocurriculum —and it makes no matter whether they are athletic, dramatic, journalistic, or musical, or whether they are pursued alone or in groups—are designed to function as laboratories for the curriculum. In these activities students can put into practice—especially with respect to character formation—the principles of knowledge relative to good conduct they have learned in the curriculum . Unless the cocurriculum provides an opportunity for extending the formative purposes of the curriculum, it could hardly be justified as a legitimate scholastic function. But educators following this line of thought believe implicitly in the ability of the cocurriculum to make a positive contribution to sound learning, decent character, and wholesome personality.

Curricular Authority

Earlier in American educational history, in fact, in all educational history everywhere, schools were organized and curricula were deployed for the explicit purpose of communicating the knowledge and values that society, then and there, considered most important for informing and forming oncoming generations. No one stopped to debate the issue of curricular authority. Now, however, in an educational age when student rights are idealized, the question should be put: Who should design the school's curriculum?

The question is not frequently asked or answered along philosophical lines, but the possible alternatives are easy enough to recite: the state, the church, the family, students themselves, teachers, school administrators, curricular experts, social engineers. The list could be extended, but the point is clear; all kinds of persons and all kinds of interests have some stake in the school's curriculum. And the stake frequently generates tensions not easily suppressed or compromised.

Educational philosophy supplies only a general answer to this question of curricular authority, although the answer is good enough to find application and prudent use in any educational situation. Curricular authority should be exercised by persons who know most about education, who know what its means are and what, in the last analysis, education is capable of doing. Although educational philosophy should be expected to honor this principle without intimidation, we must nevertheless understand that nothing in educational philosophy tells us who in a particular case should be appointed to the curriculum committee of any school or school system.

Educational Alternatives

We have followed the various avenues of education too far to now begin to believe that schools on any or all levels should have, or can have, custody of the whole of learning. Other social agencies, even the inchoate forces of society itself, are constantly performing a variety of educational functions. No educational philosopher and no educational philosophy disputes the possibility of a great deal of exceptionally worthwhile learning occurring outside the schoolhouse walls.

But this, although not entirely beside the point, does not speak directly to the contemporary issue of educational alternatives. Promoters of alternative education are frequently sympathetic to the arguments made for deschooling. In this case, they are recommending not an alternative to education, for there could be none, but a substitution of out-of-school learning activities of all kinds for school-ing. Sometimes these alternatives to regular schooling are intended to be super-vised by the school, but in other cases they are expected to proceed with complete independence of the school.[21] To ensure a general adoption of alternative educa-tion, the impediment posed in compulsory attendance laws would have to be removed. Educational alternatives—or, more exactly, alternatives to schooling—are illustrated on a grand scale in the report of the Carnegie Commission.[22]

The evidence is overwhelming and convincing: Students by the score, espe-cially in high schools, suffer from educational bewilderment, are impatient to escape from the school's clutches, and lacking a basic good will toward learning, spend a profitless four or more years in the school's custody. While they may be unready for schooling, they are also unready for life. Something is left for them to learn, both for their own and for society's good. Profitable alternatives to schooling can be designed and, to the extent they prove useful, can be counte-nanced.

Risks, however, are implicit in alternative education and should not be mini-mized. One risk is personal. Removed from the mainstream of schooling, alterna-tive education students are in a position of being exposed to a kind of learning with a limited range. They may master knowledge and skill directly associated with their out-of-school experience, but except by accident they will not be exposed to essential knowledge and skill for the broader obligations of life. Another risk is social. If, as is so often supposed, schooling is committed to the transmission of the cultural heritage, alternative education students will be ex-

FIGURE 8.2
Conflicting Issues in Curriculum

Education for Utility	The curriculum should be filled with useful knowledge.
Education for Discipline	The curriculum should contain elements capable of strengthening minds so they will be ready to meet the problems of life and learning.
Core Curriculum	Curricula should be constructed around those central themes wherein all knowledge may be unified and integrated.
Electivism	All knowledge is of equal worth: Curricular choice should rest on interest and need.
Relevance	Curricula should be organized and studies selected on principles of personal preference.
Innovation	Change in education and elsewhere is inevitable, but is innovation for the sake of innovation or to promote an image of currency educationally sound?
Social Control	In promoting social and political values can curricula avoid the contagion of social and political control?
Cocurriculum	Should the cocurriculum provide opportunities for leisure or should it be committed to sound learning?
Curricular Authority	Who should be responsible for building and maintaining the school's curriculum?
Alternative Education	Out-of-school experience, as an alternative to schooling, if care-fully supervised, promises to contribute to human formation.

cused from imbibing this heritage and will, in consequence, be out of touch with the social legacy whose principal worth is demonstrated in the contribution it can make to social solidarity. The risk, to phrase it differently, is one involving cultural illiteracy. In programming for educational alternatives, serious consideration must be given to ways of immunizing students to these risks.

THE CURRICULUM AND PHILOSOPHIES OF EDUCATION

We have wrestled with the question of what to teach and have seen it explored from various sides. Now, we should listen to what systematic educational philosophy is prepared to say about the content of the curriculum.

Idealism

Idealists are ready to send students to the books, although, as Horne says, books "are but temporary earthen vessels in which the treasures of natural and human truth are kept."[23] The curriculum should be organized around bodies of knowledge—and idealists have no hesitation about calling this knowledge truth—which, if they are cultivated prudently and artistically, will be translated by the student from mere information to knowledge. Books are the best tools for ensuring this translation because they contain not only information but interpretation of meaning for the shaping of ideas. In the end, the best ideas, Horne says, will become ideals. And ideals are both guides and safeguards to the decency of human life.[24]

Neither Horne nor, for that matter, any other idealist, instructs us to stay always with our books. Other needs are apparent—vocational training, for example. Schools should have curricular means for handling all manner of needs effectively. However, they should be careful to keep their priorities intact, and the kind of learning entitled to the highest priority is liberal and intellectual.

Horne's idealist voice is eloquent, and he is worth listening to if we want to know what idealism recommends for the curriculum. Other idealists speak of a curriculum designed to satisfy the need human beings have for knowing their physical environment. Subjects in the curriculum delegated to communicate knowledge about the physical world will vary necessarily from scholastic level to scholastic level and according to the intellectual maturity of their students, but every curriculum should contain such knowledge.

Idealism, we should think, would demur from concentrating the whole of its curricular attention on physical science, so provision must be made in the curriculum for those subjects dealing with human civilization (social science), with culture (language, literature, and art), and with personality (human science).[25]

Yet idealism can have still another curricular emphasis: on the communication of knowledge and skill for the promotion of further, independently based learning; on knowledge for the advancement of personal and social welfare; and on the development of sound moral and intellectual habits.[26]

Idealism's approach to the curriculum is at once both academic and traditional. Time is left for self-activity, because in the absence of self-activity the fundamental purpose of learning could never be achieved; however, in the last analysis, the school's curriculum must commit itself to a communication of the tested intellectual and social inheritance. Unless this commitment is clear, a curriculum is unworthy of the name.

Yet, even within this context of academic preoccupation, idealism hears at least one unconventional, perhaps liberal, voice. It is a voice challenging the separation, Greene calls it "the cleavage," of the curriculum from the cocurriculum.[27] In his view all activities supervised by the school and coming under its control are essentially learning activities, and all can contribute something to the full and complete development of personality. Why encumber one group of activities (cocurricular) with a nomenclature almost certain to be diminishing?

Realism

When realists answer the question about what schools should teach, they give the appearance of being uncompromising in their allegiance to a communication of knowledge. Realists, it is true, have a great deal of confidence in informed and disciplined minds, but their educational convictions are not as harsh as they sound. In any case, realists are fully aware of the need to modify and adjust the content of the curriculum to the age, maturity, cultural background, and ability of students in the schools.

Two general views of the curriculum are extant in contemporary realism. The first declares clearly and forthrightly the need that every person aspiring to educational decency has for basic instruction. Basic instruction consists of language (realists mean to begin with the vernacular), of the fundamental elements of logic, and of elementary mathematics. From this beginning, and keeping in mind the need for the curriculum to accommodate students' capacity for achievement, the avenue is open for instruction, first, in the methods of science and, then, in the basic facts of physics, chemistry, and biology. Next come the social sciences and history, followed by the classics in literature and art. There is a pause in this curricular rendition to include at least one foreign language. The concluding recommendation caps all this learning with philosophy, the discipline delegated to impose meaning and order on learning. This, John Wild, a leading spokesman for realism said, is appropriate education for everyone and for every school level.[28] The implication, of course, is evident: The various school levels will be expected to handle this essential curricular content in different, but always instructionally suitable, ways.

The other commonly held realist position on curriculum commits it to the formation of certain essential human habits. Broudy lists them as: symbolic habits, study habits, and habits of research, observation, experimentation, analysis, criticism, discussion, application, and enjoyment.[29] These habits are the primary outcomes toward which the curricula of all schools should aspire. How should schools deploy their instructional resources in order to enhance the possibility of the achievement of these habits?

In its construction, because the cultural and intellectual inheritance is so broad and comprehensive, the school's curriculum must be selective. Principles of selection are essential for superintending the curriculum. The principles are these: What is most generally applicable? What is most urgently needed by students? Answering these questions in the context of the whole corpus of knowledge reveals curricula that, according to Broudy, may be organized around content— the traditional plan—or around problems, a plan with an avant-garde, experimentalistic ring. The point is, though, a problem-oriented curriculum is not an experience curriculum concocted by students out of the froth and foam of their own interests. Both the problem and the content approach to curriculum are intended to promote the development of essential habits. These habits, in the last analysis, are the genius of learning.[30]

Settled, although not always comfortably, in the general camp of realism, we meet behaviorism again. We know where behaviorism takes exception to conventional realism, so those points need not be repeated. But to discover exactly where behaviorism stands on the curriculum is not an easy exercise.

In the first place, those bodies of knowledge that have been accumulated over the decades—both scientific and rational knowledge—must be submitted to tests of verification before they can be included in the curriculum. The test of verification, however, is not intended for certification of truth (as in conventional realism) but for ratification as a behavioral objective. Does this knowledge or do these skills qualify on the score of personal and social suitability? If the curriculum contains what students ought to know and be able to do, then the methodology of behaviorism (and methodology or technology of education is supreme) is put to work.

Yet this matter of deciding what should be taught may be less difficult than it sounds. We have the means, behaviorists say, to discover the objectives most useful for a good personal and social life. Once these objectives are certified by the realities of life itself, we have only to seek their development through any curricular organization that proves its effectiveness.

Religious Humanism

We should begin with this admission: Educators with a commitment to religion are not obliged by any article of religious faith to adopt the curricular principles of religious humanism. True, its principles are most generally compatible with broadly conceived religious education, but other curricular positions are also adopted by educators whose religious devotion is zealous and profound. Some religious educators may pay allegiance to idealism and follow its general curricular thrust; some may be religious existentialists; and others may embrace realism. Still, the appeal of religious humanism is seductive, and most religious educators, we think, find its curricular paradigms satisfying.

Beginning with the assumption, one seldom challenged by any philosophy of education, that education is both an individual and a social process, religious humanism maintains, on a level of principle, that the content of the curriculum must speak, first, to those elements in education certified by the essential nature of human beings. Human nature has certain permanent features totally independent of social evolution. Thus, certain fields of concentration and certain subjects must be handled in the curriculum because they bear directly on the nature of human beings. And essential human character is divinely bestowed. This thesis religious humanists hold with supreme confidence, for the ultimate authority is God himself; and the source for this divinely inspired knowledge is revelation.

Yet men and women live in the world and are to a great extent products of social evolution. What they need in order to live effectively in society changes according to the changing conditions in the social world. In consequence, the curriculum must contain elements speaking directly to men and women whose feet are planted in a historical period with its own peculiar social requirements and circumstances.

No religious humanist would argue that the curriculum of the schools in the late twentieth century should be a replica of the schools of, say, the thirteenth century, regardless of the way some theologians and philosophers idealize the intellectual excellence of the medieval genre.

This view of persons in society recommends the ratification of certain priorities of educational purpose, as we have seen, and it admonishes educators to organize a curriculum with an explicit hierarchy. Those things most important to the essential character of human beings must be taught first and most solicitously; then things that contribute to the effectiveness of life should be cultivated.

Religious humanism's curricular theory recognizes and uses the principles of permanence and change to guide the construction of the school's curriculum. The calendar of human life turns; none of history's clocks stands still. The school's curriculum, while not likely to change abruptly from year to year or even from generation to generation is, nevertheless, amenable to change.

What guidance do these curricular principles give to religious humanists? They suggest, first, that the school should aim at the development of the permanent human abilities—thought and expression. Although these abilities may vary from person to person, one more and one less able, everyone possesses them in some measure. Curricula, therefore, must make provision for the development of thought and expression, taking into account the fact of individual differences in capacity and motive to learn. It must also make provision for the person living in society, and this provision is two-dimensional: Social need, although it may not flow directly from human nature itself, is nevertheless imperative. The curriculum must keep abreast of the time. It must, moreover, keep abreast of additions and amendments to the intellectual inheritance.[31]

The common characterization of religious humanism as a theory paralyzed by perennialism is out of focus, although parts, but only parts, of the curriculum are unamenable to change.

What areas of knowledge should be included in the curriculum? Without detail, here are the principal areas designated for serious study: natural science, human science, metaphysical science (philosophy and theology), fine arts, and language arts.

Finally, a word should be added about the issue of freedom (the freedom of students to have some control over the curriculum) and authority (the final authority on what a curriculum should be when there is dispute about its construction). A responsible path between freedom and authority is narrow and often hard to follow. Students are not authorized to pick and choose from among those subjects in the curriculum designed to form their human abilities, nor are they ever allowed to ignore them. And curricular elements distilled from legitimate social need make the same imperative demand. Yet there is room for some maneuver. Not everything in a curriculum is essential, and students are permitted to choose among the unessential. A curriculum, moreover, may range well beyond the essentials to border on scholarly specialization. Religious humanism encourages students with motivation and capacity to engage in scholarship and thus to satisfy their personal propensities for learning; it encourages them, moreover, to appraise knowledge in a liberal manner. This means that religious humanism admonishes students to regard knowledge as rewarding in its own right. Knowing for the sake of knowing is not only approved, it is recommended.

Rational Humanism

Rational humanists are impressed by the accumulated wisdom of human beings, and they are fairly certain that the best of this wisdom should be used to shape minds and characters and whet intellectual appetites of intelligent students. In consequence, an association between rational humanism and a curriculum composed of the great books is almost inevitable.

Accumulated wisdom, call it the intellectual inheritance, is conveniently organized into a curriculum under the general headings of science, politics, philosophy, art, and literature. After the needs of literacy are accounted for in the elementary school, these subjects should occupy the time and talent of the best minds. But what about the rest of the students, those whose talent or motive is insufficient to carry them to and through such a rigorous regimen of study? It is possible, of course, to shape a scholastic formula for individual differences and make it compatible with rational humanism, although exponents of rational humanism have only infrequently been tempted to do so. Rational humanism as a philosophy of education, and more particularly in its theory of curriculum, labors under the heavy burden of apparent elitism.

Yet, as we have implied, rational humanism can, up to a point, adopt the curricular theses of religious humanism. This point, which turns out to be critical, is where revealed religious knowledge is introduced. Rational humanism finds it philosophically impossible to embrace revealed knowledge, although rational humanists generally evidence no hostility to religion.

Finally, the curricular issue of freedom and authority must be appraised. Any curriculum, we are told, has three masters to satisfy, although all three do not have an equal claim on the allegiance of any curriculum. The three masters are knowledge itself, legitimate social need, and personal aspiration. When the requirements of authentic knowledge are satisfied in the school—and they always operate under the superintendence of reason—social need may be tested for credibility and thereafter be ushered into the instructional syllabus. With these two masters satisfied, students may then articulate their expectations for learning. Under no circumstance, though, does rational humanism authorize any kind of student dogmatism over the curriculum of any school on any educational level. Schooling is a time for learning, for preparing for life. When school days are over, students may map out their own courses of interest and inquiry. While they are in school they should study what reason and the intellectual and social tradition tell them is important.

Pragmatism

Pragmatism is a complex, sophisticated philosophy of education. It is seldom either doctrinaire or dogmatic. There are few uniform philosophical positions to which all pragmatists are expected to cling. And what can be said about pragmatism's philosophy in general applies especially to its curricular theory. About the only thesis amenable to all pragmatists is that education is primarily a social function, and we should therefore expect the curriculum of any school to contain elements contributing directly to social effectiveness.

Still, it appears, there are two general curricular hypotheses in pragmatism and, while they could hardly be called contradictory, neither are they entirely compatible. The first hypothesis, one that even pragmatists sometimes characterize as a kind of tired liberalism, can best be illustrated by quoting directly from William Heard Kilpatrick.

In the sense formerly understood by subject-matter requirements there is not much that I should care to name in advance that must in the end be learned and still less should I wish to state when it will be learned. I know that there is a considerable body of common knowledge and common skills that any decently educated group will show; but I don't believe that naming this body in advance is the helpful way to begin.[32]

After this preface Kilpatrick goes on to recommend a curriculum with the means to improve students' quality of life and to develop their creative abilities. Such a curriculum, he wrote, "may be called the *emerging curriculum.* "[33] It has its source in the interests and needs students bring to school with them, and if the school is good, students will discover ways to satisfy these needs. He is careful to concede that many of his pragmatic confreres do not agree with his conception of the curriculum. And he is right.

The other pragmatic hypothesis concentrates on growth and on the means the curriculum contains for promoting desirable growth. To qualify growth as desirable implies the existence of some standard against which scholastic growth may be measured. This standard, although often hard to discover, must exist, if it exists at all, in a social consensus. Yet, social consensus need not be merely vulgar popular opinion or a kind of mindless conventionality; it can be safeguarded by scientific technique and rigorous reflective thought.

Now, however, the pragmatist must tell us how growth is to be cultivated. This camp of pragmatism, despite Kilpatrick's pronouncement, lacks confidence in unsuperintended growth and is absolutely convinced of the impossibility of desirable growth occurring unless means for generating it are in the curriculum.

Means to stimulate growth, Geiger reminds us,[34] may be found in the problems of life itself: not just personal and ephemeral problems, but legitimate and serious social, human problems. The problem approach to curricular organization has no monopoly though. Growth may be organized around content, and curricular content in this context may look very traditional and conventional. Conventionalism is pared away, however, when we realize that this content, in a perfectly logical application of pragmatic epistemology, lacks intrinsic validity. It is merely a means to stimulate growth of a certain kind. No subject in the curriculum, then, can be credited with distinctive dignity, and the content of the curriculum should not have the appellation truth applied to it. Yet, either problem or content must be employed, because nothing else is available for inspiring growth.

If one is to choose between a problem and a content curriculum, the basis for choice must be effectiveness. Which curriculum best stimulates a class of students to grow intellectually, morally, and socially? Choice is ratified by consequence. Dominated by this view, pragmatism naturally enough is unwilling to certify any distinction between liberal and servile learning or between liberal and vocational education.

Pragmatic spokesmen are frequently critical of abuses in vocational education, but nevertheless find it impossible to adopt a stance where learning for making a living is accorded less dignity than any other kind of learning.[35] All learning, they aver, must be placed in a context, otherwise it is learning without meaning or significance. They, of course, have no time whatever for the doctrine that knowledge can be its own end or that learning for the sake of learning is good in itself. Nor are they sympathetic to the pleading for liberal learning that promises, once the internal principles are grasped, to enable persons to apply these principles to real problems arising in life. Such antiseptic learning is not likely to be effective. Yet the principles promised from liberal learning can be forged by starting with real-life issues and, in consequence, learning to think, the ultimate genius of decent learning, will be enhanced in the practice of solving authentic rather than artificial problems.

In this conception of the curriculum the issue of freedom and authority is hardly ever so discrete as, say, in religious or rational humanism. Social need must, of course, be filtered through the lives of students, and in this connection cannot be ignored. No educator is authorized to stand indifferent to student need, regardless of the inarticulateness of its expression. Yet, society is larger and more complex than the simple addition of multiple individual needs. The social group itself has some right to a voice in the determination of curricular ends and means. Both sets of rights—personal and social—are legitimate. One is not necessarily subservient to the other, although depending on a variety of circumstances, which no one is always able to predict, one set of rights may attain temporary precedence. In any case, there are inevitable tensions between personal and social right, and the curriculum must learn to live with them. The better the educational program and the more versatile the teachers, the better these tensions will be handled and adjudicated without, in an exercise of arbitrariness, the elimination of one or the other source of tension.

Surveying the contemporary educational scene, one can hardly miss a principal tension, one lodged in affirmations of cultural pluralism, whose impact on curricular design is considerable. In a culturally pluralistic society, the decision relative to selecting one culture from among many for the curriculum is difficult. We have seen some of the difficulties surrounding an educational program steeped in cultural pluralism and need not review them here. But the curriculum theory in pragmatism defends with a good deal of vigor the thesis that every social group has a right to grow in every possible educational way by using the most formative experiences at its disposal. One's native culture, the most obvious sign of which is language, is recommended as being fundamentally most formative. It should, therefore, be in the curriculum of the school and available as a means for growth for those students whose association with it is most intimate.

The curriculum of the school should not conspire to change native cultural habits or those appurtenances to culture that contribute to its distinctive character. Instead of seeking cultural metamorphosis or amalgamation, the school's curriculum should flow with the student's cultural current. By staying on entirely familiar experiential ground the opportunities for growth are best, so this theory goes. What is sacrificed, some argue, is a common cultural base that over the generations becomes an indelible characteristic of a society.

The point cultural pluralists like to make, however, basing their contention on a pragmatic theory of knowledge, is that culture lacks intrinsic value. We should not embrace any one culture for curricular cultivation because it is supposed to be superior, for none has qualifications of superiority. Curricular culture or cultures are defended in only one way: Their value is found and justified in their capacity to stimulate individual and social growth. At the same time, we must remember, no cultural pluralist takes the position that teaching must cater exclusively to a student's native cultural background. Native culture is the place to begin, and the record of this native culture should be available for careful curricular perusal. But other cultures belong in the curriculum too. An educational program with a broad cultural base, along with the latitude of experience itself, is likely to make students conversant with cultures other than their own. As a result of direct instruction or simply through social contact, cultural blending is both inevitable and rewarding.

Under the auspices of cultural pluralism, promises are made not only for a more effective society but for a more decent and sensitive one as well.

Existentialism

If existentialism has a supreme educational commitment, it must be phrased along these lines: learning to live well now. The past is inconsequential and the future is unpredictable, so we are left with the present and must learn to cope with it. The school's curriculum can help us.

But what should the school's curriculum contain? What kinds of knowledge and skill—and both are admitted to be essential—are most likely to enable us to live well now? Human beings are, so existential theory runs, capable of everything; no absolute limit can be set with respect to either human accomplishment or aspiration. But there is, nevertheless, one fly in the existential curricular ointment: Time to accomplish everything is lacking, so aspiration for accomplishing everything is bound to be futile. Existentialism recommends the formation of the curriculum out of those common human experiences that, history tells us, are most likely to contribute to the formation of human personality. Immature, untutored students need some help to realize personal genius, whatever it may be. And they should be able to look to the school with confidence that it will offer them responsible aid.

The curriculum then, according to one line of existentialistic thought, is the one thing in education that teachers and pupils have in common.[36] It is with the content of the curriculum that teachers help students toward the objective of self-realization and personal formation. By immersing themselves in curricular existences, in those real things that can be brought into focus in school life, students can develop their inner talent to the point where it is possible for them to realize their potential. Yet when students and teachers make the curriculum of the school their common meeting place, they must be careful to use the curriculum as a means for development and not allow it to enslave them. This is a safeguard, of course, and from any point of view it makes good sense, but we know, as do existentialists, that it is a safeguard whose management is extraordinarily difficult. Knowledge may come to dominate thought instead of cultivating it; and it may lead to conformity rather than to personal freedom. Still, the existentialist admits, this is an educational risk worth taking, for the only other alternative is totally unacceptable: educational anarchy.

Still, as we have heard so often, existentialism idealizes freedom and places a high premium on the student's freedom to learn—freedom to have experiences of all kinds in and out of the curriculum. But freedom has rules, for without them both intellectual and moral anarchy are almost inevitable. Certainly every kind of learning should be given a chance, but there are points of reference. These points of reference, which can only be interpreted as restrictions or limits on personal freedom, are found in common human need. Some things, grounded on the bedrock of common need, must be taught to everyone if we are to pretend to educational decency. So, making the full circle, there are points on which existentialism and essentialism appear to agree.

It is this element of agreement—where the existentialist asserts the priority of certain kinds of basic knowledge and skill—that makes it hard to affirm an indelible relationship between existentialism and romantic humanism. We have heard educational philosophers saying that humanism's association with existentialism is intimate, and they base this assertion on what may be called existentialism's open-door policy with respect to the expanse of experience as a shaper of human personality and its allegiance to the fulfillment of personal motive. Yet, when we examine existentialism's curricular stand more closely, we find that its compatibility with humanism is either fictional or fleeting. Existentialists do not campaign for deschooling; they do not undermine the essentials of learning or call them inconsequential; and they declare unhesitatingly that freedom has rules which, if dishonored, will enslave us in ignorance and moral turpitude. Existentialism and humanism share some common ground, we admit, but this common ground is narrow and, at least on curricular theory, does not make humanism a synonym for existentialism.

Analytic Philosophy

When analytic philosophy first began to make its mark on education, its adherents were little disposed to spend time on curricular theory. This, we think, was not because the curriculum was judged unimportant. Faced with establishing its philosophical credentials, traditional programs of study were accepted as being satisfactory if they aimed at mastery and also encouraged students to recognize the difference between reality of all kinds and the symbols (usually language) employed to report, analyze, and verify reality.

Although a curriculum constructed along traditional lines is adequate if it contains the full corpus of knowledge, the best studies are always those leading to a grasp of meaning and an understanding of reality. Such studies and the discipline of precision associated with them are language and its various uses; logic with its tools for discernment, classification, and cogency; and the scientific method.

Beginning with the assumption that schools are commissioned to teach, analytic philosophers now spend a good deal of time trying to sort out what should be taught. In concert they complain about determining curricular content on the precarious foundation of cultural bias. They prefer an approach guided by rigorous rational technique and challenge the validity of curricula produced by educators who proceed from unexamined assumptions about what knowledge is, its worth, and whether and by what means it can be communicated.

No analytic pronouncement tells us to reconstruct the curriculum or pare from it any of the conventional and by now well-authenticated disciplines. It does tell us, however, to reexamine all of the assumptions on which such disciplines are based. It asks for a critical analysis of such commonly used phrases as core curriculum, integration of knowledge, unity of knowledge, liberal education, relevant study, competency-based curricula, accountability, and consumer education. As often as not these phrases are merely slogans. They confuse rather than clarify the work of students and teachers. It asks for a closer, more meticulous examination of the traditional view that curriculum is a means to an end. It is possible, some analysts assert, that the curriculum may itself be an end. In any case, what does it signify to make a distinction between ends and means?

Finally, all branches of analysis want clarification with respect to the credentials of persons who shape curricula, and they want assurances with respect to the logical process involved in determining who has responsibility for making curricular decisions. The thrust of analysis is to use the curriculum in such a way that the intellectual outcome will enable us to communicate bodies of knowledge whose verification is sound, with precise and exact meaning. After some years of neglect, the curriculum is now becoming a preoccupation of contemporary analytic philosophers.

FIGURE 8.3
Educational Philosophy and Curricular Emphasis

Idealism	The curriculum should contain those experiences capable of providing a comprehensive view of the world.
Realism	The curriculum should contain verified knowledge about physical and social reality and should also pay attention to habits associated with learning.
Religious Humanism	The curriculum should exhibit an allegiance to the arts and sciences and give religion a fair hearing.
Rational Humanism	The curriculum should be built mainly on the literary inheritance: the great books.
Pragmatism	The curriculum should be filled with experiences for promoting social effectiveness.
Existentialism	The curriculum is the one thing students and teachers have in common. It should contain knowledge and experience for cultivating a realization of self.
Analysis	The curriculum should concentrate on the kind of experience and knowledge leading to the development of a scientific perspective.

NOTES

1. ARISTOTLE (*Politics,* VIII) anticipated prophetically when he wrote: "For mankind are by no means agreed about the things to be taught, whether we look to virtue or the best life. Neither is it clear whether education is more concerned with intellectual or with moral virtue. The existing practice is perplexing; no one knows on what principle we should proceed—should the useful in life, or should virtue, or should the higher knowledge be the aim of our training; all three opinions have been entertained."

2. JOHN HOLT, *How Children Fail* (New York: Dell Publishing Co., Inc. 1965), p. 208; and Ivan Illich, *Deschooling Society* (New York: Harper & Row, Publishers, Inc., 1971).

3. BERNARD DAVIS, "Why Teaching Isn't Possible," *Educational Theory,* 27 (Fall 1977), 307. It should be added, I think, that Davis' argument revives the famous paradox expressed in St. Augustine, *The Teacher,* translated and edited by George Howie (Chicago: Henry Regnery and Company, 1969), without noticing Augustine's solution.

4. THOMAS GREEN, *The Activities of Teaching* (New York: McGraw-Hill Book Company, 1971), p. 140.

5. CARL ROGERS, *Freedom to Learn* (Columbus, Ohio: Charles E. Merrill Publishing Company, 1969), p. 103; and CARL BEREITER, *Must We Educate?* (Englewood Cliffs, N.J.: Prentice-Hall, Inc., 1974), pp. 6–7; 22–34.

6. ISRAEL SCHEFFLER, *Reason and Teaching* (London: Routledge & Kegan Paul, Ltd., 1973), pp. 67–80.

7. JOHN LOCKE, *An Essay Concerning Human Understanding,* 28th ed. (London: T. Tegg and Son, 1838), II, i, 24.

8. ST. AUGUSTINE, *The Teacher,* p. 78.

9. IMMANUEL KANT, *Critique of Pure Reason,* trans. Norman Kemp Smith (New York: St. Martin's Press, Inc., 1961), p. 147.

10. This is a conclusion that by no means elicits universal agreement. MICHAEL W. APPLE and PHILIP WEXLER, for example, in "Cultural Capital and Educational Transmissions," *Educational Theory,* 28 (Winter 1978), 43, believe that making such choices puts all of us in a dilemma. J. THEODORE KLEIN is more optimistic about cultural variety in the curriculum, "A Pluralistic Model for Educational Policy Making," *Educational Theory,* 28 (Spring 1978), 85–89.

11. Many authors have written about social evolution. Among them are: SEYMOUR W. ITZKOFF, *Cultural Patterns in American Education* (New York: Harper & Row, Publishers, Inc., 1969); ISAAC B. BERKSON, *The Idea and the Community* (New York: Harper & Row, Publishers, Inc., 1958); CLARENCE J. KARIER, PAUL VIOLAS, and JOEL SPRING, *Roots of Crisis* (Chicago: Rand McNally & Company, 1973); and JOHN DEWEY, *The Public and Its Problems* (Denver: Alan Swallow, 1927, 1954).

12 BARRY M. FRANKLIN, "Curricular Thought and Social Meaning," *Educational Theory,* 26 (Summer 1976), 298–309, deals perceptively with the issue of choice.

13. The earliest writer to stress the "melting-pot conception of the American race" was MICHAEL GUILLAUME JEAN DE CREVECOEUR, a French colonist in eighteenth-century New York, in *Letters to an American Farmer.* It was elevated to the level of a social theory in ISRAEL ZANGWILL'S, *The Melting-Pot: Drama in Four Acts* (New York: Macmillan, Inc., 1909).

14. Mastery of language is seldom stressed in the literature dealing with bilingualism. See Nell Keddie, ed., *The Myth of Cultural Deprivation* (Baltimore: Penguin Books, 1973); J. L. DILLARD, *Black English* (New York: Random House, Inc., 1972); and JANE TORREY, "Illiteracy in the Ghetto," *Harvard Educational Review*, 40 (May 1970), 254.

15. TOM DEATS, "Educational Futures: What Do We Need to Know?" *Educational Theory*, 26 (Winter 1976), 81–92.

16. JOHN T. GRASSO and JOHN R. SHEA, *Vocational Education and Training: Impact on Youth* (Berkeley, Calif.: The Carnegie Foundation for the Advancement of Teaching, 1979), p. 161.

17. JEROME S. BRUNER, "The Skill of Relevance or the Relevance of Skills," *Saturday Review* (April 18, 1970), pp. 66–68; 78–79.

18. WILLIAM HARE, "The Concept of Innovation in Education," *Educational Theory*, 28 (Winter 1978), 68.

19. Although there may be some difficulty interpreting precisely the meaning of the phrase "defensible partiality," Theodore Brameld's analysis of indoctrination is superb in *Patterns of Educational Philosophy* (New York: World Book Company, 1950), pp. 558–566. See also, I. A. Snook, ed., *Concepts of Indoctrination* (London: Routledge & Kegan Paul, 1972).

20. THEODORE GREENE, "A Liberal Christian Idealist Philosophy of Education," in the Fifty-fourth Yearbook of the National Society for the Study of Education, *Modern Philosophies and Education* (Chicago: University of Chicago Press, 1955), p. 119.

21. PAUL GOODMAN, *Compulsory Mis-education* (New York: Horizon Press, 1964), pp. 31–34.

22. GRASSO and SHEA, *Vocational Education and Training*, pp. 154–157.

23. HERMAN H. HORNE, *The Philosophy of Education* (New York: Macmillan, Inc., 1927), pp. 144–145.

24. HERMAN H. HORNE, *This New Education* (New York: The Abingdon Press, 1931), p. 120 .

25. B. B. BOGOSLOVSKY, *The Ideal School* (New York: Macmillan, Inc., 1936), pp. 133–134.

26. MICHAEL DEMIASHKEVITCH, *An Introduction to the Philosophy of Education* (New York: American Book Company, 1935), pp. 279–280.

27. THEODORE GREENE, "Liberal Christian Idealist Philosophy," p. 119.

28. JOHN WILD, "Education and Human Society: A Realistic View," in the Fifty-fourth Yearbook of the National Society for the Study of Education, *Modern Philosophies and Education* (Chicago: University of Chicago Press, 1955), pp. 34–35.

29. HARRY S. BROUDY, *Building a Philosophy of Education* (Englewood Cliffs, N. J.: Prentice-Hall, Inc., 1961), pp. 300–309.

30. Ibid., pp. 285–289.

31. WILLIAM F. CUNNINGHAM, *The Pivotal Problems of Education* (New York: Macmillan, Inc., 1940), p. 285.

32. WILLIAM H. KILPATRICK, "Philosophy of Education from the Experimentalist Outlook," in the Forty-first Yearbook of the National Society for the Study of Education, *Philosophies of Education* (Chicago: University of Chicago Press, 1942), p. 77.

33. Ibid.

34. GEORGE R. GEIGER, "An Experimentalist Approach to Education," in the Fifty-fourth Yearbook of the National Society for the Study of Education, *Modern Philoso-*

phies and Education (Chicago: University of Chicago Press, 1955), p. 153.

35.   Ibid.

36.   RALPH HARPER, "Significance of Existence and Recognition for Education," in the Fifty-fourth Yearbook of the National Society for the Study of Education, *Modern Philosophies and Education* (Chicago: University of Chicago Press, 1955), p. 229.

READINGS

ANDERSON, RICHARD C., RAND J. SPIRO, and WILLIAM E. MONTAGUE, eds., *Schooling and the Acquisition of Knowledge.* New York: John Wiley & Sons, Inc., 1977. Chapter 1, by Harry Broudy, on "Types of Knowledge and Purposes of Education," puts curricular issues in philosophical perspective.

FETHE, CHARLES, "Curriculum Theory: A Proposal for Unity," *Educational Theory,* 27 (Spring 1977), 96–102. A renewed plea is made for an integrated curriculum, and special attention is given to the college curriculum.

GRASSO, JOHN T., and JOHN R. SHEA, *Vocational Education and Training: Impact on Youth.* Berkeley, Calif.: The Carnegie Foundation for the Advancement of Teaching, 1979. Chapter 8, "Conclusions and Recommendations," challenges the assumption that vocational curricula are dumping grounds for high school students.

HARE, WILLIAM, "The Concept of Innovation in Education," *Educational Theory,* 28 (Winter 1978), 68–74. Although the author is sympathetic to innovation, and perceives its need, he maintains that educational leadership can be displayed by those who seek to preserve what is valuable in educational practice.

HIRST, PAUL, *Knowledge and the Curriculum.* London: Routledge & Kegan Paul, 1974. The author takes the position that when curricula are validly ratified the various pressures in society, which tend to justify certain kinds of opinions and beliefs, can be resisted.

HOOK, SIDNEY, "Illich's Deschooled Utopia," in Cornelius J. Troost, ed., *Radical School Reform.* Boston: Little, Brown & Company, 1973. The worth of Ivan Illich's innovative view in education is called into question.

HOOK, SIDNEY, PAUL KURTZ, and MILO TODOROVICH, eds., *The Philosophy of Curriculum.* Buffalo: Prometheus Books, Inc., 1975. Various, sometimes conflicting, views of the curriculum are represented.

PALARDY, J. MICHAEL, ed., *Elementary School Curriculum: An Anthology of Trends and Challenges.* New York: Macmillan, Inc., 1971. Pages 5–70 treat goals and objectives. The section on "Behavioral Objectives in Curriculum Design" should interest readers disposed to take a critical view of behaviorism in education.

PASSOW, A. HARRY, *American Secondary Education: The Conant Influence.* Reston, Va.: National Association of Secondary School Principals, 1977. The study of American secondary education, initiated by James B. Conant, is examined in the light of contemporary educational issues.

RICH, JOHN MARTIN, "On Educating the Emotions," *Educational Theory,* 27 (Fall 1977), 291–296. Taking into account the common opinion that formal education should be concerned primarily with intellectual development, the author offers suggestions for emotional education.

SCHEFFLER, ISRAEL, *Reason and Teaching.* London: Routledge & Kegan Paul, 1973. Chapter 6 treats of philosophical models of teaching. Chapter 10 examines the issue of revelance in education.

SCHWAB, JOSEPH, *Science, Curriculum and Liberal Education: Selected Essays,* edited by Ian Westbury and Neil J. Wilkof. Chicago: University of Chicago Press, 1978. The relationships between scientific knowledge and liberal education form the discussion in Chapter 2.

SPENCER, HERBERT, *Education: Intellectual, Moral, and Physical.* New York: D. Appleton and Company, 1914. The first chapter of this famous book contains the essay: "What Knowledge Is of Most Worth?"

WEGNER, CHARLES, *Liberal Education and the Modern University.* Chicago: University of Chicago Press, 1978. Chapter 4, "The Liberal Curriculum," revives the issue of the need and purpose of liberal learning.

9

EDUCATIONAL PHILOSOPHY AND METHOD

We have spent some time considering the nature of the student, the purposes of education, and the curricular means employed for the realization of personal formation, information, and skill. Now it is time to think about how materials of instruction are used to attain the purposes certified by philosophical analysis. When educational purpose and content vary, a single, uniform method could hardly be justified, for method—or, to use a more contemporary word, strategy—is always designed to seek already established objectives. Method is totally occupied with implementation; it is never normative. The function of method is clear, and it is hard to believe that it could ever be defined as anything other than the way to do something in order to achieve an objective.

If curriculum is the "what" of formal education, method is the "how." So far we have seen the role educational philosophy has to play in connection with objectives and curricula. What we have yet to see is to what extent method, the "how" of education, has a relationship to educational philosophy. It is possible for six teachers to be teaching a lesson in, say, reading in precisely the same way, using all the same pedagogic techniques and yet these same six teachers could adhere to different philosophies of education. Philosophy, we know, makes a difference on the level of educational policy and practice, but we are far from being convinced of educational philosophy's ability to prescribe particular methods for the classroom. If eclecticism has an unassailable place in education, it must be on the level of method.

The ultimate test for any instructional technique is made outside the borders of educational philosophy. The test is one of suitability and effectiveness. Only an obtuse teacher would persist in using techniques ineffective for stimulating learning or ignore techniques with an unblemished record for promoting sound instruction. The philosophical conclusion is almost inevitable: Teachers should be methodological pragmatists, using instructional techniques that work and discarding those found wanting.

Yet a word of caution should be added as we embrace this bold assertion of methodological pragmatism: No method can be justified, whatever its consequences, if it impairs personal dignity, and no method violative of the integrity of educational purpose should be employed. As a guardian of dignity and integrity educational philosophy establishes a relationship with method, but the development of instructional technique is the business of educational science.

METHOD AND EDUCATIONAL PURPOSE

By now we should all probably agree that education has many sides and, moreover, occurs in many places. The place of most concern to educational philosophy is the school. Both in and out of school, education is preoccupied with providing opportunity for personal formation, a personal formation aimed toward the good, the true, and the beautiful. We should pay some attention to method as it bears on these educational purposes.

Intellectual Education

Not all philosophies of education, we know, embrace the objective of intellectual education with the same degree of fervor. Although none rejects intellectual development as an objective, we have seen enough of educational philosophy at work to know how differently intellectual formation can be interpreted. For one philosophy of education, intellectual growth means the freedom of students to follow their own interests and motives; for another, intellectual growth means a mastery of bodies of knowledge organized into a curriculum.

For one philosophy of education, the human mind is a complex part of the physical organism whose capacity for intellectual development is sustained by entirely natural processes. For another, the human mind is primarily a spiritual power capable of operating in ways unrestricted by physiology. In an interpretation of human nature where human beings are solely the products of a biological evolutionary process, learning must inevitably proceed from a strictly physiological foundation. But when the nature of human beings is interpreted in a lofty, spiritual fashion, the mind is dependent on the senses for data from experience but is never limited by these data in what the spiritual power of reason can do with them.

What has this to do with method? Whatever our philosophy of education, we are all dependent on experience for what we know. When we talk about intellectual development, we must first acknowledge the imperative need for experience, either (as in the case of idealism) to cultivate our intuition or (as in the case of realism) to supply the mind with raw material. The problem of method in connection with intellectual development is to find the most effective means for supplying us with the kind of experience we need. Clearly, determinations relative to the kind of experience we need is a philosophical issue; how to handle experience in the classroom or elsewhere—once decisions have been made about kind—belongs to the province of the science of education.

Character Education

Scholastic tradition has made knowing what ought to be done the burden of intellectual education. The supposition is evident in every philosophy of education that conclusions about what ought to be done can be reached and, in general, agreed to. Teaching for doing what ought to be done is the difficult and, some say, impossible responsibility of character education. Doing what ought to be done—or, put differently, following in the conduct of life a set of worthy ideals—is learned, we think, in the same way that anything else is learned: by doing it. We learn to act prudently and justly, temperately and tolerantly by practicing these virtues. Therefore, the method for forming character, or for making the translation from knowing what ought to be done to doing what ought to be done, must be primarily a method involving the activities in life itself. Only in this way, by doing, can we expect to form those dispositions and habits which, in the end, add up to decent and dependable character.

To the extent that schools can contribute to character development (without at the same time being saddled with total responsibility for it), they must have at their disposal the means for students to practice those values of personal and social life that can be certified by moral philosophy. At this point, we need not be told, all kinds of conundrums appear, for moral philosophies are by no means in agreement either with respect to the definition of value or its ultimate source. Educational philosophies, moreover, never speak with one voice about the method and the discipline associated with the inculcation of moral habit.

Aesthetic Education

We should love beauty and scorn ugliness. Our motivation to do so, however, is disinterested, for beauty is its own reward. It may, in fact, be incapable of offering any other compensation. But beauty may be perceived in different ways: It may, for example, be perceived in its adherence to form or in the perfection of its execution; it may be perceived in the sensation of pleasure it provokes; or it may be perceived to the degree it attains the absolute perfection of an ideal.[1] In any case and in any way, the ability of persons to appreciate beauty in its various forms is a characteristic putting them in a distinctive category of all reality. This ability, moreover, to the degree that men and women cultivate it, raises them above the brute conventions of the physical and social world. It adds an aesthetic dimension making life pleasurable and more worth living. All this may be granted, but it leaves us still with the problem of shaping techniques for knowing and loving the beautiful.

This is not the place for a long, abstruse discourse on the techniques essential to whetting our appetites for beauty in its various forms, but general principles can be laid down.[2] First, some technical knowledge of art form is essential, and this knowledge can be communicated as part of intellectual education. From this point on, however, experience with various art forms is imperative, for in the last analysis it is impossible for us to love what we do not know. The method here is elusive, but it must always rest heavily on opportunities for experiencing beauty in all its forms, so the burden is shifted to the curriculum, which must, if it is entirely adequate, provide ample experience in the fine arts.[3]

Traditional and Progressive Method

It is not always easy to be sure what traditional method is or, on the other hand, to recognize progressive method when we see it in operation, for over the years, and especially in the hands of skillful teachers, traditional and progressive methods have been blended. And this blending has occurred, not with any particular philosophy of education or theory of schooling in mind, but simply in the interest of pedagogical effectiveness. There are, we have learned, few philosophical purists on the level of method.

Emphases in each method are fairly clear in theory and can be stated quickly and directly. Traditional method makes the teacher the main actor in the drama of education, and teachers always occupy the center of the instructional stage. The teacher's responsibility is to create and conduct situations conducive to learning and to direct learning activities in the classroom and laboratory. Progressive method, on the other hand, is child-centered. Students are commissioned, if this method has its way, to manage their learning activities and to call on teachers for help when help is needed.

The shift in emphasis from traditional to progressive method may sound more dramatic than it is in actual school practice, for, despite all the brave talk over the decades about child-centered schools, the weight of American educational practice has consistently been on the side where teachers assume a directive role in determining both what to teach and how to teach.

THE TEACHER

One should not go too far in a discussion of method without stopping to consider the preparation and personality of teachers on one hand and the relationship between teachers and students on the other.

Personality and Preparation of Teachers

The old saying, "Teachers are born not made," although subject to serious flaws, nevertheless contains elements of truth. Superior teachers exhibit in their disposition a genuine interest in their students and a sense of awe with respect to the content and process of instruction. It is hardly possible to expect students to kindle feelings of worth about their studies if their teachers are either unenthusiastic about or indifferent to the process of discovery they are expected to superintend. By the very nature of their work, teachers are molders of minds and characters; their sense of mission, without succumbing to sentimentality, is the foundation for their art. And this foundation, for all that can be said about the importance of teacher preparation, is almost entirely a product of personality.

We know, although we may not know why, that some persons appear to be especially well-tailored for their work. Whenever persons in any profession are well suited by their personalities for the demands and responsibilities of their profession, they are likely to be successful in it. What is true generally is true also of teachers. So far no one has discovered any dependable means for altering personality sufficiently to make persons amenable to professions or vocations for which they have no internal calling. Personality is important, and it is probably the place to begin when considering a person's aptitude for teaching. But for all the ancient wisdom with respect to teachers being born, personality alone is an insufficient qualification for a teacher's success. Careful preparation is imperative.

Philosophy of Teacher Education. It is instructive to review the history of teacher education in America, for it tells us, if it tells us nothing else, how much progress had been made over the decades in preparing teachers to fulfill their professional responsibilities in the classroom.[4]

During these decades of progress, from the humble, mid-nineteenth-century normal school to the twentieth-century university college of education, certain basic theses bearing on the proper preparation of teachers were distilled. In the end, they add up to philosophies of teacher education. Although a good deal of melding occurred as these philosophies were elaborated by scholarly expositors, there are, safe to say, two main philosophies of teacher education.

One stands firmly on the proposition that teachers, first of all, must be masters of the content of instruction, and because they are to a great extent creators of students' educational environments, they must be exceptionally well educated. This view summarily dismisses the old dogma that teachers need be versed only in the subjects they teach, for their responsibilities to their students are limited to these subjects. No distinction is made here between teachers on the lower and higher levels of schooling. It may be unrealistic to expect elementary-school teachers to be scholars; it is not too much to ask that they be broadly and decently educated. The first and foremost qualification is, therefore, that teachers, as experts in knowledge, know what to teach. With this qualification secure, they must then be technically competent, for however much they may know and however well they may be educated, their effectiveness in the classroom inevitably depends on their ability to interest, motivate, and instruct their students. Should they fail on this level, they do injury not only to themselves and the profession they represent but, more importantly, they may do irreparable injury to their students.

The coin of teacher education has another side, and now attention is riveted on technical competence, on the teacher's ability to function effectively in the classroom. Reverence for learning and for the significance of sound scholarship is paid lip service but in the end is sold at discount, for the teacher is not considered to be the creator of the student's educational environment, but a guide in the learning process. As a guide it is more important for teachers to know methods for promoting and engaging in discovery than it is to have a mastery of knowledge from which the instruction of students can proceed.

Competency-based teacher education is illustrative of this second philosophy of teacher education.[5] And, safe to say, this philosophy has achieved near dominance in American colleges and universities engaged in the education of teachers. Too often the emphasis is placed heavily on training teachers rather than educating them, although this is not necessarily true of every program of teacher education associated in theory with doctrines of competency. It is possible to define decent educational competence in general or liberal learning and thus to ensure the soundness of a teacher's education, but there is the ever-present danger, because technical competence fits more easily and naturally into a training and field-experience perspective, that decent learning will be discounted in the preparation of teachers. Many such indictments have been made against competency-based teacher education, but such indictments are hard to prove, especially when presumption is naturally on the side of teacher competence. What educational philosopher or philosophy can be persuasive in mounting an attack on competence?

In any case, a philosophy of teacher education that promotes learning by doing at the expense of careful and perceptive scholarship, one that idealizes what students preparing for teaching can learn by going into the field and using the field as their learning laboratory, is almost certain to weaken the fabric of learning in the schools. Not only will teachers prepared along such lines be undereducated, poorly educated, or not educated at all, but their students, who should always be the beneficiaries of a teacher's scholarship, insight, and soundly informed judgment, will be deprived of fundamental opportunities for a legitimate education.

The Relationship Between Teachers and Students

Some philosophies of education expect teachers to assume a dominant role in the instructional process—in other words, to conduct teacher-centered schools; others understand the role of the teacher to be that of a facilitator.

Without exception, although appearances sometimes deceive us, every educational philosophy makes students the principal agents in the educational process. Whether schools are teacher-centered or child-centered, the focus always stays close to this principle: Any education worthy of the name seeks to promote change. Desirable change is easy enough to identify, although not always easy to realize in particular cases: change from ignorance to knowledge, change from capacities to abilities, and change from impulses to ideals.

To say that students are ignorant is to say only that they lack knowledge. Such an assertion is not an indictment of their aptitude nor is it demeaning. Persons begin with capacities, with aptitudes for doing something. Experience gives evidence of all kinds of variations in capacity from one to another person, but experience also tells us that education is engaged in the process of translating an aptitude for doing something to an actual ability to do it. The shift here, to put the point differently, is from potentiality to actuality.

Finally, we should define an impulse as the tendency on the part of a person to act when given the opportunity to act or when stimulated to act. Such action, almost purely accidental in consequence, can be moral, immoral, or morally neutral. But accident is risky business. The change education seeks is for action to be superintended by ideals and for our conduct to be safeguarded by them.

These changes, educational philosophy says, should be promoted by teachers who recognize that the educational process is being conducted for students and their welfare must always be uppermost in teachers' minds. But while teachers have clear responsibilities to their students in the interest of educational decency and professional standard, students have a responsibility to their teachers, too, and they fulfill it by exhibiting good will toward learning and by adopting an attitude of docility in their approach to learning.

Lacking student good will toward learning, neither the pedagogic efficiency of teachers nor abundant opportunity for learning makes much difference. Under such circumstances, the process of instruction is bound to be fatally defective. Besides, we have heard for centuries, at least as far back as Socrates, that learning begins only with a confession of ignorance. While we should hardly expect students to ratify this Socratic premise theoretically, they must nevertheless display a willingness, if not an eagerness, to submit to the instruction of their teachers. Should they refuse, or remain indifferent, no teaching artistry is good enough to prompt the changes leading to education's fundamental purpose: intellectual and moral autonomy.

In addition to promoting change, to the extent that objectives of moral and intellectual autonomy are understood with the seriousness they deserve, method should be designed to encourage the art of prudent pedagogic withdrawal. Unquestionably, first-grade pupils need the teacher's attention and guidance more than high-school students, and high-school students more than college juniors and seniors. So independence from teachers should be promoted step by step to ensure that at the end of the educational process students will be practiced in forming their own judgments, making their own decisions, and directing their own intellectual energy toward the discovery of knowledge and skill essential to meeting personal problems successfully. Unless method is adept at surrendering responsibility to students, at the end of their schooling they will have life's problems heaped on them, but in the course of their education will have been immunized from dealing directly with these problems. As students climb the educational ladder, teachers on each successive step must know how and when to step aside, allowing students to practice personal independence. Should the art of withdrawal go unrecognized by teachers, the objectives of moral and intellectual autonomy are bound to have a hollow sound.

THE NATURE OF TEACHING

In Chapter 8 we adverted to the possibility of teaching and gave illustrations of teaching models supplied by John Locke, St. Augustine, and Immanuel Kant. Here we will look more closely at the nature of teaching, experience as a teacher, and maturation, motivation, and self-activity vis-á-vis teaching.

Teaching as a Cooperative Art

After listening to spokesmen who alleged, for various reasons, that teaching is impossible, we discovered, on closer examination, their argument rested on the proposition that teaching cannot be the cause of learning; one person cannot cause the education of another. Following Aristotle's definition of cause and distinguishing formal, material, efficient, and final cause,[6] they are right, for nothing in the nature of teaching enables teachers to cause learning. But must the argument rest here?

Farmers do not cause their crops to grow. Physicians are not the cause of restoring health in their patients. Yet both farmers and physicians aid perfectly natural processes to proceed either more quickly or more efficiently. When they do, they are engaged in the performance of cooperative art.[7]

Learning is an entirely natural process. Persons, we know, learn without the benefit of teaching. It is possible, but very difficult, for a person to be completely self-educated. The condition essential for self-education is highly unlikely in society, for the condition is total isolation. Human intervention (teaching) is not absolutely essential for learning to occur, but human intervention (again, teaching) makes the results of learning more likely and brings about their realization in ways more nearly satisfying to human need and expectation. So teachers are cooperative artists working with students and with natural learning processes to assist natural processes toward the achievement of desirable consequences. In the absence of the functioning of nature, either with teachers, farmers, or physicians, and without regard to anything they might do, nothing could happen. Students would not learn, crops would not grow, and patients would not have their health restored.

To understand the nature of teaching one must be ready to make a clear distinction between cooperative and operative art. The former, we understand, only assists nature; the latter is completely productive and is an indispensable element in the realization of its objective.

Should teachers misinterpret the nature of their art, thinking it operative rather than cooperative, they will at once inflate their own importance out of all reasonable proportion and also inflate the significance of educational technology to a point where it may endanger educational decency. There are, in the end, definite limits to the responsibility teachers can assume for the learning of their students. If educational philosophy instructs teachers in nothing more than this, it has taught them an important, essential lesson.[8]

Experience: The Best Teacher

Seeing the declaration "experience is the best teacher" makes some readers cringe. They are aghast at the assertion that "experience is the only teacher." To endorse either assertion appears to undermine the profession of teaching and, at the outset, seems to run counter to the lessons of common sense.

If we pause for a moment to think about these assertions, we see that not much in them is audacious. Unless we are prepared to embrace intuitive knowledge, we can hardly escape the conclusion that everything we learn is learned from experience. Everything we learn is learned by discovery. But experience can be either direct or vicarious, and discovery can be either aided or unaided. Introducing aided discovery introduces the art of teaching.

It is a common opinion among educators that direct experience and pure discovery lead to ideal learning, but both can have serious contingent flaws: Direct experience, should we be restricted to it, would shrink the scope of experience and make us victims of a provincial, personal reality. And pure discovery, for all its merit, is so time-consuming as to lodge us in a condition of perpetual childhood. To escape the clutches of these obvious shortcomings, the bulk of formal education rests solidly on the foundation of vicarious experience. Almost everything we read in books, see on film, or hear from our teachers is vicarious experience, and without it the scope of experience would be severely restricted. Pure discovery, despite the enthusiasm contemporary romantic humanists display for it, if carried beyond reasonable limits, is hardly more than an embrace of educational paralysis. Knowledge, our intellectual heritage demonstrates, is progressive and cumulative: We stand on the shoulders of preceding generations; we learn from our ancestors and from those whose experience qualifies them to teach. Were this otherwise, and were we all confined to the experience of pure discovery, we should be intellectual and social primitives.

Method, Maturation, Motivation,
and Self-Activity

In exercising their art, teachers must take into account the readiness of their students to experience the materials of instruction. At this point the psychological method should be brought into play, for it is pointless and profitless for teachers to undertake instruction when students are neither psychologically nor experientially ready. Teachers have two choices: one, to wait for students to reach a necessary level of maturity; two, to modify teaching to accommodate students on their maturational and experiential level.

Motivation for learning is an elusive concept.[9] For decades psychologists have been debating the nature and source of motivation and even now are diffident in their pronouncements about either. Yet teachers must capitalize on the motivation, the interest, the good will, and the desire to learn that students bring to school with them, and they must find some way to motivate them to learn when natural motives are ineffective or insufficient. Whether motivation is intrinsic (natural) or extrinsic (supplied by teachers), it stands as an incontrovertible and indispensable preamble to learning.

Now, however, educational philosophy enters the picture and, depending upon its philosophical stance, either affirms or discredits any motivation not coming directly and naturally from students themselves. We shall see more of this later, but the thesis is advanced in some educational philosophies that motivation supplied or generated by the teacher's art is subversive of student freedom and is intolerable. It leads, so the allegation reads, to a kind of control over students that is destructive of genuine educational and social democracy. On the other side of the coin, educational philosophies maintain that teachers are able to predict, because they are translators of social wisdom, what students need to know, and any dignified means for stimulating students to master this essential knowledge are authorized. Responsible and morally sensitive teachers will never jeopardize their students' freedom, so the apparition of social control is either minimized or ignored.

It is commonly believed that some philosophies of education countenance a teaching method ignoring the activity of students and count on an instructional process where learning is merely a matter of pouring in information. Under such circumstances, students' minds are passive receptacles to be filled by energetic teachers. This is caricature. Every philosophy of education affirms the necessity of activity on the part of students: Without activity learning is impossible. But what is the nature of activity? At this point philosophies lack agreement.

If learning is mainly or entirely a physiological process, activity must be overt; students must be physically engaged in doing something. Such a view is consistent with any philosophy of education that defines human nature in purely material terms. Clearly, self-activity leads to self-development, but is it essential to restrict the meaning of activity to physical movement? Is it possible for students to be mentally active without engaging in overt expression? Many educational philosophers believe implicitly in mental activity. In art appreciation, for example, although appreciation may appear to be passive, the student engaged in mental occupation may feel as much activity as if he were actually creating a work of art.[10]

However activity is interpreted, the general principle is sound and finds universal endorsement from educational philosophy: Self-activity is essential to learning.

THE ADMINISTRATION OF TEACHING

When the art of teaching is considered philosophically, a distinction should be made between the technique of teaching, elements of which we have examined, and the administration of teaching. Technique centers on the direction of learning activities in classrooms and laboratories; administration, on creating and maintaining conditions favorable to learning. Normally, administration of teaching anticipates, or prepares the way for, technique.

Creating Conditions Favorable to Learning

The art of teaching, we have seen, is mainly a matter of providing opportunities for learning to occur, and to ensure the realization of this objective teachers are obliged to heed the administration of teaching. When they do, they concentrate attention on individual differences, on the education of children with special needs, on grading and grouping, and on competition.

Individualization of Instruction. With the popularization of education in the United States every state enacted and enforced compulsory attendance laws; classrooms were filled with students of varying ability and, the evidence suggests, with vast differences in motives for learning. Some students were nurtured in homes and social settings where achievement in school was encouraged and praised; others came from culturally deprived homes where academic achievement was neither understood nor appreciated.

For the past several decades social scientists have been declaring that education is one way to redress economic deprivation, and for a long time in America the promise has been made that a good education enables persons to climb the social and economic ladder. Education is recommended as a principal means for promoting social mobility. Faced with these sometimes exaggerated expectations teachers are asked to find means for organizing their instruction to accommodate the various interests, needs, aspirations, and aptitudes students bring to school with them. Some social scientists are optimistic about altering and upgrading interest, aptitude, and aspiration, but regardless of the optimism of social theorists, the classroom teacher has no choice but to meet instructional reality face to face. Teachers must take students as they find them and then do their best to deploy instructional opportunity, to individualize instruction, and to maintain a common foundation in order to promote the eminently desirable objective of social solidarity.

Personal disposition, aspiration, and ability are entitled to teachers' recognition, but every student is expected to become a decent member of society and a responsible citizen. So as teachers make provision for individual development, taking into account the special talent or the special disability of students, they must aim also at promoting in their students a common social bond. Without a social bond, society is almost certain to founder.

Disagreement in educational policy is infrequent with respect to the instructional objective of social solidarity. Yet a good deal of disagreement surfaces over what provision should be made for the development of gifted students or those with special disability.

Opportunity for Children with Special Needs. Federal law (PL 94–142) and state law in many states require schools to mount programs of instruction for children with special needs. Such laws, we should say at the outset, can find support or lack of support on the level of educational principle, but their embrace or rejection belongs entirely to the realm of educational policy. So while educational philosophy can analyze such policies and either justify or countermand them, their adoption in law is authorized by educational policy rather than educational principle.

Yet philosophical analysis can be of some help in dealing with issues that appear to occupy a borderline between principle and policy. If, it can be maintained, society has the resources to educate everyone according to personal ability or disability, then a policy with special reference to physically or mentally handicapped students can be ratified. But if resources are limited (and weighing adequacy of resource is not a philosophical issue), what part of society's resources for education should be allocated for the instruction of disadvantaged or handicapped children?

The democratic policy of equality of educational opportunity has been applied to all children, and this means a standard of opportunity is defined and all students, regardless of disability or handicap, are allowed to meet it.[11] Such a policy is humane, respectable, and decent. And while a good deal of sentiment usually accompanies its support, it is, nevertheless, a policy capable of sober and reasoned justification. But there is another side, one that educational policy makers should not miss: How great is society's reward from this investment of time, energy, and educational resource in the instruction of children with special need? Can the argument be advanced and defended that children whose talent is superior should be entitled first to the resources society allocates for education? If society expects a return from its educational investment, the evidence is overwhelming that its return will be greater from students with superior talent than from those whose talent is limited by physical, mental, and social disability.[12]

Yet the allocation of economic resource for the education and training of children with special need can be justified by a broader interpretation of social benefit. When the allegation is made that society cannot afford the cost of educational provision for mentally or physically handicapped children, a rejoinder along these lines can be heard: Society cannot afford to withhold such opportunity, for in withholding it the cost to society will end up being greater. Such persons, untrained and uneducated, will become social burdens, and the cost of supporting them with welfare or other social programs will be far greater than the money spent to educate them; trained and educated they will become productive members of society.

In the last analysis, however, the adjudication of claim and counterclaim with respect to the education of children with special need is a matter for social policy and must be ratified or rejected on policy grounds. Educational philosophy can ferret out issues for clarification and analysis with respect to social policy, but educational philosophy, by itself, is incapable of shaping social policy.

Grading and Grouping.   After educational practice crossed the threshold of the modern world—sometime in the fifteenth century—teachers began to make use of a novel instructional idea: grading. Whether Comenius, in connection with his declarations on natural method, was responsible for grading can be debated, although clearly he recommended the organization of studies accommodated to student age and achievement.[13] From that time on the grading of curricular materials and students was nothing more than a practice everyone justified on the basis of common pedagogic sense.

In early American schools grading was frequently ignored, for good practical reasons, and all students whatever their age or ability were taught in a common classroom. Had they already mastered the lesson, repetition was assumed to be good for them. But when conditions for education improved and when resources for supporting schools became more abundant, grading became the common currency of educational practice. It had the appearance of psychological soundness and instructional efficiency.

Despite the fact that grading, as a part of the administration of teaching, has its basis in the science of education, educational philosophies have something to say about it, and theories of schooling quite clearly take one or the other side. Pragmatists and romantic humanists raise doubts in teachers' minds about the efficacy of grading, but on the other side of the pedagogical picture conservative philosophies of education and essential and behavioral theories of schooling take grading to be only an expression of true instructional wisdom.

Grouping is endorsed or rejected by various philosophies and theories. But whereas grading is confirmed or opposed on the basis of interpretation of scientific evidence, grouping is praised or blamed on grounds of social theory. Grouping is said by its critics to be a despotic way of controlling children and submitting them to the dominance of social conspirators determined to keep them in their proper social and economic place. Grouping, moreover, is alleged to be demeaning to and destructive of self-image. If persons are treated as if they lack worth and dignity, they will act that way. But the purpose of education, it is averred, is to promote individuality and to enhance personal conviction of worth. Grouping, then, can accomplish only educational and personal harm.

Yet grouping, assuming sound instruction is the purpose of formal schooling, contributes to the efficiency of teaching. It enables teachers to concentrate their effort and attention on the instruction of children with similar aptitudes and needs. Ability grouping, the evidence suggests, contributes to academic achievement, although, it must be admitted, it is capable of intimidating social education and, perhaps, personality development. The pros and cons of ability grouping put teachers in a dilemma.

Competition.   Should teachers depend upon competition to stimulate learning activities? One need read only a few of method's old tomes to recognize how much competition was prized and praised by our pedagogical ancestors. Its principal justification, in addition to its spurring of learning activity, was found in the conditions of life. In life, it was alleged, competition was nothing more than a natural expression of human nature. And should educational method neglect any opportunity to capitalize on natural disposition?

In more recent educational genres, however, competition as a part of teaching's administration has been criticized and generally curtailed. It lacks, the charge against it reads, both intellectual and moral soundness. It is deficient from the point of view of intellectual development because it exposes children to unfair treatment. Too often they are made to compete when their chance of success is remote or absent. They are assigned to competitions unequal to their ability, their interest, their background, or their maturity. Failure is an almost certain consequence, and failure retards rather than promotes learning.

Competition is indicted for moral deficiencies too. A superior quality of good character, we are told, is cooperation, an ability to work with others toward common social goals. But when school method uses competition, it inevitably teaches students that competition in the interest of personal success and self-aggrandizement is personally and socially praiseworthy. In effect, such a method promotes the very opposite of what moral education should be intent on encouraging—cooperation.

Some educational philosophies are adamantly opposed to competition in the administration of teaching, judging it to be personally undignified and socially harmful. Other philosophies, however, find some justification for competition if it is used prudently. By prudent use they mean that students are encouraged to compete with themselves, with their own past record of accomplishment. Less often, although frequently enough to attract our notice, competition is endorsed when students are made to compete with one another, or when they are made to compete with an absolute standard set by the teacher. Appraisals of competition in systematic philosophies of education are varied, but they are prone to reject competition.

Assessment of Achievement

Unless teachers assess student achievement they will be unable to determine the effectiveness of instruction. But this, the critics of measurement declare, is an educational activity carried on for the benefit of teachers rather than students. Yet there is a side to assessment enabling teachers to discover where, either in method or content, their students need help. Under such circumstances tests or other means for appraising achievement are designed for diagnostic use. Their purpose is less to measure performance than to disclose student need for help.

Still, we should say, the testing movement in American education has fallen on hard times. Once thought a panacea, standardized tests of intelligence and achievement are now frequently condemned. Almost nothing in education in recent decades has stimulated more controversy, and more hostility toward measurement, than the proposed introduction of state-wide competency tests as a precondition to high-school graduation. And these are only tests of achievement.[14]

Equally abhorrent to many modern educators and social theorists are intelligence tests. Once administered to almost every child in American schools, intelligence tests are now either severely restricted in their use or are banned altogether. Objected to largely on social grounds, their critics claim they brand children with a statement of IQ, and from then on whatever children do becomes a self-fulfilling prophecy. In addition, in a society extraordinarily sensitive to ethnic disadvantage in schooling, the results of intelligence tests are alleged to be illustrative of cultural exposure rather than native ability. Students from certain ethnic or cultural groups are penalized for their background, and with this penalty assessed at the outset of their schooling, are never able to overcome it.[15]

From its inception in the United States, the measurement movement, beginning with the 1916 *Stanford Revision of the Binet Scale,* or even earlier with the publication of Edward L. Thorndike's *Theory of Mental and Social Measurements* (1904),[16] has been subject to criticism and doubt among educators, but faced with contemporary indictments, indictments with more social than educational support, it has never been in more serious jeopardy.

SPECIAL PROBLEMS OF METHOD

Can the effectiveness of teachers in the performance of their instructional responsibilities be evaluated? Can they be held accountable for the achievement of their students? These issues, although others could be cited, are illustrative of analytic philosophy's substantial interest in conducting a critical examination of methodological policy and practice.

Evaluation of Teaching

In faculty rooms and at teachers' meetings, statements are sometimes made about teaching being too complex a process for evaluation. Although such statements appear to have a defensive ring, they contain elements of truth. If teaching is a cooperative art, learning must necessarily be an outcome of the activity, effort, and ability of students. The teacher is merely assisting a natural process. When the outcome of the learning process is measured, who is to say how much was contributed by the assistance of teachers and how much by the personal activity of students? The outcome of teaching, moreover, may not be directly and immediately observable. The consequence of learning may be deferred until suddenly and unexpectedly students recognize the benefit in skill, knowledge, and attitude they have derived from pedagogical cultivation.

Yet even when teaching is defined as a cooperative art—as we think it should be—it should be possible to make some judgment about a teacher's performance in promoting learning. Reasoning by analogy, it is possible to assess the way a farmer—also a cooperative artist—tills the soil, plants the crops, and harvests the fields. Farmers can demonstrate the efficiency, skill, and knowledge that contribute to a bountiful harvest, or they can demonstrate ineptitude. Cooperative art is capable of assisting nature toward natural results;[17] it can also hinder natural processes and impede them. So the question can be rephrased: are some teachers better cooperative artists than others? Do some have both teaching skill and knowledge setting them apart from and above their colleagues? Conversely, are some teachers lacking in both artistry and knowledge and thus ineffective stimulators of the learning process?

It is hard to believe that human activity—teaching or anything else—cannot be evaluated, so confidence in any conclusion rejecting teacher evaluation is low. Yet admitting the possibility of teacher evaluation leaves unanswered two vitally significant, but subordinate, questions. What should be evaluated and by whom?

The Process of Evaluation. Without introducing specific instruments employed for evaluating teaching, we can consider an issue that must always be central to teacher evaluation: What is being evaluated? Is the teacher's command of subject matter being judged? Is the teacher's fluency with techniques of teaching being weighed? Is the outcome of the learning process, the accomplishment of students, being measured?

For philosophies of education confident about the objectivity of knowledge, judgment about a teacher's intellectual competence is possible. If we take seriously the old dictum that teaching is impossible without a command of knowledge, we can also take seriously any responsible effort made to ascertain the level of a teacher's scholarship. If teachers are found to be deficient in their command of the subjects they are expected to teach, if they lack dependable knowledge both of their discipline and methods of instruction associated with it, any evaluation of their work is bound to be low. But for theories of schooling or philosophies of education whose theory of knowledge begins by discrediting objectivity, or whose theory of knowledge is lodged in pure relativism, who could make a sound judgment about a teacher's command of knowledge?

In philosophies of education where knowledge is discounted, technique counts most, so we should expect any evaluation of teaching to center on a teacher's ability to manipulate pedagogic technique skillfully enough to stimulate learning. But how much should skill in technique count? We have heard pronouncements in philosophies of teacher education where knowing what to teach is fundamental, but we have heard the other side, too, where teaching skill is supreme.

Knowledge and technique aside, the ultimate goal of teaching is promotion of learning, so in the last analysis, it could be argued, evaluation of teaching should be primarily a judgment with respect to what has happened to students. To what extent have the educational changes mentioned earlier in the chapter been cultivated? In the evaluation of teaching we should look first to the knowledge, the ability, and the ideals aroused in students before we concern ourselves with the teacher's pedagogic performance. The efficacy of a teacher's artistry is found, if found at all, in what students learn rather than in what we hear about a teacher's intellectual or technical competence.

Who Should Evaluate Teaching?   A moral issue is evident when judgments are made about other persons. Since it is impossible to know and weigh motive, we must depend on appraising action. When we make judgments about teaching, we gather evidence by observing teachers in their classrooms, we listen to reports from their colleagues and students, and we examine the consequences of their work. We are on most solid ground when we judge teachers by the product of their work. But this is more difficult than it sounds, for motivation and ability in students are more important to achievement than any teacher's artistry, and we should be on morally precarious ground were we to blame teachers for the inadequacies of their students. Is there no middle ground where educators can stand? Must they in the end confess to the impossibility of evaluating teaching?

At this point experience and judgment count most. So if we are to have dependable evaluations of teaching they must be made by persons who know most about education and teaching, and whose experience enables them to make prudent and fair judgments. On the basis of this principle it may not be easy to designate who in a school system should be assigned this responsibility, but in the nature of school organization we should expect to find them among department supervisors and principals.

Peer evaluation is sometimes recommended as is student evaluation, but from a philosophical point of view neither can be endorsed with the same degree of enthusiasm as evaluation by supervisors and principals. Evaluations by other teachers are almost certain to be erratic and episodic. Besides, there is the human tendency to judge the skill of others by our own. Since the art of teaching is highly personal, caution should be exercised in putting confidence in such evaluations.

In recent years greater interest has been shown in student evaluation of teaching. Various evaluation forms are used and students are asked to complete them.

Computers process the data gathered and teachers are rated. All this is precise and neat; in the end we have an objective measure. Justifications for student evaluation of teachers abound, some bordering on hyperbole, and one has little doubt that something can be learned about a teacher's methods, habits, disposition, and personality directly from students. But nowhere is the moral issue in connection with evaluation more pronounced: Students are asked to make a judgment, if the evaluation forms call for anything more than obvious personal traits apparent to anyone, that in the final analysis they are unprepared to make. Do teachers know their subjects? Are students in a position to know? Does the course have properly designed objectives? How can students tell unless they already possess the knowledge enabling them to determine proper objectives for the course?

Student evaluation of teaching, especially in an age when student freedom is idealized, is exceptionally popular the country over, but educational philosophers know, or should learn, the serious moral issue involved. This is not an argument for the abandonment of teacher evaluation; it is a plea to delegate evaluation to persons with the experience, judgment, and prudence to evaluate justly and responsibly.

Professional Responsibility and Accountability

To say that teachers—indeed, anyone engaged in the educational enterprise—should be professionally responsible is one thing; to say that schools and teachers are accountable for their students' learning is another.

Professional Responsibility. When educators are professionally responsible, as all should be, they understand their scholastic role and do their best to fulfill it. For teachers this means they equip themselves with both knowledge and technique for directing the learning of their students; moreover, it means that they invest their best effort to cultivate desirable learning objectives. It means that they have the best interests of their students at heart and that they recognize the worth of education both for persons and for society. They know they are architects in building the minds and characters of oncoming generations, and they neither skimp nor shirk their duty to their students or to the public.

Accountability. Accountability in education has an appealing sound but is not always realistic. On the most basic level accountability means that schools are responsible for the decent education of American youth, and since they use vast portions of public resources to accomplish this broad objective, they should demonstrate their success in the use of these resources. No educational philosopher can think of any reason why schools should be immunized from responsibility (accountability) to the public supporting them. Schools, after all, are not independent entities; rather, they are the educational arms of society, and their goal is the realization of objectives that society values. One would be on weak ground arguing that schools have a commission authorizing them to ignore society. Up to this point little fault can be found with the theory of accountability.

But accountability does not stay always on the institutional level. It is commonly translated to the classroom itself. And now teachers are made accountable for the learning of their students.[18] If students attain the objectives set for the class, teachers have passed their first test. If they fail, or if anyone fails, teachers too have failed. In consequence, teachers' positions, promotions, tenure, and salaries are made to depend on the application of the doctrine of accountability.

From the point of view of educational philosophy, accountability is based on a simplistic and unrealistic understanding of teaching. It distorts the meaning of the art of teaching from one where the teacher cooperates with nature to achieve certain natural learning outcomes to one where the teacher is a productive artist directly responsible for learning. Although teaching continues to be surrounded by many mysteries, our knowledge or the art and science of teaching is sufficient to warn us away from believing that teachers are agents for producing learning in their students. While educational philosophy is prepared to reject accountability as a reasonable proposition with respect to teaching, educational philosophy is nevertheless eager to endorse professional responsibility.

PHILOSOPHIES OF EDUCATION AND METHOD

Because method lacks an intimate and essential relationship to educational philosophy, we should not expect to find any method monopolized by one or another philosophy. Yet even in common adoption, philosophy adds intention to method, and both methodological emphases and preferences are likely to appear in discourses on the different philosophies of education. The universal methodological thrust, however, recognized in all philosophies of education is the activity of the learner. Despite assertions to the contrary, made, we think, more for purposes of propaganda than illumination, every philosophy of education embraces unstintingly the principle of self-activity as the bedrock of learning. Moving beyond this universally acknowledged principle, methodological preference and emphasis in the various philosophies of education can be illustrated.

Idealism

Searching through the literature on idealism, one looks in vain for any declaration that one pedagogical method is superior to all others. Idealist educators are convinced, of course, of the worth of dependable knowledge, so they expect method to contribute directly to sound instruction. And in hardly any other philosophy of education are teachers accorded a place of greater respect and dignity and, one should add, responsibility. Teachers are mainly responsible for creating the educational environment for students, especially on early scholastic levels, so idealists are extraordinarily solicitous of the personality and preparation of teachers.

Idealists show a decided preference for the method of informal dialectic.[19] In following this preference, however, they are careful to safeguard it with dependable knowledge: Students should never be allowed merely to embark on discussion. Under the direction of their teachers they should be encouraged to use discussion techniques to enlarge their intellectual horizons, always fortified with dependable information from which to proceed. Informal dialectic for idealists is neither aimless nor empty talk, and it must never descend to a pooling of vulgar or uninformed opinion.

Despite a preference for informal dialectic, idealists recognize how much precious time can be spent searching for knowledge by means of unaided discovery. Although spending time is not the same as wasting it, idealists find it hard to justify methods of self-directed learning where what is learned in hours could be taught in minutes.

Realism

When realists speak of learning they mean the acquisition of dependable knowledge, the provision for personal accommodation to natural reality (it can be called life adjustment), and discipline, which on one hand includes an intellectual and moral disposition to seek for learning and on the other, good order in the classroom. They expect teachers to teach with zeal and devotion. Realism never makes excuses for learning being hard work or for discipline sometimes being arduous, recognizing that discipline is essential to any degree of excellence.

All this, realists declare, stands on a foundation of authority in education, an authority indispensable to sound, decent, and useful learning. In schools, teachers are the agents who must possess this authority. Any method, any process in education, must begin with respect for the teacher. If respect lacks spontaneity in generation, it must be encouraged by persuasion and demonstration. On some educational levels, realists approve the use of reward and punishment, but when they do they are looking to the future when, as a result of habits toward learning inculcated by these means, students, with greater maturity, will maintain these same habits through self-directed action. Realism's general method, whatever particular techniques may be employed, calls for humility from both teachers and students. "Above them," John Wild says, "stands the truth."[20]

Religious Humanism

Religious humanism shares a good deal of common epistemological and educational ground with realism. In consequence, religious humanism's view of method comes close to duplicating realism's.

There is a difference worth noting, however, and this difference is found in the teachers' intention for the development of their pupils: While recognizing that learning's content has a natural, material side, teaching aims ultimately at a higher, supernatural purpose. Teachers who follow this philosophy of education must encourage their students toward the realization of human and temporal learning objectives, all the while keeping their attention riveted on spiritual and eternal goals.

We should expect a classroom illustrating the methodological preferences of religious humanism to be teacher- and knowledge-centered. Teachers have the clear and important commission to instruct their students and to correct nature's faults, but they are not authorized to allow their students to be passive receptacles of instruction. In this connection, Jacques Maritain, perhaps the last great modern exponent of religious humanism, made an eloquent plea for problem-solving technique as a contributor to what he called contemplative learning.[21]

Rational Humanism

While not dismissing method as inconsequential, rational humanists have paid it scant heed in their books on education. Being epistemological realists with a profound reverence for truth and for the superiority of reason, they have, we know, concentrated the bulk of their attention on the curriculum. Therein the great books have pride of place. The methodological preferences and emphases in rational humanism, one can fairly state, are generally consistent with those in realism, if we allow for a persistent and adamant opposition to behaviorism.

Pragmatism

No philosophy of education displays more enthusiasm for method than pragmatism, and we know enough about pragmatism to understand the reason for this enthusiasm. With a relativistic theory of knowledge, pragmatic teachers cannot invest their educational capital in the acquisition of knowledge, in what realists are disposed to call truth. They are left with method and, in consequence, undertake to hoist it to scholastic prominence.

In centering attention on method, pragmatism gives the impression of having invented the technique of learning by doing. Although we would recognize as exaggeration any claim along these lines, pragmatism nevertheless has a decided preference for learning by doing and therefore idealizes any method where learning is matched with experience. Put another way, method is only a means for having experience, so any truly effective method must allow students to immerse themselves fully in the experience of experiencing.

Pragmatists are excited about creativity in learning, which we should interpret as discovery, and they expect discovery to be enhanced when students construct projects exhumed from their own need and experience. No pragmatist, perhaps no educator in America, has spent more effort promoting and refining the project method than William Heard Kilpatrick.[22] In the last analysis, though, the project must be interpreted as an illustration of problem solving. And in this connection, despite its general endorsement by pragmatists, harsh disclaimers have come from the pragmatic camp. Bode used strong language when he criticized problem solving: "The emphasis on initiative and purposeful activity frequently suggests a mystic faith in a process of 'inner development' which requires nothing from the [teaching] environment except that it be let alone."[23]

Pragmatism sees method as a means for stimulating experience, so teachers, while they should be skillful in creating conditions wherein experience can range, are cautioned against intruding too much on the privacy and therefore the genuineness of student experience. Students must learn to be self-active; they must learn to formulate their own problems and projects; but they cannot achieve independence if teachers are constantly interposing themselves between students and the learning process. Yet there are times, pragmatists admit, when students may need and want a teacher's help. Then it should be given. When students appeal to them, teachers are expected to be versatile and fluent in all sides of educational technique.

Existentialism

"The good educator knows that he is educating individuals, not just man, and will use any method that will educate the whole man."[24] If this is genuinely illustrative of existentialism's approach to method (and it may not be the stance of every existentialist), it means that existentialism has no particular methodological emphasis or preference. Yet other existential voices can be heard. Some sound enthusiastic about the Socratic method, a preference putting them close to idealism. Others express opposition to the view that pupils are more important than teachers and the curriculum, because the pupils are the beneficiaries of teaching. While the assertion is incontrovertible that the students are the object of teaching, the corollary sometimes following, existentialists declare, can be dangerous to educational decency: The student should be in charge of his own education.[25]

Existentialism refuses to dismiss teachers or strip from them their teaching prerogatives; moreover, it refuses to allow students to define their own educational needs. This side of existentialism, a side contradicting its popular image, puts it close to realism.

Stressing the importance of common needs and discounting somewhat the idealization of individual needs, insisting that it is imperative to teach everyone to read, write, and count and to go beyond these basics to a healthy conversance with the whole of the intellectual legacy, and demanding achievement in all school subjects appears to put existentialism at odds with the objectives we have so often heard them say are important: freedom and the development of self. Can the authority of knowledge, represented in a good education, stand side by side with an existential commitment to personal dynamism? Ralph Harper's response, phrased this way, is positive: "But even in subjecting himself, the pupil retains his freedom of observation, inquiry, and release. The world and truth are for him to explore, but they are also for him to commit himself to as one commits one's self to a community which not only permits freedom but enlarges the self."[26]

FIGURE 9.1

Methodological Preferences in Educational Philosophy

Idealism	Informal dialectic with the precaution that participants in the dialectical process be informed is preferred.
Realism	Any method capable of promoting sound instruction and discipline is authorized. Behaviorists (who are realists) recommend conditioning.
Religious Humanism	Any method that ensures the dignity of the person and encourages critical intellectual activity is acceptable.
Rational Humanism	Great books contain knowledge and ideals that have been certified by the test of time: Imitation is the best method.
Pragmatism	Learning by doing is the ideal method.
Existentialism	The method of realism is adopted with the proviso that students have freedom for intellectual exploration.
Analysis	The scientific method is preferred because it lays the most substantial foundation for meaning.

Analytic Philosophy

Earlier in the chapter we illustrated analytic philosophy's approach to method and were left with the impression that it is not disposed to formulate or endorse method apart from direct experience with it. It sees its proper role in subjecting methods to analysis in order to disclose their strengths and weaknesses.[27] Exponents of analytic philosophy never pretend to any commission to elaborate general and prescriptive educational directions for method or anything else.

Our interpretation of analytic philosophy, recognizing the possibility of demurral, puts it in close relationship with realism on the point of educational method. Linguistic analysts usually recommend pedagogical technique that concentrates on developing language and logic; logical empiricists endorse the same technique but shift the bulk of their attention to mathematics and science. In any case, to take analytic philosophers at their word, "logical empiricism is essentially a methodology, [and] its educational consequences can be derived only indirectly. . . ."[28]

NOTES

1. JACQUES MARITAIN, *Creative Intuition in Art and Poetry* (New York: Pantheon Books, 1953), p. 161.
2. DONALD ARNSTINE, "Learning, Aesthetics, and Schooling: The Popular Arts as Textbooks on America," *Educational Theory,* 27 (Fall 1977), 261–273.
3. ARISTOTLE, *Politics,* in *The Works of Aristotle,* trans. and ed. by W. D. Ross (Oxford: Clarendon Press, 1908–1931), 1340b 23, said: "It is difficult, if not impossible, for those who do not perform to be good judges of the performance of others."

4. See MERLE L. BORROWMAN, ed., *Teacher Education in America* (New York: Teachers College Press, 1965).

5. STANLEY ELAM, *Performance-Based Teacher Education*, PBTE Series: No. 1 (Washington, D. C.: American Association of Colleges for Teacher Education, 1971), pp. 1–18.

6. ARISTOTLE, *Physics*, in *The Works of Aristotle*, trans. and ed. by W. D. Ross, (Oxford: Clarendon Press, 1908–1931), II, 3, 194b–195b. Formal cause: form; material cause: matter; efficient cause: maker; final cause: purpose.

7. The teacher's artistic role is stressed by HERMAN H. HORNE, *The Psychological Principles of Education* (New York: Macmillan, Inc., 1908), p. 33.

8. Education as a cooperative enterprise·is handled with extraordinary skill by Mortimer Adler, "In Defense of the Philosophy of Education," in the Forty-first Yearbook of the National Society for the Study of Education, *Philosophies of Education* (Chicago: University of Chicago Press, 1942), pp. 210–212. Theodore M. Greene, "A Liberal Christian Idealist Philosophy of Education," in the Fifty-fourth Yearbook of the National Society for the Study of Education, *Modern Philosophies and Education* (Chicago: University of Chicago Press, 1955), p. 124, calls teaching "both a science and an art and the great teacher is great because he excels in both respects."

9. Amply demonstrated by Jerome Bruner, *Toward a Theory of Instruction* (Cambridge, Mass.:, The Belknap Press of Harvard University Press, 1966) pp. 124–125.

10. JOHN DEWEY, *Art as Experience* (New York: Minton, Balch and Co., 1934), p. 54.

11. ROBERT H. ENNIS, "Equality of Educational Opportunity," *Educational Theory*, 26 (Winter, 1976), 5.

12. B. M. SHEA, "Schooling and Its Antecedents: Substantive and Methodological Issues in the Status Attainment Process," *Review of Educational Research*, 46 (1976), 463–526.

13. JOHN AMOS COMENIUS, *The Analytical Didactic*, trans. V. Jelinek (Chicago: University of Chicago Press, 1953), pp. 168–169.

14. ARTHUR R. JENSEN, *Bias in Mental Testing*, (New York: The Free Press, 1980), pp. 724–725; George F. Madaus, Peter W. Airasian, and Thomas Kellaghan, *School Effectiveness: A Reassessment of the Evidence*, (New York: McGraw-Hill, 1980), pp. 166–169; and George F. Madaus and Peter W. Airasian, "Issues in Evaluating Student Outcomes in Competency Based Graduation Programs," *Journal of Research and Development in Education*, 10 (1977), 79–91.

15. JENSEN, *Bias in Mental Testing*, pp. 370–373, notes these allegations and repudiates them.

16. EDWARD L. THORNDIKE, *An Introduction to the Theory of Mental and Social Measurements* (New York: Teachers College Press, 1904). The 1913 edition of this book is more readily accessible.

17. ADLER, "In Defense of the Philosophy of Education," p. 210.

18. Accountability is usually associated with competence or performance-based techniques and, of course, behavioral objectives. See Leon Lessinger, "Accountability for Results: A Basic Challenge to American Schools," in Leon M. Lessinger and Ralph W. Tyler, eds., *Accountability in Education* (Worthington, Ohio: C. A. Jones Publishing Company, 1971).

19. J. DONALD BUTLER, *Four Philosophies: And Their Practice in Education and Religion*, p. 259.

20. JOHN WILD, "Education and Human Society: A Realistic View," in the Fifty-fourth

Yearbook of the National Society for the Study of Education, *Modern Philosophies and Education* (Chicago: University of Chicago Press, 1955), p. 52.

21. JACQUES MARITAIN, "Thomist Views on Education," in the Fifty-fourth Yearbook of the National Society for the Study of Education, *Modern Philosophies and Education* (Chicago: University of Chicago Press, 1955), p. 68.

22. WILLIAM HEARD KILPATRICK, *The Foundation of Method* (New York: Macmillan, Inc., 1925); *Education for a Changing Civilization* (New York: Macmillan, Inc., 1926); and *Selfhood and Civilization: A Study of the Self-Other Process* (New York: Macmillan, Inc., 1941).

23. BOYD H. BODE, *Modern Educational Theories* (New York: Macmillan, Inc., 1927), p. 163.

24. RALPH HARPER, "Significance of Existence and Recognition for Education," in the Fifty-fourth Yearbook of the National Society for the Study of Education, *Modern Philosophies and Education* (Chicago: University of Chicago Press, 1955), p. 236.

25. Ibid., p. 235.

26. Ibid., p. 234.

27. For illustrations of work on method, see Jonas F. Soltis, *An Introduction to the Analysis of Educational Concepts* (Reading, Mass.: Addison-Wesley Publishing Co., Inc., 1968).

28. HERBERT FEIGL, "Aims of Education for Our Age of Science: Reflections of a Logical Empiricist," in the Fifty-fourth Yearbook of the National Society for the Study of Education, *Modern Philosophies and Education* (Chicago: University of Chicago Press, 1955), p. 304.

READINGS

BACON, WILLIAM, *Public Accountability and the Schooling System: A Sociology of School Board Democracy.* New York: Harper & Row, Publishers, Inc., 1978. Although the British school system is the one the author has in mind, the two issues—who controls the schools and how should they be governed and managed—have meaning for American education as well.

BARROW, ROBIN, *Radical Education: A Critique of Freeschooling and Deschooling.* New York: John Wiley & Sons, Inc., 1978. Contains good material on educational innovation and free schools.

BRUNER, JEROME, *Toward a Theory of Instruction.* Cambridge, Mass., The Belknap Press of Harvard University Press, 1966. Chapter 6 deals with the will to learn—a problem, the author says, that cannot be avoided, although it can be managed.

BUTLER, J. DONALD, *Four Philosophies: And Their Practice in Education and Religion.* New York: Harper & Row, Publishers, Inc., 1968. The educative process from the point of view of idealism, realism, and pragmatism is discussed in turn on pages 238–254, 366–377, and 490–499.

CHAMBLISS, J. J., *Boyd H. Bode's Philosophy of Education.* Columbus: Ohio State University Press, 1963. Pages 80–85 contain an analysis of Bode's approach to logical and psychological organization of subject matter.

CUMMINGS, SCOTT, *Black Children in Northern Schools: The Pedagogy and Politics of Failure*. San Francisco: R & E Research Associates, 1977. This study examines the various hypotheses advanced with respect to the academic performance of black youth.

DERR, RICHARD L., "The Logical Outcomes of Teaching," *Educational Theory*, 29 (Spring 1979), 139–148. Teaching is distinguished from "showing, telling, presenting, trying to teach, or doing something else." All topics other than the meaning of teaching, the author says, are secondary in teacher-education programs.

DUNN, LLOYD, M., ed., *Exceptional Children in the Schools: Special Education in Transition*. New York: Holt, Rinehart & Winston, 1973. Chapter 1 is an overview of the character and scope of the education of exceptional children.

HAMMILL, DONALD D., and NETTIE R. BARTEL, *Teaching Children with Learning and Behavioral Problems*. Boston: Allyn & Bacon, Inc., 1975. Chapter 6 is concerned with the reason for, and assessment of, behavior problems in the classroom.

HILLS, PHILIP J., *Teaching and Learning as a Communication Process*. New York: John Wiley & Sons, Inc., 1979. This short book is concerned with teaching and learning in higher education, further education, and continuing education. The principles of method, though, have general application in schooling.

JENSEN, ARTHUR R., *Bias in Mental Testing*. New York: The Free Press, 1980. This is a huge volume. Chapter 1, "Mental Testing Under Fire," can be recommended for the general reader.

KIRK, SAMUEL A., and JAMES J. GALLAGHER, *Educating Exceptional Children*, 3rd edition. Boston: Houghton Mifflin Company, 1979. Chapter 13 considers the role of parents, state and federal legislation, and the courts in relation to directions for educating exceptional children.

KOWALSKI, JOAN P. S., *Evaluating Teacher Performance*. Arlington, Va.: Educational Research Service, Inc., 1978. The introduction deals with who should evaluate teaching and the various problems associated with assessing teachers' performance and effectiveness.

MADAUS, GEORGE F., PETER W. AIRASIAN, and THOMAS KELLAGHAN, *School Effectiveness: A Reassessment of the Evidence*. New York: McGraw-Hill Book Company, 1980. Chapter 5, "School Outcomes: Standardized Tests of Ability," and Chapter 6, "Standardized Tests of Achievement," are excellent expositions.

PFEIFFER, RAYMOND S., "The Scientific Concept of Creativity," *Educational Theory*, 29 (Spring 1979), 129–137. Creativity, a favorite word in some educational circles, is often misunderstood and misused. This article goes a long way toward clarifying its meaning.

POSTMAN, NEIL, *Teaching as a Conserving Activity*. New York: Delacorte Press, 1979. Chapter 7, "Redefining Relevance," is done well by an author who admits to having been a rider on the bandwagon of relevance.

TURNBULL, ANN P., BONNIE B. STRICKLAND, and JOHN C. BRANTLEY *Developing and Implementing Individualized Educational Programs*. Columbus, Ohio: Charles E. Merrill Publishing Company, 1978. The section on individualized instruction is well done, although it tends to focus on exceptional children.

VALLENTUTTI, PETER J., and ANTHONY O. SALPINO, *Individualizing Educational Objectives and Programs: A Modular Approach*. Baltimore: University Park Press, 1979. In the first module prevailing educational goals and objectives of the school district and general community are illustrated. The teacher is shown how to use this knowledge to "establish individualized educational objectives for each pupil."

IV

CONTEMPORARY ISSUES IN EDUCATIONAL POLICY

10

FUNDAMENTALS
OF
EDUCATIONAL
POLICY

Authentic principles of education speak with a clear voice to all human beings throughout the whole of history. Educational policy, although hardly less important, is less ambitious: Its commission is to translate principle to the education of persons in particular historical, political, social, and economic settings.

Were this chapter on educational policy written for a European or Asian country, its content, we can well imagine, would turn out to be remarkably different. As it is, the fundamentals of educational policy distilled here belong to American education. They were shaped, and are being reshaped, within the American experience by principles philosophy articulates for the management of the human enterprise of education and by the prudence and judgment of men and women whose experience in life and education equips them to say how the education of human beings should proceed at this time in this place.

A word about policy's stability should be appended: Educational policy is constantly evolving; its fundamentals, reacting to life's pressure, are subject to inevitable metamorphosis. New problems arise, new conditions are fixed. Educational policy must be fluid, flexible, and precocious enough to keep abreast of them. Under these circumstances, one should anticipate amendment in this chapter's outlook and constitution as the calendar turns. Approaching them now, the fundamentals of policy can be classified as political, social, and organizational. Quite likely these same classifications, or ones substantially similar, could be used with confidence a decade hence, but the issues subsumed to them would illustrate preoccupations in educational policy introduced by the reconstructing force of time.

POLITICAL POLICY AND EDUCATION

Plato appears to have been the first political philosopher to recognize education's significance to politics. To illustrate this significance he wrote *The Republic,* a book that, while sometimes characterized as a treatise on education, is in fact a book on political philosophy.[1] Education figures large in Plato's great book because, in the nature of things, education has a huge part to play in the destiny of political states. Although the lesson Plato taught was not always mastered, we know from only a cursory reading of history that sometime in the eighteenth century national states, prompted by their leaders' thirst for power, came to understand how education could contribute to the national good. It was only then, when education was assumed to have a positive civic purpose, that political states began to pay close heed to Plato's political philosophy as it erected and sustained an intimate compact between education and political policy. Our nation's forefathers learned their first political lessons from Europe, so it is not surprising that they too discovered a role for education in an American political system being carved from a wilderness.

State Educational Authority

Despite the lesson history taught about education and European nationalism, neither the American colonies nor the architects of the new American political system were entirely sure just where authority for education belonged. Safe to say, the American colonial educational experience exhibited a residue of conviction, with its source mainly European, making education a collective responsibility. Had this conviction been translated directly to public policy, our books on American educational history would contain accounts of how the colonies and then the first states erected and maintained state systems of education. But this conviction, as it turned out, marked time.

On the other side of the policy coin was the preference for making education an individual responsibility, with the state standing aside either doing nothing at all or acting only when certain persons, for example, orphans or indigents, required training or education to keep them from swamping public poor rolls. For a long time, under the flag of educational freedom, persons rather than states or local communities were charged with the responsibility for their own and their children's education.

Yet men of political vision and prudence soon came to see educational individualism as an impediment to the kind of political society America wanted and needed. Although the United States Constitution is silent about education, the first states recognized education's fortifying influence on the common good and gave their legislatures a constitutional commission to establish and maintain systems of public education. It took a long time, we know, to clarify the precise meaning of public education but the original states took the first step in affirming state authority in education. An interpolation here is apt: Our political ancestors could have reserved educational authority to the federal government, making it a national responsibility. They demurred, however, largely on grounds that centralization of authority in a national state, a political practice with which they were all too familiar, was inimical to good government, so whenever possible they curtailed the authority of the centfal government.

A State's Legitimate Right to Sustain Itself. Plato supposed he had written the charter for an ideal state, one granting citizens an opportunity to realize personal talent and ambition. He expected, moreover, that state-controlled education would be capable of preparing citizens for personal success and, at the same time, would protect the ideal and fundamental foundations of the state. It never occurred to him that the state would authorize a subversive brand of education containing the seeds for its overthrow or destruction.

All contemporary national states adopt the same policy: They refuse to countenance political subversion in education or elsewhere. This clear policy is exhibited in all political ideologies and systems ranging from totalitarianism to democracy. In totalitarian states education is subjected to strict control, and no departure from official policy is permitted in the operation of schools. In democracies every effort is made to blend freedom and authority by delegating schools to promote in their teaching the virtues of political democracy and by eliciting from students a voluntary embrace of its rational principles.

Pursuing a legitimate right, some say an obligation, to sustain itself, the state is authorized to promote civic order and tranquility through educational and other means. This, critics may argue, is only an organized conspiracy to infringe freedom by an outright endorsement of indoctrination.[2]

In democratic societies schools are encouraged to teach about various political systems and philosophies. Marxism, for example, rather than being ostracized from the curriculum of American schools, is included in the syllabus of social studies courses. Issues at political controversy are handled in the schools, sometimes in the face of considerable vocal opposition, without endangering or subverting the common good. And this liberal practice is justified by the conviction that the best safeguard to misunderstanding and misinterpretation is an abundance of information. Yet, to the extent that the full arsenal of political thought can be represented, there is clearly a point in American educational policy to which all teachers are expected to subscribe and follow: Truth is our best ally, but it must be taught in such a way that it is both recognized as truth and allied to our best interests. In this connection educational philosophers offer wise counsel when, as a fundamental in educational policy, they tell us to teach and justify the democratic charter with zeal and devotion.[3]

Does such a policy have implications for the freedom of inquiry? Does it, in fact, advance or retard the correlative policy of academic freedom?

Academic Freedom. Academic freedom safeguards the road of investigation leading to dependable knowledge (truth) from intimidation by alien intruder and arbitrary fiat. It is sometimes, although incorrectly, interpreted to mean a teacher's unbridled right to teach anyone anything.

In elementary and secondary schools the policy of academic freedom is seldom assaulted, for on these levels of instruction teachers are engaged principally in instructing students in methods essential to particular fields of knowledge and in the knowledge unearthed by these methods. They are delegated to provide their students with a decent educational foundation, and this commission, although heavy, does not usually tempt them to enter the borderland between the known and the unknown or to challenge the authenticity of an existing corpus of knowledge. Their principal obligation is to communicate the intellectual legacy, or those parts of it appropriate to the age and maturity of their students, without undertaking to challenge, repudiate, or contradict this legacy.

It is possible, of course, for some teachers to reject either the whole or great parts of the social and intellectual legacy, and we should neither expect nor require them to teach what they do not believe. Our respect for intellectual honesty should protect them from authoritarian compulsion. If teachers find it impossible to comply with the scholastic commission of elementary and secondary schools to teach bodies of knowledge organized into the curriculum, they should seek positions on the higher levels of education, where freedom of investigation and latitude in teaching with criticism and originality are countenanced, or they should turn to some other occupation. A student's natural right to decent opportunity for learning inhibits teachers from departing from commonly accepted principles of knowledge, and it inhibits them, too, from a kind of educational militancy that undermines a student's confidence in knowledge and confuses a student's purposes for engaging in the serious business of learning.

In colleges and universities, where students with greater maturity have supposedly mastered the fundamentals of knowledge and the methods associated with them, teaching is more nearly aligned to discovery. We should expect the faculties of colleges and universities to exhibit a reasonable anxiety about the adequacy and dependability of knowledge. We should expect scholars to probe the mysteries of their disciplines, and we should also expect them to hold up to searching inquiry even the conventional wisdom of their studies. But how far are they entitled to go? Where, if anywhere, must they call a halt to the novelties of their teaching and research? If they are unready to curb their own appetites for inquisitiveness, who is authorized to issue directives for them to cease and desist? Even in higher education, it must be clear, the rule of reason refuses to authorize academic licentiousness. An appointment to a college faculty is not a commission to make any pronouncement, whatever its merit, with impunity.

When academic freedom is honored in public educational policy, it is an internal rather than an external scholastic control. Academic freedom is a necessary condition for discovery. Without freedom to discover, without the freedom to go beyond what is already known, even to invade those areas of scientific and philosophical knowledge where truth appears to be positive and incontrovertible, intellectual progress is pulled up short and knowledge becomes a stagnant pool. A policy of academic freedom encourages scholars to research, discover, reexamine, and reinterpret standard conviction, but it says too that they must do all these things honestly and responsibly. A judgment of honest and responsible scholarship can of course be rendered. Scholars' findings can be either praised or blamed, affirmed or refuted, but such judgments must be rendered by experts in the field and not by politicians, bureaucrats, or academic intruders. Academic freedom allows scholars to follow the truth wherever it may lead, but it should not be confused with free speech, a civil liberty guaranteed in the Constitution. And even this civil liberty has restrictions surrounding it. Citizens can speak and write freely, but excesses in speech and writing are penalized by laws on slander and libel. A scholar has full range in his field of specialization, but the protection of academic freedom is enjoyed only when what is said or written is supported by a disciplined study of the evidence. Scholars can be controverted but, again, only by the results of genuine research and unfettered criticism. Their freedom of expression can be curtailed only by the authority of bodies of evidence mustered by scholars of equal knowledge and standing. Academic freedom is a perquisite of the scholar's office; it is not a passport to intellectual anarchy.[4]

Compulsory Education: An Illustration of State Educational Authority. An exercise of state educational authority can be illustrated in various ways, but one way with special appeal to us, because it finds justification in its contribution to the common good, is compulsory education.

It is important to be precise when we speak of compulsory education, for its evolution in policy evidences different sides. We have to go well back in American educational history to find an authentic compulsory education law, all the way to colonial Massachusetts, where the first such law was enacted in 1642. In 1852, more than two centuries after the first educational law was passed in the colonies, Massachusetts again took the lead and translated state educational authority into compulsory attendance legislation.

The Massachusetts law became a model for other states, until eventually all states required all children to attend school. Public policy was expressed in educational law, and this expression was always justified in terms of the common good. Compulsory attendance became, in fact, one of the most obvious expressions of American educational policy.

But policy, we know, does not command allegiance or assent merely by its expression, and nowhere is this more clearly demonstrated than in compulsory attendance laws. Americans by the thousands applauded such laws, for in them they saw the foundations being laid for a more progressive economic and political society. For these people education was a common faith, and now at long last public policy was on their side. But alongside almost every enthusiastic advocate of compulsory attendance stood a vocal and intransigent foe. The state, opponents averred, lacked the authority to require school attendance; moreover, they asserted, every citizen has the natural right to remain ignorant. In the end, however, when compulsory attendance statutes were subjected to constitutional tests, the state was authorized to require school attendance. So the matter remains today, despite concerted effort in some quarters to amend compulsory attendance laws and allow children to seek their education in those places and under those conditions judged best for them.

State educational policy is expressed in law or in regulation based upon law. But before laws are enacted, and this applies to educational as well as all other law, sentiment supporting policies from which law is forged is already present in the community. Normally, law is a codification of belief held by most people to be both good and true. It would be unusual for law to be in the vanguard of public opinion and on those rare occasions when in fact it is, such laws are enormously difficult to enforce.

Limitation on State Educational Authority

Public policy confers on states extensive authority to establish, maintain, control, and superintend various means for education within their borders. In an expression of educational policy, states can, for example, define the official curriculum for elementary and secondary schools, establish standards for the certification of teachers, set the length of the school year, and delegate authority to local jurisdictions to conduct and support schools. Yet, state authority has limits, and these limits are further expressions of public policy.

It is instructive to look at a few illustrations to gain a clear vision of limitations on state authority. In the American political system such limitations are usually imposed by the judicial branch of government. In any case, the courts have given us the most vivid illustrations of restricting state authority, and here, by way of additional illustration, we shall review three court decisions rendered by the United States Supreme Court: *Pierce* v. *Society of Sisters, and the Hill Military Academy; Meyer* v. *Nebraska;* and *Brown* v. *Board of Education of Topeka.*

Pierce v. Society of Sisters, and the Hill Military Academy. In 1922 Oregon enacted a law requiring all normal children to fulfill their legal obligation of compulsory attendance by enrolling in public schools. Such a law, its exponents declared, would ensure social solidarity, uproot crime and political dissent, and contribute materially to the general welfare. The implication was evident: Private schools could not be trusted to make a full and fair contribution to the common good.

Before the law's effective date, 1925, two educational corporations conducting schools in Oregon—the Society of Sisters and the Hill Military Academy—went to court to seek relief from the law, which, they maintained, was an infringement of their property rights protected by the Fourteenth Amendment. They were, they contended, being deprived of property without due process of law. The United States Supreme Court, recognizing the state's usurpation of authority, declared the Oregon law unconstitutional. In its decision the court wrote that the state enjoys considerable latitude in exercising its entirely legitimate right to conduct, control, and supervise education within its borders, but that such right does not extend so far as to allow the state, either directly or indirectly, to suppress schools not conducted by the state. This law, the court declared, was an arbitrary exercise of power, which indeed deprived these corporations of property without due process of law.[5]

Meyer v. Nebraska. In 1919, after the experience of World War I had revived an American spirit of suspicion and isolation, Nebraska enacted a law prohibiting the teaching of any foreign language in any public, private, or parochial elementary school in the state. The law was justified on the ground that the common good required everyone to know and understand the English language. Studying other languages in elementary schools consumed time that otherwise could be used to study English and, in addition, displaced English's status as a common idiom. Proponents of this legislation and, as it turned out, the lower courts too, interpreted the law as being nothing more than a legitimate exercise of the state's police power.

A teacher in a Lutheran parochial school, Meyer, conducted classes giving instruction in German. Being in violation of the law, he was arrested, tried, and found guilty. He appealed to the state courts and eventually, because state courts found no fault with the law and upheld his conviction, to the United States Supreme Court. In a 1922 decision the Court declared that the state of Nebraska had exceeded its authority in depriving a person of the liberty to pursue a lawful occupation without due process of law. Teaching, including the teaching of ancient and modern languages, the court held, has universal recognition as a lawful, honest, and praiseworthy occupation. For the state to legislate otherwise was an arbitrary exercise of its power, so the law was declared unconstitutional.[6]

Brown v. Board of Education of Topeka. From shortly after the Civil War to the middle of the twentieth century several states conducted what can best be called dual school systems: One system of schools for black children and another for white children. This policy of race segregation ranged beyond schools and was specifically ratified by the United States Supreme Court in *Plessy* v. *Ferguson* (1896).[7] But the lower courts had spoken directly to the issue of scholastic segregation of the races dozens of times and in every instance had upheld the constitutionality of the "separate but equal" practice.

Until 1954 it was well established in many cases decided in both state and federal courts that legislation providing for separate schools for white and black children did not violate any provision of the Constitution. From time to time the allegation had been made that race segregation in the schools violated the Fourteenth Amendment clause prohibiting any state from making or enforcing "any law which shall abridge the privileges and immunities of citizens of the United States." This allegation lacked force, however, because the courts distinguished between privileges and immunities based on state citizenship from those based on federal citizenship. It was argued, moreover, that education is a privilege conferred by the states and, therefore, not one of the privileges safeguarded by the Fourteenth Amendment. Besides, it was maintained, race segregation in the school violated the provision in the Fourteenth Amendment making it unlawful for any state to "deny to any person within its jurisdiction the equal protection of the law." The courts were in agreement, however, that when separate schools were provided for white and black children, no one was denied the equal protection of the law so long as both classes of children were afforded substantially the same educational opportunities.

The 1954 decision in the *Brown* case, while not mustering new legal insights with respect to race segregation in public schools (the legal objections to segregation were all on the record), broke new ground for educational policy by declaring that equality of educational opportunity, whatever a state might do to provide equal learning facilities, is inherently impossible when children are segregated on the basis of race alone. Segregation itself is a deprivation incapable of being redressed by the provision of equal facilities.[8]

In the wake of the *Brown* decision, American educational policy was destined to wear a new face, and American educational policy, for so long expressed in terms of separate but equal educational opportunity, became thereafter straightforward and unqualified equality of educational opportunity. The policy was clear and unconditional; however, practice carrying it to full realization in the nation's schools was encumbered by numerous social and political obstacles.

In these three precedent-setting decisions we have heard the courts affirm that state educational authority is extensive and comprehensive, but we have also heard them say that the exercise of this authority is subject to educational and legal principles capable of countermanding educational policies that stray away from reason, prudence, and justice.

Private Education

The school more than any other major social institution is dependent upon the state, and the school more than any other social institution has the responsibility for preparing persons for effective citizenship and social resourcefulness and integrity. In the American scholastic experience the educational policy of public-private dualism has been forged and ratified. This means that public and private schools operate in partnership to implement the policies of democratic education.

As provision for American education evolved, it found its basis in private education, for this was the kind of education our forefathers knew best, and it was, moreover, the kind of education in which they exhibited most confidence. Their fear of an autocratic or despotic state controlling the means of education was justified by their recollections of European educational practice and, to a great extent, this fear of educational despotism prompted the architects of the republic to leave unmentioned in the Constitution any national prerogatives for education. So from the beginning of the American nation, it could be argued, educational policy was one of laissez faire, with either the several states or the people themselves engineering the means whereby educational opportunity might be provided.

In time, of course, the states themselves assumed responsibility for the education of the people, most likely following the bold thesis advanced by Thomas Jefferson, for without a decent level of education distributed among the citizens of the land the novel experiment with a republican form of government could never succeed. In the absence of informed opinion, citizens could hardly be expected to shape public policy. The political policy embracing popular sovereignty was unconditional; in consequence, literacy and learning, education's most obvious and basic appurtenances, were imperative. So toward the middle of the nineteenth century, public schools—then called common schools—made their first appearance. Almost immediately they began a half-century-long competition with private schools whose record of accomplishment in America was by that time almost two centuries old.

State constitutions authorized their legislatures to establish and maintain systems of public education, and when they did they neglected to make any substantial legal provision for private schools. Private education in the United States was left to stand or fall entirely on the precarious ground of tradition, for tradition rather than law justified its claim for recognition.

Public education entered American society as a weak, undernourished, and often unloved stepchild of private education, but as it matured and found its proper place in American society, it became more and more acquisitive. Eventually, proponents of public education were expressing the opinion that private education was inimical to the best interests of American education and society. Hasty steps were taken to immunize children from the contagion of private schools, first in Michigan and then in Oregon, and to convert public education into a monopoly. This movement, hasty as it was, was a major threat to private educational initiative, but it was halted by the decision of the United States Supreme Court in *Pierce* v. *Society of Sisters*.[9] Yet this decision, one giving private education an explicit legal foundation, did not immediately halt the mounting antipathy to private education. Public schools alone, the placards read, were capable of promoting and safeguarding the fundamental principles of American democracy. Private schools, by implication, were subversive of the common good. Besides, it was declared with a good deal of fervor, if private schools wanted to operate in the mainstream of American life, they would not isolate themselves from the public arena and insulate their students from the benefits of public schooling.

It would be pure hyperbole to maintain that private education is today under assault from public education monopolists, yet it is no secret that private education on all levels is in serious financial jeopardy. One by one private schools disappear from the American educational landscape. As they do the American public is becoming increasingly alarmed, for whatever avant-garde expositors for public education may assert, educational pluralism for a pluriform American society has almost unassailable justification in educational and political philosophy.

Although it cannot be said that the financing of American schools is a matter for philosophy, the principles on which educational pluralism, or public-private dualism, stands can be stated clearly. These principles may be insufficient to maintain the health of private schools, but they can guide educational policy with respect to the merit and necessity of preserving private education in a free society.

The principles authenticating public-private dualism are not hard to find: First, any free society, which is also pluralistic in its expectations from education, must permit responsible groups and individuals to provide education outside the public school system; otherwise, both freedom and democratic right are mocked. Second, private education must accept and teach the fundamentals of the American democratic way of life and maintain scholastic standards equal to those of public institutions. Third, public policy must guarantee parents the right of choice to select either public or private schools for their children.

The foregoing propositions do nothing to undermine public education or anyone's confidence in it—who could seriously argue that public education has not been a great boon to American society?—but they do establish private education on a solid theoretical foundation, thus enabling parents to exercise a democratic right to make educational choices and direct the education of their children. Once this parental right is asserted, as it has been in both law and political theory, it would be difficult to see how it could be exercised in the absence of sufficient educational means. In the disappearance of private education with a consequent monopoly for public education, parents' educational right of choice would become patently meaningless.

Religious Education

Any perceptive analysis of Western culture offers two profoundly important conclusions with respect to religion: One, many of our cultural attitudes and ideals have their source in our religious inheritance and, to some extent at least, American culture and civilization are indebted to religion for a synthesis of personal and social life. Two, the long and turbulent history of the relationship between church and state has left a residue of perennial and persistent suspicion about the church's commitment to the preservation of freedom. Theocratic states, both now and in the past, exhibit tendencies more toward suppression of personal freedom and social autonomy than toward sustaining conditions for freedom of conscience and personal responsibility. Being beneficiaries of a culture infused with religious ethic and ideal, the American public entertains a sympathetic view toward religion, and this sympathy from time to time discloses itself in educational policy. Yet the American dread of religion's intruding into politics has resulted in the elaboration of a public policy that erects a high and impregnable wall of separation between church and state.[10]

Educational policy, in turn, tries to strike a balance of compromise between these two apparently conflicting positions. The school, one can maintain with confidence, is a civilizing institution, and to function effectively it should undertake to communicate to its students the principal stanchions of the social legacy. Incontrovertibly, religion is one of these principal stanchions. Its imprint on American life and institutions is indelible, so it is hardly acceptable for the schools of the nation to adopt a policy authorizing or requiring religious illiteracy.

Yet, one should be clear, religious literacy, which educational policy can endorse with impunity, does not imply that public schools engage in teaching denominational or sectarian doctrine. Schools can function as civilizing institutions without becoming religious institutes.

Although public policy clearly authorizes private schools wherein the articles of religious belief can be taught, one should not overlook the religious rights and responsibilities of the family itself. It may very well be true that religious perspective permeates all school subjects, as exponents of religious education declare, but it would also appear to be true that the home is where seeds of faith are planted most deeply and cultivated most effectively. The school, especially the officially religious school, can contribute, we would suppose materially, to the home's religious objective, but it can hardly be expected to assume responsibility for it. In the final analysis, American educational policy declares, the obligation of teaching sectarian religious doctrine and cultivating it in the minds of youth is the business of the home. Should it choose to seek help, it can call on private schools and churches, but it cannot expect public schools to adopt its teaching function.

At the same time, the home has every right, and public policy should secure this right, to expect public education on all levels to abstain from any direct or indirect subversion of religious belief. The school should not be expected to replace the family as a religious teacher, but it must scrupulously avoid undermining the family's religious commitment.

This public educational policy, one of friendly neutrality toward religion, took a long time to forge. It, along with other educational policies, evolved over the decades. We know, for example, a good deal about the religious convictions of our colonial ancestors, and we know, too, of their idealization of religious education. For a century or more in this frontier land, all education was religious in both content and purpose, and no one apologized for a school where the tenets of a religious sect were taught with zeal and devotion. But this policy of educational sectarianism could not succeed in the temperate religious climate of a new, progressive nation whose commitment to personal, political, and religious liberty was supreme.

Educational sectarianism did retreat, although its retreat was impeded by the widely held conviction that religion was an essential plank in the platform of public morality, and educational policy embraced nonsectarianism. One after another the states enacted laws and issued regulations excluding denominational instruction from public schools. This policy was far from flawless in its execution, for the meaning of nonsectarianism was often misunderstood, and this misunderstanding permitted a kind of instruction clearly detrimental to the status of some religious denominations. Too often, social historians of the nineteenth century tell us, this policy was translated to mean a Protestant nonsectarianism, which could, when prompted, take a harsh and strident position of opposition to Jews and Roman Catholics. But these evidences of intolerance passed with the evolution of a more liberal and generous American religious spirit. American social policy continued its forward march and with it, almost step for step, educational policy advanced toward religious tolerance.

Public policy is prepared to encourage religion and religious disposition among citizens without, at the same time, contributing any direct support to religious schools or institutions. In tandem with the policy of nonsectarian instruction in public schools, the states, one after another, instituted policies withholding public money from both churches and religiously established schools. We need not illustrate such statutory restrictions here, but all had the same effect in declaring that public money could not be used for the support of religion or religious education.

Yet in its execution, this policy denying public support for religious education refused to exhibit hostility to religion. On this point the best evidence may be obtained by reviewing court decisions. Public policy endorses the use of public money for transporting children to religious schools[11] and for supplying students in religious schools with essential instructional materials.[12] In permitting children to leave the public school during regular school time to obtain religious instruction, public policy demonstrates its willingness to encourage a spirit of religion among the citizens of the country.[13]

Yet public policy drew the line, again in court decision, when religious instruction was introduced to public schools and students were released during part of the official school day to take courses in religion taught by representatives of various religious creeds. Students were free, of course, to elect or reject these courses, and the teachers of religion were not compensated by the public school. School time and property were used, however, and this was enough to invalidate the practice.[14] Along the same line, public policy rejects the adoption of official school prayer as well as the reading of the Bible as a nonsectarian scholastic practice.[15]

Where, we can ask finally, does this leave the school as a civilizing institution? It cannot, we see, engage in denominational teaching nor can it use the Bible as a means for cultivating religious literacy. How, then, can schools teach anything about the religious inheritance?

Few educational philosophers declare the religious experience unimportant in the transmission of culture. Almost with one voice they subscribe to the proposition that schools should do their best to persuade their students by means of competent instruction to take life seriously and to seek for something worthy of their allegiance. Religious experience and religious institutions are vital parts of our culture; neither should be dismissed from education. The school's approach to religion should be one of official neutrality, but neutrality should not be confused with neglect or indifference. Religion should not be ignored. It should be studied and discussed in a spirit of honest inquiry. Courses in history and literature should be used to convey reliable information about religion, but complete confidence should not be placed in secondary sources. The classics of the world's great religions should be studied as illustrations of what can be given meaning and value in human life, and they should be studied in a way calculated to inculcate respect for sincere conviction about ultimate belief.

Doctrinal teaching, the expression of religious preference, or attempts to indoctrinate students in a general religious spirit are not parts of the business of public schools. If this kind of instruction is desirable, it should be left to the church, the private school, or the home.

Tensions in Local Support

Equality of educational opportunity has been ratified time and again in educational and social theory. In the famous *Brown* decision of 1954 a policy of equality of educational opportunity became part of the nation's basic law.[16] No one need have any doubt whatever where educational policy in the United States stands on this traditionally troublesome point. But does this settle the matter?

Even a hasty review of resources available for educational support from one to another state or from one to another community within a state reveals vast, almost insurmountable, differences. With public education in the United States dependent mainly on local support, can equality of opportunity be realized?

The supreme courts of California, in 1971, and Texas, in 1973, gave a clear and precise answer.[17] So long as schools must depend largely on the resources of the local community for support, equality of educational opportunity, these courts declared, is seriously impeded. How can this situation be corrected in order to ensure equality of educational opportunity? One way, of course, is to increase the level of state aid and thus to more nearly approach equality of support from community to community within a state. And we know, without probing the issues of state equalization practices, that this is presently being done and on a large scale. But anyone who takes the trouble to do so can discover that the states are unequal in their ability to support education. Simply put, some states are richer than others. This leaves the solution, if one is to be found, on the national level, and it suggests that equality of support can be obtained by a program of federal financing of the schools.

On the surface this solution is attractive, and it is entirely possible that federal financing of schools would result in the provision of equal, or nearly equal, resources for education on local levels. But solving the financial problem could generate another. The signs of history are all too obvious to ignore: Control inexorably follows the dollar. Adopting a solution where schools would be financed from the national level could leave them in the unenviable position of being controlled from the national level. If history has taught educational policy makers anything, it has taught them of the dangers inherent in a centralized system of national education. Equality of educational opportunity might be obtained in a program of federal financing of the schools, but in obtaining fiscal equality the equally attractive feature of decentralization of educational control might be lost in the bargain.

At least since the middle years of the nineteenth century, Americans have regularly exhibited an immense amount of faith in education. This faith persuades them that education has the means to weld society to common purpose, and in the growth of the nation from a small, weak, and incoherent confederation to a powerful, wealthy, and politically stable country, most social historians acknowledge education's profound influence. The contribution education can make to society is seldom disputed, nor is doubt common that education has a part to play in upgrading the status of individuals. The record is too clear to erase: Millions of Americans over the past century have used education as a lever to hoist them to higher social, economic, and political positions.

When we turn to the general question of education and social progress and look at the principal current issues subsumed to it, the point is not whether education is a veritable panacea, but how it can be used. How can it be used to achieve desirable economic mobility for hundreds of thousands of disadvantaged youth? How can education be used to repair either the deficiencies of talent or environment and thus put certain disadvantaged classes in the mainstream of American life? How can education play a part in the enormously complicated issue of social integration in American society? And, finally, how can education be employed to correct or modify the faults of the past as those faults depress the opportunity of millions of people to obtain their fair share of the nation's economic and political bounty?

The social record may very well prove that too much has been expected from education, yet educational policy should try to sort out the possible from the impossible and then set the compass of education in a direction where reasonable expectations can be realized. It may be pure exaggeration to characterize education as a social and economic panacea; it is not unreasonable, however, to expect education to make a positive contribution to social progress.

Economic Mobility and Education

However personal and social motives are tested—and we should suppose such motives vary according to differences among persons—one obvious universal human motive is economic security. In a democratic society committed to a policy of equality of educational opportunity, how much can education be expected to contribute to the ability of persons to enjoy economic security and to improve themselves by making steady progress up the economic ladder? Must persons now occupying menial economic positions always remain in them, and must their children follow in their footsteps? Must certain ethnic and racial classes be sentenced perpetually to economic disadvantage with the ominous prospect that their children's future will be no better?[18]

The Economic Opportunity Act of 1964 declared war on poverty and under its various titles provided for equality of social, economic, political, and educational opportunity for minorities and others who traditionally were poor and underprivileged. It commissioned education, with an abundance of financial support, to invent new and insightful programs for the education of these citizens, enabling them to obtain their fair share of the nation's wealth and influence. The fundamental altruism evident in this legislation speaks well for the sensitivity of the public conscience to the problem of economic inequality, but for all this altruism, for all this determination to eliminate poverty and put all disadvantaged classes on a footing allowing them to compete favorably, the consequences of programs sponsored in this legislation were, at best, mixed.

Appraisals of educational means to eliminate poverty and provide for equality of economic opportunity extend from confident endorsement to mild disapproval. Assessments clearly supportive of education as a means for upgrading the economic chances of underprivileged and minority classes can be found. Such assessments declare that better schools, better teachers, smaller classes, progressive teaching methods, and more abundant resources for learning contribute directly to the improvement of academic achievement. And such conclusions endorse the whole array of practice aimed at better education, fortified by entirely adequate educational resources, for it is clear, they allege, that better educational opportunity puts students in a more competitive position in the economic marketplace.[19]

Other assessments, however, are less optimistic. They do not dispute the fact that a certain level of educational opportunity is essential to an upgrading of economic mobility, and that this opportunity can be secured by adequate financial support for schooling, but they bristle at the assumption that the correlation between the amount of money spent on education and the achievement of students in schools is both high and positive. Economic success, some social scientists tell us, depends less on schooling than on a number of elusive social and personal factors. Besides such elements as luck and personality, which would seem to be unrelated to school achievement, figure into the equation that adds up to success.[20]

If social scientists studying the effects of schooling on economic success cannot agree, what direction should educational policy take?[21] Whatever special studies in this enigmatic field demonstrate, educational philosophers know that personal talent cannot be realized in the absence of opportunity. They know, moreover, that opportunity by itself does not guarantee success. Yet, educational policy, if it is to be true to the broad commitment to equality in American society, must infuse educational practice with the conviction that the means for achievement must be provided to all classes of citizens. And these means, it would seem, should vary according to the disposition, motivation, and talent of students. What is called for is a diversified and comprehensive educational opportunity built upon a foundation of decent basic education. The results of sociological research are not needed to prove that basic literacy is essential to succeed on any level in

American economic society, that technical skill is required, and that motivation to succeed is imperative. Education can do a great deal about literacy and technical skill, so education's role in contributing to economic security should not be discounted. Education may also be able to stimulate and clarify motive, although prediction on this point is hazardous, for we are as yet unsure about the generation and preservation of motive in particular cases. We should be wrong to abandon education as a means to securing social and economic betterment, but we should probably be wrong, too, in adopting a policy making education wholly responsible for economic security.

With, we are told, a dropout rate in American secondary schools of about 25 percent, the schools must seek ways to whet the motivation of disadvantaged students; the schools must encourage students, by introducing attractive programs of learning, to remain in school until they have achieved enough skill and maturity to meet the economic world face to face. But education can, and probably should raise its sights beyond students presently in school, taking into account and appealing to persons who over the past decade or so have left school without either literary or technical skill essential to their finding positions of worth and satisfaction in economic society. And now the solution, for all its uncomplimentary sound, must be compensatory education. Educational policy should authorize schools to mount programs, mainly on the level of adult education, to give persons lacking essential skills an opportunity to obtain them. No magic economic or political solution can be found to redress personal inability; sponsoring a change from capacity to ability is the proper function of schools. They can teach essential skill if educational policy and their students give them a chance.

Nature-Nurture and Education

Opinion of educators, psychologists, social scientists, and social philosophers is divided, often sharply, on whether intelligence is genetically determined—and therefore invariable—or whether it is cultivated by environment and thus able to be permanently and quickly improved in the proper educational setting.

Leading the field among spokesmen for the genetic-determination camp is Arthur Jensen. In a much-noticed article in the *Harvard Educational Review,* "How Much Can We Boost I.Q. and Scholastic Achievement?",[22] his conclusion, one subjected to intense criticism, was: not much, if at all. Children come to school with their basic capacity already defined, and this is all the school has to work with. The notion that educational intervention can alter a child's capacity is rejected as an extreme and naive environmentalism.

The antithesis of Jensen's position was represented most notably by proponents of "Project Head Start," a program sponsored by the Office of Economic Opportunity. In its inception Head Start held out the promising prospect of improving the capacity of children, especially if conventional school programs were anticipated and preschool experiences were introduced before age five. In addition, it was supposed that by resting on this foundation of early training, education could be a critical tool for eliminating poverty. In its first years Head Start was saddled with unrealistic expectations among politicians, the public, and sometimes, educators. President Lyndon Johnson contributed a good deal of ammunition to this optimistic theme in his pronouncement that the lives of the children involved in Head Start would be spent "productively and rewardingly, rather than wasted in tax-supported institutions or in welfare-supported lethargy."

Promoters of Head Start and other programs to improve educational readiness who urged the powerful influence of environment did not mean to dismiss genetic constitution as irrelevant, nor did they believe that all children could become geniuses as a result of educational intervention. Nevertheless, inflated expectation circulated, and the public was swamped by claims that children could be taught to read by age two and that the IQ could be raised by twenty points in a year. When it became clear that these were exaggerations, the reputation of Head Start declined precipitously.[23]

Yet, with a nearly twenty-year experience with Head Start, cautious evaluation points in this direction: Low-income children who participate in such programs are less likely to be held back in school and are less likely to be assigned to special classes for slow learners than children who have not had a preschool educational experience. Although programs such as Head Start are incapable of eliminating poverty and of permanently reshaping a child's capacity for learning, educational gain is registered when such programs pay special attention to the teaching of cognitive skills and when subsequent schooling continues to emphasize the same kind of teaching. What Head Start and similar programs illustrate is that while nurture alone is incapable of redeeming nature, such programs add new dimensions to the educational enterprise and can be of considerable benefit for improving the health, nutrition, and educational readiness of millions of the nation's children. This in itself is an important achievement.

Experience with Head Start, even admitting to what its critics call a modest contribution to later educational achievement, recommends an educational policy taking into account the benefit in learning to be gained by introducing preschool educational experiences to children, especially to disadvantaged children, on a large scale. The point to be remembered, though, is that such an educational policy should be introduced without any discounting of authentic scholastic objectives. Preschool experience, in other words, is not a substitute for decent schooling.

Social Integration

In the late twentieth century, some educational philosophers contend, the educational enterprise is perilously close to being swamped by an overabundance of objectives. It has been asked to help eliminate poverty and to improve the capacity of children. It has been charged with the care of children's nutrition and health. And it has been commissioned to promote social integration.

The efficacy of social integration is undebatable, for it must be the destiny of human beings to live together in concord and harmony, otherwise the supreme objective of human happiness will be sacrificed on the altar of social discord. We know where educational policy in the United States stands on the question of equality of opportunity. The *Brown* decision is legally definitive, and progressive, enlightened social policy and conscience are firmly on the side of human equality. This policy declares against segregation. It clearly and steadfastly refuses to countenance segregation in public education. But a policy of desegregation is not the same as a policy of integration. Schools are called upon to promote integration. How can they do so?

In its teaching, in its climate, and in the composition of its student body the school can make a positive contribution to social understanding, harmony, and integration. So much can be taken for granted. It can also be taken for granted that, given the time, education can be a powerful influence in shaping and reshaping public opinion. What cannot be taken for granted is that the school can directly and almost immediately remake society and revise existing social attitudes, biases, and prejudices. Hostility to various experiments intended to pave the way for social integration in the schools, notably experiments with busing to achieve racial balance in some of the nation's urban schools, illustrate how little schools can do to uproot intransigent public opinion even when they adopt progressive social policies toward the composition of their student bodies.

The Coleman Report, *Equality of Educational Opportunity,*[24] took the lead in declaring that the solution to the problem of social integration was not so much a matter of improving the schools, and thus by means of better educational facilities improving the educational and social status of students from disadvantaged classes in society, but rather was a matter of altering the composition of school populations. According to the report, social education by indirect rather than direct means, exposure to various social groups and meeting their values face to face, rather than by teaching about their differences, is the solution to social integration.

Yet, when students in such integrated schools leave for home at the end of the day, they do not always find their homes and communities ready to ratify the social values promoted in the schools' climate. And this condition testifies to the validity of an educational proposition educators have always known, and now appear to have forgotten: that social education in the community at large is probably more impressive and convincing than any scholastic instruction.[25]

Educational policy is on solid ground, nevertheless, in taking a stand against schools being either neutral in their approach to social integration or in justifying the status quo in their teaching and social demeanor. Educational policy should be fully supportive of social integration and should take an assertive position on its side. Still, despite George Counts' bold assertion more than a half-century ago,[26] schools alone are incapable of building a new social order. Society has room for many teachers, and the school, for good or ill, is only one.

Theory of Access to Schooling

Another issue bearing heavily on education in the United States, one, it would seem, occupying that foggy borderland between principle and policy, is access to schooling. In considering a theory of access to schooling, a matter involving what is currently called affirmative action, three points attract our attention: equality of educational opportunity, compensatory justice, and distributive justice.

If opportunities for schooling—and here schooling usually means special programs in higher education—were unlimited, and if everyone who applied to a graduate or professional school could be admitted, the problem would disappear and any consideration of a theory of access to schooling would be unnecessary.

Some of the nation's great colleges and universities have adopted a policy of open admissions. Anyone who applies, with or without the conventional academic prerequisites to higher learning, is admitted. Whether open admissions policies are justified by the liberal doctrine of "the right to fail" or are introduced to avoid litigation and controversy can be debated. In the end, however, whatever its real or imagined contribution to equality of educational opportunity, open admissions alters the character of higher education. Some critics of open admissions call this alteration an educational disaster; others are more sanguine, for they see the dismantling of traditional educational standard as one way to distribute the experience of higher study more generously and more democratically.[27]

More commonly, however, programs in higher education, especially in the professional schools, have only a limited number of places for students. Traditionally, of course, such schools committed themselves to a policy of admitting students whose qualifications predicted high academic performance. Qualifications were judged on the basis of past scholastic achievement and, in some schools, on special aptitude tests.

Equality of Educational Opportunity. The thesis here, although it may be regarded as conservative or, in some quarters, discriminatory, follows the line of thought that equality means a similar treatment of similar persons. Therefore, in developing a theory of access to schooling, if this principle is followed, those students whose academic record and aptitude are most promising will be admitted. The admissions process is indifferent to any factors other than the academic quality of the applicants.[28]

Compensatory Justice. Among applicants for special educational programs may be some who represent groups in the population who have undergone a number of social, cultural, and educational disadvantages. Following principles of compensatory justice, the admissions process would take such disadvantages into account. In consequence, applicants whose aptitude for success, or whose demonstrated qualifications for admission, are nearly equal to those of other applicants who are assumed not to have suffered from such deprivations will be admitted. Characterized as compensatory justice by some, such a policy is called preferential treatment or reverse discrimination by others.[29]

Distributive Justice. According to the hypothesis of distributive justice, every group in society—racial and ethnic minorities, women, and others—has a right to its fair share of society's goods and services. Various kinds of higher education offer a service to society, and students who are able to take advantage of this educational service end up likely to harvest their fair share of society's goods. Every group in society should thus be entitled to its fair, or proportionate, share of doctors, lawyers, dentists, engineers, and teachers. Following this theory to its logical conclusion, educational policy is directed to employ what amounts to a quota system in its admissions practices for higher and professional education.[30]

Sensitivity to past inequality should encourage Americans to adopt an educational policy giving qualified students from traditionally disadvantaged classes in society every chance to enter higher schools, and it should clearly discourage and prohibit any continuing discrimination against them. On this point educational policy can be clear and direct. From this point on, however, policy evaporates into personal evaluation and judgment. Far from being a settled issue as the Supreme Court's decision in *University of California* v. *Bakke*[31] demonstrates, educational policy, divided as it is on this issue of access to schooling, can only recommend a preservation of educational integrity on one hand and a close allegiance to principles of equality and justice for all citizens on the other.

POLICY CONSIDERATIONS AND
EDUCATIONAL ORGANIZATION

Population shift over the past several decades has put more and more of the nation's schoolchildren in urban areas, and for a number of economic and social reasons minorities have flocked to the cities. This challenge to the educational enterprise is not entirely new. It was faced before and met, some say, successfully when waves of immigrants crossed the Atlantic Ocean to land on America's shores in the late years of the nineteenth and the early years of the twentieth centuries. Faced with Americanizing millions of children of foreign-born parents, American schools committed themselves to two principal instructional objectives: one, to teach English as a common idiom and, two, to inculcate allegiance to the American economic and political system. For the most part, these objectives were cultivated without opposition either from the general public or from persons intended to benefit from this kind of instruction. In the end, some social historians allege, this educational policy paid huge dividends.

But the social and educational climate has changed. American society in the 1980s only faintly resembles its turn-of-the-century counterpart. The simple, straightforward instructional objectives of former times, which may or may not have been praiseworthy, are no longer considered adequate. And the needs and aspirations of the contemporary educational clientele differ in many fundamental ways from the people who came to America from Europe determined to become and have their children become fully integrated in American life and society. Cultural pluralism was even then a fact of social life, but pluralism fought a losing battle with idealizations of cultural homogeneity, and determined effort was spent to erase linguistic and cultural differences.

Once "the schools of America [were called] the temples of a living democracy,"[32] but such a bold assertion is today charged with blindness or timidity. Education has made gigantic strides in the direction of technological efficiency but, critics charge, it has suffered from its neglect of basic conflict in social ideology. Cultural homogeneity, once the proud boast of the American school, is under assault and education's mission is being reworded. All this and more has burdened American education, especially urban education, with immensely complicated problems, and we should spend some time examining the policies, or projected policies, designed to cope with them.

In urban schools and in others as well, new questions about the worth of schooling have surfaced. We hear talk about deschooling American society and, while the prospects of a deschooling movement do not appear to be either desirable or imminent (some commentators describe deschooling as a step toward social anarchy or educational insanity), alternatives to the kind of educational organization now in place have been proposed. A return to educational voluntaryism is one; the voucher plan for supporting and, by indirection, reorganizing education is another.

In all American schools, but especially in urban schools, the issue of discipline stands out. Large city schools sometimes resemble armed camps with hostile forces preparing for battle. Sound instruction, it must be obvious to all, goes forfeit in the face of an educational climate where basic good order is absent. But school discipline, however large it may loom, is not the only problem burdening the schools. Scholastic standard, too, becomes a pawn in a conflict over educational policy. How effective are the schools? And is it possible for them to be effective when they continue to follow what in some quarters is called an archaic scholastic practice: grading? Finally, from state to state the competence-testing movement is gaining momentum. These issues need the illumination of policy as American education faces the future.

Urban and Minority Education

Neither urbanization in American society nor a preponderance of minorities in urban centers is in prospect of disappearing, so educational policy must try to strike a balance between amelioration of the problems inherent in urbanization and a decent educational opportunity for all classes of citizens. What are the choices?

Even in the face of competing hypotheses advanced by social scientists engaging in empirical and statistical studies, the choices now appear to be: compensatory education; the development of magnet or beacon schools; community action programs giving citizens of the community more voice in the direction of local school programs; redistricting and consolidation of school systems in order to broaden the social base of urban schools; and a more extensive use of various techniques, the most controversial of which is busing, to introduce a more democratic social mix to the population of urban schools.

Compensatory Education.   Hundreds of thousands of students leave high school before graduation. Leaving, they too often lack basic skills for competing successfully in American society. Their leaving may, in fact, be prompted by a lack of basic skill, for without the tools of learning, educational experience afforded in any school is almost certain to be unrewarding. Students unable to read or write are not likely to find much motivation for studying history, literature, mathematics, or science, nor are they likely to make much progress in mastering vocational or occupational skills.

In his *Aims of Education* Alfred North Whitehead said education should prepare us to know some things very well and to do some things very well.[33] In the absence of basic skill neither objective has much chance of being realized, for one of the principles of learning, readiness to learn, is being violated. The fundamental purpose of compensatory education, with all its pejorative social and personal features stripped way, is to cultivate readiness and open the way for the acquisition of essential literacy and technical skill. The solution to educational disadvantage is within educational policy's reach. Adopting the solution and implementing it in a humane, confident, equitable, and educationally sound way are the issues with which educational policy must wrestle.[34]

Community Control.   Justification for community control of schools is found in the popular thesis that schools are more effective in addressing vital educational needs of the community if the educational policies governing the operating of local schools are distilled on the level of the immediate community.

Community control is presently lacking, so one argument goes, for despite what appearances may suggest, educational control is actually in the hands of an educational bureaucracy. How American schools came to be controlled by an educational bureaucracy finds an answer in a revisionist interpretation of educational history.[35] In order to maintain social, political, and economic control, vested interest made a bold assault on the schools. With an abundance of resources for molding public opinion at its disposal, vested interest convinced or cajoled the public to divest itself of educational sovereignty. In turn, control, now in the strong hands of vested interest, was delegated to an educational bureaucracy, which the political power brokers could trust, ranging from a state department of education to the administrators in local school systems. Rather than heeding community educational need, this bureaucracy caters to the preferences of an entrenched and powerful vested interest. As a result the schools no longer belong to the people nor are they answerable to them for the policies enforced. The schools are pawns of an establishment in American society which, while seldom obvious in its exercise of fundamental control, nevertheless holds in its hands the reins of economic and political power and, as it turns out, educational power too.[36]

All this has a conspiratorial ring, and it is meant to. To wrest control from the establishment and strip the bureaucracy of its authority to return control to the hands of the people is one way, a revolutionary way, of introducing genuine democracy to policies of educational organization and control. But this is not the only way to look at the matter of community control, and it is not essential for us to adopt the conspiratorial theory to redress the limited voice the people of the community sometimes have in the direction of policy for their schools. Another thesis is more palatable to an appetite unimpressed by conspiracy theory. It maintains in a forthright manner the doctrine that popular sovereignty, one common enough to political theory, be applied to education. In the last analysis, such a theory declares, the people are sovereign in the development and ratification of educational policy. So if schools are ever to speak directly to legitimate educational need as that need is discovered and defined on the local level, every school must have its own policy council. Parents, students, and teachers must be given a direct voice in the definition of objectives, in the development of curriculum, and in every side of the management of education on the local level.

Redistricting and Consolidation. So long as urban school districts are organized along urban government lines, urban schools will be populated mainly by minority and poor children, for the inner city is a haven for such families. Unless the social composition of cities is altered, educational policy can recommend changing school district boundaries to include suburban areas. Policy recommending redistricting and consolidation—the metropolitan school district would be the outcome—has a good deal of support among educational theorists, social scientists and, sometimes, federal judges, but it also faces stiff opposition, not to mention hostility. Critics of redistricting and consolidation maintain, on one hand, that such a policy sacrifices the values inherent in the neighborhood school and, on the other, that in order to implement such a policy schools would have to resort to busing on a large scale.

Transporting children to and from school is a common practice in hundreds of American school districts, especially in rural areas, and under such circumstances is regarded as an entirely antiseptic educational policy. Yet, as we have observed over the past decade, when geography shifts to the city, transporting children to and from school can be interpreted and criticized as an unacceptable, invidious social policy.

Alternatives to Conventional School Organization

Leaving behind us the difficult policy questions related to schools in the cities, we meet new ones related to the fundamental value of schooling itself. They are revealed in alternatives to conventional school organization and can be listed as proposals for deschooling, for voluntaryism either in organizing schools or attending them, and in a voucher plan for school support.

Deschooling. Schooling is a waste of time, proponents of deschooling assert, and they counsel us to resort to more imaginative ways for educating the children of the land. But schooling can be worse than a waste of time. It can, we are told, make us prisoners of social institutions, so that we become their victims rather than their masters.[37] Schools have become institutions conspiring to exercise social control and to manipulate values and ideals rather than places where the basic needs of human beings in a democratic society can be met. Expressed in the strongest language, schools are institutions of enslavement.[38]

Undoubtedly a great deal in American education is surrounded by myth. Much more is expected from schools than they can ever hope to accomplish. But is the whole of American education, and is all schooling, a myth, as the most outspoken and extreme critics of the American educational system declare? If we are to abandon the schools, are substitute learning networks available for providing suitable opportunity for learning? And have we good reason for believing that these networks would be more efficacious in husbanding decent learning than the schools?

We know, of course, that the school is not the only place where learning occurs, and we suspect that sometimes it is not the best place for certain kinds of learning, but it is unquestionably one place where means for directing and conducting learning activities are made readily available. Can a sound and liberal educational policy, and can a progressive and sensitive social policy seriously countenance the abandonment of schools in American society?

Voluntaryism.   Scholastic voluntaryism as we meet it on the contemporary scene has two sides: One side makes attendance in schools voluntary but does not disturb the regular organization of schools. The other side, without declaring for the abandonment of schools, divorces them from the public arena, where they are controlled and supported, and makes them institutions of private enterprise. In other words, government goes out of the business of schooling, and all formal education is left in the hands of academic entrepreneurs.

In company with all other private enterprises voluntaryism would put schools in a position of competing for students; success or failure would depend upon the schools' ability to satisfy their scholastic customers. The element of competition, as we introduce it now, has an ominous, forbidding sound, for it is unconventional to describe schooling as a commodity to be bartered in the marketplace where it must subscribe to the law of supply and demand. Yet if we look more closely we see that elements of competition have always been operative in the broad arena of American private education and especially higher education.

The Voucher Plan.   The voucher plan would not seek to disturb public or private schools as they presently exist. But it would change methods of school support drastically: No public school would be an automatic recipient of public money, and private schools, if students elected to attend them, would be eligible to receive public money.

All public financial allocations for education would be made not to schools but directly to students in the form of vouchers. Students could choose to attend either public or private schools and give their vouchers, thus paying for their education, to the school selected. The school, in turn, would present its vouchers, collected from students, to the public treasury and receive money for them.

Following this plan, schools would be supported on the basis of the number of students enrolled in them.

Supporters of the voucher plan are confident that this is the best way to restore integrity to American education and to eliminate the financial monopoly public schools now enjoy. Over the past several years the voucher plan has been given attention in the educational literature, but for the most part the plan has been regarded as being either eccentric or avant-garde. More recently, however, voucher-plan activists have moved from the level of educational promotion to the level of politics. In January 1980, for example, promoters of the voucher plan circulated petitions in the state of California seeking a sufficient number of signatures for an initiative measure authorizing its public test. Had this tactic succeeded, the voucher-plan proposal would have been put on the ballot and the voters would have been given a chance to accept or reject it. As it was, the petition movement failed, yet a sufficient amount of interest appears to remain current, so we are tempted to believe that American education has not heard the last of the voucher plan.

Educational Standard

Extreme critics of American education call it a disaster. They point, for example, to colleges and universities instituting courses in remedial reading; they call attention to the enormous number of students who leave high schools before graduation, and they collect testimony on the poor reading performance of children in elementary schools. All this and more, they declare, is sufficient evidence to convict educational standard of severe decline.

Graded and Nongraded Schools.   A litany of complaint about the decline in educational standard is, if not endless, at least too long to recite here. The source of trouble, conservative opinion asserts, can be found in the general abrogation of a teaching commitment to fundamental skill and to an absence of academic rigor in the schools. Liberal opinion, going in the other direction, indicts the practice of grading, where students are classified according to age and are assigned to grades in school. What they are taught in these grades may have little or nothing to do with what they are capable of, or are interested in, learning. The solution to this persistent impediment to learning, it is alleged, is to introduce the nongraded school, where students, without consideration for their age or grade, will be permitted to advance according to their talent by being taught according to their individual needs.

Although the abandonment of grading is most commonly recommended for elementary education, grading has its critics in high schools too. Yet nongraded schools may be too unconventional to satisfy the public taste. When they are, the open classroom may be offered as a suitable substitute. In either case, the basis for these educational reforms is lodged in the creed of instructional individualization.

Testing for Competence.   Several states have either enacted or are on the verge of enacting legislation requiring tests of competence before high school diplomas are awarded. The argument for the competency test is simple and straightforward: The high school diploma represents a certain level of educational accomplishment; if students are unable to demonstrate this level of accomplishment, diplomas should be withheld.[39]

A litany of the pros and cons of competency testing is easy enough to recite, but the important point is this: What are schools expected to accomplish, and what is the high-school diploma expected to represent? If it represents a prescription of academic achievement, then competency testers are on the right track; if it represents personal growth and maturity and an ability to cope with the realities of life, then testing for prescribed competencies may be out of order.

In the final analysis, educational policy must be clear with respect to its expectations from all levels of schooling. It must be clear about its objectives and the means schools should use to help students attain them. Moreover, it must be careful not to allow educational practice to narrow the definition of standard achievement to the point where elitism corrodes the educational common good.

School Discipline.   Teachers beginning their professional careers complain that lack of school discipline is the principal and most serious impediment to their work, and experienced teachers frequently confirm such testimony. Disciplinary problems range from misbehavior in the classroom—disruptive of effective instruction—to an atmosphere of extreme hostility and physical violence. Earlier we adverted to schools, especially inner-city schools, that sometimes resemble armed camps. Too often, we hear, students in such schools lack a degree of commendable docility essential to learning, and some students prove to be destructive, if not actually dangerous. The daily press contains running accounts of personal duels between students, and it tells us, too, of teachers being molested in the schools. In such a climate, how is learning possible?

Neither educational principle nor policy, those essential constituents of educational philosophy, give exact directions for handling disciplinary problems, but they do provide some alternatives to consider. They may not tell us which disciplinary theory to follow, but they do tell us that we must follow one.

Policy can range from a theory of no control, reminding us that children have their own lives to lead and that they should therefore be free to determine their own modes of behavior, to a theory of strict control, which ends up in practices of behavior modification or drug therapy. The theory of no control, which had its most popular expression in A. S. Neill's *Summerhill,* may be extended so far as to assert that disciplinary problems have their origin in the effort of adults to impose their values and goals on children. The source of disciplinary problems is not in the behavior of children but in an adult behavior that, in seeking to exercise control, creates tensions confusing and upsetting the school's moral climate.

Between these extreme positions we find a theory of discipline centering on value clarification. The explanation to the tension and friction that turn out to be unacceptable social behavior and an impediment to instruction is that students come to school with values (and who knows their source) either not fully understood or different in substance from those adopted by schools. This theory of discipline tells us to find alternatives to punishment, for punishment diminishes self-image, by instituting counseling programs aimed at value clarification and accommodation. Value clarification vis-à-vis discipline has considerable support in the work of Carl Rogers and Abraham Maslow.[40]

Another theory maintains that misbehavior or flawed discipline has its genesis in the failure students experience in school. Underlying this theory is the conviction that schools do not meet the social and intellectual needs of their students and thus almost certainly make some degree of failure inevitable for the majority of students and especially for students coming from cultural and social backgrounds differing from those conventionally represented in the schools. The solution to the problem of discipline, William Glasser tells us, is to discover ways of conducting schools where failure is unknown and impossible.[41]

Moral behavior, still another theory maintains, is learned behavior, so discipline has a clear cognitive dimension. And the school must begin with this dimension if it is to succeed in sustaining a disciplinary climate conducive to instruction. Lawrence Kohlberg's theory of moral development, one centering on moral reasoning, aims finally at the development of a personal moral-value system. Largely a matter of cognitive development, conventional deportment and appraisals of moral worth must be taught and justified. In consequence of this teaching and justification, it is expected that students will comply with the reasonable and fully comprehended standards of behavior demanded for citizenship in the schools. This is called conventional moral development. But moral formation should not stop at this level. It should proceed to what are called postconventional moral and ethical standards. These are personal standards and are most likely to give direction to the behavior of students while they are in school and in their lives thereafter. Following Kohlberg's paradigm of moral reasoning, or character education, the problem of school discipline is ameliorated and a solid foundation is laid for a permanent personal system of moral values.[42]

The theory of behavior modification, advanced most especially in the work of B. F. Skinner, makes school discipline and all human behavior an outcome of conditioning and reinforcement. There is nothing extraordinary in the proposition that learning can modify behavior, for it would seem that all educators down through the ages have entertained such a view, but the methods embraced in behaviorism to modify behavior—in this case school discipline—are rejected by many educators as being inconsistent with the fundamental dignity of human beings.

Finally, what can be described as a conservative view of school discipline is expressed and, it should be said, finds substantial support in educational policy. Children in American society have a right to educational opportunity—political and educational policy is definite on this point—but students who have no interest in or intention to profit from educational opportunity and students whose conduct in school is flagrantly disruptive of good order and, in some cases, public safety have no place in the school. Public policy, the assertion continues, must be firm

Contemporary Issues

enough in its conviction to exclude such students, and educational policy must not be dominated by a naive and mindless sentimentalism promoting the right of the recalcitrant person to remain in school. Educators, spokesman for this view declare, have known for centuries, but are sometimes tempted to forget, that the person who refuses to learn cannot be taught.

NOTES

1. HENRY J. PERKINSON, *Since Socrates: Studies in the History of Western Educational Thought* (New York: Longman, Inc., 1980), p. 15.
2. See MICHAEL B. KATZ, *Class, Bureaucracy, and Schools: Illusion of Educational Change in America* (New York: Holt, Rinehart and Winston, 1971), pp. 108–109; and Samuel Bowles and Herbert Gintis, *Schooling in Capitalist America: Educational Reform and the Contradictions of Economic Life* (New York: Basic Books, 1976), pp. 266–267.
3. JACQUES MARITAIN, "Thomist Views on Education," in the Fifty-fourth Yearbook of the National Society for the Study of Education, *Modern Philosophies and Education* (Chicago: University of Chicago Press, 1955), p. 74.
4. For an insightful account of academic freedom in American educational history, see Richard Hofstadter and Walter P. Metzger, *The Development of Academic Freedom in the United States* (New York: Columbia University Press, 1955).
5. Pierce v. Society of Sisters, 268 U.S. 510.
6. Meyer v. Nebraska, 262 U.S. 390.
7. Plessy v. Ferguson, 163 U.S. 537.
8. Brown v. Board of Education, 347 U.S. 483.
9. Pierce v. Society of Sisters, 268 U.S. 510.
10. Everson v. Board of Education, 330 U.S. 1.
11. Ibid.
12. Cochran v. Board of Education, 281 U.S. 370.
13. Zorach v. Clauson, 343 U.S. 306.
14. McCollum v. Board of Education, 333 U.S. 203.
15. School District of Abington Township v. Schempp, 347 U.S. 203; and Engel v. Vitale, 370 U.S. 421.
16. Brown v. Board of Education, 347 U.S. 483.
17. Serrano v. Priest, 96 California Reporter 601–626 (1971). In San Antonio Independent School District v. Rodriguez, 411 U.S. 1, 58 (1973), although the Texas court had endorsed the idea that local support was an obstacle to equality of opportunity, the United States Supreme Court refused to affirm the decisions of the California and Texas courts.
18. SAMUEL BOWLES, "Unequal Education and the Reproduction of the Social Division of Labor," *Review of Radical Political Economics,* 3 (Fall 1971), 266, concludes that power to equalize education is largely outside the state's authority. Inequality, he declares, has its origin in "associated differences in class culture."

19. CHRISTOPHER JENCKS and DAVID RIESMAN, *The Academic Revolution* (New York: Doubleday & Co., Inc., 1968), p. 150.

20. CHRISTOPHER JENCKS et al., *Inequality: A Reassessment of the Effect of Family and Schooling in America* (New York: Basic Books, Inc., Publishers, 1972), p. 227.

21. For critiques of *Inequality* and Jencks' rejoinder, see the symposiums in the *Harvard Educational Review* (Fall 1973), *Sociology of Education* (Winter 1973), and *The American Educational Research Journal* (Spring 1974).

22. *Harvard Educational Review,* 39 (Winter 1969), 1–123. The genetic explanation of intelligence and, thus, social and educational inequality was employed by Richard Herrnstein, "I.Q.," *Atlantic Monthly* (September 1971), pp. 43–64; and by Hans Eysenck, *Race, Intelligence and Education* (London: Temple Smith, 1971).

23. EDWARD ZIGLER and JEANETTE VALENTINE, *Project Head Start: A Legacy of the War on Poverty* (New York: The Free Press, 1980), pp. 15–23.

24. JAMES COLEMAN et al., *Equality of Educational Opportunity* (Washington, D. C.: Government Printing Office, 1966). This study, initiated by Section 402 of the Civil Rights Act of 1964, ordered the Commissioner of Education to "conduct a survey and make a report to the President and the Congress, within two years of the enactment of this title, concerning the lack of availability of equality of educational opportunity for individuals by reasons of race, and color, religion, or national origin in public educational institutions on all levels in the United States."

25. It is interesting, and probably important, to note that Christopher Jencks began the study of *Inequality* using the title "The Limits of Schooling" (Jencks et al., *Inequality,* p. vi.).

26. GEORGE S. COUNTS, *Dare the School Build a New Social Order?* (Carbondale, Ill: Southern Illinois University Press, 1978). Over a long and illustrious academic career, Counts apparently never altered his view that they should. See William E. Sheerin, "Educational Scholarship and the Legacy of George S. Counts," *Educational Theory,* 26 (Winter 1976), 107–112.

27. THEODORE L. GROSS, "How to Kill a College: The Private Papers of a Campus Dean," *Saturday Review* (February 4, 1978), pp. 13–20.

28. This interpretation was expressed most prominently by the plantiff in DeFunis v. Odegaard, 414 U.S. 1038.

29. ROBERT D. HESLEP, "Preferential Treatment and Compensatory Justice," *Educational Theory,* 26 (Spring 1976), 148–149.

30. Ibid., p. 150; and Donald M. Levine and Mary Jo Bane, eds., *The Inequality Controversy,* (New York: Basic Books, Inc., 1975), pp. 66–71.

31. Regents of the University of California v. Bakke, 438 U.S. 265.

32. ANGELO PATRI, *The Problems of Childhood* (New York: D. Appleton and Company, 1922), p. 10.

33. ALFRED NORTH WHITEHEAD, *Aims of Education* (New York: Macmillan, Inc., 1929), p. 12.

34. One should not neglect noticing the strong opposition to compensatory, or remedial, education. See Robert J. Panos, "Picking Winners or Developing Potential," *School Review,* 81 (May 1973), 440–442; and George S. Rothbart, "The Legitimation of Inequality: Objective Scholarship vs. Black Militance," *Sociology of Education,* 43 (Spring 1970), 159–174.

35. Represented best in Michael B. Katz, *Class, Bureaucracy, and Schools* (New York: Holt, Rinehart & Winston 1971); and David B. Tyack, *The One Best System: A*

History of American Urban Education (Cambridge, Mass.: Harvard University Press, 1974).

36.   BOWLES and GINTIS, *Schooling in Capitalist America* p. 266; and Samuel Bowles and Herbert Gintis, "I.Q. in the U.S. Class Structure," *Social Policy,* 3 (November-December 1972, January/February, 1973), 78.

37.   Everett Reimer, *School Is Dead* (Garden City, N. Y.: Doubleday & Co., Inc., 1971), p. 96.

38.   IVAN ILLICH, *Deschooling Society* (New York: Harper & Row, Publishers, Inc., 1971), p. 157.

39.   GEORGE F. MADAUS, PETER W. AIRASIAN, and THOMAS KELLAGHAN, *School Effectiveness: A Reassessment of the Evidence* (New York: McGraw-Hill Book Company, 1980), p. 166.

40.   CARL ROGERS, *Freedom to Learn* (Columbus, Ohio: Charles E. Merrill Publishing Company, 1969); and Abraham Maslow, *Motivation and Personality* (New York: Harper & Row, Publishers, Inc., 1970).

41.   WILLIAM GLASSER, *Schools Without Failure* (New York: Harper & Row, Publishers, Inc., 1969); and *The Identity Society* (Harper & Row, Publishers, Inc., 1972).

42.   LAWRENCE KOHLBERG, "The Child as a Moral Philosopher," *Psychology Today,* 2 (September 1968), 25–30. Kohlberg's theory is challenged by Betty A. Sichel, "Can Kohlberg Respond to Critics?" *Educational Theory,* 26 (Fall 1976), 337–347. Kohlberg's stages of moral reasoning are described well in Jack Braeden Arbuthnot and David Faust, *Teaching Moral Reasoning: Theory and Practice* (New York: Harper and Row, 1981), pp. 49–67.

READINGS

BOWLES, SAMUEL and HERBERT GINTIS, *Schooling in Capitalist America: Educational Reform and the Contradictions of Economic Life.* New York: Basic Books, Inc., Publishers, 1976. The authors carry the conflict theory into acute ideological controversies in education.

CATALDO, EVERETT F., MICHAEL W. GILES, and DOUGLAS S. GATLIN, *School Desegregation Policy: Compliance, Avoidance, and the Metropolitan Remedy.* Lexington, Mass.: D. C. Heath & Co., 1978. Chapter 5 deals with such volatile issues as busing and school quality.

COLEMAN, JAMES S., and others, *Equality of Educational Opportunity.* Washington, D. C.: Government Printing Office, 1966. The general conclusion of this famous study appears to be that the character of schools for minority children may not be the critical factor in their academic success or failure.

DITTMER, A., "Assault with a Deadly Mandate: The Minimal Competency Movement," *Media and Methods,* 15 (Summer 1979), 26–29. The flaws in this movement are stressed.

DODSON, FITZHUGH, *How to Discipline with Love.* New York: Rawson Associates, 1977. Interesting views on school discipline are presented.

ELVIN, LIONEL, *The Place of Commonsense in Educational Thought.* London: George Allen & Unwin, 1977. Although the context is British, the author considers the question of religion in public education in Chapter 4. The approach is analytical.

FLEMING, JOHN E., GERALD R. GILL, and DAVID H. SWINTON, *The Case for Affirmative Action for Blacks in Higher Education.* Washington, D. C.: Howard University Press, 1978. This is a report of several studies of affirmative action as it is now caught, according to the authors, in a shift of public opinion from liberalism to neoconservatism.

GOODMAN, PAUL, *Compulsory Mis-education.* New York: Horizon Press, 1964. An eloquent criticism of compulsory education. Worth reading even for the person who has no sympathy for educational alternatives or deschooling.

GRANT, CARL A., ed., *Multicultural Education: Commitments, Issues, and Applications.* Washington, D. C.: Association for Supervision and Curriculum Development. Although all the chapters are good, Chapter 12 deals with the philosophy supporting multicultural education.

HEDMAN, CARL G., "The 'Deschooling' Controversy Revisited: A Defense of Illich's 'Participatory Socialism,'" *Educational Theory,* 29 (Spring 1979), 109–116. This is a sympathetic treatment of what has come to be known as the alternative school movement.

HESLEP, ROBERT D., "Preferential Treatment and Compensatory Justice," *Educational Theory,* 26 (Spring 1976), 147–153. The author concludes that the argument advanced to support compensatory justice does not support contemporary educational policies.

LEVINE, DONALD M., and MARY JO BANE, eds., *The Inequality Controversy: Schooling and Distributive Justice.* New York: Basic Books, Inc., Publishers, 1975. This book contains sections that should be read for the other side of the issue as it is presented by Robert Heslep.

STRIKE, KENNETH A., "The Role of Theories of Justice in Evaluation: Why a House is Not a Home," *Educational Theory,* 29 (Winter 1979), 1–10. The author maintains that while evaluation of educational and other social welfare programs is not in itself a philosophical issue, philosophy nevertheless can contribute to sharpening the sensitivity and intuitions of evaluators to principles of justice.

TIMPANE, MICHAEL, ed., *The Federal Interest in Financing Schooling.* Cambridge, Mass.: Ballinger Publishing Co., 1978. The federal role in financing elementary and secondary education is acknowledged to be a matter of dispute. The several chapters of this book undertake to establish a broad framework of federal educational policy.

TROOST, CORNELIUS J., ed., *Radical School Reform: Critique and Alternatives.* Boston: Little, Brown & Company, 1973. The book has four parts: critique of the new education, the learner and the curriculum, the teaching of values, and alternatives to extremism. This is an immensely interesting and worthwhile anthology.

WEINBERG, LOIS TUCKERMAN, "An Answer to the 'Liberal' Objection to Special Admissions," *Educational Theory,* 29 (Winter 1979), 21–30. On three controversial points relative to special admissions, the author finds such procedures reasonable and justifiable.

ZIGLER, EDWARD and JEANETTE VALENTINE, *Project Head Start: A Legacy of the War on Poverty.* New York: The Free Press, 1980. Although the authors readily admit the hyperbolic claims made for Head Start, they admit, too, the positive outcomes of the program.

II
EDUCATION
IN
CONTEMPORARY
SOCIETY

Every society has a huge stake in education. Whether in or out of school, education is a principal means for preserving and improving the social structure that makes civilized life possible. Idealizations of education are common enough, and on occasion we meet people who articulate them with a missionary zeal, but it is unnecessary to idealize education in order to recognize its imperative character.

When we pause to consider the stature of education in contemporary American society, we find that, although its worth is stated with varying degrees of fervor, only the most myopic critic contests its fundamental worth. The necessity of education in contemporary American society comes close to being a self-evident proposition. Agreement on this level is easy. It becomes more and more difficult, however, when we move on to consider education's nature and purpose and when we are asked to describe the kind of education we are prepared to endorse.

Stating the nature, the purpose, and the means for education and then shaping these statements into policies to implement them is the principal business of educational philosophy. In the preceding chapters we have seen what various philosophical systems assert about education. What they have to say is consequential, although it would be pure exaggeration to maintain that philosophical literacy is ubiquitous and that in the final analysis it penetrates every attitude with respect to the broad mission of education in American society. We say, in other words, that while philosophy is important, probably essential, to the functioning of the educational enterprise, philosophy is not always capable of a kind of eloquence enlisting the body politic to the logic of its propositions. If the voice of the philosopher is not persuasive enough to give direction to American education, whose voice is heeded?

In a nation taking seriously the doctrine of popular sovereignty, the voice is the collective voice of the citizens. And here, while philosophical foundation and conviction may have a place, broad social hypotheses are, in the end, more effective for introducing attitudes with respect to what education should be. The people of the country are the ones who define education. So far we are on safe ground. But going on, we find fluctuations in educational mood: The people themselves are not always sure of the proper educational prescription. They do not express common educational convictions, and the reason they do not must be found, if it is to be found at all, in discrete social and educational hypotheses.[1]

If there were just one hypothesis we would have a right to expect it to dominate educational policy and, with some luck, to immunize educational practice from the infection of discord so as to form a common consensus as to the direction all education, in and out of school, should take. In such a happy circumstance, practical decision would be easy to forge, and schooling following upon it would be easy to organize. But instead of one broad hypothesis, there are two. And these hypotheses—we characterize them as conservative and liberal—contend for supremacy in American education. They are lodged in both principle and policy, but they extend to that borderland beyond principle and policy where educational philosophy seldom penetrates and depend for their sustenance on what can be called a diverse educational spirit of the age.

The words *liberal* and *conservative* are subject to all kinds of interpretation, and we know how ineffective they are in educational philosophy for defining substantial difference. Even in politics, where these terms are regularly used, their meaning is frequently obscure. They are handy labels, but unless they are used with precision they are not useful to us in educational discourse.

Let us see if we can be more precise in identifying the differences between what we have called conservative and liberal hypotheses about American education. When we do our attention is riveted on educational aim first, for here the difference in approach is most evident.

CONSERVATIVE AND LIBERAL EDUCATIONAL AIMS

Without a formal commitment to any philosophical system, and sometimes without what could be called philosophical literacy, educational aims are represented from sharply divergent points of view. Without exhausting every possibility for different assignments of educational aim, we can nevertheless elaborate the most obvious aims that add up to either conservative or liberal educational hypotheses.

Transmission of Culture

Throughout the greater part of its Western history, and surely in the American experience, formal education has been regarded as the primary means for continuing the cultural legacy, for insulating men and women from ignorance, and for contributing to a civility making possible the effective functioning of society. In addition, particularly in American education, the realization is clear that democracy rests upon a fragile charter that in the last analysis must be expressed as the consent of the people to live according to its code. This code's authority is grounded in the cultural legacy. If such a foundation is precarious, it is nevertheless the one on which American democracy stands.

Recent history, in counterculture movements, in intemperate attacks on established policy, and in outright terrorism or only its threat, has demonstrated how fragile the democratic compact is. Although the school alone, depending mainly upon its instructional capabilities, cannot be expected to ensure respect for the democratic charter, the school has a positive role to play, and the conservative hypothesis emphasizes this role. The schools are agents for society, and their principal commission, twofold as it turns out, is to concentrate on sound instruction—that is, teaching what can be taught—and to generate a commitment in all students to the general welfare. The general welfare is interpreted to mean good citizenship and an embrace of those ideals that contribute directly to democracy.[2]

The liberal educational hypothesis exhibits little enthusiasm for the school's role in cultural transmission. Culture is not discounted, but because it is enormously elusive and constantly subject to reinterpretation and amendment, cultural transmission, if carried too far, will inevitably result in social control. The liberal hypothesis makes formal education a vehicle for communicating ways of living successfully, so the genius of education is found in the experience of democratic living, in the give and take of school life itself, in the inquiring and questioning preceding the adoption of workable values, and not in rescuing ideas and ideals from the past. Liberalism neither discounts civility nor repudiates democratic ideals, but it puts much less confidence in positive teaching to secure these entirely worthwhile objectives than does conservativism. If there is a way to capsulize all this, even recognizing the hazard in trying, the conservative approach capitalizes on instruction and imitation to the end that the cultural legacy will be perpetuated; the liberal approach capitalizes on the real or imagined ability contemporary education has for introducing reform to society and for reconstructing the social order.[3]

The Place of Knowledge

Conservative educators spend no time worrying about the possibility of obtaining and then communicating dependable knowledge.[4] Although dependability may be certified in a number of ways by various theories of knowledge, cultivators of this hypothesis seldom ask the help of theory. Common sense tells them that knowledge is possible and, with proper safeguards, is dependable. Common sense, they say, is good enough.

The educator's responsibility, because presumably educators know most about the educational process, is to select from this body of dependable knowledge those parts most likely to result in the proper formation of students in school. Everything cannot be taught, everything cannot be organized into the curriculum of even the best school, so selection must be employed to sort out the knowledge that the test of time demonstrates to be of most worth.[5]

Liberalism is unconvinced that common sense is good enough to ensure and certify the validity of knowledge. In this educational camp, the general attitude prevails that truth is at best relative. Although there is some knowledge and some skill that every decently educated group of citizens must have, neither knowledge nor skill must be invested with universal worth or dependability. What is truth? If the answer to this question is indecisive, as it is among liberals, the educational solution is to provide experience in dependable methods for having worthwhile experience. So schooling, rather than being a process where students acquire an abundance of information, is one where they learn how to have experiences conducive to living a satisfying and productive life.[6]

The Nature of Reality

Conservative views on reality belong to the long tradition of realism. We may be spectators vis-á-vis the universe, but as spectators we are able to have experience with physical and social reality, and this reality is neither phantom nor ephemeral. The world is a world of order and regularity whose secrets, while grudgingly revealed, are nevertheless possible to unravel. We can know the world as it is.

Liberals are far less confident about order and regularity in the social and physical world. For the most part they take evolution seriously and find reality in a process that has not been terminated but is in a state of flux and manufacture. What we know today may last until tomorrow and beyond, but we cannot count on it. So where the conservative is prepared to meet the order in the universe face to face and do his best to adjust to it, the liberal tries to prepare himself to live in a world of perpetual change.

The Fundamentals of Human Life

Conservative attitudes toward education are based on the conviction that human nature is a duality of body and mind. Even in a rejection of supernaturalism, the conservative approach regards human beings as having a spiritual mental capacity unaccounted for solely in the explanations given by the sciences of biology and physiology. Human beings are unique because they have a spiritual power of rationality, and the extent of their rationality—their disability or ability—is for the most part genetically determined. This view of human nature declares the educational practices consistent with behaviorism either unattractive or unacceptable.

Liberals acknowledge that human beings are unique but this uniqueness is found not in any dualistic interpretation of human nature but in the fact that human beings have become, over the course of centuries, complex, complicated organisms capable of reflective thinking. They are what they are not because of some mysterious spiritual power but because an evolutionary process has conferred a distinctive nature on them.

The Spirit of Idealism

The human spirit, conservatives say, is captivated by ideals, and these ideals, fortified by the wisdom of the ages, are the dominant themes of life. They inspire us to great and good things; they invest us with a spirit of humanity and altruism and in the last analysis contain the fundamentals making life worth living. The genius of human spirit is not generated in education, and surely not in any school, but the school, sharing in this spirit of humanity, is an important agent for promoting it.

Liberals are pragmatic. Rather than investing confidence in anything so elusive as the spirit of humanity, they prefer to interpret human goals as translations of self-interest into a commitment to the common good. The common good is neither defined in advance nor filtered through tradition, which, from the liberal point of view, tends to be regressive rather than progressive, but is elaborated in the actual experience of life.

Ethical Choice and Responsibility

The conservative view of morals, or ethics, is straightforward and clear: Values to all of life are distilled by rational processes and, in the end, come to have a prescriptive character. In other words, the differences between right and wrong, between ethical and unethical behavior, between responsibility and irresponsibility are capable of clear definition and description. Once these differences have been defined and described, it is up to human beings to abide by them. They have the means—freedom—to choose to do what they ought or to do something else. They are responsible for their conduct. In consequence, society and its various instrumentalities and agencies can hold them responsible and accountable for their behavior and, if need be, punish them for infractions of the social and moral code. We may not be the captains of our fate, but we are responsible for what we do or refuse to do.

Sometimes bordering on a social sentimentality tempted to absolve men and women from responsibility for their actions but going too far beyond it to be characterized as only inflated sentiment, liberal approaches to education are based largely on ethical determinism. We play some part in directing our behavior, but only a part. Forces outside of us figure large too. One can never be entirely sure where responsibility for a specific human act lies. Under the circumstances it is not only hazardous but probably wrong to penalize persons for behavior for which they are only partly responsible or not responsible at all. If liberals are uncomfortable with the proposition that we are captives of our environment, they are equally uncomfortable with the thesis that we are masters of our fate.

Translating these attitudes toward human responsibility to the level of school instruction, we find conservatives calling for an educational program placing a high premium on discipline, on the development of habits of personal and social behavior predisposing us to do what we ought to do, and the corollary therefrom: If we refuse to do what we ought to do, we should be penalized. Liberalism, while not an enemy of discipline, is unimpressed by the effectiveness of externally imposed discipline. It calls for the development of self-discipline without the threat of punishment or the artificiality of reward.[7]

AIMS AND THEIR PRIORITY

The trouble with American education, conservative critics allege, is that with too many aims an assignment of priority is difficult or impossible. Which aims are more and which are less important? Which should have priority in the schools? We have observed conflicting positions, and it is easy to imagine that with a broad array of aims dealing with the fundamentals of education a good deal of confusion is inevitable.

Schools, conservatives say, are asked to do too much. They are asked to instruct students, but the commission does not end with this. They are asked to contribute to vocational efficiency, so they become centers for technical training. They are asked to shape and reshape social convictions and attitudes. They are asked to promote political values. They are asked to become health centers, and they are asked to promote adult education. All too frequently, so the argument goes, they are asked to do all of these things at once. With such a broad commission how can they be expected to do anything well?

The positive values of schooling, liberals assert, are to be found precisely in the flexibility of schools to do what society needs. It may be true, they continue, that schools function best in the absence of preordained aims. Schools follow the main currents of society and keep abreast of broad need, not just the instructional need of the societies they serve.

With all these aims, some subject to conflict, how are educators to make choices, and what should guide them? When they choose, can they be confident of the support of their clientele? It is axiomatic that when society is clear in the commission it gives to schools, the educators' role is easily fulfilled, but when society's goals are unclear or uncertain, scholastic aims are hard to sort out.

Finally, the conservative critic declares, educational aims for twentieth-century American schools are vague. One cannot be entirely certain about what is expected of schools, and students who go to school are given conflicting signs about what to expect from the time and effort they invest there. Progressive spokesmen are not at all sure that vagueness is a deficiency. Prescriptive aims for schooling, and aims stated with an inflexible priority, may in the end conspire to make impossible the realization of legitimate personal learning objectives.

Educational aim, as we have seen, is influenced by different hypotheses with respect to human capacity and the nature of the world. And these hypotheses can be translated to the level of educational policy and practice. When they are, they end up in an assignment of scholastic priority ranging from liberal to technical and occupational to consumer-oriented education.

Liberal Education

Liberal education, to which the conservative educational hypothesis pays particular attention, is concerned primarily with the development of distinctive human abilities. Its concentration is not on the preparation of men and women for the economic world, although nothing in liberal learning cancels out vocational and professional education. It concentrates instead on preparing men and women for the role they are to play in society by aiming at their ability to think and express themselves. Ultimately, it essays to use educational means to make life genuinely human.[8]

In aiming at the development of the human abilities of thought and expression, liberal education depends heavily, sometimes exclusively, upon literary means. More than in any other definition of education's purpose, liberal education makes reading, writing, and thinking the principal stanchions of an instructional program.

Studies capable of contributing to reading with understanding, writing and speaking clearly and persuasively, and thinking logically and cogently are organized into a core curriculum. This is an instructional program—a set of required courses—for everyone. This is the kind of educational formation every person in society is entitled to, because every person possesses the distinctive human abilities of thought and expression.

This commitment to liberal education is made for all levels of education, beginning in the elementary school and continuing through the college, but liberal education, for all the charges of lack of relevance leveled at it by its critics, need not stop with the subjects in the core curriculum. Standing on a foundation of liberal knowledge, boys and girls, men and women with literary and intellectual accomplishments can move on to other fields of study that are recommended by their ability or their interest. They can go into the professions, or they can turn to hundreds of vocations and, with the liberalizing influence of their education, seek success and satisfaction. When they work at earning a living and when they try to be influential in shaping social and political policy, they have in their possession the intellectual and educational qualifications giving them full membership in a genuinely human society.

Liberal education is accused of being exclusively intellectual in outlook, and with such an emphasis, its critics charge, it neglects other imperative human needs. There is more to life, they say, than cultural ornamentation. Defenders of liberal learning admit that the commission they give to education is to life in general and not to any one of its particular needs. Still, they promise, liberal learning contains a huge bonus: It is capable of cultivating ethical character. The pedagogy associated with liberal learning and character is not entirely clear, for liberal educators do not distinguish themselves as methodologists, yet they are content to embrace a long tradition where character formation and liberal education go hand in hand.

Technical or Occupational Education

The popular rejoinder coming from educators whose base is in the technical or occupational camp to affirmations idealizing liberal education is that liberal learning is almost totally a waste of time. In the first place, it puts too heavy a dependence on the traditional culture, which, while it may have had meaning at one time, is now either largely archaic or is superseded by the introduction of cultural pluralism. In any case, contemporary American society has too little need for the kinds of literary skills promoted in liberal education. In an age when oral expression is paramount, reading does not qualify for a high place in scholastic purpose; writing is probably unnecessary, or at least unimportant, in a society where all one has to do is pick up a telephone. Thinking is undoubtedly important, but again the point is made: Is thinking best stimulated by reading the ancient authors or is it better cultivated by dealing with the burning issues of the day?

Moreover, its critics continue, liberal education represents an aristocratic tradition. It caters to and promotes elitism by concentrating on educational goals having little or no relevance to persons who must make their living by the sweat of their brow. Everyone needs salable skill, technical knowledge, and an occupational disposition enabling them to work intelligently and productively in economic society. To this end education should make ample provision for supervised work experience as well as instruction in the skill and knowledge fitting persons for various occupations.

It is unlikely, in any case, that a core curriculum can be defended, for human need is too diverse to be accounted for with any degree of adequacy in a litany of required courses. Preparation for life, on one hand, and life adjustment, on the other, are not likely to be achieved by separating life from learning as is done— or so the indictment reads—by adopting a platform of liberal education.

In the absence of any general need that can be authenticated by the experience of life itself, educational policy must reject liberal education to concentrate on the needs people have, and are able to demonstrate, in contemporary society. These needs are principally economic and social, and they are without peer in any definition of educational priority.

The extent to which schooling can contribute to economic mobility and social status is debated.[9] Although we find the assumption current that schooling contributes to economic and social mobility and betterment, studies conducted by social scientists sometimes give us pause. Their findings would seem to sustain a conclusion that both economic and social status are altered relatively little by schooling, and that both are more dependent on factors over which education has no direct control and can do little to change. Yet even admitting that neither economic nor social status can be altered by schooling, instruction aimed at the development of social and economic skill can be justified, for social and economic needs are both obvious and imperative in contemporary society. So whether this concentration of attention on such needs can ameliorate social and economic disadvantage is beside the point to anyone embracing this definition of educational priority.

Consumer-Oriented Education

Literacy and culture may have their place in a broad array of educational purpose. Preparing for economic and social life with an abundance of skill essential to it is also important. But, in the final analysis, every person in American society is a consumer of goods and services, and the education bound to have the most significance is an education preparing members of this society to make consumer decisions with intelligence and prudence. So priority in schooling should be given to instruction in how to purchase and use goods and services intelligently, understanding both the values received by consumers and the economic consequences of their acts.

How much the school's curriculum would have to change if this aim were given priority is hard to say, but the emphasis to all instruction, nevertheless, should be fixed on the education of consumers. Along this line, as part of the same definition of priority, attention should be given to the use of leisure time prudently so as to balance those activities yielding personal satisfaction with those that are socially useful. In addition, instruction should attend to the rights and duties of citizens in a democratic society. They should be taught to be diligent and competent in the performance of their obligations as members of the community and citizens of the state and nation. Finally, the same definition of priority authorizes instructional attention on the significance of the family in society and the conditions conducive to successful family life.

On a most basic level, education should undertake to conform to those instructional aims giving priority to preparation for life and for life adjustment, but both should always be interpreted in the light of men and women as consumers.

In an educational age where different educational aims compete for priority, it is the difficult commission of educational policy, enlightened by principles husbanded by educational philosophy, to design and follow a prudent educational course through this thicket of educational purpose.

APPRAISALS OF EDUCATIONAL STANDARD

How should we read the record of contemporary educational achievement? Are American schools, overwhelmed by an abundance of scholastic aims, unable to do anything well? Has preoccupation with captivating student interest and motivation by introducing almost endless variety to instructional programs led to a deterioration in conventional academic achievement?

Reading the record one way, we find testimony to the pitiful condition of reading and writing skill among students in elementary and secondary schools. With so many tempting distractions, such as television, students are indisposed to read and, with an absence of standards demanding definite levels of achievement in reading skill, they slide through school missing the very accomplishment most essential to their success in society. This deficiency becomes an almost insurmountable obstacle to subsequent learning.

Students, some critics allege, enter college without mastery of reading skill. If they are to succeed in college, remedial reading courses—which would seem to belong in the elementary school—must be offered. Writing and speaking, to move on from reading, are arts of expression whose development, we are told, comes only from practice. Where in the schools, these critics continue, is ample attention given to the cultivation of clarity and fluency in oral and written expression?

These deficiencies in the basics, in the tools of learning, are alleged to bring American educational standards to the verge of disaster. Fault is found with the tendency of contemporary education to neglect the basics while investing time and attention in such things as personality formation, creativity, social training, and an abundance of other nonacademic aims that are bound to undermine decent standards of achievement.[10]

There is another side to the coin, however, and we should look at it before we come to any conclusion about the status of standard in contemporary schooling. In the first place, the more optimistic appraisers of American education allege, these indictments of contemporary educational standard are based on false evidence. Most of what we know about educational achievement comes from the results of tests. But tests for measuring achievement are too filled with cultural and educational bias to be dependable.[11]

Adopting this thesis, regardless of whatever statistical validity can be claimed for standardized achievement tests, they lack social and cultural validity. Despite their results, which sometimes make the accomplishments of American students look bad, it is unfair to claim on the basis of such tests that standards are going down. If educational testers were more solicitous about the design and use of their tests, if they tested for what really counts, they would discover that standards whose relevance can be authenticated on a scale of social reality are improving.[12]

There is another side: Apart from any comment on the measurement movement, the assertion is made that standards are shaped from outdated and over-worn educational values and are perpetuated in the schools by myopic educators and an inapt public. Rather than pandering to a backward public opinion on educational standard, educators should mount a campaign against arbitrary, impersonal, and irrelevant standards. Such standards, if enforced, separate the genius of life from the joy and benefit of learning. They are impediments to cultural progress in an open society rather than guarantees of educational decency. For the most part, say the most outspoken critics of the restoration of standard thesis, arbitrary, impersonal, and irrelevant standards are illustrative of a vacant and decadent intellectualism. They are unrepresentative of life and should be jettisoned in the interest of superior instruction.[13]

This rejoinder does not convince persons who worry about the deteriorating quality of American education, so they respond: We need not make a decision with respect to a hierarchy of educational priorities—in other words, we need not say whether schools should endorse liberal, occupational, or consumer educational aims—in order to defend basic educational standards. The needs of life in society supply the necessary evidence. Without decent literary skill, liberal learning becomes impossible, occupational success a hopeless quest, and intelligent, prudent consumerism an empty promise.

All this pessimism about the character and quality of American education, it is said by way of demurral, finds its source in an idealization of elitist cultural values. Thousands of children come to school from homes and social backgrounds where traditional standards of education are neither practiced nor endorsed. Standards supplanting traditional ones, although too frequently judged inferior, are in reality only different. If American education is to ensure justice for all classes of citizens, to poor, socially and economically disadvantaged, and minority children alike, it must redefine standard along lines of appropriateness and flexibility. Standards set, if any are needed, must be capable of cultural and social accommodation. Appropriate education for the middle-class child from a suburban home may be the worst kind of education for the child from a family in the inner-city ghetto.

This theme of educational and cultural accommodation is familiar to contemporary educational discourse, and it has an intrinsic appeal to a socially sensitive society that, despite all the charges leveled against it, is nevertheless basically decent and just. Concealed by argument and counterargument this point may go unnoticed: Poor and minority parents are very likely more interested in having their children receive good schooling—as good schooling is conventionally defined—than they are in having their deprived social and cultural backgrounds catered to. Parental economic and social aspiration for children must be taken into account. When it is, we may find that they reject poor schooling, mixtures of scholastic motive, and the lack of educational standard for their children. They may see good education as a principal means for rescuing their children from the contagion of cultural and economic isolation. If so, practical educational reality should replace academic sentimentalism in appraising both the objectives and standards of achievement schools should be expected to adopt and enforce.

Finally, innovation comes to our attention. It may be the most overused word in the educator's vocabulary. On the contemporary scene it comes close to being the badge of educational respectability. Being receptive to change, in attitude, in aim, in pedagogic technique, should be praised. Only the most insensitive teachers embrace educational paralysis. But innovation (the word *change* may be good enough) must be justified by its educational consequences, and even then it should be superintended with a prudence only sound experience supplies. The question is good and educators swept along by a tide of innovation should prepare an answer: Why does innovative practice so often appear to drift toward a discounting of decent, conventional educational standard?

FREEDOM AND AUTHORITY

Agreement should be easy on this assertion: The ultimate purpose of education is to enable persons to achieve intellectual and moral autonomy. Along the way, however, on this long and often precarious route to autonomy, boys and girls, men and women searching for freedom must submit to genuine authority if the object of their quest is to be realized. An apparent paradox makes us uncomfortable: To gain freedom we must begin by surrendering it. Is this what is required?

The history of childhood contains hundreds of curious demonstrations, but among them one stands out particularly. Parents love their children and sometimes worry about loving them too much. So each generation somehow tries to make things easier and better for the one following. This affection for children and a determination to make their lives better takes its toll on discipline. The reins of control are loosened a bit, old ways of acting are jettisoned, and old formulas of discipline are discarded. This is sometimes cause for worry and anxiety: Are children being given too much freedom? With all this freedom can they be expected to become fully responsible members of society? Can they be depended on?

Anxiety over the care and upbringing of children sometimes led our ancestors to design novel ways to provide for their education and training. Concerned that a lack of parental discipline, bred of too much affection, would contaminate the morals of youth, they frequently resorted to the practice of apprenticing their children to the custody of friends or relatives who would be capable of enforcing strict control and administering a sterner discipline. But sometimes, in the absence of a family to whom they might farm out their children, parents called upon the schools to exert the moral authority they themselves were somewhat reluctant to impose. So the principle of *in loco parentis,* where teachers take the place of parents and guide the formation of children with all the authority of their parents, was destined to have a long, and sometimes hectic, record in the history of education.

Parents continue to worry about the formation of their children, and they never cease to wonder if their affection for them does not block an exertion of the kind of authority necessary for their proper development. Yet the old apprenticeship system is filed away on history's scrapheap, and the doctrine of *in loco parentis* turns out to be only an imprecise reminiscence in the history of education. The school has an obvious role to play in the moral and intellectual education of children, although definitions of this role, as we have seen, are subject to debate. Children need freedom to grow, they need a latitude enabling them to discover their interests and talents; but they need genuine guidance to help them map out the proper routes to satisfy these interests and talents. How much freedom should they have? And when does guidance become restrictive of formation and coercive of freedom?

Against this background of uncertainty, teachers and the public alike entertain anxiety that contemporary education, so entranced by the permissive spirit of the age, has surrendered its legitimate function of exercising genuine authority. In this surrender students are accorded a freedom bordering on license, which makes the realization of personal autonomy—the ultimate goal of education—almost impossible. If students reject scholastic discipline and authority, and if educational theory endorses this rejection, the result is likely to be educational confusion. As a result, the authority of teachers to instruct their students in necessary knowledge is eroded, chaos results, educational standard goes forfeit, and the genuine formative function of education atrophies.

Some critics of contemporary education paint this dark a picture; others, however, are more sanguine about the prospect of melding authority and freedom. They regard the imposition of discipline, so common to the old-fashioned school, as being repressive of motivation and interest; they declare the dominance of the curriculum, reflected so often in an array of required courses, a kind of academic imperialism subversive of true intellectual and moral growth; and they find it difficult to subscribe to any theory of classroom management where, if the doctrine of *in loco parentis* is reinstated, the teachers become drill sergeants. Still, they are optimistic about the authority of common purpose percolating to a level where it can introduce direction and coherence to the educational enterprise. The generation of the authority of common purpose must come, if it is to come at all, from the freedom of students to be themselves and to seek for their full development as distinctive persons. It must come from experience uninhibited by an authority imposed either by parents or an educational bureaucracy.

A more balanced appraisal of the contemporary educational scene in the United States does not lead us to suppose that it is either so bleak as its critics allege or so bright as the promoters of student right and freedom maintain. Schools exercise their authority over instruction, although it is sometimes blemished, and students enjoy a degree of freedom, even when it is expressed obtrusively, consistent with their objective of having worthwhile and personally meaningful, relevant instruction.

We should be able, though, to establish a basis in policy for balancing the claim of freedom with the necessity of authority. It is hard to believe that one could for long sustain any hypothesis underwriting either the abandonment of genuine authority or the repression of freedom.

The source of authority commissioning schools to maintain conditions conducive to learning may come, depending upon philosophical assumption, from divine injunction, rational imperative, or pragmatic consensus. In some interpretations genuine educational authority finds its basis in a blending of all three sources.

In any case, any one of these sources of authority, or all together, concedes the immaturity of students, their need for discipline, and the right they have to sound instruction. Entering school, where they will remain for a long time, they are unready to make decisions about the nature of their learning and how it should proceed. These important decisions must be made by persons equipped with the necessary experience and education. Authority here, in the hands of the educator, must always be infused with genuine affection and care for students who are to be the beneficiaries of an educational environment created for them.

Inexperience and lack of knowledge about the demands of life are poor recommendations, in any rational appraisal of educational authority and freedom, for an uninhibited freedom of students to make their own choices. Yet, as students ascend the educational ladder, as they gain more experience and have a clearer vision of their own motives and interests, as they find ways to assess their own ability, their voices become more authoritative. So it is philosophically impossible to certify the freedom of students at the beginning of the educational process to make all their own decisions about the direction and substance of their education. Yet it is philosophically unacceptable to withhold from students, as they come closer and closer to the end of formal education, the legitimate responsibility they have to themselves. Freedom is progressive, and as it proceeds in education authority recedes.

Without authority guiding students to gain a secure foothold on the first rungs of the educational ladder and without the freedom of students to assert their own educational prerogatives as they near the top of the educational ladder, the universally acknowledged objective for education being an excursion into moral and intellectual autonomy has an empty and meaningless sound.

Even in an idealization of a progressive approach to autonomy, where freedom is earned step by step, we know that all the tensions between authority and freedom, between the standards of society, the marketplace, the school itself, and the disposition of students to make their own decisions will not disappear. These tensions remain; likely they are perennial. Philosophically astute, sensitive, experienced educators should have the virtue of prudence equipping them to balance an exercise of responsible educational authority with the legitimate right of human freedom.[14]

EDUCATIONAL PHILOSOPHY AND THE
EDUCATION OF TEACHERS

Perusing the latest books on educational philosophy looking for reasons why teachers and prospective teachers should spend valuable time studying the subject, we find all too frequently this or similarly stated justifications: The principal outcome from such a scholastic experience enables teachers and students of education to build their own philosophy of education. The assumption is evident, and apparently sincere: Students in a course in educational philosophy are counted to be apprentice or novice educational philosophers, and by the time their craft is mastered they will have a systematic philosophy of their own. Sometimes explicit, although more often implicit, in these litanies of justification is the recommendation that such personal systems be built by picking and choosing various propositions from organized philosophies.

Eclecticism and Educational Philosophy

Apparently, philosophical images are more open and liberal, and therefore popular, if eclecticism is endorsed and if the myth that every philosophy has mixed elements of truth and error is allowed wide circulation. The philosophic trick, should students succeed in mastering it, is to find the elements of truth and incorporate them into their own system of beliefs about education.

How this advice differs from telling students to satisfy their philosophical taste is not entirely clear, but when such advice comes from serious, practicing scholars of educational philosophy it is bound to be disquieting and confusing. In the absence of definite formulas for finding and mining these deposits of widely scattered truths, the embrace of eclecticism is all the more puzzling. Such advice, in the end, conspires to undermine fundamental philosophical knowledge about education by calling a halt to genuine inquiry before it has a chance to begin.

Two sides to this eclectic fashion are prominent, and we should take their measure carefully. One side implies a lack of validity to knowledge unless it is personalized, unless somehow it is produced from the froth and foam of our own experience. All this has a convincing ring, especially when we are absorbed in a subject whose dimensions are essentially practical.

Still, haste should be made slowly here, for neither knowledge's validity nor its applicability depends on the kind of subjectivity expressed in the ancient sophistic creed: "Man is the measure of all things." While the futility of trying to apply knowledge one lacks is obvious, no universal cognitive principle requires the study of educational philosophy to be a solitary journey into scholastic faith or an existential experience wherein educational truth is disclosed in an academic trance. Why students should be encouraged to approach the study of educational philosophy in any other way than by employing the usual conventions of scholarity is a curious, but unexplained, academic affectation.

Philosophy's Personal Appeal

The other side has an ominous sound too, and if taken seriously, it makes us wonder whether a subject whose personal character is trumpeted merits academic standing and is worth studying at all. The ominous sound comes from the broadcast of various opinions about education, all assigned approximately equal value, coupled with the petition for students to seek out and adopt the ones with the greatest appeal.

If educational philosophy is only opinion about education, such an approach would have prudence to recommend it. But if personal appeal is the criterion to be satisfied by scholarship here, how different the scholastic credentials of educational philosophy must be from other subjects capable of verifying the data in their syllabi. If educational philosophy has something to teach, if it possesses knowledge worth having about education, students should not be abandoned from the start to find and assess the merit of this knowledge for themselves.

Somewhere along the line as we study educational philosophy, we shall have to make a decision about the worth and use of philosophical knowledge. If knowledge, as distinguished from opinion, about educational ends and means is possible, then it should be respected and studied as knowledge. If educational philosophy contains propositions whose truth can be demonstrated, one should be extremely diffident about accepting or rejecting them on the basis of opinion and then go on searching for more appealing substitutes.

In connection with educational philosophy, the point is the same as with any other subject purporting to be knowledge rather than opinion: Acceptance or rejection is made on evidence and demonstration rather than on whim or appeal, personal attraction or distaste.

Philosophies of education stand or fall, and should be accepted or rejected, on their facility for taking evidence from the nature of reality, knowledge, value, and persons and translating it into educational programs whose ends and means conform to canons of reason, logic, and empirical evidence. Nothing short of this should motivate students entering courses in educational philosophy. Their purpose is not to confirm preconceived opinions about education or to cement attractions to teaching and learning supplied from a student's educational experience, but to follow the dependable routes of educational philosophy and science and establish a code for education that will be intellectually certifiable and scholastically trustworthy.

Philosophy's Use

When students of educational philosophy have in their possession dependable knowledge about educational ends and means, when they have practice in analyzing various propositions produced by different philosophies of education, what are they to do with this knowledge and skill? Is there merit in the assertion that teachers need a philosophy of education in order to be effective? Must every classroom teacher be an educational philosopher with mastery over sets of intricate and complex arguments about educational ends and means?

Were we disposed to argue for an essential relationship between superior pedagogic technique and philosophical erudition, we would have to explain away an abundance of contemporary and historical illustration testifying otherwise. We would have to explain, for example, how in the schools of our forefathers, in the classrooms of America's common schools less than a century ago, teachers without much education or skill in the propositions of educational or, for that matter, any other kind of philosophy functioned with a rustic but commendable efficiency. As these early teachers practiced the art of teaching, intuition may have supplied what instruction withheld; nevertheless, the fact remains that such teachers were effective enough to instruct most of the nation's children without putting on display any systematic philosophical knowledge about education. Almost certainly they made basic assumptions about their work and, following them faithfully, taught lessons from a crude syllabus, but they spent almost no time pondering those issues that for centuries had been paraded across the pages of every educational discourse.

Philosophy of Education and Pedagogy

It is important to set the record of scholastic expectation straight: The objective of courses in educational philosophy is not to produce educational philosophers; it may not even be to give prospective teachers a chance to develop their own philosophies of education. It may be only to introduce prospective teachers, or anyone else connected with education, to those imperative, perennial questions about education that should be probed by anyone answering muster to the ranks of professional educators.

Here language must be used with precision. Can one be persuasive in maintaining that the person who essays only to give instruction in reading and writing or, on a more advanced level, to teach, say, the higher mathematics and nothing more, needs help from educational philosophy? Such persons may face their work as a simple craft, lacking both depth and design, with the sole purpose of communicating knowledge and skill. And such teaching, stripped of all artistry, can be carried on. The situation is altered though, by replacing the schoolmaster with an educator, by giving our attention to the qualifications of a professional person whose commitments to education are broader and more profound than those of hearers of lessons, to one who, engaging in the art of teaching, pays heed to the whole process of forming boys and girls.

Teachers who regard the business of education as mere work, a kind of high-class day labor, are probably benefited little by what educational philosophy has to teach. Yet teachers who elevate the education of human beings to a professional level and regard themselves as cooperative artists, complementing nature as it works toward appropriate ends, are not only favorably disposed toward educational philosophy but embrace it as an indispensable supplement to their art-istry.[15]

In any case, although there is a certain satisfaction in justifying the place of educational theory in connection with teachers' artistry, it is probably not neces-sary to do so. In an educational age filled with dispute about what a proper education is and about what schools should teach, knowledge about the philoso-phy of education, which is different from a commitment to a systematic philoso-phy of education, should seem to have an imperative character.[16]

Educational Philosophy's Professional Dimension

Teachers in the schools today suffer considerable disadvantage when they lack simple literacy in the philosophy of education, for there are hundreds of times in a professional career when they will be called on—in teachers' meetings, in PTA meetings, in curriculum and disciplinary committee meetings, and in boards of education meetings, to cite only a few—to deal with problems where an ability to handle educational questions in a philosophically judicious way will be im-mensely useful. Besides these important uses for educational philosophy in teach-ers' custody, we should remind ourselves that if teachers are ill-equipped to philosophize about education or are prone to dismiss it as lacking relevance for their work, they will have left forfeit to professional educational philosophers the ultimate definition of their professional responsibilities.

What they choose to neglect will be done for them by a cadre of educational philosophers in the country's colleges and universities. There are, perhaps, two thousand colleges and universities in the United States that offer courses in educational philosophy, and we are safe in assuming that among the two thou-sand or so professors teaching such courses fewer than ten percent will be in the vanguard of philosophical scholarship with voices eloquent enough to be heard the country over. Should votes on vital educational decisions—where theory meets practice face to face—be cast by so few?

In this historical genre, moreover, where the contest between educational change and preservation goes on without interruption, where debate rages over whether the purpose of education is to reform and reconstruct society or to preserve and transmit a tested intellectual and social legacy, where the choice so often is between innovation and convention, the need for teachers to range beyond the simple pedagogies of their classrooms appears obvious.

Reward of Philosophical Study

To say that every teacher must be a systematic educational philosopher is proba-bly hyperbole, but it is not asking too much to expect teachers to distill meaning from educational definition and to infuse their day-to-day professional functions with meaning and design. Nowhere more than in analyzing educational definition and purpose do teachers need facility for philosophizing about education. So the study of educational philosophy has two rewards: One is knowing about a variety of educational ends and means and how they are arrived at; the other is conversance with philosophical technique enabling teachers to distill meaning from educational discourse. Without such knowledge they are likely to belong always to a second rank of educators.

NOTES

1. R. FREEMAN BUTTS, "Public Education in a Pluralistic Society," *Educational Theory*, 27 (Winter 1977), 3–11, adverts to this point, although he is preoccupied with what he calls "a deep disenchantment" with public education, which has its origin in the people's belief "that the schools no longer belong to them."

2. ARTHUR E. BESTOR, *The Restoration of Learning* (New York: Alfred A. Knopf, Inc., 1955), expressed this view as well as anyone.

3. HOWARD OZMON and SAM CRAVER, *Philosophical Foundations of Education* (Columbus: Charles E. Merrill Publishing Company, 1981), pp. 105–108, call reconstructionism a philosophy of education and undertake to rehearse its historical background. Their point is debatable. Reconstruction appears to be more a hypothesis than a philosophy and probably had its American origin with the work of George S. Counts. The contemporary exponent of the hypothesis is THEODORE BRAMELD, *Patterns of Educational Philosophy: Divergence and Convergence in Culturological Perspective* (New York: Holt, Rinehart & Winston, 1971).

4. This appears to be PAUL HIRST'S thesis in *Knowledge and the Curriculum* (London: Routledge & Kegan Paul, 1974), p. 22.

5. Ibid., p. 85.

6. This position is illustrated well in JOHN DEWEY, *Human Nature and Conduct: An Introduction to Social Psychology* (New York: Holt, Rinehart & Winston 1922), p. 265. It is also called ethnomethodological epistemology. See DAVID GORBUTT, "The New Sociology of Education," *Education for Teaching*, 89 (Autumn 1972), 7.

7. Without subscribing to either liberal or conservative theses, CHARLES FETHE, "Curriculum Theory: A Proposal for Unity," *Educational Theory*, 27 (Spring 1977), 101–102, discusses the role of discipline in the curriculum.

8. Although not without its critics (for example, Hirst, *Knowledge and the Curriculum*, p. 35) *General Education in a Free Society*, Harvard Committee Report, may be taken as a contemporary manifesto on liberal education.

9. The following are but illustrative of the scope of this debate: PETER M. BLAU and OTIS D. DUNCAN, *The American Occupational Structure* (New York: John Wiley & Sons, Inc., 1967), pp. 429–430; CHRISTOPHER JENCKS et al., *Inequality: A Reassessment of the Effect of Family and Schooling in America* (New York: Basic Books, Inc., Publishers, 1972), p. 160 and p. 227; J. W. B. DOUGLAS, *The Home and the School* (London: MacGibbon and Kee, 1964); RANDALL COLLINS, "Functional and Conflict Theories of Educational Stratification," *American Sociological Review*, 36 (December 1971), 1010; SAMUEL BOWLES and HERBERT GINTIS, *Schooling in Capitalistic Amer-*

ica: Educational Reform and the Contradictions of Economic Life (New York: Basic Books, Inc., 1976); and CAROL LOPATE, "Approaches to Schools: The Perfect Fit," *Liberation* (September-October 1974), pp. 26–32.

10. THEORDORE L. GROSS, "How to Kill a College: The Private Papers of a Campus Dean," *Saturday Review* (February 4, 1978), pp. 13–20.

11. ARTHUR R. JENSEN, *Bias in Mental Testing* (New York: The Free Press, 1980), pp. 370–373, undertakes to supply a comprehensive answer to this controversial subject.

12. AARON V. CICOUREL et al., *Language Use and School Performance* (New York: Academic Press, 1974).

13. Free or freedom schools would be the ideal substitutes, according to some scholars. See JONATHAN KOZOL, *Free Schools* (Boston: Houghton Mifflin Company, 1972), p. 14.

14. DAVID N. SILK, "Aspects of the Concept of Authority in Education," *Educational Theory,* 26 (Summer 1976), 271–278.

15. HAROLD TAYLOR, "The Need for Radical Reform," *Saturday Review* (November 20, 1965), p. 76, called teaching a "creative art, a healing art . . . "

16. This is the position taken by the Task Force on Academic Standards of the American Educational Studies Association, "Standards for Academic and Professional Instruction in Foundations of Education," *Educational Studies,* 8 (Winter 1977–78). These standards were adopted by the American Educational Studies Association in 1977, by the Society of Professors of Education, and the Philosophy of Education Society in 1979.

READINGS

ADLER, MORTIMER J., *Reforming Education: The Schooling of the People and Their Education Beyond Schooling.* Boulder, Colo: Westview Press, 1977. In Chapter 3 Adler maintains that true freedom as education's aim has been lost; false liberalism, the worst enemy of freedom, is still destroying liberal education.

BERNIER, NORMAND R., and JACK E. WILLIAMS, *Beyond Beliefs: Ideological Foundations of American Education.* Englewood Cliffs, N.J.: Prentice-Hall, Inc., 1973. Chapter 1 is an excellent discourse on the nature of ideology.

BRANN, EVA T. H., *Paradoxes of Education in a Republic.* Chicago: University of Chicago Press, 1979. This perceptive book deals with the relationships between education and the state.

General Education in a Free Society, Report of the Harvard Committee. Cambridge, Mass.: Harvard University Press, 1945. One should look carefully at this study to see if it is possible to make a clear distinction between liberal and general education.

GREENE, MAXINE, *Teacher as Stranger: Educational Philosophy for the Modern Age.* Belmont, Calif.: Wadsworth Publishing Co., Inc., 1973. Written from the perspective of phenomenological existentialism, Chapter 1 considers the place of philosophy in the teacher's vocation.

JONSEN, RICHARD W., *Small Liberal Arts Colleges: Diversity at the Crossroads.* Washington, D.C.: American Association for Higher Education, 1978. This short work seeks to establish a framework for understanding the changes small liberal arts colleges have undergone in the "light of their past, present, and future roles in our society."

KERR, DONNA H., *Educational Policy: Analysis, Structure, and Justification.* New York: David McKay Co., Inc., 1976. Chapter 2 is concerned with the nature of educational policy and the problem of identifying educational policy among a variety of social and political policies.

LLOYD, D. I., ed., *Philosophy and the Teacher.* London: Routledge & Kegan Paul, 1976. Chapter 8, although referring to them as traditional and progressive, deals with what we have called liberal and conservative educational views. Chapter 11 considers the issue of authority in education.

NASH, PAUL, *Authority and Freedom in Education.* New York: John Wiley & Sons, Inc., 1966. An introduction to educational philosophy that pays close attention to authority and freedom in the educational process.

NOLL, JAMES W., ed., *Taking Sides: Clashing Views on Controversial Educational Issues.* Guilford, Conn.: The Dushkin Publishing Group, Inc., 1980. The following are good reading in connection with this chapter: Issue 6, have the schools met their social goals? Issue 8, how can opportunity be equalized? Issue 11, what power should teachers have? and Issue 12, what rights do students have?

PETERS, RICHARD S., *Education and the Education of Teachers.* London: Routledge & Kegan Paul, 1977. See Chapter 7 for a view of the place of philosophy "in the training of teachers."

PHILLIPS, NORMAN R., *The Quest for Excellence: The Neo-Conservative Critique of Educational Mediocrity.* New York: Philosophical Library, 1978. See Chapter 7 for reflections on the role of neoconservatism in American education.

RAVITCH, DIANE, *The Revisionists Revised: A Critique of the Radical Attack on the Schools.* New York: Basic Books, Inc., 1978. While one could not describe this book as a conservative defense of education, it is nevertheless an effort to restore some equilibrium to what may be called extreme liberal views and interpretations.

STARK, JOAN S., and Associates, *The Many Faces of Educational Consumerism.* Lexington, Mass.: D. C. Heath and Company, 1977. Although the focus is mainly on higher education, Part 1—about fifty pages—characterizes consumerism as an emerging issue in education.

STRIKE, KENNETH A., and KIERAN EGAN, eds., *Ethics and Educational Policy.* London: Routledge & Kegan Paul, 1978. Two selections, pp. 105–146, deal with autonomy, freedom, and schooling.

WEGENER, CHARLES, *Liberal Education and the Modern University.* Chicago: University of Chicago Press, 1978. The worth of the liberal curriculum is illustrated in Chapter 4.

Additional Readings

General

Bandman, Bertram, *The Place of Reason in Education.* Columbus: Ohio State University Press, 1967.

Bantock, G. H., *Freedom and Authority in Education.* Chicago: Henry Regnery and Company, 1953.

Barrow, Robin, *Plato, Utilitarianism and Education.* London: Routledge & Kegan Paul, 1975.

Barth, Roland S., *Open Education and the American School.* New York: Agathon Press, 1972.

Belth, Marc, *The New World of Education: A Philosophical Analysis of Concepts of Teaching.* Boston: Allyn & Bacon, Inc., 1970.

Benne, Kenneth D., *A Conception of Authority.* New York: Teachers College Press, 1943.

Bereiter, Carl, *Must We Educate?* Englewood Cliffs, N.J.: Prentice-Hall, Inc. 1974.

Berkson, Isaac B., *The Idea and the Community.* New York: Harper & Row, Publishers, Inc. 1958.

Blanshard, Brand, *The Uses of Liberal Education.* Chicago: Open Court Publishing Company, 1973.

Bobbitt, Franklin, *The Curriculum.* New York: Arno Press, 1972.

Bosanquet, Bernard, *Three Lectures on Aesthetics.* New York: Macmillan, Inc., 1915.

Bower, William C., *Moral and Spiritual Values in Education.* Lexington: University of Kentucky Press, 1952.

367

Bowyer, Carlton, H., *Philosophical Perspectives for Education*. Glenview, Ill.: Scott, Foresman & Company, 1970.

Boyd, William, *The Emile of Jean Jacques Rousseau*. New York: Teachers College Press, 1962.

Bruner, Jerome, *The Process of Education*. Cambridge, Mass.: Harvard University Press, 1960.

Bryant, William M., *Hegel's Educational Ideas*. New York: AMS Press, 1971.

Butts, R. Freeman, *The American Tradition in Religion and Education*. Boston: Beacon Press, 1950.

Charters, W. W., *Curriculum Construction*. New York: Arno Press, 1972.

Combs, Arthur W., *Myths in Education: Beliefs That Hinder Progress and Their Alternatives*. Boston: Allyn & Bacon, Inc., 1979.

Conant, James B., *The American High School Today*. New York: McGraw-Hill Book Company, 1959.

Conant, James B., *Education and Liberty*. Cambridge, Mass.: Harvard University Press, 1953.

Cordasco, Francesco, ed., *Bilingualism and the Bilingual Child: Challenges and Problems*. New York: Arno Press, 1978.

Cowen, Emory L., and others, *New Ways in School Mental Health*. New York: Human Science Press, 1975.

Crary, Ryland W., *Humanizing the School: Curriculum Development and Theory*. New York: Alfred A. Knopf, 1969.

Curwin, Richard L., and Barbara Fuhrmann, *Discovering Your Teaching Self: Humanistic Approaches to Effective Teaching*. Englewood Cliffs, N.J.: Prentice-Hall, Inc., 1975.

Dalin, Per, *Limits to Educational Change*. New York: St. Martin's Press, Inc., 1978.

Dollar, Barry, *Humanizing Classroom Discipline: A Behavioral Approach*. New York: Harper & Row, Publishers, Inc., 1972.

Feinberg, Walter, *Reason and Rhetoric: The Intellectual Foundations of Twentieth-Century Liberal Educational Policy*. New York: John Wiley & Sons, Inc., 1975.

Fuller, Richard Buckminster, *R. Buckminster Fuller on Education*. Amherst: University of Massachusetts Press, 1979.

General Education in a Free Society, Report of the Harvard Committee. Cambridge, Mass.: Harvard University Press, 1945.

Glasser, William, *Schools Without Failure*. New York: Harper & Row, Publishers, Inc., 1969.

Gray, J. Glenn, *The Promise of Wisdom*. Philadelphia: J. B. Lippincott Company, 1968.

Green, Thomas, *The Activities of Teaching*. New York: McGraw-Hill Book Company, 1971.

Greene, Maxine, *Landscapes of Learning*. New York: Teachers College Press, 1978.

Gutek, Gerald L., *Philosophical Alternatives in Education*. Columbus, Ohio: Charles E. Merrill Publishing Company, 1974.

Guttchen Robert S., ed., *Philosophical Essays on Curriculum*. Philadelphia: J. B. Lippincott Company, 1969.

Hamm, Russell L., *Philosophy and Education: Alternatives in Theory and Practice*. Danville, Ill.: The Interstate Printers & Publishers, Inc., 1974.

Hart, Harold H., ed., *Summerhill: For and Against*. New York: Hart Publishing Company 1970.

Holt, John, *How Children Fail*. New York: New American Library, 1967.

Holt, John, *Instead of Education*. New York: E. P. Dutton, 1976.

Illich, Ivan, *Deschooling Society*. New York: Harper & Row, Publishers, Inc., 1970.

Itzkoff, Seymour W., *Cultural Pluralism in American Education*. New York: Harper & Row Publishers, Inc., 1969.

Karier, Clarence J., Paul Violas, and Joel Spring, *Roots of Crisis: American Education in the Twentieth Century*. Chicago: Rand McNally Company, 1973.

Katz, Michael B., *Class, Bureaucracy, and Schools*. New York: Holt, Rinehart & Winston, 1971.

King, Roger B., "Education and Educational Policies," *Educational Theory*, 29 (Winter 1979), 53–66.

Kirkorian, Y. H., ed., *Naturalism and the Human Spirit*. New York: Columbia University Press, 1944.

Kozol, Jonathan, *Death at an Early Age*. Boston: Houghton Mifflin Company, 1967.

Kozol, Jonathan, *Free Schools*. Boston: Houghton Mifflin Company, 1972.

Lang, Ossian H., ed., *Educational Creeds of the Nineteenth Century*. New York: Arno Press, 1972.

Langer, Susanne K., *Feeling and Form: A Theory of Art*. New York: Charles Scribner's Sons, 1953.

Langford, Glenn, and D. J. O'Connor, eds., *New Essays in the Philosophy of Education*. London: Routledge & Kegan Paul, 1978.

Larkin, Ralph W., *Suburban Youth in Cultural Crisis*. New York: Oxford University Press, 1979.

Leonard, George, *Education and Ecstasy*. New York: Delacorte Press, 1968.

McKenzie, Richard B., *The Political Economy of the Educational Process*. Boston: Martinus Nijhoff Publishing, 1979.

Mackenzie, Millicent, *Hegel's Educational Theory and Practice*. New York: Haskell House Publishers, Ltd., 1971.

Martin, Jane R., *Explaining, Understanding, and Teaching*. New York: McGraw-Hill Book Company, 1970.

Mason, R. E., *Educational Ideals in American Society*. Boston: Allyn & Bacon, Inc., 1960.

Mason, R. E., *Moral Values and Secular Education*. New York: Columbia University Press, 1950.

Mead, Margaret, *The School in American Culture*. Cambridge, Mass.: Harvard University Press, 1951.

Metcalf, Lawrence C., ed., *Value Education: Rationale, Strategies, and Procedures*. Washington, D.C.: National Council for the Social Studies, 1971.

Metzger, Walter P., ed., *The Constitutional Status of Academic Freedom*. New York: Arno Press, 1977.

O'Neill, James M., *Religion and Education Under the Constitution*. New York: Harper & Row, Publishers, Inc., 1949.

Ozman, Howard, *Comtemporary Critics of Education*. Danville, Ill.: The Interstate Printers & Publishers, 1970.

Ozman, Howard, *Utopias and Education*. Minneapolis: Burgess Publishing Company, 1969.

Parker, Francis W., *Talks on Pedagogics: An Outline of the Theory of Concentration*. New York: Arno Press, 1972.

Peddiwell, J. Abner [pseud.], *The Saber Tooth Curriculum*. New York: McGraw-Hill Book Company, 1939.

Pekarsky, Daniel, "Rights and Love in Education: An Essay on the Politicization of the School," *Educational Theory*, 29 (Winter 1979), 11–20.

Perkinson, Henry J., *The Possibilities of Error: An Approach to Education.* New York: David McKay Co., Inc., 1971.

Pfeiffer, Raymond S., "The Scientific Concept of Creativity," *Educational Theory,* 29 (Spring 1979), 129–137.

Phenix, Philip H., *Education and the Common Good: A Moral Philosophy of the Curriculum.* New York: Harper & Row, Publishers, Inc., 1961.

Postman, Neil, and Charles Weingartner, *Teaching as a Subversive Activity.* New York: Dell Publishing Company, Inc., 1969.

Pratte, Richard, *Ideology and Education.* New York: David McKay Co., Inc., 1977.

Rader, Melvin M., ed., *A Modern Book of Esthetics.* New York: Holt, Rinehart & Winston, Inc., 1952.

Rafferty, Max, *What Are They Doing to Our Children?* New York: New American Library, 1963.

Raths, Louis E., Merrill Harmin, and Sidney B. Simon, *Values and Teaching: Working with Values in the Classroom.* Columbus, Ohio: Charles E. Merrill Publishing Company, 1966.

Reimer, Everett, *The School Is Dead.* Garden City, N.Y.: Doubleday & Co., 1971.

Rich, John M., *Humanistic Foundations of Education.* Worthington, Ohio: C. A. Jones Publishing Company, 1971.

Rickover, Hyman G., *Education and Freedom.* New York: New American Library, 1963.

Rousseau, Jean Jacques, *Émile.* Translated by Barbara Foxley. New York: E. P. Dutton, 1938.

Schwartz, Adina, "Aristotle on Education and Choice," *Educational Theory,* 29 (Spring 1979), 97–107.

Silberman, Charles E., *Crisis in the Classroom: The Remaking of American Education.* New York: Random House, Inc., 1970.

Simon, Sidney B., Leland W. Howe, and Howard Kirschenbaum, *Values Clarification.* New York: Hart Publishing Company, 1972.

Smith, Philip G., *Philosophy of Education: Introductory Studies.* New York: Harper & Row, Publishers, Inc., 1964.

Smith, Ralph A., ed., *Aesthetic Concepts and Education.* Urbana: University of Illinois Press, 1970.

Snook, I. A., *Indoctrination and Education.* London: Routledge & Kegan Paul, 1972.

Spring, Joel H., *A Primer of Libertarian Education.* New York: Free Life Edition, 1975.

Tyack, David B., *The One Best System: A History of American Urban Education.* Cambridge, Mass.: Harvard University Press, 1974.

Wales, John N., *Prologue to Education: An Enquiry into Ends and Means.* London: Routledge & Kegan Paul, 1979.

Warren, Donald R., *History, Education, and Public Policy.* Berkeley, Calif.: McCutchan Publishing Corporation, 1978.

Weinstein, Gerald, and Mario Fantini, *Toward Humanistic Education: A Curriculum of Affect.* New York: Holt, Rinehart & Winston, 1970.

Analytic Philosophy

Ayer, A. J., *Language, Truth, and Logic.* London: Victor Gollancz, 1950.

Ayer, A. J., *The Problem of Knowledge.* Baltimore: Penguin Books, 1956.

Ayer, A. J., *Russell and Moore.* Cambridge, Mass.: Harvard University Press, 1971.

Feigl, H., and W. Sellars, eds., *Readings in Philosophical Analysis.* New York: Appleton-Century-Crofts, 1953.

Hospers, John, *An Introduction to Philosophical Analysis.* Englewood Cliffs, N.J.: Prentice-Hall, Inc., 1967.

Moore, George E., *Ethics.* New York: Holt, Rinehart & Winston, 1912.

Moore, George E., *Philosophical Papers.* London: Allen & Unwin, 1959.

Moore, George E., *Philosophical Studies.* London: Routledge & Kegan Paul, 1922.

Moore, George E., *Some Main Problems in Philosophy.* New York: Macmillan, Inc., 1953.

Peters, Richard S., *Authority, Responsibility and Education.* London: Allen and Unwin, 1973.

Peters, Richard S., *Ethics and Education.* Glenview, Ill.: Scott, Foresman & Company, 1967.

Russell, Bertrand, *The Basic Writings of Bertrand Russell,* ed. by R. E. Enger and L. E. Denonn. London: Allen and Unwin, 1961.

Russell, Bertrand, *Education and the Good Life.* New York: Boni & Liveright, 1926.

Russell, Bertrand, *Education and the Modern World.* New York: W. W. Norton & Co., Inc., 1932.

Russell, Bertrand, *Education and the Social Order.* London: Allen and Unwin, 1932.

Russell, Bertrand, *The Impact of Science on Society.* New York: Simon & Schuster, Inc., 1953.

Russell, Bertrand, *The Philosophy of Bertrand Russell,* ed. by P. A. Schilpp. Evanston, Ill.: Northwestern University Press, The Library of Living Philosophers, vol. 5, 1946.

Russell, Bertrand, *Science and Religion.* London: Butterworth, 1935.

Ryle, Gilbert, *Concept of Mind.* New York: Barnes and Noble Books, 1949.

Scheffler, Israel, *Conditions of Knowledge: An Introduction to Epistemology and Education.* Chicago: Scott, Foresman & Company, 1965.

Scheffler, Israel, *The Language of Education.* Springfield, Ill.: Charles C Thomas, Publisher, 1960.

Smith, B. O., and Robert H. Ennis, *Language and Concepts in Education.* Chicago: Rand McNally & Company, 1961.

Wittgenstein, Ludwig, *Philosophical Investigations.* New York: Macmillan, Inc., 1968.

Wittgenstein, Ludwig, *Tractatus Logico-Philosophicus.* New York: Humanities Press, Inc., 1961.

Existentialism

Blackham, H. J., *Six Existentialist Thinkers.* London: Routledge & Kegan Paul, 1952.

Buber, Martin, *I and Thou,* trans. by R. G. Smith. Edinburgh: T. & T. Clark, 1937.

Camus, Albert, *The Myth of Sisyphus.* Paris: Gallimard, 1942.

Collins, James, *The Existentialists.* Chicago: Henry Regnery Company, 1952.

Harper, Ralph, *Existentialism.* Cambridge, Mass.: Harvard University Press, 1948.

Heidegger, Martin, *Existence and Being.* Chicago: Henry Regnery Company, 1968.

Jaspers, Karl, *Man in the Modern Age,* trans. by E. & C. Paul. London: Routledge & Sons, Ltd., 1933.

Kneller, George F., *Education and Economic Thought.* New York: John Wiley & Sons, Inc., 1968.

Kneller, George F., *Existentialism and Education.* New York: John Wiley & Sons, Inc., 1958.

Manheimer, Ronald J., *Kierkegaard as Educator.* Berkeley: University of California Press, 1977.

Sartre, Jean-Paul, *Existentialism,* trans. by B. Frechtman. New York: Philosophical Library, Inc., 1947.

Vandenberg, Donald, *Being and Education: An Essay in Existential Phenomenology.* Englewood Cliffs, N.J.: Prentice-Hall, Inc., 1971.

Idealism

Adamson, John E., *The Theory of Education in Plato's Republic.* New York: Macmillan, Inc., 1903.

Barrett, Clifford, *Contemporary Idealism in America.* New York: Macmillan, Inc., 1932.

Berkeley, George, *Principles of Human Knowledge.* New York: E. P. Dutton, 1910.

Bogoslovsky, B. B., *The Ideal School.* New York: Macmillan Inc., 1936.

Butler, J. Donald, *Four Philosophies: And Their Practice in Education and Religion,* 3rd ed., New York: Harper & Row, Publishers, Inc., 1968.

Butler, J. Donald, *Idealism in Education.* New York: Harper & Row, Publishers, Inc., 1966.

Demiashkevitch, Michael, *An Introduction to the Philosophy of Education.* New York: American Book Company, 1935.

Froebel, Friedrich, *The Education of Man,* trans. by W. N. Hailman. New York: D. Appleton and Company, 1899.

Harris, William T., *Psychologic Foundations of Education.* New York: D. Appleton and Company, 1898.

Horne, Herman H., *The Democratic Philosophy of Education.* New York: Macmillan, Inc., 1932.

Horne, Herman H., *Idealism in Education.* New York: Macmillan, Inc., 1910.

Horne, Herman H., *Philosophy of Education.* New York: Macmillan, Inc., 1927.

Horne, Herman H., *The Psychological Principles of Education.* New York: Macmillan, Inc., 1908.

Horne, Herman H., *This New Education.* New York: The Abingdon Press, 1931.

Livingstone, Richard, *On Education.* New York: Macmillan, Inc., 1944.

Maguire, G. P., *Plato's Theory of Natural Law.* New Haven, Conn.: Yale University Press, 1947.

Moberly, Walter, *Plato's Conception of Education and Its Meaning Today.* New York: Oxford University Press, 1944.

Plato, *The Republic.* Cambridge, Mass.: Loeb Classical Library, Harvard University Press, 1930-1935.

Royce, Josiah, *Lectures on Modern Idealism.* New Haven: Yale University Press, 1919.

Ulich, Robert, *Conditions of Civilized Living.* New York: E. P. Dutton, 1946.

Ulich, Robert, *Fundamentals of Democratic Education.* New York: American Book Company, 1940.

Wild, John, *Plato's Modern Enemies and the Theory of Natural Law.* Chicago: University of Chicago Press, 1953.

Wild, John, *Plato's Theory of Man.* Cambridge, Mass.: Harvard University Press, 1946.

Pragmatism

Baker, Melvin C., *Foundations of John Dewey's Educational Theory.* New York: King's Crown Press, 1955.

Bayles, E. E., *Democratic Educational Theory.* New York: Harper & Row, Publishers, Inc., 1960.

Bayles, E. E., *Pragmatism in Education.* New York: Harper & Row, Publishers, Inc., 1966.

Bode, Boyd H., *How We Learn.* Lexington, Mass.: D. C. Heath & Co., 1940.

Bode, Boyd H., *Modern Educational Theories.* New York: Macmillan, Inc., 1927.

Bode, Boyd H., *Progressive Education at the Crossroads.* New York: Newson Company, 1938.

Brameld, Theodore, *Ends and Means in Education.* New York: Harper & Row, Publishers, Inc., 1949.

Brameld, Theodore, *Patterns of Educational Philosophy.* New York: Holt, Rinehart & Winston, 1971.

Brameld, Theodore, *Toward a Reconstructed Philosophy of Education.* New York: The Dryden Press, 1956.

Childs, John L., *American Pragmatism and Education.* New York: Holt, Rinehart & Winston, 1956.

Childs, John L., *Education and Morals.* New York: Appleton-Century-Crofts, 1950.

Childs, John L., *Education and the Philosophy of Experimentalism.* New York: Century Company, 1931.

Counts, George S., *Education and the Promise of America.* New York: Macmillan, Inc., 1946.

Dewey, John, *Art as Experience.* New York: Minton, Balch & Co., 1934.

Dewey, John, *Experience and Education.* New York: Macmillan, Inc., 1938.

Dewey, John, *Experience and Nature.* Chicago: Open Court Publishing Company, 1926.

Dewey, John, *How We Think.* Boston: D. C. Heath & Company, 1933.

Dewey, John, *Human Nature and Conduct.* New York: Holt, Rinehart & Winston, 1922.

Dewey, John, *Influence of Darwin on Philosophy.* New York: Holt, Rinehart & Winston, 1910.

Dewey, John, *Moral Principles in Education.* New York: The Wisdom Library, 1959.

Dewey, John, *The Quest for Certainty: A Study of the Relation of Knowledge and Action.* New York: G. P. Putnam's Sons, 1960.

Dewey, John, *Reconstruction in Philosophy.* New York: Holt, Rinehart & Winston, 1920.

Dewey, John, *Theory of Valuation.* Chicago: University of Chicago Press, 1939.

Fiebleman, James, *An Introduction to Peirce's Philosophy.* New York: Harper & Row, Publishers, Inc., 1946.

Fletcher, Joseph, *Moral Responsibility: Situation Ethics at Work.* Philadelphia: The Westminister Press, 1967.

Geiger, George R., *Philosophy and the Social Order.* Boston: Houghton Mifflin Company, 1947.

Hook, Sidney, *Education for Modern Man.* New York: Dial Press, Inc., 1946.

Hook, Sidney, *The Metaphysics of Pragmatism.* Chicago: Open Court Publishing Company, 1927.

James, William, *Essays in Radical Empiricism.* New York: Longmans, Green & Co., 1912.

James, William, *A Pluralistic Universe.* New York: Longmans, Green & Co., 1909.

James, William, *Pragmatism.* Cambridge, Mass.: Harvard University Press, 1975.

James, William, *Talks to Teachers.* New York: Holt, Rinehart & Winston, 1946.

James, William, *Varieties of Religious Experience.* New York: Longmans, Green & Co., 1916.

Jarrett, James L., *The Educational Theories of the Sophistis.* New York: Teachers College Press, Columbia University, 1969.

Kilpatrick, William H., *Education for a Changing Civilization.* New York: Macmillan, Inc., 1951.

Kilpatrick, William H., *Philosophy of Education.* New York: Macmillan, Inc., 1951.

Pai, Young, *Teaching, Learning, and the Mind.* Boston: Houghton Mifflin Company, 1973.

Peirce, Charles S., *Philosophy and Human Nature.* New York: New York University Press, 1971.

Spencer, Herbert, *Education: Intellectual, Moral, and Physical.* New York: D. Appleton Company, 1914.

Wynne, John P., *Philosophies of Education From the Standpoint of Experimentalism.* Englewood Cliffs, N.J.: Prentice-Hall, Inc., 1947.

Realism

Aristotle, *The Works of Aristotle,* trans. and ed. by W. D. Ross. Oxford: Clarendon Press, 1908–1931.

Broudy, Harry S., *Building a Philosophy of Education.* Englewood Cliffs, N.J.: Prentice-Hall, Inc., 1961.

Drake, Durant, ed., *Essays in Critical Realism.* New York: Macmillan, Inc., 1920.

Finney, Ross L., *A Sociological Philosophy of Education.* New York: Macmillan, Inc., 1928.

Holt, E. B., ed., *The New Realism.* New York: Macmillan, Inc., 1912.

Jaeger, Werner, *Aristotle: Fundamentals of the History of His Development.* trans. by R. Robinson. Oxford: Clarendon Press, 1934.

Lynch, John P., *Aristotle's School: A Study of a Greek Educational Institution.* Berkeley: University of California Press, 1972.

Perry, Ralph Barton, *General Theory of Value: Its Meanings and Basic Principles Construed in Terms of Interest.* New York: Longmans, Green & Co., 1926.

Skinner, B. F., *The Technology of Teaching.* Englewood Cliffs, N.J.: Prentice-Hall, Inc., 1968.

Skinner, B. F., *Walden Two.* New York: Macmillan, Inc., 1948.

Smith, M. Daniel, *Theoretical Foundations of Learning and Teaching.* Waltham, Mass.: Xerox College Publishing, 1971.

Watson, John B., *Behaviorism.* New York: W. W. Norton & Co., Inc., 1924.

Wegener, Frank, *An Organic Philosophy of Education.* Dubuque, Iowa.: William C. Brown Co., Publishers, 1957.

Wild, John, *Introduction to Realistic Philosophy.* New York: Harper & Row, Publishers, Inc., 1948.

Wild, John, ed., *The Return to Reason.* Chicago: Henry Regnery Company, 1953.

Religious and Rational Humanism

Adler, Mortimer J., and Milton Mayer, *The Revolution in Education.* Chicago: University of Chicago Press, 1958.

Aquinas, St. Thomas, *The Teacher—The Mind.* Chicago: Henry Regnery Company, 1953.

Augustine, St., *St. Augustine on Education,* ed. and trans. by George Howie. Chicago: Henry Regnery Company, 1969.

Augustine, St., *Concerning the Teacher.* New York: Appleton-Century-Crofts, 1939.

Cunningham, William F., *General Education and the Liberal College.* St. Louis: B. Herder Book Company, 1953.

Cunningham, William F., *The Pivotal Problems of Education.* New York: Macmillan, Inc., 1940.

Fitzpatrick, Edward A., *How to Educate Human Beings.* Milwaukee: Bruce Publishing Company, 1953.

Gilson, Etienne, *The Breakdown of Morals and Christian Education.* Toronto: St. Michael's College Press, 1952.

Gilson, Etienne, *History of Philosophy and Philosophical Education.* Milwaukee: Marquette University Press, 1948.

Gilson, Etienne, *Reason and Revelation.* New York: Charles Scribner's Sons, 1938.

Houvre, Franz de, *Philosophy and Education,* trans. by Edward B. Jordan. New York: Benziger Brothers, 1931.

Hutchins, Robert M., *The Conflict in Education in a Democratic Society.* New York: Harper & Row, Publishers, Inc., 1953.

Hutchins, Robert M., *Education for Freedom.* Baton Rouge: Louisiana State University Press, 1943.

Hutchins, Robert M., *The Higher Learning in America.* New Haven, Conn.: Yale University Press, 1936.

Hutchins, Robert M., *No Friendly Voice.* Chicago: University of Chicago Press, 1936.

Kandel, I. L., *The Cult of Uncertainty.* New York: Arno Press, 1972.

McGucken, William J., *The Catholic Way in Education.* Milwaukee: Bruce Publishing Company, 1934.

Marique, Pierre J., *Philosophy of Christian Education.* Englewood Cliffs, N.J.: Prentice-Hall, Inc., 1939.

Maritain, Jacques, *The Degrees of Knowledge.* New York: Charles Scribner's Sons, 1938.

Maritain, Jacques, *Existence and the Existent,* trans. by L. Galantiere and G. B. Phelan. New York: Belgrove, 1948.

Maritain, Jacques, *Man and the State.* Chicago: University of Chicago Press, 1951.

Maritain, Jacques, *A Preface to Metaphysics.* New York: Sheed Andrews & McMeel, Inc., 1948.

Maritain, Jacques, *The Range of Reason.* New York: Charles Scribner's Sons, 1952.

Maritain, Jacques, *True Humanism.* New York: Charles Scribner's Sons, 1938.

Newman, John Henry, *The Idea of a University.* New York: Doubleday & Company, Inc., 1959.

Niebuhr, Rheinhold, *The Nature and Destiny of Man.* New York: Charles Scribner's Sons, 1919.

Redden, John D., and Francis A. Ryan, *A Catholic Philosophy of Education.* Milwaukee: Bruce Publishing Company, 1942.

Shields, Thomas E., *Philosophy of Education.* Washington, D.C.: The Catholic Education Press, 1921.

INDEX